JOURNAL FOR THE STUDY OF THE OLD TESTAMENT
SUPPLEMENT SERIES
401

Editors
Claudia V. Camp, Texas Christian University
and
Andrew Mein, Westcott House, Cambridge

Founding Editors
David J.A. Clines, Philip R. Davies and David M. Gunn

Editorial Board
Richard J. Coggins, Alan Cooper, John Goldingay,
Robert P. Gordon, Norman K. Gottwald, John Jarick,
Andrew D.H. Mayes, Carol Meyers, Patrick D. Miller

BIBLE IN THE TWENTY-FIRST CENTURY SERIES
4

Editor
Athalya Brenner

Dedicated to:

AB

אשה גדולה

(1 Kgs 4)

and in the memory of the one and only
Nicole Loraux

Between Woman, Man and God

A New Interpretation of the Ten Commandments

Hagith Sivan

T & T CLARK INTERNATIONAL
A Continuum imprint
LONDON • NEW YORK

Copyright © 2004 T&T Clark International
A Continuum imprint

Published by T&T Clark International
The Tower Building, 11 York Road, London SE1 7NX
15 East 26th Street, Suite 1703, New York, NY 10010

www.tandtclark.com

British Library Cataloguing-in-Publication Data
A catalogue record for this book is available from the British Library

Typeset and edited for Continuum by Forthcoming Publications Ltd
www.forthcomingpublications.com

Printed on acid-free paper in Great Britain by The Bath Press, Bath

ISBN 0-567-08045-5 (hardback)
    0-567-08055-2 (paperback)

CONTENTS

SERIES EDITOR'S PREFACE

Athalya Brenner

This volume is the fourth in the 'The Bible in the 21st Century' series. This is the title of our collective research project in the Biblical Studies Section, within the Department of Art, Religion and Culture at the University of Amsterdam, with the support of NOSTER (Netherlands School for Advanced Studies in Theology and Religion) and ASCA (Amsterdam School of Cultural Analysis). In this research program, as can be seen from its Internet formulations,[1] together with our international research partners, we endeavour to problematize contemporaneous authoritative and cultural meanings of bibles by focusing upon the processes of transmission, readership and actualization of biblical texts up to and including the Twenty-First Century.

We started the project together with our corresponding department at the University of Glasgow in 2000. The first book of the BTC series, *Bible Translation on the Threshold of the Twenty-First Century: Authority, Reception, Culture and Religion* (A. Brenner and J.W. van Henten [eds], 2002), is a collection of papers problematizing contemporary biblical translations as cultural phenomena. Subsequent BTC volumes, be they collections or monographs by single authors, have followed and will follow a similar pattern and present work done locally as well as by international research partners and colleagues.

The present volume, *Between Woman, Man and God*, is a monograph written by Hagith Sivan (University of Kansas). It constitutes an engagement with the Ten Commandments as a foundational text of faith, exploring the implications of Decalogue formulations and related narrative texts for the construction and gendering of the biblical communities of faith—and of ours. The Hebrew Bible delineates the essence of wo/manhood through both platitudes and paradoxes. It uses women as a category of exegesis to advance a platform of manhood that depends on a regular and assiduous performance of what is 'right' and on careful avoidance of what is 'wrong'. Women are taken as emblematic contradictions (piety–impiety; compliance–contravention; correct–unacceptable behaviour), which necessitates the weighing of texts both on their own merits and against the wider context of the Decalogue's ramifications. This is what Sivan does in her book and, as such, this is a truly pioneering project with ramifications for biblical literary criticism as well for feminist criticism.

---

1. Visit <http://www.theo.uu.nl/noster/> for the Dutch version, and <http://cf.hum.uva.nl/bijbelwetenschappen/english/index.html> for the English (following the 'Research' link).

To quote from our local research program,

> The cultural-historical significance of 'the bible' results from the fact that bibles function as canons, i.e. networks or collections of intensely mediated texts that are considered sources for forms, values and norms by people. The canonical status of these texts leads to an ongoing process of re-interpretation and actualization, during which the biblical text is read selectively… Elements that are considered meaningful are being connected with actual views of life. Fragments of biblical texts function as a source of common values and interests. They form a point of attachment for the formulation of common identities and a reservoir of images, archetypes, topoi and model texts that inspire new texts and other forms of expression.

Broadly speaking, this is the mission of the present series. Hopefully, this volume as well as others will explore features and issues that are oriented to contemporary culture and the bible's (and religion's) place within it, issues that are gaining ground but—perhaps—still get less academic attention than they deserve.

ACKNOWLEDGMENTS

The magnificent mind of Nicole Loraux continues to exercise its magic over me. Athalya Brenner provided intellectual and spiritual sustenance throughout. I am grateful to the Hall Center at the University of Kansas for a Hall fellowship and to the Graduate Research Fund at the University of Kansas for its continuous assistance. I am also, as ever, in the debt of Pam LeRow and the late Lynn Porter, of the Word Processing Center at the University of Kansas. I had the opportunity to share my thoughts with a group of women assembled in the house of my dear friend, Aliza Rodnitzky, in Tel Aviv in summer 2003. To their lively reactions I owe a few reflections.

This book forms a sequel to my *Dinah's Daughters: Gender and Judaism from the Hebrew Bible to Late Antiquity* (published under the name of Helena Zlotnick). As can be seen, my exploration of Jewish/Israelite identities has been progressing counter-clockwise to conventional chronology.

ABBREVIATIONS

AASOR	Annual of the American Schools of Oriental Research
AB	Anchor Bible
ABD	David Noel Freedman (ed.), *The Anchor Bible Dictionary* (5 vols.; New York: Doubleday, 1992)
ANET	James B. Pritchard (ed.), *Ancient Near Eastern Texts Relating to the Old Testament* (3 vols.; Princeton: Princeton University Press, 3rd edn, 1969)
ATLA	American Theological Library Association
ATR	*Anglican Theological Review*
AusBR	*Australian Biblical Review*
AUSS	*Andrews University Seminary Studies*
BA	*Biblical Archaeologist*
Bib	*Biblica*
BibInt	*Biblical Interpretation: A Journal of Contemporary Approaches*
BibRes	*Biblical Research*
BJRL	*Bulletin of the John Rylands University Library of Manchester*
BN	*Biblische Notizen*
BR	*Bible Review*
BT	*The Bible Translator*
BTB	*Biblical Theology Bulletin*
BZ	*Biblische Zeitschrift*
CBQ	*Catholic Biblical Quarterly*
CRBS	*Currents in Research: Biblical Studies*
ETR	*Etudes théologiques et religieuses*
EvQ	*Evangelical Quarterly*
ExpTim	*Expository Times*
FemTh	*Feminist Theology*
HAR	*Hebrew Annual Review*
HBT	*Horizons in Biblical Theology*
HR	*History of Religions*
HTR	*Harvard Theological Review*
HUCA	*Hebrew Union College Annual*
IB	*Interpreter's Bible*
ICC	The International Critical Commentary
Int	*Interpretation*
JBL	*Journal of Biblical Literature*
JBQ	*Jewish Bible Quarterly*
JES	*Journal of Ecumenical Studies*
JETS	*Journal of the Evangelical Theological Society*
JJS	*Journal of Jewish Studies*
JNES	*Journal of Near Eastern Studies*

JNSL	*Journal of Northwest Semitic Languages*
JQR	*Jewish Quarterly Review*
JR	*Journal of Religion*
JSNT	*Journal for the Study of the New Testament*
JSNTSup	*Journal for the Study of the New Testament*, Supplement Series
JSOT	*Journal for the Study of the Old Testament*
JSOTSup	*Journal for the Study of the Old Testament*, Supplement Series
JSS	*Journal of Semitic Studies*
NCBC	New Century Bible Commentary
OTL	Old Testament Library
PAAJR	*Proceedings of the American Academy of Jewish Research*
RB	*Revue biblique*
REJ	*Revue des études juives*
RelS	*Religious Studies*
RelSRev	*Religious Studies Review*
RevScRel	*Revue des sciences religieuses*
RivB	*Rivista biblica*
RSV	Revised Standard Version
RTR	*Reformed Theological Review*
SBLSP	SBL Seminar Papers
SBLSS	SBL Semeia Studies
ScEs	*Science et esprit*
SJOT	*Scandinavian Journal of the Old Testament*
SR	*Studies in Religion/Sciences religieuses*
TDOT	G.J. Botterweck and H. Ringgren (eds.), *Theological Dictionary of the Old Testament* (trans. John T. Willis; 11 vols.; Grand Rapids: Eerdmans, 1995)
THAT	Ernst Jenni and Claus Westermann (eds.), *Theologisches Handwörterbuch zum Alten Testament* (Munich: Chr. Kaiser Verlag, 1971–76)
ThWAT	G.J. Botterweck and H. Ringgren (eds.), *Theologisches Wörterbuch zum Alten Testament* (Stuttgart: W. Kohlhammer, 1970–)
TLOT	G.J. Botterweck and H. Ringgren (eds.), *Theological Lexicon of the Old Testament* (trans. Mark E. Biddle; 3 vols.; Peabody, MA: Hendrickson, 1997)
TynBul	*Tyndale Bulletin*
UF	*Ugarit-Forschungen*
USQR	*Union Seminary Quarterly Review*
VT	*Vetus Testamentum*
WBC	Word Biblical Commentary
ZABR	*Zeitschrift für altorientalische und biblische Rechtsgeschichte*

Chapter 1

THE WINDING PATHS OF BIBLICAL WO/MANHOOD

And the women,
Our women:
Their terrible and blessed hands,
Their small and delicate chins, their large Eyes,
Our mothers, wives, lovers,
They are dead, as though they had never lived.
Their place at our table,
Their place at our homes,
Walking behind the oxen,
Them we will abduct to the mountains,
On their account we will sit in jail,
They are those who walk behind the plow,
Toil over the grain, tobacco, and fire,
Crowd the markets and cut the trees;
Them we will conquer in the cow sheds
With shining knives,
On their heavy and round thighs,
On their clinging ear hangings,
Women,
Our women.

—Nazim Hikmet, *Our Women*[1]

1. *The Decalogue: Scholarly Controversies and Consensus*

The Pentateuch transmits two (by some counts three, with Exod. 34) full 'versions' of the Decalogue (Exod. 20.2-17; Deut. 5.6-21).[2] These are substantially similar but their differences are so striking as to make one ponder on questions of provenance, chronology, emendation and redaction, not to mention the flexibility and malleability of the text itself.[3] To this day, moreover, there is no agreement regarding the

---

1.   My translation into English was made from a Hebrew translation of the poem.
2.   See, among many other treatments, Stanley A. Cook, 'A Pre-Masoretic Biblical Papyrus', *Proceedings of the Society of Biblical Archaeology* 5 (1903), pp. 34-56. On the relations between the two versions, see Fèlix García López, 'Analyze littéraire de Deutéronomie V–XI', *RB* 85 (1978), pp. 37-39.
3.   For discussions see the standard commentaries, as well as the huge bibliography provided by ATLA electronic database under the Ten Commandments. A good summary is provided in

precise divisions of the Decalogue itself. Jews, Catholics and Protestants have a different way of numbering the Commandments. The varying systems reflect both credal disagreements and scholarly confusion over the precise meaning of each of the Commandments, and over the respective history of each prohibition prior to its 'codification' or insertion into the redacted text.[4]

In spite of the Decalogue's textual economy there are certain redundancies that hint at either a haphazard selection of contents or specific intentions.[5] Nor is it clear what guiding principles had provided a basis of textual unity or disunity. Scholars espousing the Decalogue's inner harmony construct it as a fundamental criminal code which further forms the center of all other Pentateuchal 'laws'.[6] In this interpretation, the centrality of the Decalogue as a milestone in the history of the relations between Yahweh and Israel is reinforced by the positioning of the text(s) as a fountainhead of ancient Israelite (criminal) legal system.

As 'law', the Decalogue is unique among the multitude of Pentateuchal regulations because Yahweh conveyed the Sinaitic precepts directly to the people (Exod. 20.1), using sounds and without mediation. Moreover, God even applied a finger to write these rules on tablets of stone to ensure memorialization (Exod. 24.12; 31.18; 34.1; cf. Deut. 5.4). Voice, language and gesture, then, were crucial components of

Richard Freund, 'The Decalogue in Early Judaism and Christianity', in Craig A. Evans and James A. Sanders (eds.), *The Function of Scripture in Early Jewish and Christian Tradition* (JSNTSup, 154; Sheffield: Sheffield Academic Press, 1998), pp. 124-41. See also James H. Watts, *Reading Law: The Rhetorical Shaping of the Pentateuch* (The Biblical Seminar, 59; Sheffield: Sheffield Academic Press, 1999), and Cyril S. Rodd, *Glimpses of a Strange Land: Studies in Old Testament Ethics* (Edinburgh: T. & T. Clark, 2001), *passim*. On Exod. 20 as a Deuteronomistic insertion, Andrew D.H. Mayes, 'Deuteronomy 5 and the Decalogue', *Proceedings of the Irish Biblical Association* 4 (1980), pp. 68-83. The flexibility and malleability of the text is strikingly reflected in a Samaritan version of the First Word, Yitzhak Magen, 'Mount Gerizim during the Roman and Byzantine Period', *Qadmoniot* 120 (2000), pp. 133-43 (143) (Hebrew).

4.   These problems are discussed in the standard commentaries as well as in specific treatments of the Decalogue, such as Jakob J. Stamm and Maurice E. Andrew, *The Ten Commandments in Recent Research* (London: SCM Press, 1967); Eduard Nielsen, *The Ten Commandments in New Perspective: A Traditio-Historical Approach* (Naperville, IL: Allenson, 1968); Walter Harrelson, *The Ten Commandments and Human Rights* (Philadelphia: Fortress Press, 1980); Dale Patrick, *Old Testament Law* (Atlanta: John Knox Press, 1985); and William Johnstone, 'The Ten Commandments: Some Recent Interpretations', *Expository Times* 100 (1988–89), pp. 453-61, to mention but a few. On 'Words', דברים, as either the Decalogue alone or the whole Torah, see Jacob Chinitz, 'The Ten and the Torah', *JBQ* 27 (1999), pp. 186-91. For a comprehensive overview, see Cornelis Houtman, *Exodus* (Historical Commentary on the Old Testament; 3 vols.; Leuven: Peeters, 1993–2000), III, pp. 16-30. I am following the order found in the Hebrew Bible.

5.   See Rodd, *Glimpses*, p. 78, for the former view, although the redactor could have made a better or more acute choice, if indeed the 'laws' were picked to create a 'decalogue' at any cost.

6.   Anthony Phillips, *Ancient Israel's Criminal Law: A New Approach to the Decalogue* (Oxford: Basil Blackwell, 1970), *passim*, esp. p. 10. But see Rodd's reservations regarding the implied chronological priority of the Decalogue *vis-à-vis* other Pentateuchal laws (*Glimpses*, p. 79). The Decalogue, however, like Deborah's 'Song', has been long regarded as a very old text, Amelie Kuhrt, 'Israel: The Formation of a Small Levantine State c. 1200–900', in *idem*, *The Ancient Near East* (2 vols.; London: Routledge, 1995), II, p. 422.

communication between the divine and humans during the Sinaitic epiphany. Much is left unsaid, or rather unwritten. The clauses of the Decalogue are brief to the point of obscurity. They are devoid of penalty and precision, and they represent (even with the Covenant Code of Exod. 21–23) a tiny fraction of the kind of legal regulations that are vital for the functioning of an orderly and humane society.

Based on modern perceptions of legality, the Decalogue, by itself, would imply that its recipients had already been familiar with its basic ethical, theological and legal stance. Such a narrow approach neglects, however, the striking fact that in biblical sequence the Ten Words do not form an independent legal manifesto like the Code of Hammurabi or the great legal codices of late Roman antiquity.[7] Nor does the Decalogue stake a claim to comprehensiveness. Its comprehension depends on mental evocation of the links which it forges, directly and indirectly, with surrounding legal and narrative strata.[8]

Discussions of the Decalogue have revolved around a variety of issues, including its sources, the relationship between the Decalogue and the literature of ancient Near East, as well as affinities between the Pentateuchal Decalogues and Pentateuchal laws.[9] What hands were at work when an 'original' text (if any) was redacted and inserted into the narrative of the Exodus, and into its 'resumption' in Deuteronomy? Some scholars believe an *Ur*-Decalogue to be as early as the sixteenth century BCE; others postpone its redacted version to a post-exilic period. Several scholars detect the hand of the Deuteronomic school in a reworking of an Exodus Decalogue to fit into a Deuteronomic humanistic mold; others prefer a prophetic shaping of the same text.[10] Another view regards the final form of the Sinaitic pericope in Exodus, Decalogue inclusive, as a P(riestly) revision of an underlying Deuteronomic edition.[11]

Desirable as it might appear to pursue an analysis of the Decalogue within a conventional historical context, such a desideratum remains, at present at least,

---

7.   On the latter see the important contribution of Catherine Hezser, 'The Codification of Legal Knowledge in Late Antiquity: The Talmud Yerushalmi and Roman Law Codes', in Peter Schäfer (ed.), *The Talmud Yerushalmi and Graeco-Roman Culture* (Tübingen: J.C.B. Mohr [Paul Siebeck], 1998), pp. 581-641; and Jill Harries, *Law and Empire in Late Antiquity* (Cambridge: Cambridge University Press, 1999).

8.   In other words, it is neither 'law' nor 'custom', but a diagram of categories of human–Hebrew behavior.

9.   Yair Hoffman, *The Doctrine of the Exodus in the Bible* (Tel Aviv: Tel Aviv University Press, 1983 [Hebrew]), p. 116 and *passim*, with Nielsen, *The Ten Commandments, passim*. Cf. Timo Veijola, 'Bundestheologische Redaktion im Deuteronomium', in *idem, Das Deuteronomium und seine Querbeziehungen* (Helsinki: Finnische Exegetische Gesellschaft, 1996), pp. 258-60, for a covenantal theology redactor.

10.   Moshe Weinfeld, *Deuteronomy and the Deuteronomic School* (Oxford: Clarendon Press, 1972), *passim*; Arvid S. Kapelrud, 'Some Recent Points of View on the Time and Origin of the Decalogue', *Studia Theologica* 18 (1964), pp. 81-90 (repr. in *idem, God and His Friends in the Old Testament* [Aarhus: Universitetsforlaget, 1979], pp. 11-20).

11.   William Johnstone, 'The Decalogue and the Redaction of the Sinai Pericope in Exodus', *ZAW* 100 (1988), pp. 361-85 (370-71).

unreachable.[12] Scholarly allocations of dates to the Decalogue have met with universal disapprobation.[13] The range of eras attached to each of the presumed stages of the Decalogues, either an 'original' (Mosaic?) or a 'final' (exilic? Post-exilic?) redacted version, is nothing short of astonishing. A singular lack of balance in the Decalogue itself between expansive commands (such as the Sabbath Commandment) and terse prohibitions (such as 'thou shalt not murder; kill; or commit adultery'), renders even more complex the debate about the precise form and length of an 'original' Decalogue. Nor does the absence of penalty clauses facilitate an assessment of the roots and development of the Decalogue document(s).

By one scholarly interpretation, the Decalogue provides a charter which guarantees male freedom of action delineated, somewhat paradoxically, by a series of constraints and admonitions.[14] In this reading, the Decalogue epitomizes manhood by formulating concerns and directing them at, primarily, individual males, Israelites, who are married with children but also have living parents, and who, in addition, live in an urban milieu of sorts, own property and slaves, are active in the cult and in administering justice, and are capable of, or may be tempted to commit everything that the Commandments forbid.[15] A different scholarly opinion regards the Decalogue as a document addressed to 'Israel as a nation', or one extended family, presumably regardless of gender.[16] A third prefers to envisage the Ten

---

12.   See Houtman, *Exodus*, III, for an overview.

13.   See my 'Dating the Decalogue' (forthcoming) for a comparative examination of scenes of law-giving in ancient Israel and Sparta, with a focus on Moses and Lycurgus. Briefly summarized, the Exodus account and Lycurgus' life (as 'recounted' by Plutarch) suggest striking biographical commonalities gathered into a tissue of narratives woven around the two lawgivers. Among the elements that 'link' Moses with Lycurgus are: a royal background; renunciation of royal position; 'exile'; 'return' to become law-givers at moment of 'national' crisis; and the content and purpose of their laws. In the eyes of the Spartans (and other Greeks) Lycurgus' legal reforms engineered the ascent of their city-state into a position of dominance and exclusivity; the Penatateuch commemorates Moses as the crafter of Israelite identity. On Sparta and Lycurgus, see W.G. Forrest, *A History of Sparta 950–192 BC* (New York: Norton, 1968); and Robin Osborne, *Greece in the Making, 1200–479* (London: Routledge, 1996), pp. 187-200. Especially interesting are the Lycurgean laws which aim at equalizing the position of all freeborn Spartans by injecting a sense of belonging and solidarity and by promoting the education of the young. Ancient Greek estimates placed 'Lykourgos' in the early ninth century BCE; modern calculations place the reforms associated with his name in the seventh century BCE.

14.   Frank Crüsemann, *Bewahrung der Freiheit: Das Thema des Dekalogs in socialgeschichlicher Perspektive* (Munich: Chr. Kaiser Verlag, 1983), *passim*, with Johnstone, 'The Ten Commandments', pp. 453-61. Crüsemann's views have been recently upheld by Rodd, *Glimpses*, pp. 86-87.

15.   David J.A. Clines, 'The Ten Commandments: Reading from Left to Right', in Jon Davies, Graham Harvey and Wilfred G.E. Watson (eds.), *Words Remembered, Texts Renewed: Essays in Honor of John F.A. Sawyer* (JSOTSup, 195; Sheffield: Sheffield Academic Press, 1995), pp. 97-112.

16.   Walter Zimmerli, *Old Testament Theology in Outline* (Edinburgh: T. & T. Clark, 1978), p. 138. See also Moshe Weinfeld, 'The Decalogue: Its Significance, Uniqueness, and Place in Israel's Tradition', in Edwin Firmage, Bernard G. Weiss and John W. Welch (eds.), *Religion and Law: Biblical-Judaic and Islamic Perspectives* (Winona Lake, IN: Eisenbrauns, 1990), pp. 3-47,

Words as a manifesto aimed at 'every man', a universal charter of (male?) human-ity.[17] Was Athalya Brenner, then, correct in decrying the apparent exclusion of women not only as passive participants in the Sinaitic theophany, but also as active sharers of responsibility and identity?[18] Otherwise phrased, how ethically norma-tive is the Decalogue?[19] And in terms of the present study, how gender specific is it?

If the Decalogue's series of prohibitions is a central feature of the ethics of Israel-ite manhood, as modern critics seem to imply, it must be examined as a cultural proposition within biblical 'history'.[20] Embodied in the biblical text are expanses that join biblical characters and episodes through ideological plans (or 'laws') and 'historical' antecedents (or narratives). And although men constantly aspire to occupy a space devoid of women, if not altogether anterior to sexuality, the very range of representation of mortal manhood, from aggression to helplessness, and from brutality to tenderness, doubles and depends on the vision of women as a 'traumatic kernel' or a 'Thing'.[21] A perpetual striving to appear to be good winds

and *idem*, 'The Uniqueness of the Decalogue and its Place in Jewish Tradition', in Ben-Zion Segal and Gerson Levi (eds.), *The Ten Commandments in History and Tradition* (Jerusalem: Magnes Press, 1990), pp. 1-44. The use of the second person singular or plural in legal formulations recalls the style of exhortation and homily rather than of ordinary laws and implies a view of Israel as an extended family and of law as common patrimony, as Jean L. Ska argues in 'Biblical Law and the Origins of Democracy' (unpublished paper delivered at SBL 2001, electronic version available from <www.biblicallaw.org>, pp. 7-8).

17. Brevard S. Childs, *The Book of Exodus: A Critical, Theological Commentary* (OTL; Philadelphia: Westminster Press, 1974), pp. 399-400.

18. 'The Decalogue—Am I an Addressee?', in *idem* (ed.), *A Feminist Companion to Exodus–Deuteronomy* (The Feminist Companion to the Bible, 6; Sheffield: Sheffield Academic Press, 1994), pp. 255-58. See the analysis of Judith Plaskow, *Standing Again at Sinai: Judaism from a Feminist Perspective* (San Francisco: Harper & Row, 1990).

19. Echoing Rodd, *Strange Land*, p. 81, who questions the Decalogue's privotal position, perhaps unnecessarily. We can only judge its historical primacy on the basis of the redacted text. Cf. Gerhard von Rad, *Old Testament Theology* (trans. D.M.G. Stalker; 2 vols.; Edinburgh: Oliver & Boyd, 1962), I, pp. 250-51, who claims that Israel could never consider the Decalogue as an absolute moral law but rather as a revelation in a specific historical moment. See also Patrick D. Miller, 'The Place of the Decalogue in the Old Testament and its Law', *Int* 43 (1989), pp. 229-42 (230).

20. I will be avoiding, deliberately, questions relating to the thorny issues of biblical chronol-ogy, the 'historicity' (or lack of it) of the episodes narrated, and the dating of the legal or narrative strata of the Pentateuch. For a brief review of scholarly theories, each with its strengths and weaknesses, see the intelligent summary of Kuhrt, 'Israel', pp. 417-35, who concludes, on the basis of careful examination of conflicting theories, that the biblical beginnings of Israel are woven together (in the seventh century or later) into a complex narrative from a variety of source material, none of which can be dated with any certainty, but all supporting a position that reconstructed the past to fit 'contemporary' understanding of the self.

21. Martha C. Nussbaum, *The Therapy of Desire: Theory and Practice in Hellenistic Ethics* (Princeton, NJ: Princeton University Press, 1994), and Slavoz Žižek, *The Sublime Object of Ideol-ogy* (London: Verso, 1989), on women as a (Lacanian) 'Thing' and a traumatic kernel. See also Žižek's *The Metastases of Enjoyment: Six Essays on Women and Causality* (London: Verso, 1994), *passim*. I do not deal with gender attributes of the divine in this study.

its deviant and divisive course through the ideologies of wo/manhood that require sifting, but not separation. If narrative politics provide models of behavior which explain what wo/man is all about, legal poetics account for the ethos that fashions the ideology of wo/manly codes of conduct.

2. *Making Wo/Men*

What, then, is 'wo/manhood'? In terms of modern anthropological research, manhood is a subject of battles, subtle yet potent, which rage daily in villages even in present day Mediterranean.[22] In such rural communities manhood is a demonstrable 'achievement', publicly performed, man-to-man.[23] The terms of 'triumph', ever changing, ever elusive, are nevertheless within clear parameters: manhood is measured in terms of 'being good at being a man'.[24] 'Being a good man', by contrast, hardly counts. Performance, then, and not ethics, determines masculinity; the place of man in society; relations among males; and the interaction between man and the environment, human, animate and inanimate.

This is the reality of 'manliness', at least as captured through the observations of anthropologists. It charts an all-male territory, overlaid with projections of public image, and undergirded by an invisible net of male–female and female-to-female communications. In this ecology, womanhood is molded to fit an ideology of manhood (and vice versa) through a collective exercise of verbal aggression (especially gossip and public shaming).[25] Since the meaning of 'being good at being a man' deludes definition, the framing of the interpretative design of womanhood, by contrast, is drawn along specific and limiting behavioral contours. And whereas women's words and actions reveal but also conceal, support but also subvert social and ethical norms, the ideology of womanhood is both complementary and contradictory to norms of manhood.[26]

---

22. Michael Herzfeld, *The Poetics of Manhood: Contest and Identity in a Cretan Mountain Village* (Princeton, NJ: Princeton University Press, 1985), p. 17.

23. Cf. contemporary Bedouin societies, Lila Abu Lughod, *Veiled Sentiments: Honor and Poetry in a Bedouin Society* (Berkeley: University of California Press, 1986), and *Writing Women's World: Bedouin Stories* (Berkeley: University of California Press, 1993).

24. Herzfeld, *Poetics of Manhood*, p. 17.

25. Cf. David D. Gilmore, *Aggression and Community: Paradoxes of Andalusian Culture* (New Haven: Yale University Press, 1987), and *idem*, *Manhood in the Making: Cultural Concepts of Masculinity* (New Haven: Yale University Press, 1990). For striking parallels from Roman antiquity, David Wray, *Catullus and the Poetics of Roman Manhood* (Cambridge: Cambridge University Press, 2001). Cf. Lyn Bechtel, 'Shame as a Sanction of Social Control in Biblical Israel: Judicial, Political and Social Shaming', *JSOT* 49 (1991), pp. 47-76; see also the articles gathered in Victor H. Matthews and Don C. Benjamin, *Honor and Shame in the World of the Bible* (Semeia, 68; Atlanta, GA: Scholars Press, 1994). More specifically, Shane Kirkpatrick, 'Questions of Honor in the Book of Judges', *Koinonia* 10 (1998), pp. 19-40.

26. Cf. Danna N. Fewell and David M. Gunn, *Gender, Power and Promise* (Nashville: Abingdon Press, 1992), p. 159: 'politics are written on the bodies of women…war is written on women's bodies'. On the volatility of gender concepts, Judith Butler, *Gender Trouble: Feminism and the Subversion of Identity* (London: Routledge, 1990), *passim*.

In societies where cultural concepts of masculinity dictate certain modes of female conduct in both public and private, a young woman must become 'modest and upright' if she is to allay fears and suspicions, whether founded or unfounded.[27] Under a threat of exposure, and of worse things to come, the hegemony of gossip induces women to become exemplary models of the feminine probity.[28] This tyranny of communal verbal aggression extends to women as well as to men. While in public, men extol neighborly solidarity and mutually loyal friendship based on masculine honor, their behavior in private suggests that such declarations are merely 'prophylactic formulae to ward off suspicion, betrayal, and anxiety'.[29]

In spite of obvious differences between dwellers of a rural Mediterranean orbit in the twentieth century and the communities described in the Hebrew Bible, similar structures and concerns appear as generative factors of relational codes of wo/manly comportment. Remote as the 'reality' that the Hebrew Bible projects may appear by analogy with that of contemporary Crete or Spain, all ideologies of masculinity and of femininity are motivated by fear of violating basic social and religious prohibitions, written and mostly unwritten.

From the start of both 'universal' (Gen. 1–11) and specific Hebrew/Israelite 'history' (Gen. 12 onwards), manhood is defined on the basis of demonstrative obedience to God's precepts. Womanhood implies obedience to males and, of course, to Yahweh. Disobedience defines deviation. To marginalize and to stigmatize those who would not or could not conform to its rules, the Hebrew Bible devises a language that represents normativity and transgression in terms of masculine and feminine modes of behavior. If manhood means compliance, female defiance concretizes acceptable types of communication between men and the environment. Words, a crucial male weapon, enforce consensus and have remained the means of fashioning orthodoxy and unanimity of action.

Genesis provides two manners of molding men. One, pre-Israelite and post-flood, promises life to all descendants of the post-deluvian family of Noah (Gen. 9.8-16). Women, however, are the vital means that ensure the viability of the divine assurance. There is no ark for single males, or for single females. To seal the 'covenant' of human perpetuity, God draws a rainbow across the sky, harnessing nature to words. With Abraham, the object of the second model of constructing males, Yahweh enters a 'covenant of fertility', 'signed' in the blood of male circumcision (Gen. 15.5-21; 17.1-9).[30] The Exodus Decalogue provides a third archetype, a wholesale contract between all(?) Israelites and God, marked by the construction of a center of sanctity (the tabernacle).[31] Taken together, the covenants reinforce a

---

27. Gilmore, *Aggression*, p. 53, for the story of Conchita whose public necking with her fiancé in an alley during a festival opened a factory of rumors that threatened to undermine her wedding and her family.

28. Wray, *Catullus*, p. 133.

29. Gilmore, *Aggression*, p. 5.

30. Mary Douglas, *Leviticus as Literature* (Oxford: Oxford University Press, 1999), p. 88, for the expression. See also the remarks of Lawrence A. Hoffman, *Covenant of Blood: Circumcision and Gender in Rabbinic Judaism* (Chicago: University of Chicago Press, 1996), *passim*.

31. On the tabernacle, Ralph W. Klein, 'Back to the Future: The Tabernacle in the Book of Exodus' (unpublished paper available from Klein's web site <www.ot-studies.com.>)

unilateral course of human reproduction, from male seed to women's closed or open bodies, depending on the divine will *vis-à-vis* the womb. Yet, the language of the covenant, and the emphasis on exclusivity, also echo the description of the divinely inspired human marital bond which Gen. 2.24 so poignantly captures and which biblical idealization of monogamy reflects.[32] The body of Israel *vis-à-vis* Yahweh is virginal and must remain closed to others, as is the covenant itself.[33]

Like the universe itself (Gen. 1), the first identifiable Hebrew male is made by a verbal fiat (Gen. 12). In return for unquestioned obedience, Yahweh promises Abra(ha)m procreation and paternity (Gen. 12.2; 13.15-16; 15.5-21). The pledge undermines the archetypal image of womanhood, namely motherhood.[34] An all male covenantal genealogy must, however, remain a fantasy, even in the fertile mind of biblical narrators. But the stretching of biblical 'horizons of fertility' beyond basic gender functioning conjures a terrifying specter of feminine sexuality, tempered only by inducing the ban of female sterility.[35] The presence of Sarah and of Hagar indicates an admission of the indispensability of woman in the Genesis scheme of manhood.

To instill the desired discipline in woman's womb, the weapon of mortal 'creation', Yahweh reinforces Eve's 'curse' by increasing female pain and passion through a game of sterility and fertility.[36] In the conceptualization of Genesis's womanhood, battles over the womb take place between Yahweh and woman. Female sterility breeds discipline, and discipline breeds an awareness that human passion, or the toil of labor are, in themselves, insufficient. In Genesis terms, the *agon* of 'being good at being a woman' focuses on the performance of the womb and is doubly dependent, on God and on man.[37] In biblical discourse about the feminine, beauty and barrenness are two configurations that shape female discourse and male–female dialogues.[38]

Because in Israelite history the inextricable tie between man and soil is specific and limited to Israelites and to Canaan, the history of the Genesis ancestors, in spite of intimacy with Yahweh, ends in Egypt and on a note of failure. To sever the Egyptian bond the book of Exodus reverses the ancient amity between Israel and

32. Etan Levine, 'On Exodus 21,10: Onah and Biblical Marriage', *ZABR* 5 (1999), pp. 133-64 (161 and *passim*).

33. Job 31.1, with a word-play that no translation can convey.

34. On paternity as a concomitant concept of the relegation of maternity, Nancy Jay, *Throughout Your Generations Forever: Sacrifice, Religion and Paternity* (Chicago: University Chicago of Press, 1992), *passim*.

35. Expression borrowed from Nicole Loraux, *The Children of Athena: Athenian Ideas about Citizenship and the Division between the Sexes* (trans. C. Levine; Princeton, NJ: Princeton University Press, 1993), p. 241.

36. Carol L. Meyers, *Discovering Eve: Ancient Israelite Women in Context* (New York: Oxford University Press, 1988).

37. As nicely illustrated in the double blessing bestowed on Rebecca, once by her family (Gen. 24.60) and once by God (25.23). Note also the appropriation of the terminology of fertility of 12.1-3.

38. James G. Williams, 'The Beautiful and the Barren: Conventions in Biblical Type-Scenes', *JSOT* 17 (1980), pp. 107-19.

Egypt. The battle between the hostile Egyptian government and its Hebrew subjects become a contest of wit between midwives and Pharaoh, and revolves around the womb.[39] The 'warriors' are all women, mothers, sisters, daughters.[40] At the dawn of Israelite history, disobedience and defiance characterize feminine words and actions. Women emerge as perpetual dissidents *vis-à-vis* the social and political context.[41] But they also guarantee preservation.

The biblical discourse of Israel as a common 'race' that can be traced back to a single Abrahamic ancestry necessitated the recasting of the ideology of manhood, as well as the 'naturalization' of women. This double process is sublimated in the metaphorical parturition of the nation itself as outlined in the Exodus narrative. Placed in a desert, an inhospitable territory unfit for human habitation, the trials and tribulations of the Israelites in the Sinai trace the birth pangs of a new entity out of an inchoate human substance.[42] Like Eve, a late comer to paradise of Genesis 2, the Israelites are cast as foreigners to the land destined to become theirs. And like the painful coming of humanity in Genesis 3, through knowledge and expulsion, the making of Israel in the Sinai is marked by endless misdemeanors.

The exodus, the story that envelops the Decalogue, unfolds a quest for land and for identity.[43] In the book of Exodus, Canaan becomes a mirage, or a narrated entity constructed with care through reminiscences of the past. To bridge over many generations that the narrative consigns to oblivion (between the death of Jacob and the birth of Moses), the self-appointed divinity of Israel is styled as the 'God of Abraham, Isaac and Jacob' (Exod. 3.6). God of men, then, dangling a specter of a land flowing of milk and honey. Yet, the first encounter of Israelite males with the inhabitants of the promised territory (Josh. 2) is affected through sexual intercourse and verbal exchange with a gentile trader of bodies (= prostitute).[44] The geography of the as yet unknown promised land, then, must be learnt through intimacy with the topography of a foreign female's body.

39. See my, 'Moses the Persian? Exodus 2, the "Other" and Biblical "Mnemohistory"', *ZAW* (2004 [in print]).

40. Is this a parody on basic male criteria of war and impregnation? For the two see Harry A. Hoffner, 'Symbols for Masculinity and Femininity: Their Use in Ancient Near Eastern Sympathetic Magic', *JBL* 85 (1966), pp. 326-34. See also the exhaustive analysis of Joppie Siebert-Hommes, *Let the Daughters Live: The Literary Architecture of Exodus 1–2 as a Key for Interpretation* (Leiden: E.J. Brill, 1998).

41. Josette Féral, 'The Powers of Difference', in Hester Eisenstein and Alice Jardine (eds.), *The Future of Difference* (New Brunswick, NJ: Rutgers University Press, 1985), pp. 88-94 (92), quoting Julia Kristeva's *Polylogues* (Collection Tel quel; Paris: Seuil, 1977), p. 498. On the Bible as a tissue of obedience/disobedience moralities, see Walter Brueggemann, 'The Shrill Voice of the Wounded Party', *Horizons in Biblical Theology* 21 (1999), pp. 1-25.

42. Cf. Ska's observation on landscape and law, 'Biblical Law', p. 6.

43. Thomas B. Dozeman, *God on the Mountain: A Study of the Redaction, Theology and Canon in Exodus 19–24* (Atlanta: Scholars Press, 1989), *passim*. See also Suzanne Boorer, *The Promise of the Land as Oath: A Key to the Formation of the Pentateuch* (Berlin: W. de Gruyter, 1992).

44. Cf. the version of Num. 13 which focuses on learning about the nature of the land, as though geography is solely a male matter. On Rahab, see below, Chapter 3 §5 and Chapter 4 §6.

To the Israelites about to receive the Ten Commandments, Moses prescribes temporary sexual abstinence. The three days of separating from sex and from women (Exod. 19.15), although a banal figure in biblical annals, correlate both with the three months of concealment which Moses' mother secured for her newly born, and with the three months that the Israelites had spent in the desert since leaving Egypt (Exod. 19.1).[45] The book of Exodus enjoins the Israelites to remember the Exodus and to transmit its collective memory to posterity (Exod. 34.18; cf. Deut. 5.2-4) by an annual 'acting out'. At the heart of the performance is a recitation of the Decalogue, a 'contract' between Yahweh and Israel that inscribes the latter into the fabric of human societies, while emphasizing its uniqueness through Yahweh.[46] The Israel of the Decalogue partakes in the ordinary through a series of conventional prohibitions. Yahweh's Israel is carefully distinguished from its environment by a series of injunctions that express loyalty to a specific God, a specific cult and worship. If 'being good at being a man' entails, according to the demands of the Decalogue, the avoidance of stealing, killing and coveting, not to mention apostasy and violation of the Sabbath and other men's property, what would be the essence of womanhood, if different?

Encapsulating an important locale for the self-definition of the Israelite male, the Decalogue is religiously charged yet aesthetically planned. In a way, it represents an osmosis between ideology and reality, or between a legal 'arcadia' and human existence. Its prohibitions are regularly repeated throughout the Bible not only because bans, by their very nature, often fail to achieve the desired effects, but also because a rhetoric of repetition is an essential characteristic of humans, in general, and of manhood in particular.

The Decalogue stands for public and domestic comfort. It defines deviation and conformity through basic standards which are, in themselves, insufficient to encompass the complexities of real life interaction. A true Israelite, to judge by the Decalogue, is a man who swerves perilously along a hazardous road which can turn at any moment either right or left (= wrong). And since an Israelite comes into being in two distinct stages, at birth, and at the moment of the collective covenant, the indispensability of women for the first renders their ostensible absence from the second all the more palpable.

Within the Israelite covenantal entity, social relations are measured against moral standards which revolve around perceptions of the human body. Thus, 'love' is not so much an emotion as a signified behavior that must be acquired through learning.[47] The covenant ceremony of monogamy emphasizes women's participation (Deut. 29.9-10, 17), and Deut. 31.12 calls on women, as well as on every member

---

45. Cf. the three days fast which Esther proclaims (Est. 4.16) and the three rainy days of the Jerusalem assembly in Ezra 10.9, both signaling a momentous event.

46. See Nahum M. Sarna, *Exploring Exodus: The Heritage of Biblical Israel* (New York: Schocken Books, 1986), pp. 140-44, on the Decalogue as 'self-enforcing code' (p. 142) which expands and modifies Near Eastern treaties

47. William L. Moran, 'The Ancient Near Eastern Background of the Love of God in Deuteronomy', *CBQ* 25 (1963), pp. 77-87.

of the Israelite congregation, to listen and to learn the Torah (cf. Josh. 8.35).[48] The presence of women at the tent of the assembly is attested (somewhat controversially), but an emphasis on separation remains.[49]

At the center of its map of morals, the Decalogue projects the contours of male identity. Materializing out of Yahweh's roaming voice, the precepts address individual Israelite males only, in the second person masculine singular.[50] They prohibit rather than permit. They aspire to redefine the relationship between the individual and God as a personal one, and at the same time the public link between God and Israel as a whole. In the Exodus' scheme of 'creation', the Decalogue officiates as a textual midwife who gives birth to a 'kingdom of priests and a sacred people' (Exod. 19.5-6). But if the midwives of Exodus 1 deflate masculine values, the Decalogue appears to espouse gender difference by codifying manhood. Within complex constellations of conflicting and shifting biblical identities (Israelite–gentiles; male–female; Hebrew–Israelite), the Decalogue provides an important example of the organization of human relations through specific (written?) guidelines. Its centrality in the present arrangement of the early 'histories' of Israel, suggests its indispensability for any investigation of the moral and ideological message of the Hebrew Bible.

3. *A New Reading of the Decalogue and Some Old Problems*

Three basic assumptions guide my investigation of the Ten Commandments:

1. There are intimate and, indeed, inseparable links that tie together narrative and legal discourses in the Hebrew Bible. Such connections make any exploration of the Decalogue plausible, if not vital, only within a large canvass of biblical 'history' comprising both legal and narratological layers.

2. There are (at least) two distinct 'histories' in the Hebrew Bible, each with its own moral and theological outlook, each requiring a separate treatment. One follows the formation of Israel from the age of the ancestors to the conquest of Canaan (Genesis–Numbers); the other traces the vicissitudes of Israel in the promised land (Joshua–2 Kings or the so-called Deuteronomic [Dtr] History). Since the Decalogue features in both 'histories', this redactional choice supports the viability of constructing separate analyses around each of the Decalogues as independent expressions of two worldviews.

---

48. Cf. William Horbury, 'Women in the Synagogue', in *idem et al.* (eds.), *The Cambridge History of Judaism* (3 vols.; Cambridge: Cambridge University Press, 1999), III, pp. 376-95.

49. Exod. 38.8; cf. 1 Sam. 2.22. The term צבא is variously rendered as 'fasting' (LXX) or 'praying' (Targums). Zech. 12.11-14 divides mourning clans into female and male groups.

50. On these aspects see the illuminating comments of Plaskow, *Standing Again at Sinai, passim*; and George W. Nicholson, 'The Decalogues as the Direct Address of God', *VT* 27 (1977), pp. 422-33.

3.   It is possible, indeed advantageous, to read the biblical mega-narrative (law and lore inclusive) as an attempt to come to terms with a deep-seated conflict that marks Israelite manhood as a product of specific relations with a specific god on the one hand, and as an ideology that must participate in a non-Israelite human environment on the other hand. As a foundational chart of this act of balancing, the Decalogue broadly outlines the poetics of a distinct Israelite identity. To gain insights into its contents, positioning and significance, one must peruse competing and complementary ideologies. I have chosen to focus on the ideologies of biblical womanhood as a key because these provide a rich canvass of complicity and counterbalancing in spite of clear patriarchal agenda and of andocentric biases.[51]

An inner-Pentateuchal dichotomy between a predominantly narratological part (Gen. 1–Exod. 19) and a pivotally legal landscape launched with the Decalogue (Exod. 20–Deut. 34) has dictated for decades the shaping of modern biblical scholarship.[52] Yet, both are constituents of a super-structure which may be best termed a 'historicized fiction' or 'fictionalized history'.[53] In this biblical recreation of the past, law and lore become equally indispensable mediators of veracity and credibility, as well as of the legitimacy of the Bible's theological message.[54] The

---

51.   On questions of reading texts, narrative theories and women's lives, see the articles assembled in Mieke Bal (ed.), *Anti-Covenant: Counter-Reading Women's Lives in the Hebrew Bible* (Bible and Literature, 22; Sheffield: Almond Press, 1989), especially her Introduction (pp. 11-24). Particularly important are analyses that highlight the victimization of women by advocating 'an exodus to a gynocentric counterworld', such as Athalya Brenner and Fokkelien van Dijk-Hemmes, *On Gendering Texts: Female and Male Voices in the Hebrew Bible* (Leiden: E.J. Brill, 1993), and the articles in Peggy L. Day (ed.), *Gender and Difference in Ancient Israel* (Minneapolis: Fortress Press, 1989). On strategies that stress female complicity and the close involvement of women in the history of patriarchy, see Cristina Thürmer-Rohr, *Vagabonding: Feminist Thinking Cut Loose* (trans. Lise Weil; Boston: Beacon Press, 1991). In general on feminist strategies of interpretation, see Marie-Therese Wacker, 'Historical, Hermeneutical, and Methodological Foundations', in Louise Schottroff, Silvia Schroer and Marie-Therese Wacker, *Feminist Interpretation: The Bible in Women's Perspective* (trans. Martin and Barbara Rumscheid; Minneapolis: Fortress Press, 1998), pp. 1-82 (52). See also the overview of Carol Meyers, 'The Family in Early Israel', in Leo Purdue *et al.* (eds.), *Families in Ancient Israel* (Louisville, KY: Westminster/John Knox Press, 1997), pp. 1-47, and Phyllis Trible, 'Feminist Hermeneutics and Bible Studies', in Ann Loades (ed.), *Feminist Theology: A Reader* (Louisville, KY: Westminster/John Knox Press, 1990), n.p.

52.   Frank M. Cross, *Canaanite Myth and Hebrew Epic: Essays on the History of the Religion of Israel* (Cambridge, MA: Harvard University Press, 1973), pp. 295-300, prefers Gen. 1–Exod. 40 as a basic unit.

53.   Herbert N. Schneidau, *Sacred Discontent: The Bible and Western Tradition* (Baton Rouge: Louisiana State University Press, 1976), p. 215; see also Robert Alter, 'Sacred History and Prose Fiction', in Richard E. Friedman (ed.), *The Creation of Sacred Literature: Composition and Redaction of the Biblical Text* (Berkeley: University of California Press, 1981), pp. 7-24 (8).

54.   Well termed by García López 'Res Gestae' of Yahweh (or Gestes of Yahweh), echoing the well-known *Res Gestae Divi Augusti* and medieval epics, Fèlix García López, 'Narración y ley en los escritos sacerdotales del Penateuco', *Estudios Bíblicos* 57 (1999), pp. 271-87 (272).

Bible's 'plural textuality' suggests that divorcing law from narrative, by consigning them to separate sub-disciplines, is artificial and unhelpful.[55]

Clearly it is crucial to understand how legal corpora entered a narrative framework, although the question may also be phrased in an opposite fashion. A determination of the chronological priority of these strata and of their individual components has been a subject of numerous scholarly debates which are not likely to be resolved any time soon.[56] A certain consensus, held together by Noth's publications, has held the second great biblical history (Joshua–2 Kings) as the work of one person, or rather of one (post-exilic) school.[57] But there is no agreement regarding the authorial and redactional hands of Genesis–Numbers. Recent years have also witnessed an increasing number of scholarly investigations into the relationship between Pentateuchal law, lore (or narratives) and theology, as opposed to analyses that depart from either the legal or the narrative strata.[58] Much of this work has departed from a basic presupposition that holds the narrative framework of the laws as significant as the laws themselves.[59] But this direction of research is still in its infancy. At the dawn of the twenty-first century we are experiencing a period of

55. For the quote, Richard E. Friedman, 'Sacred History and Theology: The Redaction of the Torah', in *idem* (ed.), *The Creation of Sacred Literature*, pp. 25-34 (28).

56. For a succinct summary, see Richard Coggins, *Introducing the Old Testament* (Oxford: Oxford University Press, 2nd edn, 2001). See also the summary provided by Kuhrt, 'Israel'.

57. Martin Noth, *The Deuteronomistic History* (JSOTSup, 15; Sheffield: JSOT Press, 2nd edn, 1991). See also Antony F. Campbell and Mark A. O'Brien, *Unfolding the Deuteronomistic History* (Minneapolis: Fortress Press, 2000), pp. 1-37.

58. See already the Wellhausen–Noth 'debate' over the nature of P as 'law' or 'narrative', Julius Wellhausen, *Prolegomena to the History of Ancient Israel* (Atlanta: Scholars Press, 1994 [repr. of the 1885 English trans.]), pp. 8-9 (primarily 'law'), and (primarily 'narrative'). On the intimate intertwining of law and narrative, see Mary Douglas, *In the Wilderness: The Doctrine of Defilement in the Book of Numbers* (JSOTSup, 158; Sheffield: JSOT Press, 1993), *passim*, esp. pp. 102-26. Erich Zenger, 'Die Bücher der Tora/des Pentateuch', in *idem et al.* (eds.), *Einleitung in das Alte Testament* (Stuttgart: W. Kohlhammer, 3rd edn, 1998), pp. 66-124, 142-76 (76-77), has called attention to the dialectical structure linking narrative to law; see also Nanette Stahl, *Law and Liminality in the Bible* (JSOTSup, 202; Sheffield: Sheffield Academic Press, 1995). On reading the Pentateuch by constructing distinct legal and narrative landscapes, see Jon D. Levenson, 'The Theologies of Commandment in Biblical Israel', *HTR* 73 (1980), pp. 17-33; Sean D. McBride, 'Perspective and Context in the Study of Pentateuchal Legislation', in James L. Mays *et al.* (eds.), *Old Testament Interpretation* (Nashville: Abingdon Press, 1995), pp. 47-59; and Thomas Römer, 'La formation du Penateuque selon l'exégèse historico-critique', in Christian-Bernard Amphoux and Jean Margain (eds.), *Les premières traditions de la Bible* (Lausanne: Editions du Zebre, 1996), pp. 17-55. In general, see Rolf Rendtorff, 'Directions in Pentateuchal Studies', *CRBS* 5 (1997), pp. 43-64. See also Levinson's criticism of Meir Sternberg, *The Poetics of Biblical Narrative* (Bloomington: Indiana University Press, 1987), for excluding legal texts, Bernard M. Levinson, 'The Right Chorale: From the Poetics to the Hermeneutics of the Hebrew Bible', in Jason P. Rosenblatt and Joseph C. Sitterson (eds.), *Not in Heaven: Coherence and Complexity in Biblical Narrative* (Bloomington: Indiana University Press, 1991), pp. 129-53 (131). Douglas, *Leviticus as Literature*, provides a good example of the blending of law and narrative in order to trace not only the inner logic of Leviticus but also its ideology *vis-à-vis* Deuteronomy.

59. Jean L. Ska, *Introduction à la lecture du Pentateuque. Clés pour l'interprétation des cinq premiers livres de la Bible* (Paris: Cerf, 2000), pp. 28-30.

transition in which past scholarly axioms are tumbling and none has, as yet, taken their place.[60]

There seems hardly a doubt that it is impossible to understand the Pentateuch, as it now stands, in solely legal or only in novelistic terms. One leading question, aptly phrased by Otto (in relations to the P[riestly] source), is whether we are dealing with a 'historical narration' or with a 'cultic codification'.[61] Are the laws works of literary art, even literary constructs?[62] The positioning of the Decalogue at the heart of a transition between a straightforward narrative (Gen. 1–Exod. 19) and lengthy legal excursuses renders its demands pivotal in the Pentateuch's redactional scheme.

Questions relating to the nature of the law itself pose more problems. By one reading the law represents little beyond a minimum standard of behavior which the narratives constantly aspire to surpass.[63] If this is the case, it is necessary to ask: Why does the Decalogue (and Deuteronomy) prescribe death for certain transgressions, and by some readings of the Decalogue, for all transgressions?[64] What kind

---

60. See the articles in Lester L. Grabbe (ed.), *Can a 'History of Israel' be Written?* (JSOTSup, 245; Sheffield: Sheffield Academic Press, 1997), and the seemingly interminable debate over archaeological perspectives of early Israel: Niels P. Lemche, 'Early Israel Revisted', *CRBS* 4 (1996), pp. 9-34; William G. Dever, 'Revisionist Israel Revisited: A Rejoinder to Niels Peter Lemche', *CRBS* 4 (1996), pp. 35-50; and Norman K. Gottwald, 'Triumphalist versus Anti-Triumphalist Versions of Early Israel: A Response to Articles by Lemche and Dever in Volume 4 (1996)', *CRBS* 5 (1997), pp. 15-42; see also Israel Finkelstein, 'The Archaeology of the United Monarchy: An Alternative View', *Levant* 28 (1996), pp. 177-87; and Amihai Mazar, 'Iron Age Chronology: A Reply to I. Finkelstein', *Levant* 29 (1997), pp. 157-67. I refrain, deliberately, also from delving into issue of synchronic or diachronic analysis, in spite of the reservations which Eckhard Otto, for example, leveled at Pressler's *View of Women* (see Otto's review in *Theologische Literaturzeitung* 119 [1994], pp. 983-86). A useful overview of recent trends is provided by David M. Carr, 'Controversy and Convergence in Recent studies of the Formation of the Pentateuch', *RelSRev* 23 (1997), pp. 22-31, which reviews the work of Van Seters, Blum, Crüsemann, Levin, Campbell, O'Brien and Boorer; and Jan-Wim Wesselius, 'Towards a New History of Israel', *Journal of Hebrew Scripture* 2 (2000–2001), pp. 2-21. On recent dating debates regarding the possibility of late (Hellenstic) redaction, see Hans M. Barstad, 'Is the Hebrew Bible a Hellenistic Book?, or Niels Peter Lemche, Herodotus, and the Persians', *Transeuphratène* 23 (2002), pp. 129-51.

61. Eckhard Otto, 'Forschungen zur Priesterschrift', *Theologische Rundschau* 62 (1997), pp. 1-50 (8) ('eine Geschichtserzählung' or 'Kultgesetzgebung').

62. Baruch J. Schwartz, 'The Prohibition Concerning the "Eating" of Blood in Leviticus', in Gary A. Anderson and Saul M. Olyan (eds.), *Priesthood and Cult in Ancient Israel* (JSOTSup, 125; Sheffield: JSOT Press, 1991), pp. 34-66. Cf. the view of law as scribal tradition or as a literary product in the ancient Near East, Samuel Greengus, 'A Textbook Case of Adultery in Ancient Mesopotamia', *HUCA* 40-41 (1969–70), pp. 33-44 (43-44). On traditional, mainstream scholarly approaches to the analysis of biblical laws, see Bernard S. Jackson, 'The Ceremonial and the Judicial: Biblical Law as Sign and Symbol', *JSOT* 30 (1984), pp. 25-50.

63. Gordon J. Wenham, 'The Gap Between Law and Ethics in the Bible', *JJS* 48 (1997), pp. 17-29.

64. On threats of capital punishment as an index to the world of the Deuteronomist, see Louis Stulman, 'Encroachment in Deuteronomy: An Analysis of the Social World of the D Code', *JBL* 109 (1990), pp. 613-32. On death as the (hidden) penalty of all of the Decalogue's clauses see

of 'realities' do the narratives and, for that matter, the law, represent? Moshe Greenberg has suggested that the law-codes express cultural values, and Peter Haas has elaborated by advancing the notion that legal materials presuppose endeavors to concretize values and principles through behavioral prescriptions.[65] Such views further imply that Pentateuchal alternating of law and lore provides a useful model of integrating legal investigation with an analysis of narratives.

Even this is not as simple as it may, at first, appear. Within the Pentateuch itself there are, at least, two distinct worldviews: one that had guided the redaction of the early history of Israel (Genesis–Numbers), and another that had shaped Deuteronomy, the latter also providing an inspiration for the redactor(s) of Joshua–2 Kings, the second great historical narrative of Israel's fortunes and misfortunes. Each of these Pentateuchal components contains a significant number of 'laws', representing two legal systems.[66] In this reading, if Genesis 31 and 38, for example, presuppose the absolute authority of the *paterfamilias* over the entire household, Deuteronomy's familial laws point to a systematic infraction of this control through the gradual appropriation of paternal power by communal mechanisms.[67] This

Phillips, *Ancient Israel's Criminal Law, passim.* See also below, Chapters 6 and 7, with the salubrious remarks of Martha T. Roth, '"She Will Die by the Iron Dagger": Adultery and Neo-Babylonian Marriage', *Journal of the Economic and Social History of the Orient* 31 (1988), pp. 186-206, on the multiple meaning of the threat of capital punishment. In fact, the inclusion of this type of threat in a marriage contract points to its euphemistic nature regarding female marital fidelity.

65.   Moshe Greenberg, 'Some Postulates of Biblical Criminal Law', in Menahem Haran (ed.), *Yehezkel Kaufmann Jubilee Volume* (Jerusalem: Magnes Press, 1960), pp. 5-28 (21); Peter Haas, '"Die, She Shall Surely Die": The Structure of Homicide in Biblical Law', *Semeia* 45 (1989), pp. 67-87 (84).

66.   Deuteronomy, for example, dispenses with sacral procedures (see below on the ritual of branding a person who wishes to remain a slave). In general, see Weinfeld, *Deuteronomy, passim*; Bernard S. Jackson, *Essays in Jewish and Comparative Legal History* (Leiden: E.J. Brill, 1975); and Michael Fishbane, *Biblical Interpretation in Ancient Israel* (Oxford: Basil Blackwell, 1985). On Deuteronomy as a freedom charter, freeing individuals from the authority and control of kinsmen, see Joseph Blenkinsopp, 'Deuteronomy and the Politics of Post-Mortem Existence', *VT* 45 (1995), pp. 1-16. See also the raging debate about the gender orientation of Deuteronomic legislation between Pressler, (*View of Women*), and Georg Braulik, ('Haben in Israel auch Frauen geopfert? Beobachtungen am Deuteronomium', in Siegfried Kreuzer and Kurt Lüthi [eds.], *Zur Aktualität des Alten Testaments. Festschrift für Georg Sauer* [Frankfurt: Peter Lang, 1992], pp. 19-28). On Deuteronomic distinctions *vis-à-vis* the Covenant Code, see Caroline Pressler, 'Wives and Daughters', in Victor H. Matthews, Bernard M. Levinson and Tikva Frymer-Kensky (eds.), *Gender and Law in the Hebrew Bible and the Ancient Near East* (JSOTSup, 262; Sheffield: Sheffield Academic Press, 1998), pp. 147-72 (170-71). On relating laws to landscapes, in addition to Ska, 'Biblical Law', see Eckhard Otto, 'Town and Rural Countryside in Ancient Israelite Law: Reception and Redaction in Cuneiform and Israelite Law', *JSOT* 57 (1993), pp. 3-22.

67.   See Louis Stulman, 'Sex and Familial Crimes in the D Code: A Witness to Mores in Transition', *JSOT* 53 (1992), pp. 47-63, but also see the reservations of Douglas, *Leviticus as Literature*, pp. 104-106, who regards the Deuteronomic prescriptions as an attempt to stop arbitrary self-help and violence in (post-exilic) conditions of fragmentation and collapse. See also Christopher J.H. Wright, 'The Israelite Household and the Decalogue: The Social Background and Significance of Some Commandments', *TynBul* 30 (1979), pp. 101-24.

'transition in mores' divested the *paterfamilias* of control over the bodies of members of the family by making adultery, rape, seduction (i.e. sexual transgressions), filial disrespect and homicide offences against society at large.[68] Deuteronomy, it has been repeatedly asserted, no longer regards women as chattel or personal property.[69]

Whether such distinctions between the status of women in Genesis–Numbers on the one hand, and in Deuteronomy (and the Dtr History) on the other hand, are fully justified, it is certainly advisable to treat the legal and narratological exegesis of each of the Commandments within two distinct frameworks, Genesis–Numbers and Deuteronomy–Dtr History, respectively.[70] This is precisely what I have done in this book. I have separated between the Decalogue of Exodus 20 and of Deuteronomy 5, treating each one as the centerpiece of a redactional tissue that advances specific agendas.[71] Accordingly, each chapter is divided into two sections, one centering on the Exodus' Decalogue, the other on Deuteronomy's Decalogue. Each of these divisions contains presentations and analysis of exegetical legal texts, mostly along the line of 'mainstream' scholarship, followed by allied narratives which are

68. Stulman, 'Sex', p. 62. Cf. David Daube, 'The Culture of Deuteronomy', *Orita* 3 (1969), pp. 43-50 on the culture of shame background of D which emphasizes public disgrace and implicates God in the discovery of crimes. See also Stephen Dempster, 'The Deuteronomic Formula *kî yimmatse* in the Light of Biblical and Ancient Near Eastern Law: An Evaluation of David Daube's Theory', *RB* 91 (1984), pp. 188-211, who draws attention to the kinship between Deuteronomic legislation and other Hebrew Bible laws.

69. On Deuteronomy's 'benevolence' towards women, see Weinfeld, *Deuteronomy*, pp. 285-92. See also below, Chapters 6 and 7. For women as chattel in rabbinic writings, see Judith Romney Wegner, *Chattel or Person? The Status of Women in the Mishnah* (New York: Oxford University Press, 1988).

70. For different reasons in support of the distinction of Deuteronomy, see Eckhard Otto, 'False Weights in the Scales of Biblical Justice? Different Views of Women from Patriarchal Hierarchy to Religious Equality in the Book of Deuteronomy', in Matthews, Levinson and Frymer-Kensky (eds.), *Gender and Law*, pp. 128-46, who also regards the 'pre-Deuteronomistic laws of Deuteronomy' as a revision of laws of the Covenant Code (rather than a precursor, as John Van Seters maintains in 'Comparison of Babylonian Codes with the Covenant Code and its Implications for the Study of Hebrew Law', [unpublished paper delivered at SBL 2001, electronic version available from <www.biblicallaw.org>], p. 3). For Otto, Deuteronomy advances a 'brotherly ethos' which pertains to men and women equally ('False Weights', p. 142, on basis of Deut. 15.12). In Otto's scheme the exclusion of women from the cult is interpreted as liberation from cultic obligations (p. 143).

71. I refrain from delving into the perennial problem of Deuteronomic/Deuteronomistic elements in the final redaction of the Pentateuch as a whole. See, among many, Marc Vervenne, 'The Question of "Deuteronomic" Elements in Genesis to Numbers', in Florentino García Martínez *et al.* (ed.), *Studies in Deuteronomy in Honour of C.J. Labuschagne on the Occasion of his 65th Birthday* (VTSup, 53; Leiden: E.J. Brill, 1994), pp. 243-68; and *idem*, 'Current Tendencies and Developments in the Study of the Book of Exodus', in *idem* (ed.), *Studies in the Book of Exodus: Redaction–Reception–Interpretation* (Leuven: Peeters, 1996), pp. 47-54, with ample bibliography. Nor do I deal with other vexed questions, such as the relationship between the Deuteronomy and the Dtr History, which has recently been reopened by Gary N. Knoppers in his 'Rethinking the Relationships between Deuteronomy and the Deuteronomistic History: The Case of Kings', *CBQ* 63 (2001), pp. 393-415. All this is important but irrelevant to the present inquiry.

interpreted mostly with the help of feminist methodologies.[72] To illustrate the meaning and import of the Decalogue, I have selected key legal texts and index narratives that provide, to my mind, complimentary commentaries of the driving force behind each of the individual Commandments.

I have also taken women, subjects and objects of both law and lore, as signifiers or common denominators of the worldviews propounded in each of these systems. Cautiously but consistently this study reclaims the encoded voice of womanhood, or rather the code of women, as one crucial key of comprehending the ancient Israelite mind. By selecting female characters and their tales as interpretative clues, I am presenting a reading of the Decalogue at three levels: legal, behavioral and representational. Beginning with an analysis of the legal contents of each Commandment through allied legal texts which relate to women and to the feminine, each chapter continues with an investigation of the ways in which the activities of the female and male protagonists of select narratives elucidate the range of the Commandments. Underlying the presentation is the question of how authorial/ redactional views reshaped and manipulated 'reality' in order to provide their own exegesis of the same Commandment.

A close reading of the relevant texts is an obvious point of departure. My main question when approaching these texts is: What is their relevance to the ideas and ideals of wo/manhood and, through these, to the clauses of the Decalogue? The Hebrew Bible delineates the essence of wo/manhood through both platitudes and paradoxes. It uses women as a category of exegesis to advance a platform of manhood that depends on a regular and assiduous performance of what is 'right' and on careful avoidance of what is 'wrong'.[73] Women are taken as emblematic contradictions (piety–impiety; compliance–contravention, correct–unacceptable behavior) which necessitates the weighing of texts both on their own merits and against the wider context of the Decalogue's ramifications.

Because womanhood is a fundamental axis of biblical worldviews, the exclusion of women's experience from the purview of mainstream modern biblical interpretation has resulted in imperfect comprehension of the Bible itself.[74] The traditional recasting of biblical agendas in terms of contrasts between Israelites and gentiles, or 'them' and 'us', appears insufficient because such a dichotomy is

72. For a recent summary of the latter, see Elizabeth Schüssler Fiorenza, *Wisdom Ways: Introducing Feminist Biblical Interpretation* (Maryknoll, NY: Orbis Books, 2001), and below.

73. Annelies Knoppers, 'Using the Body to Endorse Meanings about Gender', in Mary Stewart Van Leeuwen *et al.* (eds.), *After Eden: Facing the Challenge of Gender Reconciliation* (Grand Rapids: Eerdmans, 1993), pp. 268-98.

74. As has been argued by numerous feminist scholars. See the recent survey of J. Cheryl Exum, 'Feminist Study of the Old Testament', in Andrew D.H. Mayes (ed.), *Text in Context* (Oxford: Oxford University Press, 2000), pp. 86-115. Among numerous contributions which highlight the potential and achievements of feminist exegesis, see Mieke Bal, 'Reading as Empowerment: The Bible from Feminist Perspective', in Barry N. Olshen and Yael S. Feldman (eds.), *Approaches to Teaching the Hebrew Bible as Literature in Translation* (New York: Modern Language Association of America, 1989), pp. 87-92; Alice Bach, 'Reading Allowed: Feminist Biblical Criticism Approaching the Millennium', *CRBS* 1 (1993), pp. 191-215; and the excellent survey and comments of Schottroff, Schroer and Wacker, *Feminist Interpretation*.

meaningless without understanding who, exactly, is the proverbial 'other' or the perennial 'foreigner'.[75]

To this day, however, feminist biblical scholarship and so-called 'mainstream' scholarship have remained strangely apart.[76] This uneasy co-existence must be questioned especially because an integrative approach, such as the one followed in this study, that relies on methodologies developed by both exegetical strands, is bound to sharpen and to deepen our understanding of crucial texts such as the Decalogue. Nor is it possible, to my mind at least, to provide a nuanced version of how the ancient biblical world, as gleaned from its textual legacy, looked upon women, men and gender differences, without relying on both 'mainstream' and 'feminist' interpretations. As the anthropology of modern-day village life in the Mediterranean shows, 'manhood' is closely intertwined with 'womanhood', not only because masculinity itself is a construct, but also because the daily male '*agon*' over public status is a direct extension of the activities in the female/male domestic sphere.

The importance of narratives involving women for better understanding of Pentateuchal law and lore has already been suggested by Calum Carmichael in several studies, including one which examines Deuteronomic family legislation and narrative traditions in Genesis and Ruth.[77] He deems the casuistic legal corpus of Deuteronomy a literary form that provides both antiquity and meaning for the actions and/or penalties described in the narratives of named women traditions. Richard Freund believes that narratives which feature unnamed women in Judges– 2 Kings preserve lost stories which had been once well known.[78] For David Noel Freedman, the entire history of Israel, from the Exodus to Kings, had been conceived (or rather contrived) as a tissue of covenant transgressions recorded in stories which, occasionally, feature women.[79]

In my own work I have found the methodologies of feminist biblical scholarship especially appropriate.[80] Precisely because of their multileveled, multi-disciplined

---

75. See the illuminating comments of Claudia V. Camp, *Wise, Strange and Holy: The Strange Woman and the Making of the Bible* (JSOTSup, 320; Sheffield: Sheffield Academic Press, 2000), p. 188 and *passim*.

76. I note that *The Cambridge Companion to Biblical Interpretation* (Cambridge: Cambridge University Press, 1998), edited by John Barton, boasts one brief article on feminist interpretation (Ann Loades, 'Feminist Interpretation', pp. 81-94); much more space is devoted to historical, literary, political and social readings, although each of these categories could have also included a section on feminist exegesis.

77. Calum M. Carmichael, *Women, Law and the Genesis Traditions* (Edinburgh: Edinburgh University Press, 1979), p. 1 and *passim*.

78. Richard A. Freund, 'Naming Names: Some Observations on "Nameless Women" Traditions in the MT, LXX and Hellenistic Literature', *SJOT* 6 (1992), pp. 213-32 (225).

79. David Noel Freedman, *The Nine Commandments* (New York: Doubleday, 2000), an earlier version of which is criticized by Rodd, *Glimpses*, p. 82. Note the absence of covetousness, a factor that has also undermined Phillips' hypothesis regarding the Decalogue as a criminal code because intent does not appear as a punishable crime. Cf. Calum C. Carmichael, *The Origins of Biblical Law: The Decalogues and the Book of the Covenant* (Ithaca, NY: Cornell University Press, 1992).

80. Katherine D. Sakenfeld, 'Feminist Perspectives on Bible and Theology: An Introduction to Selected Issues and Literature', *Int* 42 (1988), pp. 5-18, and *idem*, 'Feminist Uses of Biblical

approaches, feminist readings have the ability to differentiate the literary, historical, religious-theological and existential dimensions of the biblical narrative.[81] Relying on a range of tools that contemporary biblical scholarship in general brings to bear on biblical texts, feminist critics have been able to produce new interpretative models which have been successfully applied to a (re)consideration of women's roles and to a reassessment of the prejudices and partiality of the sources themselves.[82] The very awareness of such biases is instrumental in this process of re-evaluation. As Cheryl Exum admirably summarizes: 'fragmenting women, leaving their stories incomplete so that they are not full characters, is typical of biblical narratives, and readers tend to fill the gaps in the easiest way; that is, according to convention and presuppositions [of patriarchal ideology]'.[83]

Feminist discussions of language have illuminated 'the pervasiveness of the male orientation of the biblical God', in itself an outcome of a general focus on men and on masculine language for God.[84] Such discussions have measured and evaluated the parameters of the patriarchy that shaped the Bible.[85] This is important especially because biblical attitudes to women, at first glance, do not appear to differ greatly from those evinced by the surrounding civilizations. Yet, the very occupation with the communal history of Israel makes the relative omission of women striking, necessitating alternative histories in order to recover the story of those who have been forgotten, silenced and repressed.[86]

Materials', in Letty M. Russel (ed.), *Feminist Interpretation of the Bible* (Philadelphia: Fortress Press, 1985), pp. 55-64.

81. Schottroff, Schroer and Wacker, *Feminist Interpretation*, p. 63.

82. Phyllis Bird, 'The Place of Women in the Israelite Cultus', in Patrick D. Miller, Paul D. Hanson and S. Dean McBride (eds.), *Ancient Israelite Religion: Essays in Honor of Frank Moore Cross* (Philadelphia: Fortress Press, 1987), pp. 397-419 (399-400). See also the assessment of traditional mainstream criticism by Mieke Bal, *Death and Dissymmetry: The Politics of Coherence in the Book of Judges* (Chicago: University of Chicago Press, 1988), and by Adele Berlin, *Poetics and the Interpretation of Biblical Narrative* (Bible and Literature, 9; Sheffield: Almond Press, 1983); as well as the contributions in Athalya Brenner and Carol Fontaine (eds.), *A Feminist Companion to Reading the Bible: Approaches, Methods and Strategies* (The Feminist Companion to the Bible, 11; Sheffield: Sheffield Academic Press, 1997); and Athalya Brenner, 'On Reading the Hebrew Bible as a Feminist Woman: Introduction to the Song of Songs', in *idem* (ed.), *A Feminist Companion to the Song of Songs* (The Feminist Companion to the Bible, 1; Sheffield: JSOT Press, 1993), pp. 11-27.

83. J. Cheryl Exum, *Fragmented Women: Feminist (Sub)versions of Biblical Narratives* (Valley Forge, PA: Trinity Press International, 1993), pp. 67-68.

84. Exum, *Fragmented Women*, pp. 15-17.

85. Tikva Frymer-Kensky, 'The Bible and Women's Studies', in Lynn Davidman and Shelly Tenenbaum (eds.), *Feminist Perspectives on Jewish Studies* (New Haven: Yale University Press, 1994), pp. 16-39.

86. Ronald Boer, 'Culture, Ethics and Identity in Reading Ruth: A Response to Donaldson, Dube, McKinlay and Brenner', in Athalya Brenner (ed.), *A Feminist Companion to Ruth and Esther* (The Feminist Companion to the Bible, 2nd Series, 3; Sheffield: Sheffield Academic Press, 1999), pp. 163-70 (167), also with comments on the evaluation criteria of these efforts. It is time, however, to move away from categorization of women as either 'victors', 'victims', 'virgins' and 'voices', the categories still used by Tikva Frymer-Kensky, *Reading the Women of the Bible* (New York: Schocken Books, 2002).

Scholars have traditionally divided the ancient social world into 'private' and 'public' domain, each further endowed with a specific gender distinction, with 'private = female' and 'public = male'.[87] This is a comforting but perhaps also a misleading dichotomy. Feminist scholars have demonstrated that 'the private is the public when the interests of individual households are reflected in the collective actions of larger groups'.[88] In fact, the examination of the domain of women, or female spheres of activity, formerly considered out of sight and away from the public, has the potential of illuminating what, exactly, is considered 'private' and how do men act or talk in public. Looking at differentials in both Pentateuchal law and biblical narratives that appear to privilege men (i.e. 'public') is, therefore, important precisely because they do not automatically imply the inferiority of Israelite women (i.e. 'private').[89]

Uncovering the lives of biblical women poses serious methodological problems that are shared by all attempts to reconstruct biblical history.[90] Threads of complex interaction between biblical redacted texts and the 'original' socio-economic-cultic-political contexts that generated them suggest multiple levels of 'reading' women. Feminist investigations of biblical women have eloquently demonstrated how patriarchal concerns manufacture female stereotypes. A social constructivist, however, must go further than this separation of fictional gender as the fiction of sex, and away from Foucault's perceptions of sexuality as metaphor for society and power.[91]

The questions that we need to pose are: What do we mean by being a man, and being a woman, in private and in public? Is this identity founded in the self or in society? One problem which all biblical scholars must face is the lack of historical specificity in which to anchor conventions of gender. We can only, with much circumspection, address issues of sexual identity, sexuality and the sex-linked protocols of social life. 'Separation of sexual identity from social identity has been and continues to be a crucial premise of women's history' and 'in theory, at least, sexuality as an interiorized defining structure of the integral self, and sexual belief and behavior as semiotic expressions of a culture's preoccupations, are now radically separate and incommensurate ways of thinking'.[92]

That women are often the imaginative constructs of men seems evident: such are biblical women of prophecy and of power, the women seen as property of men, and

87.   Michelle Z. Rosaldo, 'Women, Culture and Society: A Theoretical Overview', in Michelle Z. Rosaldo and Louise Lamphere (eds.), *Women, Culture and Society* (Stanford, CA: Stanford University Press, 1974), pp. 17-42, and, in the same collection, Peggy R. Sanday, 'Female Status in the Public Domain', pp. 189-206.

88.   Carol Meyers, '"Women of the Neighborhood" (Ruth 4.17): Informal Female Networks in Ancient Israel', in Brenner (ed.), *A Feminist Companion to Ruth and Esther*, pp. 110-27 (115); see also Karla G. Bohmbach, 'Conventions/Contraventions: The Meanings of Public and Private for the Judges 19 Concubine', *JSOT* 83 (1999), pp. 83-98.

89.   Meyers, '"Women of the Neighborhood"'.

90.   Frymer-Kensky, 'Bible and Women's Studies', p. 19.

91.   See the exposé of Nancy Partner, 'No Sex, No Gender', *Speculum* 68 (1993), pp. 419-43, to which I owe these reflections.

92.   Partner, 'No Sex, No Gender', p. 423.

the women fantasized by poets. In a way, historians of the present do exactly the same thing—imagine the women of the past. Fundamental notions of sexuality, identity and our own estimate of how deeply the cultural conventions of gender affect the way we think determine whether the 'women' we revive are human beings or cultural ideograms. Theories of social constructivism have divorced the mind from the body, elevating the latter into a metaphor map which reflects pressures of social processes determined by power relations.[93] The resultant cultural portraits hinge on a stylized mime of class, gender and economic hierarchies of the larger society. Yet, this focus on patterns of sex/status domination which are typical of all traditional societies also obscures individual and cultural variation. As long as a specific cultural pattern, such as an aspect of dominance of males over females, is made to fit a form of sexual behavior, nothing more is explored. Nor does it explain how can anyone begin to subvert any of the widely shared meanings whose production, distribution and enforcement have constructed the human 'Thing' which has no self and no personal sexuality.

The fact remains that there is no single all encompassing mode which satisfies all aims of understanding, nor can one argue for the primacy of any of the modes except by referring to criteria which are, in themselves, derivative.[94] The question for feminist scholars should not be whether the Bible offers negative or positive portrayals of women but which body of assumptions helps us to the richest, most complex and generous understanding of women—especially women of frankly misogynist societies. Which set of assumptions offers them humanity, and which reduces them to passive anthropological exhibits?[95]

4. *A Rabbinic Reading of the Decalogue*

By way of concluding remarks I recruit rabbinic reflections on the triangle of Torah–Israel–God that demonstrates the vitality of women as decoders of Israelite manhood, itself the sum total of biblical law and narratives. מדרש עשרת הדברות (*Midrash Decalogue*) provides instructive observations on the questions raised here. It highlights how the rabbis, like biblical authors and redactors, used narratives to elaborate and explicate 'legalities' and how they handled female figures to explore theology and morality:[96]

> According to the sages the Torah had been created two millennia before the world was created... Rather upset (at her isolation?) the Torah asked the Lord: Why was I created two thousand years before the world? Why don't you give me to

93. See the articles gathered in Ed Steiner (ed.), *Forms of Desire: Sexual Orientation and the Social Constructionist Controversy* (New York: Routledge, 1990), including one by Foucault.

94. Partner, 'No Sex, No Gender', p. 429; Louis O. Mink. 'Modes of Comprehension and the Unity of Knowledge', in Brian Fay *et al.* (eds.), *Historical Understanding* (Ithaca, NY: Cornell University Press, 1987), pp. 35-41 (40).

95. Partner, 'No Sex, No Gender', p. 433.

96. The date of this midrash is unclear. It may be early medieval, Miron B. Lerner, 'On the Midrashim on the Decalogue', in Yaakov Sussman and David Rosenthal (eds.), *Meḥqerei Talmud. I. Talmudic Studies* (Jerusalem: Magnes Press, 1990–93), pp. 217-36 (Hebrew).

humans? The angels told her: We are delaying handing you over because humans
will sin in you and it is best that you stay with us...

Before Moses came and gave the Torah to the people of Israel, the Lord went to
every people and language on earth to offer them the Torah so that they will not be
able to say that: Had the Lord offered us the Torah we would have gladly received
it... So the Lord went to the sons of Lot and said: Will you take the Torah? They
said: What is written in it? He said: You shall not commit adultery. They said: We
are the result of adultery and we do not want the Torah...

Thus the Lord went from one people to another and they all refused the Torah.
Then he came to Israel. Will you accept the Torah? [They asked.] What is written
in her? [The answer.] Six hundred and thirteen precepts. They said: All that the
Lord said we shall do and we will listen...

When God gave the Torah to Israel He said: Give me witnesses that you will
abide by her... [They responded: Here are Abraham, Isaac and Jacob] [all of whom
God rejected]... They then said: Here are our sons. And the Lord immediately
responded: Give them to me as a pledge and I will take them. And immediately the
Israelites brought their wives with their babies and also their pregnant wives
whose swollen belies the Lord made as transparent as glass so that they [the unborn babies] would converse with Him. And the Lord said the them: I want to give
Torah to your fathers and you have been proffered as a pledge of fulfillment. They
responded: Let it be. And he said: I am the Lord God who brought you out (Exod.
20.2). They responded: Indeed. You shall not have other gods. They said: No [we
will not]. And in this manner they responded with nay or ye...[97]

Casting Yahweh as a matchmaker and the Torah as a daughter, or a bride to be
negotiated, the midrash rearranges the universe of the biblical Exodus along gender
lines with the Torah, always feminine, at its center and the nations dwelling on
earth as prospective bridegrooms. In this midrashic version of the 'creation' tale the
Torah becomes emblematic of 'history'. The midrashic imagination reinvents the
terrain of the Exodus, constructing a symbolic order in which the Torah, in its most
succinct expression through the Decalogue, serves as a bridge between purity and
impurity and between order and chaos.

Like the first humans, the Torah is a result of a process of creation rather than of
generation. 'She' is also on intimate terms with Yahweh and with the angels.[98] The
identity of the Torah text is indelibly female. Since Exodus 20 (the Ten Commandments) employs a language that invests only males with the value of commitment
(above), rabbinic institutional usage designates men as the true Jews. But to become
a Jew one requires double parentage, to adopt the strictest view on the subject.
Hence the paradox of constructing Judaism on the exclusion of women while
assuming that all women who reproduce are already integrated into the commonwealth.[99]

97. Adolph Jellinek, 'Midrasch der Zehn Gebote', in *idem* (ed.), *Bet ha-Midrash Sammlung*
(2 vols.; repr., Jerusalem: Wahrmann Books, 1967), I, pp. 62-90. Unless otherwise stated, translations from Jellinek's edition (referred to simply as 'Jellinek') are mine.

98. Cf. Boyarin, *Unheroic Conduct, passim*.

99. Cf. rabbinic definitions of a 'Jew' on the basis of ascribed maternity, a dictum which renders fatherhood, paradoxically and symbolically, an irrelevant assumption. On questions of Jewish

Through a series of displacements the Torah becomes the link between Israel and Yahweh, providing a means of affirming identity and of representing the division between the sexes. Thinking about the Decalogue necessarily entails a reconsideration of this division. *Midrash Decalogue* goes beyond the biblical text of Exodus 19–20 in its diffusion of the biblical narrative to embrace several referents and to spread across several places. Expanding the play between words and meanings, the midrash engages its readers in an exploration of the bond between the people and the law, Yahweh and Israel, and between men and women.

My study, like the midrash, explores the tales of the Decalogue as a milestone in a journey that aims at the imaginative exclusion of women from the world of men. Because the Hebrew Bible makes metaphors out of the identity of male 'citizens' or members of the covenant, the mechanisms of exclusion exemplify modes of inclusion by using the feminine as the discriminating factor. When Yahweh negotiates the 'marriage' of the Torah with Israel, the latter must supply a pledge of their commitment to its precepts. Resorting to the past, the Israelites of the midrash select the three patriarchs, Abraham, Isaac and Jacob, as their symbolic token of loyalty to Yahweh and to the law. But *Midrash Decalogue* discounts the ancestral paternal figures in favor of maternal images of pregnant women.[100] The text appears to concede to women, wives and future mothers, the role of exclusive mediators between Yahweh and the Israelites of the future, bearers of the Decalogue.

Mapping the space of negotiations around transparent pregnant bellies of Jewish mothers allows a direct discourse between males (Yahweh and future sons of Jews), a mode that simultaneously elevates and reduces the role of mothers. In the midrashic appropriation of paternity rather than of maternity Yahweh communicates with fetuses through the bodies of their mothers. Fathers, like the three Genesis ancestors, cannot provide sufficient pledge of the commitment of Israel to the Torah. The midrashic understanding of the forging of the Torah bond between Yahweh and Israel through the bodies of mothers indicates that the hypothetical exclusion of women from the Sinaitic theophany could never be an accomplished fact. A reconsideration is in place.

identity see my *Dinah's Daughters: Gender and Judaism from the Hebrew Bible to Late Antiquity* (Philadelphia: University of Pennsylvania Press, 2002), Introduction and Chapters 4 and 5.
    100.   Cf. *Lamentation Rabbah* with the discussion in *Dinah's Daughters*.

Chapter 2

MONOTHEISM = MONOGAMY? TEXT, IMAGE AND PARADIGM (WORD ONE; WORD TWO)

The image of man made in God's own image.
The cruel pitiless human, justifying atrocities—
And God, indifferent about his monstrously faulty invention.
Or did we invent God to suit our merciless blind nature?
I can no longer follow the verbal glorification of prayers.
I lost my love, my admiration and fear—
All the ingredients needed for absolute obedience.
I could not find an explanation for
and have lost my acceptance of divine blamelessness.
I could not pray, nor can I ever again…

—Extract from Ava Kadishson Schieber, 'Dialogue'[1]

I am Yahweh your God who brought you out of the land of Egypt, from the house of bondage.

You shall not have other gods before me. You shall not make for yourself a graven image (or) a likeness of anything which is in heaven above or on land below or in the water beneath the earth. You shall not bow to them or venerate them because I am Yahweh your God, a jealous God who brings to bear the sin of fathers on sons, to the third and fourth generation of my enemies; [a God] who also repays with kindness the multitudes who love me and who guard my precepts. (Exod. 20.2-6; Deut. 5.6-10)

1. *Meanings of Monotheism*

Two elements determine the essence of the First Commandment.[2] One is the presentation of Yahweh as the sole and exclusive divinity of a specific group of humans. The other is the encoding of Egypt as a 'house of slavery'. The two may, at first, appear antagonistic and they are certainly agonistic. Yahweh initiates a 'divorce' from a 'home' in which the Hebrews had been demoted into a secondary social rank, like a spurned wife (Exod. 21.10). The separation from Egypt is neither clear

1. Ava Kadishson Schieber, *Soundless Roar* (Evanston: Northwestern University Press, 2002), p. 134.
2. I am counting Exod. 20.2 as a Word, according to the Jewish counting, and despite scholarly objections to the absence of an imperative in this statement.

cut nor swift. It is painful and, as it turns out, willed by Yahweh alone. In a battle of will and wit between the Egyptian pharaoh who embodies bondage, and the Hebrews' self appointed divinity who epitomizes freedom, victory is meant to secure perpetual separation. The means to win lead through an *agon* or a manly competition. To achieve a triumph Yahweh engages in a calibrated demonstration of damage and destruction which must outweigh the Pharaonic power to inflict similar ills. The Exodus narrative repeatedly recalls Yahweh's 'strong arm' (Exod. 13.3 and *passim*), and how it wins in a show of hands which delivers a final humiliation on the pharaoh.

By recalling Yahweh's prowess in the war over manumission in Egypt, the First Word is inscribed into a conventional male context in which warfare determines degrees of masculinity.[3] The Second Word postulates familiarity and distance that are uniquely biblical. It suggests that idolatry, like adultery, results from undesirable proximity to proscribed bodies.[4] And it implies that monotheism requires intimacy with Yahweh, as well as deliberate distancing from all other gods in whatever form and shape these may be.[5]

Memory motivates affiliation. To belong to the community which Yahweh's love had guided out of a house of misfortune, the Hebrews must remember at all times both God and Egypt, past and present masters. The First Commandment stretches back to a 'historical' memory which features a specific Egyptian past and the fatal intertwining of Yahweh's liberating will with pharaonic despotic desires.[6] In the Second Commandment memory becomes a personal attribute of Yahweh. For the Word that proscribes the making of images and censures apostasy also insists on Yahweh's capacious memory. Here, too, a competitive streak is concealed. Just as Yahweh of the First Word is a God who, implicitly, combats mighty mortals (like the Egyptian pharaoh), the Second Word explicitly delineates a God whose existence depends on an ongoing competition with other gods over the love and loyalty of specific mortals. If the Hebrews/Israelites must recall, without failure, the image of tyrannical Egypt, Yahweh's own recollection is directed, in the Second Word, to the iniquities of the Israelites themselves.

3.   Adrian Schenker, 'La profanation d'images cultuelles dans la guerre. Raisons explicites et raison implicites de l'aniconisme israélite dans les textes de la Bible', *RB* 108 (2001), pp. 321-30, makes the interesting suggestion that the Second Word and its allied legal texts were anchored in a desire to save Yahweh the embarrassment of profanation due to defeat on the battlefield.

4.   On idolatry and adultery as diseases or addictions which threaten the inner-freedom of will by forbidden contact, both breaking the limits of fidelity and leading to defection through a polluting contact, see Jan Assmann, *Moses the Egyptian: The Memory of Egypt in Western Monotheism* (Cambridge, MA: Harvard University Press, 1997), pp. 76-77.

5.   Cf. the so-called 'marriage metaphor' in the prophets, Renita J. Weems, *Battered Love: Marriage, Sex and Violence in the Hebrew Prophets* (Minneapolis: Fortress Press, 1995); Gail Streete, *The Strange Woman: Power and Sex in the Bible* (Louisville, KY: Westminster/John Knox Press, 1997), esp. p. 76 and *passim*, among many studies.

6.   Y. Hoffman, *The Doctrine of the Exodus in the Bible*, p. 119, regards Egypt as a late Dtr insertion. Cf. the late redaction of Exod. 2 which I have dated to the late sixth century in my, 'Moses the Persian?'

Based on the Decalogue alone, and specifically on its first two clauses, belonging, and by implication manhood, is determined on the basis of monotheism and memory alone.[7] In this structure Egypt is monochromatic, a land of bondage and of abhorred polytheism. Describing Egypt as a 'house' or a 'home' (בית) the First Word redraws a territorial chart into a familial map.[8] In this recreated 'geography' Egypt's mighty kingdom is ultimately controlled by the Creator like all created entities. Slavery and liberty in this tale of liberation are matters of divine arbitration, echoing the power of a master over members of his household. The First Word reminds the Hebrews of their separation from the Egyptians because of being singled out by a God who vies for their affection. Freedom in this instance is not an inward quality, but a form of conventional manumission. Egypt, envisaged as the embodiment of injustice, is the womb from which the chosen people emerge; and the umbilical cord is cut once and for all by Mosaic or Yahwist monotheism.[9]

Yet, the present arrangement of the Pentateuch softens the sharp dichotomy of the Decalogue's opening strictures. In the book of Genesis Egypt stands neither for polytheism nor for tyranny, but for bonds of ancestral blood. Its very evocation conjures contrasting images. Egypt symbolizes benevolence and openness to strangers, as well as temptations of illicit sexuality. Genesis' Egypt is a land of unlimited opportunities, where enterprising ancestors can find refuge and flourish, and where a Hebrew slave can rise to dizzy prominence. Ironically, the success of the ancestors in Egypt is channeled through women. By using Sarah's beauty, Abraham insinuates himself into pharaonic favors (Gen. 12). Joseph's adroit avoidance of the advances of his mistress land him in jail, whence he is saved by the Pharaoh himself (Gen. 39.40-41).

A multifaceted Egypt casts into relief Yahwist monolithic monotheism in which there is only one super power, a steadfast entity given to rewarding loyal followers

---

7.   I have no desire to enter the battlefield regarding the chronology of Yahwist or Mosaic monotheism nor, for that matter, that regarding the question of whether Moses proclaimed monotheism or monolatry—two terms which, strictly speaking, simply mean one god and the worship of one (god) respectively. Modern dictionaries define monotheism as belief that there is only one God, while monolatry signifies the worship of one god without excluding recognition of the existence of others. For further reflections on these terms, Moshe Halbertal and Avishai Margalit, *Idolatry* (trans. Naomi Goldblum; Cambridge, MA: Harvard University Press, 1992), pp. 67-70 and 182-90. See also the articles gathered in Karel van der Toorn (ed.), *The Image and the Book: Iconic Cults, Aniconism, and the Rise of Book Religion in Israel and the Ancient Near East* (Leuven: Peeters, 1997). As the Hebrew Bible demonstrates, distinctions are artificial and the centrality of Yahweh real, wished for or assumed, and rarely imply the exclusion or/and no acknowledgment of the very existence of other gods. I would agree with William F. Albright, *Archaeology and the Religion of Israel* (Baltimore: Johns Hopkins University Press, 5th edn, 1968), p. 177, on a de facto monotheism which was practical and implicit, although I disagree with his notion that Mosaic monotheism was neither intellectual nor explicit. For recent discussion regarding the absence of genuine monotheism in pre-exilic Israel, see Martin Beck, *Elia und die Monolatrie: Ein Beitrag zur religionsgeschichtlichen Rückfrage nach dem Vorprophetischen Jahwe-Glauben* (Berlin: W. de Gruyter, 1999), *passim*. Perhaps, then, the term should be written as 'Monotheism'.

8.   Cf. the use of מקדש ('sanctuary') to describe divine dwelling (Exod. 25.8) and the qualified use of the term בית ה׳ אלהיך ('house of the Lord', 23.19).

9.   Assmann, *Moses the Egyptian*, pp. 144, 209.

and to penalizing apostates. If Egypt emerges as a fickle, if not a feminized entity in Genesis and Exodus, it is because 'she' is perceived as the very antithesis of Yahweh. If Egypt is a society divided according to class, status and rank, Yahweh's group is, in the text at least, classless and devoid of distinctions. What determines membership is an unquestioned obedience to Yahwist principles.

While the First Word strives to introduce a decisive wedge between Egypt and nascent Israel, the Second aims at creating a chasm between Yahweh and all other gods. The magnitude of this 'divorce procedure' cannot be underestimated. Its very ideology seems opposite to the ideals of closeness around which disparate groups coalesced in antiquity. Indeed, the idea of monotheism must have stood in strange antagonism to the visible plurality of nature and to human reproduction itself. Yahwist society is shaped, then, on an achieved state of belonging, as well as on kinship. Because the one is gained by 'nature' and the other by 'culture', they match only by necessity and through the indispensable mediation of women. The production of more 'Hebrews' or 'Israelites' (or 'Jews' for that matter) depends on reproduction. But the making of Hebrew men depends on careful acculturation to monotheism.

The book of Genesis unfolds the history of the ancestors as a single closely related group held together by blood and by 'monotheism'. The book of Exodus traces the problems of 'indoctrinating' monotheism. And because the path to mono-theistic virtue is far from certain the First Word projects the commonality of recent experience, and not of a remote ancestral one, as the bonding matter par excellence. Only the Second Word, a correlative if not a necessary complement to the First, evokes the universal experience of the creation itself and therefore of polytheism.[10] 'Hebrews' or 'Israelites' alone can fully participate in the First Word, which is neither a prohibition nor a specific recommendation. The universality which the Second Word suggests can, potentially, incorporate anyone willing to adhere to Yahwist monotheism by renouncing idolatry.[11] Both Words indicate that there is need for a constant scrutiny of the outer and the inner self. Put otherwise, the bulk of the Decalogue focuses on the correct deportment of men which has bearing on their public performance and which, in turn, is judged by peers. At the start of the Decalogue, the focal point of the new theology is clearly stated; at its end stands a ban on covetousness which may, at first, appear an oddity within a series of com-mon and concrete prohibitions. This ban reinstates, however, Yahweh as the index

10.   In spite of Walther Zimmerli, 'Das Zweites Gebot', in *idem* (ed.), *Göttes Offenbarung: gesammelte Aufsätze zum Alten Testament* (Munich: Chr. Kaiser Verlag, 1963), pp. 234-48 (236-38), who argues that the prohibition on images had not been an 'original' part of the Decalogue at all, but a product of later redactional hands. See also William L. Moran, 'The Conclusion of the Decalogue (Exod. 20.17 = Deut. 5.21)', *CBQ* 29 (1967), pp. 543-54 (553); and Christoph Levin, 'Der Dekalog am Sinai', *VT* 35 (1985), pp. 165-91 (170). These views correspond with the widely held belief in Deuteronomic iconoclasm, as recently argued by Karel van der Toorn, 'The Iconic Book: Analogies between the Babylonian Cult of Images and the Veneration of the Torah', in *idem* (ed.), *The Image and the Book*, pp. 229-48.

11.   On early Israelite monotheism as a consequence of reordering older religious beliefs, see Ronald S. Hendel, 'Worldmaking in Ancient Israel', *JSOT* 56 (1992), pp. 3-18 (13).

of manhood, because the issue of craving what belongs to another, and of mind controlling, remains one between the individual and God alone.

Norms of membership, if not of masculinity itself, are thus measured by two contradictory criteria, adherence and rejection. One implies a wholehearted acceptance of the God that had effected a divorce from Egypt; the other implies an uncompromising rejection of visual manifestations of the divine as of other gods. Neither is a given, because there is no instinctive monotheism. Monotheism is a virtue that must be instilled through legal strictures and learnt by negative examples. Monotheism incorporates the possibility of deviation and, specifically, of idolatry and apostasy. The precise meaning of either is expressed not only in fashioning images of either other gods or of Yahweh, but also in active promotion of the worship of gods besides Yahweh.

Paradigms of believing, according to the First and the Second Words, hinge on an understated freedom of action to choose the right or the wrong path. Thus the Yahweh of the First Word is not merely a liberator from an Egyptian 'house of bondage', but also from inner human bondage. As the wilderness wanderings illustrate, the road of the liberated Hebrews to achieving this state of inner freedom was neither easy nor, in fact, ever fully achieved. Nor does separation from Egypt necessarily lead to a promised land. The absence of this longed for territory from the Decalogue itself is as remarkable as that of the common ancestors. Rather, the 'divorce' from the Egyptian past or 'depaganization', as a quest for monotheism, winds its way through no man's land, a territory in which everyone must chart his or her way to the meaning of the true God.

The Decalogue advances a comprehension of 'monotheism' by appealing to family imagery.[12] Perhaps it harks back to 'Canaanite' polytheism which scholars have termed 'reductive monotheism' since it features a primordial divine couple as a single procreative pair.[13] The First Word's 'home' (of bondage of Exod. 20.2)

---

12. Cf. the discussion of Isaiah's language in Katheryn P. Darr, *Isaiah's Vision and the Family of God* (Louisville, KY: Westminster/John Knox Press, 1994).

13. Gregorio del Olmo Lete, *Canaanite Religion according to the Liturgical Texts of Ugarit* (trans. Wilfred G.E. Watson; Bethesda: CDL Press, 1999), p. 47. Whether such an influence also accounts for references to the Asherah remains elusive in spite of an impressive Asherah industry, including Michael D. Coogan, 'Canaanite Origins and Lineage: Reflections on the Religion of Ancient Israel', in Miller, Hanson and McBride (eds.), *Ancient Israelite Religion*, pp. 115-24, and, in the same collection, both Kyle P. McCarter, 'Aspects of the Religion of the Israelite Monarchy: Biblical and Epigraphic Data', pp. 137-55, as well as Jefffrey H. Tigay, 'Israelite Religion: The Onomastic and Epigraphic Evidence', pp. 157-94. See also Saul Olyan, *Asherah and the Cult of Yahweh in Israel* (Atlanta: Scholars Press, 1988); Richard J. Pettey, *Asherah, Goddess of Israel* (New York: Peter Lang, 1990); Baruch Margalit, 'The Meaning and Significance of Asherah', *VT* 40 (1990), pp. 264-97; Steve A. Wiggins, *A Reassessment of Ashera: A Study according to the Textual Sources of the First Two Millennia BCE* (Kevelaer: Butzon & Bercker, 1993); Judith M. Hadley, *The Cult of the Asherah in Ancient Israel and Judah: Evidence for a Hebrew Goddess* (Cambridge: Cambridge University Press, 2000); C. Uehlinger, 'Anthropomorphic Cult Statuary in Iron Age Palestine and the search for Yahweh's Cult Images', in van der Toorn (ed.), *The Image and the Book*, pp. 97-155 (140-44). But see the reservations of Tikva Frymer Kensky, *In the Wake of the Goddesses: Women, Culture and the Biblical Transformation of Pagan Myth* (New York:

evokes the ubiquitous 'paternal clan' (בֵּית אָב, literally 'father's house'), and Yahweh's generational memory wreaks havoc on 'fathers', 'sons' and 'grandsons', invoking the procreative or the female aspects of the divine self. In Amos' (3.2) beautiful words, 'Only you have I known of all the families of the earth': Yahweh's complaint captures an image of fertility and reproduction. The 'earth' is the same entity which had produced, upon divine will, the first humans (Gen. 1.27). Israel in this construct is a 'family' (Amos 3.1) which, like most biblical families, is endogamous, patrilineal, patriarchal, patrilocal, extended and polygynous and often dysfunctional.[14]

Yahweh is a 'jealous' God, an emotion which suspicious husbands share.[15] The imagery reflects an exclusive male discourse in which monotheism means a constant competition between masculine gods over the heart of a fickle woman.[16] A covenant, in this discourse, is not merely a formal treaty between a suzerain and his vassals but, rather, an intimation if not an imitation of a marriage contract.[17] The divinely created marital bond and the religious covenant are two sides of the same

Schocken Books, 1992), pp. 158-61, on the Asherah not as a consort but rather as an embodiment or hypostatization of Yahweh's power to ensure prosperity and fertility, seconded by Stephen A. Geller, 'The God of the Covenant', in Barbara N. Porter (ed.), *One God or Many? Concepts of Divinity in the Ancient World* (Chebeague, ME: Casco Bay Assyriological Institute, 2000), pp. 273-319 (275 n. 2).

14. E. Levine, 'On Exodus 21,10', p. 134.

15. On this theme, see Gerlinde Baumann, *Liebe und Gewalt: die Ehe als Metapher für das Verhältnis JHWH und Israel in den Prophetenbüchern* (Stuttgart: Katholisches Bibelwerk, 2000). Perhaps the word 'those who love me' (Exod. 20.6), with its evocation of the complex term 'love', is the most ambiguous of all the Decalogue's carefully chosen words. In Genesis the verb is ordinarily used to denote conjugal or parental love, usually with far reaching consequences for the object of this love. On 'love' within the context of Deuteronomy, where it is exclusively used for the relations between Yahweh and Israel, see below. Isa. 41.8 'translates' Deuteronomic love to describe the relationship between Yahweh and Abraham; see Moshe Goshen-Gottstein, 'Abraham-Lover or Beloved of God', in John H. Marks and Robert M. Good (eds.), *Love and Death in the Ancient Near East: Essays in Honor of Marvin Pope* (Guilford, CT: Four Quarters Publishing, 1987), pp. 101-104. On the metaphor of biblical marriage as interpretative axis of idolatry, Halbertal and Margalit, *Idolatry*, pp. 9-36.

16. Cf. Pierre Bourdieu, *The Logic of Practice* (Stanford: Stanford University Press, 1990), pp. 71-72, on gender as a primary source of the metaphorical language which articulates power relations.

17. On marriage contracts and treaty formulae, see John P. Brown, 'The Role of Women and the Treaty in the Ancient World', *BZ* 25 (1981), pp. 1-28, following George E. Mendenhall, *Law and Covenant in Israel and the Ancient Near East* (Pittsburgh: The Presbyterian Board of Colportage of Western Pennsylvania, 1955), and Weinfeld, *Deuteronomy*. See also William D. Barrick, 'The Mosaic Covenant', *The Master's Seminary Journal* 10 (1999), pp. 213-32. But see the reservations regarding treaty terminology made by Geller, 'God of the Covenant', p. 281, especially on the scarcity of references to God as king in the main covenant texts of the Pentateuch (Exod. 15.18 and Num. 23.21 being the exceptions). On priestly formulations of covenant theology, Philip P. Jenson, *Graded Holiness: A Key to the Priestly Conception of the World* (JSOTSup, 106; Sheffield: JSOT Press, 1992); Israel Knohl, *The Sanctuary of Silence: The Priestly Torah and the Holiness School* (Minneapolis: Fortress Press, 1995); and Stephen A. Geller, *Sacred Enigmas: Literary Religion in the Hebrew Bible* (London: Routledge, 1996).

basic social organization, both hinging on the concept of the singular, mono/gamy/ theism. Both are also, as Levine has suggested, 'reflective consciousness' that extends its monotheistic 'logic' into the relations between the sexes, and vice versa.[18] The 'logic' of monogamy was applied to the relations between God and Israel. And since Israel is invariably a woman and Yahweh her betrayed spouse, the concept of monotheism as a cornerstone of Israelite religion implies the feminization of the Hebrew/Israelite male in relations to God.[19]

Already the Bible's 'first existential reflection on human condition' emphasizes the duality of humanity by insisting that 'it is not good for man to be alone' (Gen. 2.18).[20] Creation legends focus on a single human pair as an idyllic state, combining paradisiacal existence and monogamy (Gen. 2.24).[21] Yahwist (or Mosaic) monotheism stipulates a neat symmetry between a deity who is like a loving husband, and a community which should play the role of an obedient wife. Yet, neither love nor obedience are automatic. Like taming a shrew, loving obedience is an object of an educational campaign. Coaxed and coerced, 'love' is hedged with numerous rules that repeat the Second Word's ideology of exclusivity. Yahweh's unilateral declaration of the First Word proves, in itself, insufficient to dispel a world in which males have endless possibilities of allying with a wide array of divinities, as well as visible and tangible ways to convey wishes and fears and to assert manhood within the rickety frame of sexuality.

2. *Moses and Gendered Monotheism*

Between the 'positivism' of the First Word and the negativism of the Second stands a huge range of deviant behavior and of antagonistic and agonistic constructs. The road to monotheism appears as nebulous and complex as human nature itself. The Second Word proposes negative icons; the First Word socializes males (and females?) through the shared experience of bondage. The visible model of both, Moses, provides a striking exception and an exceptional mold. Not a participant in the past of slavery, Moses' exemplary status and nearness to Yahweh provoke fear and resentment. His marriage outside the group of Yahwist adherents incites criticism from his own siblings who may have understood monotheism in terms of endogamy, if not monogamy (Num. 12, below). Behaviors, such as the faultfinding

18. E. Levine, 'On Exodus 21,10', p. 155.

19. Howard Eilberg-Schwartz, *God's Phallus: and Other Problems for Men and Monotheism* (Boston: Beacon Press, 1994).

20. The expression is E. Levine's; see his 'On Exodus 21,10', p. 153, and pp. 154-55 for what follows.

21. As expected, this endorsement of monogamy has puzzled critics who have preferred to read it as an explanation of sexual yearning (Herman Gunkel, *Genesis* [trans. Mark E. Biddle; Macon, GA: Mercer University Press, 1997]) or as love between the sexes (Claus Westermann, *Genesis*, I [3 vols.; Neukirchen–Vluyn: Neukirchen Verlag, 1974]), rather than an allusion to marriage. But see Bernard F. Batto, 'The Institution of Marriage in Genesis 2 and in Atrahasis', *CBQ* 62 (2000), pp. 621-31, who, correctly, calls attention to the separation between marriage and reproduction.

ascribed to Miriam in Numbers 12, and the critical circumcision handled by his non-Israelite wife in Exodus 4, provide an index of the female conformity/deviation patterns that the Bible employs to shape righteous manhood.[22]

Neither the First nor the Second Word, however, hints at the agencies that may promote forms of deviation. In two classic tales of apostasy (Num. 25, below), the 'return' or regression into idolatry is linked with sex and both censure manly loss of self-control through close contact and proximity to undesirable foreign women.[23] In the hindsight of the Dtr school of history, the very division of the kingdom of David was due to Solomon's accommodation of the idols worshipped by his foreign wives (1 Kgs 11).[24]

Polarizing gender is one avenue of recapturing the desired antagonism between Israelite ecology and its immediate but rejected environment. As a prelude to the Sinaitic epiphany, Moses commands the Hebrew males to wash their garments (Exod. 19.14). The act symbolizes initiation and change.[25] It further entails sexual renunciation (19.15). This pointer of preparation, then, demands separation between males and females. Unlike the permanent partition which the opening of the Decalogue envisages between Israel and Egypt, Yahweh and other gods, Hebrews and gentiles, the one between the sexes is temporary. It lasts for three days, precisely the period which Yahweh had instructed Moses to ask of the Pharaoh (3.18), knowing full well the futility of such a request.

Through representations of deviant behavior, biblical narratives, like Exodus 32, define in what ways the objects specified in the laws deviate from the norm. In a construed world in which only the deity cannot be constructed, outward appearances must be misleading. A calf, golden as it may be, cannot be a god; nor can it represent Moses, and certainly not Yahweh. A woman, able as she may be, cannot be a sole ruler of the Israelites (2 Kgs 11); and a text, holy as it may appear, cannot become normative without due consultation with an authorized female agent of Yahweh (2 Kgs 22). Transgressions, such as worshipping other gods (Exod. 32) and defying Yahweh's trusted emissary (Num. 12), are represented as contravening community norms. They are also dangerous because they are public (as in Exod. 32),

---

22.   For Drorah O'Donnell Setel, the two women's (Miriam and Zipporah) connection with the priesthood suggests a cultic status which was forgotten or repressed ('Exodus', in Carol A. Newsom and Sharon H. Ringe [eds.], *Women's Bible Commentary* [Louisville, KY: Westminster/ John Knox Press, 1992], p. 29). On Miriam, see below, §5. On Zipporah and the enigmatic Exod. 4, see Julian Morgenstern, 'The "Bloody Husband"(?) (Exod 4:24-26) Once Again', *HUCA* 34 (1963), pp. 35-70. On biblical 'dialectics of disdain' *vis-à-vis* deviant religious groups in general, see J. Berlinerblau, 'The "Popular Religion" Paradigm in Old Testament Research: A Sociological Critique', *JSOT* 60 (1993), pp. 3-26 (17).

23.   'Biblical references to women engaging in forbidden cultic practices or in the service of forbidden deities suggest that only as Yahweh and Jerusalem became dominant did women's participation in the official cultus become circumscribed' (Meyers, '"Women of the Neighborhood"', p. 123).

24.   Gary N. Knoppers, 'Sex, Religion, and Politics: The Deuteronomist on Intermarriage', *Hebrew Annual Review* 14 (1994), pp. 121-41; and below Chapter 9.

25.   Jonathan Z. Smith, 'The Garments of Shame', in *idem, Map is Not Territory: Studies in the History of Religion* (Studies in Judaism in Late Antiquity, 23; Leiden: E.J. Brill, 1978), pp. 1-23.

and can move from the private to the public (as in Num. 12). Above all, subversion can become the norm. By exposing such deviant behavior, narrators prefigure what is to be avoided and prevented. By featuring women in the role of promoters of apostasy and agents of defiance and deviation, the ideological basis of the community is narrowly defined around male norms.

Idolatry in theses contexts is not merely the breaching of the First and Second Word. It is also a transgression of gender boundaries. The celebrants of the gold calf indulge in sexual orgies (Exod. 32.6), as do the Israelites who chase Moabite women in the wilderness (Num. 25.1). Because the envisaged audience of these narrated scenes are respectable Israelite males who share norms and values with the narrators, spectacles of aberration delineate 'righteous' and deviant men and women. The 'leprous' Miriam of Numbers 12 becomes a living symbol of disobedience by submitting to an abhorred disease. Narratives of counter-Yahwism and Mosaism become arenas of demonstrating Yahweh's power and of demonizing Yahweh's rivals. Parading the reprehensible, biblical tales of idolatry and insubordination, or of exemplary adherence, affirm and suggest standards for manhood and, by implication, for womanhood. Such visualizations contribute to the drawing of clear boundaries between Egypt and Israel, Yahweh and other gods, the licit and the illicit, and between men and women.

3. *Norms of Piety/Impiety: On Altars and Slaves in the 'Covenant Code'*

> You will not make gods of silver to be with me [alongside with me?] [in my case?][26] Neither shall you make for yourselves gods of gold. An altar of earth you will make for me to sacrifice on it your burnt offerings, peace offerings, sheep and oxen. Everywhere where I cause my name to be mentioned there I will come to bless you. If you make for me an altar of stone you will not build it of hewn stones on which you have wielded a iron tool. For this is a desecration. Neither will you mount the steps of my altar lest you expose your nakedness. (Exod. 20.23-26)

Gushing out of the smoky fog that envelopes the Sinaitic theophany, the rules which accompany the Decalogue aspire to reinforce the meaning of monotheism by focusing on matter, ritual piety and manumission. All three are components of a Yahwist worldview which incorporates nature and society into a monotheistic culture. The combination breeds uneasiness. Regulating a collective culture by prescriptions and proscriptions paradoxically complicates, rather than simplifies, the 'translation' of the Words into reality. The First Word renders untenable the very idea of Hebrew slaves in Hebrew households. The reality and ubiquity, however, of the institution of slavery dictates a series of regulations (Exod. 21.1-11) which aspire to preserve a social equilibrium among Hebrew masters and co-religionist slaves. The Second Word opposes the encapsulation and imprisonment of the divine essence in human-made shapes. But the ebullience of human desire to express homage to the divine requires restraint.

26. As suggested by Joe M. Sprinkle, *'The Book of the Covenant': A Literary Approach* (JSOTSup, 174; Sheffield: JSOT Press, 1994), p. 35, following Henri Cazelles, *Etudes sur le code de l'alliance* (Paris: Letouzey et Ané, 1946), pp. 39-40.

In the so-called Covenant Code impiety and, by implication, piety hinge on the abuse and use of valuables and of humans.[27] Exodus 20.23 incorporates a ban on the fashioning of divinities in precious metals (gold and silver).[28] The practice of using these valuables to such purpose is rarely but strikingly attested in Genesis– 2 Kings, with tales such as the construction of a calf of gold (Exod. 32, below), with earrings of Egyptian provenance, and in the account of the golden calves of Jeroboam (1 Kgs 12.28-29). While donations of gold and silver to Yahweh constitute a legally acceptable manifestation of piety (Exod. 25.2-3), contributions towards the fabrication of forbidden images become a violation of the Second Word.

To bridge between human devoutness and divine reservations regarding appropriate piety, Exod. 20.24-25 provides rules for the construction of altars.[29] These are to be made from earth, like humans themselves, and of uncut stones, material associated with the labor of humans and especially with male hands.[30] Such rudimentary structures were to enable ordinary Israelites to sacrifice and eat ritually prepared animal food without violating the Second Word.[31] Forbidden are more elaborate altars made of hewn stones, because the process involves the application of a chisel rather than one's own bare hands.[32] The term 'tool' (חרב) (Exod. 20.25) is synonymous with the word ordinarily used to describe a sword or a dagger, weapons of destruction and desolation rather than cult constituents. The coincidence seems deliberate. Yahweh's worship focuses on peaceful, domestic pursuits and no part of it should recall the blood and gore of war.

Nor should an altar be polluted with an unintentional exposure of the body. Exodus 20.26 aspires to separate sexuality from sacrifice by insisting on specific architectural features, or rather on their absence, so as to avoid unwonted display of

27. For a recent analysis of the 'Covenant Code' of Exod. 20.22–23.33, see Sprinkle, *Covenant*, in addition to the standard commentaries. For a review of the literature and of the (much contested) relationship between the Decalogue and the Covenant Code (CC), see John Van Seters, *A Law Book for the Diaspora: Revision in the Study of the Covenant Code* (Oxford: Oxford University Press, 2002), who espouses a late, exilic date for the CC. On the CC within Tetrateuch context, see Hans Ausloos, 'Exod 23.20-33 and the "War of YHWH"', *Bib* 80 (1999), pp. 555-63. For an overview, see Guy Lasserre, 'Quelques etudes recentes sur le code de l'alliance', *Revue de theologie et de philosophie* 125 (1993), pp. 267-76.

28. Cf. Isa 2.20, taken to prove that the concern for making images becomes prominent in exilic and post-exilic context; see Frank Crüsemann, *The Torah: Theology and social History of Old Testament Law* (Minneapolis: Fortress Press, 1996), pp. 198-99.

29. See Paul Heger, *The Three Biblical Altar Laws: Developments in the Sacrificial Cult in Practice and Theology; Political and Economic Background* (Berlin: W. de Gruyter, 1999), for a recent detailed discussion.

30. On מזבח אדמה as a 'natural' altar, namely an altar made from readily available 'natural' elements, see Edward Robertson, 'The Altar of Earth', *JJS* 1 (1948), pp. 12-21. On the structure of these verses, see Diethelm Conrad, *Studien zum Altargesetz: Ex 20.24-26* (Marburg: Kombacher, 1968), pp. 26-31.

31. Jerald G. Janzen, *Exodus* (Westminster Bible Companions; Louisville, KY: Westminster/ John Knox Press, 1997), p. 160.

32. Cf. Deut. 27.5; Josh. 8.31. Janzen, *Exodus*, p. 160, regards the ban on stone altars as an expression of distinction between the mandated central worship and the permitted local worship.

the intimate parts of the male body. Its call to modicum censures male nakedness in contact with Yahweh's altar. Like the ban on using iron tools in fashioning altars, the fear of pollution through bodily baring defines the horizons of pious manhood. If altars possessed gender characteristics, they would have been 'masculine', precisely because their erection demands the application of male hands while their shape prevents the exposure of male private parts.

Between individual altars and Yahweh stands a fragrant curtain of smoke, rising from sacrificed animals. This barrier has a double function: it satisfies the divine desire for visible devotion, as well as human need for nourishment. Exodus 20.4 regards altars of earth as the stage on which an Israelite may sacrifice domestic animals for survival. Incorporated in this act of fumed bonding is a blessing, for Yahweh is willing to bestow grace on this form of compliance wherever it may take place. Correct connections with the divine, then, are limited to specific venues of visible communication and to specific means. To compliment this chart of the permissible and the forbidden, Exod. 21.1-11 outlines a map of recommended relations among unequal members of the same Yahwist community:[33]

> If you purchase a Hebrew slave, he will labor for six years and on the seventh he will be set free for nothing (or: without payment of redemption money). If he had entered slavery by himself, he shall leave by himself. If he entered servitude with his wife, she will leave with him. If his master had given him a wife who had borne him sons or daughters, the woman and her children will stay with the master and the husband will leave by himself. If the slave states: 'I have loved my master, my wife and my children and will not leave them even for freedom' his master should make him approach 'the gods' (or: the deity), and at the door [or the door post], he will pierce his ear with an awl. And the man will be his slave for eternity.
>
> If a man sells his daughter to become a slave she will not leave like a slave. If she fails to give pleasure to the master for whom she had been designated she should be redeemed (or: ransomed); to foreign people he will not sell her in spite of his power over her because such sale is [evidence] of his faithlessness. If he designated her for his son, the rules pertaining to [freeborn?] daughters must be followed. If he takes another [as a wife], he should not detract from the food, clothing and marital rights [of the first 'wife']. And if he fails to follow any of these three options she will be set free for nothing (or without the payment of money).

Exodus 21.2 ordains the manumission of a Hebrew male slave after six years of labor.[34] 'Sabbatical' rules, then, apply not only to God and to free Israelites but also

---

33. The juxtaposition, as well as the insertion of these rules next to the Decalogue, and the nature of the entire 'legal' series of Exod. 19–24, have generated controversy. Opinions range from 'a loosely organized miscellany' with little purpose (John Durham, *Exodus* [WBC, 3; Waco, TX: Word Books, 1987], p. 319), through late composite insertion of several redactional hands and without exegetical significance (Childs, *Exodus*, p. 465), to a covenantal collection aimed at establishing a relationship with a god (Sprinkle, *Covenant*, p. 37).

34. The chronology is clearly reminiscent of the cycle of the creation itself as well as of the Sabbath (below Chapter 4). On this pericope, Gregory C. Chirichigno, *Debt-Slavery in Israel and the Ancient Near East* (JSOTSup, 141; Sheffield: JSOT Press, 1993); and John Van Seters, 'The Law of the Hebrew Slave', *ZAW* 108 (1996), pp. 534-46.

to the unfree. Yet, if the rule regarding 'sabbatical' manumission appears clear-cut, 21.4-5 highlights the dilemma of independence: a slave whose wife and children are not liberated with him has, evidently, the right to decide whether he wishes, or not, to adopt the opportunity of liberty.[35] The moment of freedom is circumscribed by a choice between two ostensibly unequal paths, one leading to full membership in Yahweh's community, the other to permanent subjection to another human member of the self same community.

At the heart of this 'free' choice is the family. The liberated slave, if married to a woman owned by his master, cannot leave with her or with their children. His selection, either way, is conditioned by 'love'.[36] Exodus 20.4-6 suggests that the freedom which Yahweh had secured for the Israelites from Egyptian bondage is an inherent attribute of male membership in the Yahwist community. If a liberated man prefers the love of his family and of his master to the love of liberty he is to be branded forever. Love, then, is not merely an emotion. It signifies a mode of behavior which binds humans among themselves, as well as all the Hebrews to Yahweh.[37] The ceremony that bridges between freedom and slavery for love's sake leaves a visible mark on the man's ear as a symbol of the permanence of his servile status and his innate inability to perceive freedom as a basic tenet of belonging.[38] This ritual entails the positioning of the voluntary slave next to the house's entry door in the presence of 'the gods' (or God or ancestral figurines, אלהים), and the piercing of his ear. The involvement of these hallowed witnesses implies that a judicial procedure had taken place in which a person 'guilty' (of love?) was deemed guilty by sacral adjudication, hence 'punishable' (by a permanent mark of identification).[39] The rite also raises questions regarding perceptions of marriage and

---

35. The text does not allude to the ethnicity of the wife—is she an Israelite or a foreigner? For the former, see Pressler, 'Wives and Daughters', pp. 147-72; for the inclusive nature, see Van Seters, *Law Book for the Diaspora*, pp. 90-92. I concur with Pressler.

36. Cf. Ruth 1.16-17. On 'love' as a verbal contract rather than an emotional concept, see Jack M. Sasson, *Ruth: A New Translation with a Philological Commentary and a Formalist-Folklorist Interpretation* (Baltimore: Johns Hopkins University Press, 1979 [2nd edn = Sheffield, JSOT Press, 1989]), *s.v.*

37. On biblical metaphors of love, see William Moran, 'The Ancient Near Eastern Background of the Love of God in Deuteronomy', *CBQ* 25 (1963), pp. 77-87; Yohanan Muffs, *Love and Joy: Law, Language and Religion in Ancient Israel* (New York: Jewish Theological Seminary of America, 1992), pp. 121-93; Katherine D. Sakenfeld, 'Love (Old Testament)', in *ABD*, VI, pp. 375-81. See also below.

38. Exod. 21.6's expression, 'to bring the slave closer to god', has generated controversy regarding the precise meaning of the term 'god' or 'gods'. The controversy is summarized in Sprinkle, *Covenant*, pp. 56-59, who opts for 'gods' as *teraphim* representing ancestral figurines. Whether the ceremony of marking the ear was further intended to discourage men from selecting the course of servitude, as Sprinkle (p. 59) argues, is equally unclear. See also Victor Hurowitz, 'His Master Shall Pierce his Ear with an Awl (Exodus 21.6): Marking Slaves in the Bible in Light of Akkadian Sources', *PAAJR* 58 (1992), pp. 47-77.

39. Shalom Paul, *Studies in the Book of the Covenant* (Leiden: E.J. Brill, 1970), p. 90. On the piercing the ear in general, see Ake Viberg, *Symbols of Law: A Contextual Analysis of Legal Symbolic Acts in the Old Testament* (Stockholm: Almquist & Wiksell, 1992), esp. pp. 77-88 (on Exod. 20).

personal freedom in a monotheistic society. This raises the question: Are the two in fact antithetical?

Human 'love', specifically of a man for a woman, acts as a divider in situations of impending liberty. Withdrawal of affection, if involving an enslaved woman 'married' to the master, breeds potential problems. Love, in the case of a liberated Hebrew male, may serve as a reinforcing bond of slavery. It may act as an obstacle in the path of complete manhood. Posed, for a moment, as a master of his own fate, a male Hebrew has the power to choose a path of servitude or of liberty. A female Hebrew slave in Exodus 21 is not endowed with such free will—her fate is determined by law and not by the self.

Branding the ear, of all the human organs, implies that the very ears which had heard God's message of liberty in the Sinai also act as arbiters of personal freedom. Within the framework of the feminine, the ears are not destined to bear the mark of the awl but, rather, to display golden ornaments that are removable and hence potentially suborned to foster idolatry. In biblical constructs of masculinity, the human ear translates the divine voice into terms of individual behavior. Were the translation imperfect, the ear must display the consequences of faulty understanding. Women (and children) bear shiny ornaments which carry their own brand of enslavement. If used as decorative jewelry, such earrings merely enhance the inner beauty of the ear. When applied to a transgression of the Second Word, as happened in the episode of the gold calf (below), these human artifacts emphasize deafness to the word of God.

Marking the Israelites as a group that values freedom from human bonds, the First Word suggests that the liberation from Egyptian slavery granted liberty to all of Israel. Exodus 21 acknowledges the possibility of subjection not to gentiles but to members of the same group. Monotheism, it seems, does not after all liberate *all* its practitioners from the social ties that condition the functioning of society.[40] Nor does monotheism solve a basic human dilemma of affiliation. Paradoxically, Exodus 21 shows a slave espousing the cherished bond of love at the expense of even personal liberty, thereby mirroring the loving loyalty that Yahweh constantly claims *vis-à-vis* Israel and that Israel is expected to reciprocate.[41] Perhaps, then, the pierced ear may be read as a badge of honor rather than of the shame of misplaced fidelity, at least if read against the grain.

How crucial was the moment of transition from slavery to freedom? According to the First Word, this is the defining moment of Israelite identity. The rules relating to 'purchase-marriage' of a 'Hebrew' female slave (אמה, Exod. 21.7-11) point in the same direction.[42] Here the law accompanies a female lifecycle not from birth

---

40.   Here I stand in contrast with those (like Sprinkle, *Covenant*, pp. 65, 71) who regard these rules as a promotion of humanitarian treatment of slaves in general.

41.   On 'love' as a conventional expression to denote obligation of vassals to lords in a treaty context, see Thomas W. Mann, *Deuteronomy* (WBC, 5; Louisville, KY: Westminster/John Knox Press, 1995), p. 56, and below.

42.   Van Seters, *Law Book*, p. 90. The term אמה has been variously seen as referring to a second wife, so Charles F. Fensham, 'The Son of a Handmaid in Northwest Semitic', *VT* 19 (1969),

to death, but from her forced transplantation into the house of a stranger, through alternative venues of concubinage, marriage, possible resale, to manumission.[43] Born to a free Hebrew father, the woman is, in fact, unfree because her father has the legal right to sell her. However, because of her group affiliation, the law defines the options open to her 'master/husband' if he takes another woman.

At the heart of these rules are provisions which aspire to guarantee the place of an unwanted woman in the household. Her 'master/husband' must provide her with food and clothing (Exod. 21.10), presumably in perpetuity. He must also be responsible for her עֹנָה, an elusive term that has generated much scholarly dispute, and which probably denotes marital right, or sexual due of some sort.[44] A *hapax legomenon*, the word has linguistic associations with 'opening' of both the mouth (in the course of a conversation), and the erogenous areas (during sexual intercourse). Such an assimilation of terms reflects a widespread conceptual symmetry between oral and vaginal anatomy, and between receptive and aggressive activity.[45] Through this blend of bodily parts and legal rights, the 'law' speaks on behalf of the silent or silenced woman. Exodus 21.10 seems to suggest that the master/'husband' is responsible for the physical and sexual well-being of the woman he purchased and spurned, and that he cannot resell her to another.

Read within the context of the Decalogue's first injunctions, the rules relating to co-religionist slaves provide further reflections on affinities between covenant, gender relations and marriage. It seems possible that rules, like Exod. 21.10 (of providing a rejected wife with basic needs), were calculated to promote a monogamous trend by indirectly discouraging multiple economic and sexual obligations, and by directly insisting on the enslaved woman's inalienable rights in a household taken over by another woman. Perhaps the juridical stipulation of Exod. 21.10 was derived from the fundamental biblical concept of covenant.[46] Both covenantal ideology and marital idealism extol mono/gamy/theism as two sides of the same idyllic existence. Monogamy restrains sexual competition; monotheism strives to eliminate polytheistic rivalry. But just as the Decalogue stops short of ordaining monotheism, the Hebrew Bible does not command monogamy of equality.

pp. 312-21, or to a bonded woman who is either the second wife of a free man or of a slave, so Alfred Jepsen, 'אָמָה and שִׁפְחָה', *VT* 8 (1958), pp. 293-97. In Genesis the women called אָמָה are also concubines (Sprinkle, *Covenant*, p. 51 n. 1).

43. Pressler, 'Wives and Daughters'.

44. See the brilliant survey of E. Levine, 'On Exodus 21,10', esp. pp. 143-64, from which much of what follows is drawn. Sprinkle, *Covenant*, p. 51, translates the term as 'cosmetics', following Shalom Paul, 'Exod. 21.10: A Threefold Maintenance Clause', *JNES* 28 (1969), pp. 48-53, who regards עֹנָה as oil or ointments and hence as an item linked with skin's beauty. For recent discussions, see Pressler, 'Wives and Daughters', esp. pp. 158-60 on Exod. 21.8-11; and Raymond Westbrook, 'The Female Slave', in Matthews, Levinson and Frymer-Kensky (eds.), *Gender and Law*, pp. 214-38.

45. E. Levine, 'On Exodus 21,10', p. 144, with Shalom Paul, 'Euphemistically "Speaking" and a Covetous Eye', *HUCA* 14 (1994), pp. 193-204.

46. E. Levine, 'On Exodus 21,10', p. 155.

4. *A Calf of Gold:*
The Allure of the Image and the Attraction of Apostasy

Besides interpreting the Commandments, the book of Exodus is quick to provide a narrative illustration of the meaning of the Decalogue's Second Word by painting a scene of idolatry and orgy in which sex and apostasy symbolize misplaced piety. The story is well known.[47] When Moses is engaged in receiving the Torah directly from Yahweh, the Hebrews demand a 'god' (rather 'gods', the text uses the plural) to replace their vanished leader. Their request to Aaron is couched in words that echo the First Word itself: 'Rise and make for us [a] god[s] (אלהים) who can lead (plural) us ahead (ילכו לפנינו), because this man Moses, who has brought us out of the land of Egypt, we know not what happened to him' (Exod. 32.1). Aaron constructs a gold substitute, rituals follow, Yahweh informs Moses, the angry Moses breaks the tablets of the divinely dictated mores and grinds the sparkling god to dust.[48] He then initiates a massacre of the idolatrous, prepares new tablets, goes up and down the mountain, and presents the people with a new covenant (Exod. 34). This 'testimony' (עדות) of the renewed relations is deposited in the ark, which is placed in a tent that is accompanied by Yahweh's cloud by day and by night (Exod. 40.38).

Within barely a dozen chapters (and less than six weeks), the entity that had saved Israel from Egyptian bondage changes substance and identity. In response to the Israelite quest for divine leadership, Aaron creates a heifer made of gold and presents this shiny creation as 'your god, O Israel, the one who had brought you out of the land of Egypt' (Exod. 32.4). It is, moreover, a structure wholly made with the gold which Hebrew males obtained, on Aaron's order, from the very ears of their own wives and children (32.2-3). These earrings had been among the items which

---

47. On the episode and its relevance to the thorny issues of redactional history, see Joachim Hahn, *Das 'Goldene Kalb': Die Jahwe-Verehrung bei Stierbildern in der Geschichte Israels* (Frankfurt: Peter Lang, 1981 [2nd edn = 1987]); Gary N. Knoppers, 'Aaron's Calf and Jeroboam's Calves', in Astrid B. Beck *et al.* (eds.), *Fortunate the Eyes that See: Essays in Honor of David Noel Freedman* (Grand Rapids: Eerdmans, 1995), pp. 92-104; Hans-C. Schmitt, 'Die Erzählung vom Goldenen Kalb. Ex. 32 und das Deuteronomistische Geschichtswerk', in Steven L. McKenzie and Thomas Römer (eds.), *Rethinking the Foundations: Historiography in the Ancient World and the Bible—Essays in Honor of John Van Seters* (Berlin: W. de Gruyter, 2000), pp. 235-50. It has, as has been widely acknowledged, close parallels with the account (considered by many to antedate Exod. 32) of Jeroboam's establishing a double calf cult in the kingdom of Israel (1 Kgs 12.26-30); see Wesley I. Toews, *Monarchy and Religious Institution under Jeroboam I* (Atlanta: Scholars Press, 1993), pp. 123-35. On representations of bulls in close association with a god on Iron Age II seals, see Uehlinger, 'Anthropomorphic Cult Statuary', p. 111.

48. The question of plausibility and what, exactly, did Moses grind is discussed by David Frankel, 'The Destruction of the Golden Calf: A New Solution', *VT* 44 (1994), pp. 330-39 who rejects the metaphorical explanations of Samuel E. Loewenstamm, 'The Making and Destruction of the Golden Calf', *Bib* 48 (1967), pp. 481-90; and *idem*, 'The Making and Destruction of the Golden Calf. A Rejoinder', *Bib* 56 (1975), pp. 330-43, and his followers, and argues that Moses ground the tablets (and not the calf) to powder which then became a drink and only afterwards burnt the calf. This ingenious suggestion relies on a textual emendation which rearranges Exod. 32.20.

Yahweh had suggested as an appropriate compensation to be paid by the Egyptians to their Hebrew 'neighbors' for decades of oppression (3.21-22). To be precise, (Hebrew) women were instructed to collect valuables from their female Egyptian neighbors and from any female living in their (female) neighbor's house. The intent may have been to secure future contribution to Yahweh's own shrine (25.3). Ironically, these served to violate God's own precepts.[49]

As a bridge between the Egyptian past and the wilderness interlude, the earrings provide a silent but eloquent testimony of the multiple use of female ornaments and of women's potential share in acts of apostasy.[50] Earrings were often associated with divine regalia of idols.[51] The tangible association between the ear, the communicating seat of male obedience and disobedience on the one hand, and the specific metal which promotes apostasy and graces female ears on the other hand, hints at a mental evocation of gendered idolatry scale, as does the reference to sex and dance in honor of the gold bovine (Exod. 32.6, 19). In the rules regarding male Hebrew slavery, the ear represents inverted priorities.[52] The transgressing Hebrews in Exodus 32 are guilty of abusing an organ of piety by making it into a bearer of potential impiety. They are also blameworthy because their endowment of a forbidden image with divine qualities constitutes a flagrant violation of the Second Word.

In the telling of the story of the gold calf in Exodus 32, two stages can be discerned. One is marked by Moses' absence; the other by his vindictive presence. The first phase unfolds the making of a god and the rites in this god's honor. The Israelites not only sacrifice to the calf, but also eat, drink and engage in sexual orgies (Exod. 32.6).[53] The precise purpose of their celebration is unclear. Perhaps it was a continuation of the victory feast over Egypt which had begun in Exodus 15.[54] Its sexual undertones are unmistakable. According to the Exodus 32 'etiology of sin',

49.   Another irony, as Carol Meyer notes, resides in the textual assumption that the Egyptian women who are 'neighbors' participate in a women's network with a high enough degree of solidarity and cross-group identity to accede to the rather odd request ('Women of the Neighborhood', p. 121).

50.   On ancestral links through Jacob and his iconoclastic act which involves earrings and idols (Gen. 35.2-4), see Donald E. Gowan, *Theology in Exodus: Biblical Theology in the Form of a Commentary* (Louisville, KY: Westminster/John Knox Press, 1994), p. 219, who draws attention to divine mercy vs. divine wrath in Exod. 34 and 32 respectively. See also R.W.L. Moberly, *At the Mountain of God: Story and Theology in Exodus 32–34* (JSOTSup, 22; Sheffield: JSOT Press, 1983), *passim*.

51.   Hurowitz, 'His Master', *passim*.

52.   Herbert C. Brichto, 'The Worship of the Golden Calf: A Literary Analysis of a Fable on Idolatry', *HUCA* 54 (1983), pp. 1-44.

53.   The meaning of 'to play' (לצחק) here is to engage in conjugal caresses; see E. Levine, 'On Exodus 21,10', p. 147, with BDB, p. 850, and Gen. 26.8; 39.14, 17.

54.   As R.J. Burns, *Has the Lord Indeed Spoken Only Through Moses? A Study of the Biblical Portrait of Miriam* (Atlanta: Scholars Press, 1987), p. 20, and Jerald G. Janzen, 'The Character of the Calf and its Cult in Exodus 32', *CBQ* 52 (1990), pp. 597-607, have argued. Janzen, *Exodus*, p. 228, further argues against a fertility ritual in favor of one centering on the divine warrior. If this is the case I wonder whether the Exod. 32 references are meant as a parody rather than a prolongation.

the Israelites indulge in sex and apostasy, both profoundly offensive to Yahweh's sensibilities.[55]

The second stage is set when Moses is ready to rejoin the camp. Already at a distance he hears loud voices as though fighting has broken out. Then correction comes: 'It is not a sound of victory cheers, nor one of the vanquished, but rather the sound of an orgy' (Exod. 32.18).[56] On approaching, Moses beholds the people dancing. He breaks the tablets of the law, destroys the calf and turns to Aaron, blaming him for the sin. In Aaron's version the making of the calf was miraculous: the gold which the Israelites had donated had miraculously materialized into an icon out of the flaming conflagration (32.24).[57]

According to Yahweh's vocabulary, the events mark a shift of identity: the celebrants become Moses' own people' whom Moses (and not Yahweh) had brought out of Egypt (Exod. 32.7-8). Yahweh also proposes a seemingly neat solution to the problem of inveterate idolatry in the camp: eliminate the idolatrous 'traitors' and make Moses in the mold of Abraham, a new father of a new nation (32.10). Rejecting the proposal, Moses pleads for the people, reminding Yahweh of the First Word: 'Why should Yahweh be angry with your people whom you had brought out of the land of Egypt?' (32.11).

By the time Moses implores God on the behalf of the delinquent Israelites, the calf is no more than a textual reference. Moses' first reaction, even before accosting Aaron, had been to burn and grind the calf to dust.[58] According to Exod. 32.20, Moses scattered the dust in water and made the Israelites drink the apparently deadly concoction.[59] He kills others with the help of the Levites, and Yahweh sends a plague to do away with the rest (32.28, 35). Already in antiquity the description bred doubts, and the Talmuds transmit a query of an erudite woman regarding the

---

55. The expression is taken from Jerarld G. Janzen, 'Song of Moses, Song of Miriam: Who is Seconding Whom?', in Brenner (ed.), *A Feminist Companion to Exodus–Deuteronomy*, pp. 187-99 (198). Cf. Num. 25, with my 'The Rape of Cozbi', *VT* 51 (2001), pp. 69-80.

56. Following E. Levine, 'On Exodus 21,10', p. 147, rather than the standard 'sound of singing' or 'sound of laughing'. The אֹנות here stands for opening or entering, in other words for sexual activities. The phrase is difficult and has elicited different interpretations. For the sense of an 'orgy' deriving from אֹנה ('to make love') and linked with the name of the goddess of love and war, Anath, see Ariella Deem, 'The Goddess Anath and Some Biblical Hebrew Cruces', *JSS* 23 (1978), pp. 25-30. On connecting Exod. 32.18 to the goddess, see Ronald Edelmann, 'Exodus 32:18', *JTS* 1 (1950), p. 56 and *idem*, 'To ענות: Exodus xxxii 18', *VT* 16 (1966), p. 355. For a different translation ('It is not the sound of a hero song, nor the sound of a coward's taunt. I hear the sound of reversal'), which connects the verses not only with a reversal but also with the voice of Anat (i.e. sexual innuendo), see Robert M. Good, 'Exodus 32.18', in Good and Marks (eds.), *Love and Death in the Ancient Near East*, pp. 137-42.

57. Aaron's incrimination has been usually taken to detect an argument relating to rival claims of priestly houses in which Exod. 32 promotes the Levites at the expense of Aaron while Num. 25 does the opposite (Cross, *Canaanite Myth*, pp. 198-200).

58. Or the tablets, as Frankel, 'Destruction', argues.

59. Loewenstamm, 'The Making and Destruction of the Golden Calf', presents ancient Near Eastern parallels to account for a ritual of burning, grinding and scattering which he sees as devoid of realism. But see Frankel, 'Destruction', for another interpretation. See also Jack M. Sasson, 'Bovine Symbolism in the Exodus Narrative', *VT* 18 (1968), pp. 380-87.

discrepancies between the crime and its punishments.[60] She wondered why Exodus 32 referred to no less than three types of death (by drinking, implicitly; by the sword and through a plague, explicitly) for those who committed the exact same sin.

Rabbinic reflections on this biblical text also detect an affinity between idolatry and adultery through the commonality of an ordeal procedure.[61] Numbers 5 prescribes a ritual, intended to reveal concealed adulteresses, which bears curious similarities to the settlement of scores in the gold calf episode.[62] Through a mixture of earth from the sanctuary and 'holy water' (Num. 5.17), a priest is supposed to detect whether a marriage bed had been 'polluted' (5.19-20). Moses' purpose in administering the gold powder to the Israelites is not stated. Perhaps it was to act as a cleansing agent since Moses charges Aaron with causing the people to sin (Exod. 32.21). Perhaps it was a test of loyalty to Yahweh.[63] In either case the husband and Yahweh pose as the injured party, imbued with 'a spirit of jealousy' (Num. 5.14, 30).

Both tales assume that the sinners had been prone to sin. Aaron claims in his justification that the Israelites had been, by nature, bent on evil (Exod. 32.22). The trial of the *soṭah* in Numbers 5 assumes that a woman is inclined to embark on extramarital affairs. In such situations only a specific combination of the holy and the mundane (earth-dust/water) can uncover marital impiety, or become a catalyst of sin and purification. In the constructed landscapes of idolatry (Exod. 32) and adultery (Num. 5) the latter, if true, becomes a debasement of the ideology of manhood, while the former stands for a defilement of the ideology of Mosaic Yahwism. Marital fidelity requires the woman to remain in monogamous relations; monotheistic faith requires a male Israelite to stay faithful to Yahweh alone.

Perhaps the most dramatic result of the defection of the Israelites was the dismemberment of the tablets which contained God's precepts. The need to refashion these enabled the redactor to project a new covenant, with its own set of rules. Exodus 34 provides a select 'repetition' of the Decalogue of Exodus 20, likewise featuring Yahweh as a deity of memory, especially with regards to sin (34.7).[64] But in Exodus 34 the Egyptian past of the First Word recedes in favor of an ancestral-Canaanite one in order to highlight the divine promises of land. Thus 34.10-11

60. See *b. Yom.* 66b; *y. Soṭ.* 3.4, with Judith Hauptman, 'Women Reading Talmud', in Rina Levine-Melammed (ed.), *Lift Up Your Voice: Women's Voices and Feminist Interpretation in Jewish Studies* (Tel Aviv: Yedioth, 2001), pp. 28-40 (28-34) (Hebrew).

61. This implied association is also suggested by the insertion of this pericope into the tractate dealing with the *soṭah* (= suspected adulteress) in the Palestinian Talmud (vs. its insertion into the tractate *b. Yom.*), Hauptman, 'Women Reading Talmud', pp. 31-32. See also my comments in *Dinah's Daughters*, Chapter 5.

62. Below, Chapter 7. In this, as in much else, the rabbis anticipated modern scholarship and medieval biblical commentaries.

63. As Frankel, 'Destruction', p. 336, argues, also on the basis of its similarities with the *soṭah* ordeal and on the basis of *b. 'Abod. Zar.* 44a (not referring to the sources quoted above in n. 60). He also makes the interesting suggestion that both potions included erased words, based on Num. 5.23, and on the assumption that Moses ground not the calf but the tablets.

64. Gowan, *Theology in Exodus*, p. 219, draws attention to divine mercy vs. divine wrath in Exod. 34 and 32 respectively. Cf. Moberly, *At the Mountain of God, passim*.

envisages an imminent materialization of a return to that territory (34.10-11). In this projected context, marriage with locals becomes a threat not only because the community that engendered Exodus 34 views intermarriage with disfavor, but also because such alliances result in the dissolution of the covenant with Yahweh in favor of another with other gods.[65] The correct form of marriage for an Israelite remains 'monogamy', namely marriage within the group of faith or endogamy.

5. *Purity, Pollution and Piety: Leviticus and Numbers on 'Leprosy'*

The issue of 'monogamy' as an earthly reflection of idealized monotheism raises questions about the articulation of identity. Calves of gold transmit images of the forbidden and map a path which leads from a straightforward violation of the Second Word to veneration of idols, sin and punishment. In this interpretation of the Commandment there is room neither for penitence nor for expiation. A literal recasting of the Decalogue in the wake of the calf's episode calls for a ban on marriage between 'Israelites' and 'locals' (Exod. 34.16). The prohibition discourages exogamy when linked with apostasy. It does not necessarily enforce endogamy, monogamy or monotheism. But it assumes the presence in the camp of an inherent and fatal weakness which entices Israelite males to follow gentile female partners (rather than the other way around), and it accredits the latter with a propensity to direct the unwary into deviant apostasy.

To what extent are Yahwist principles of monotheism cum 'monogamy' to be applied, and to whom? Where do the forbidden and the permitted begin? Or end, for that matter?[66] Although the ancestral clan, in Genesis, follows a carefully charted diagram of desirable marriages, the last recorded alliance (Gen. 41.45, Joseph and Aseneth) is one between a Hebrew and an Egyptian. Yet, Dinah's (un)desired partner in Genesis 34, like the gold calf, symbolizes a corporeal sin and vice incarnate.[67] The distinction of Shechem and of the calf consists of perceptions of their very inferiority.

Interpreters of the First Word required, in addition to a map of negativities, a figure that would embody the positive idealism of the opening statement of the Decalogue. If Yahweh is God of liberation and of loyalty, a Yahwist is a humanized reflection that can serve as a model of manhood and an exemplar of Yahwist monotheism. To judge by the sheer space which the Pentateuch allocates to Moses, there is hardly a doubt that he, of all men, is the chosen paradigm.[68] Yet, Moses is also endlessly challenged. The most serious reservation regarding his preferred status comes from within his textual(?) family. Against an unusual familial quarrel,

---

65. The regulation may also echo the events at Baal Peor (Num. 25), which, in turn, are invoked in Exod. 32.25 (Aaron has driven Israel wild) and the sexual aspect of the offence of idolatry. On this link, see Hugo Gressman, *Mose und seine Zeit: ein Kommentar zu den Mose-Sagen* (Göttingen: Vandenhoeck & Ruprecht, 1913), pp. 199-218.

66. See the study of Deborah F. Sawyer, *God, Gender and the Bible* (London: Routledge, 2002), *passim*.

67. *Dinah's Daughters*, Chapters 1 and 3.

68. Material multiplies rapidly. For starters ATLA electronic database is useful.

Moses' humility, the indefinable quality which renders him unique in the annals of Yahwism, emerges. It is publicly revealed not in his dealings with either Israel or Yahweh but with his own siblings. The catalyst of the clash over the meaning of manly 'humility' and its manifestations is a woman—Moses' own sister; the bone of contention may have been another woman—Moses' wife.[69]

Numbers 12 transmits a peculiar narrative.[70] It begins with a reference to Moses' marriage with a 'Kushite' woman. This woman, of whom nothing else is known, and/or the marriage itself, become the subject of a family feud between Miriam and Aaron on the one hand, and Moses on the other hand.[71] Leaving matrimony aside, the tale turns to a complaint about Moses' status *vis-à-vis* Yahweh and Yahweh's community. Miriam and Aaron contest Moses' exclusive access to the divine word and will. Yahweh intervenes. In the course of the enforced resolution one family member, Miriam, is inflicted with 'leprosy'.[72] Brother Aaron remains as unscathed as he had been in the aftermath of the affair of the gold calf.[73] Moses' unique standing is reasserted. Miriam must undergo the shame of parental penalty and of publicly administered admonition before cure comes through separation and demotion.

What, exactly, is this fragmentary narrative about? Embedded within a general recital of communal recalcitrance, the episode appears to convey yet another

69. See Phyllis Trible, 'Bringing Miriam Out of the Shadows', in Brenner (ed.), *A Feminist Companion to Exodus–Deuteronomy*, pp. 166-86 (175) (first published in *BR* 5 [1989], pp. 14-25, 34), for a list of questions regarding the possible bones of contention, especially whether the concepts of cleanliness and uncleanliness are violated by this marriage. On Miriam see the sophisticated analysis of Camp, *Wise, Strange and Holy*, Chapters 5–7 and *passim*.

70. On Num. 12's 'hopeless conflation', see Burns, *Has the Lord Indeed Spoken?*, pp. 77-78. Martin Noth, *Numbers: A Commentary* (trans. J.D. Martin; OTL; London: SCM Press, 1968), p. 93, and *idem*, *A History of Pentateuchal Traditions* (trans. Bernhard W. Anderson; Englewood Cliffs: Prentice Hall, 1972), p. 32 n. 120, espouses a J nucleus vs. George B. Gray, *A Critical and Exegetical Commentary on Numbers* (ICC; Edinburgh: T. & T. Clark, 1903), p. 124, and Norman H. Snaith, *Leviticus and Numbers* (The Century Bible; London: Thomas Nelson, 1967), pp. 234-35, who prefer an E source.

71. Scholarly speculations about the identity of the Cushite usually range between a Midianite (i.e. Zipporah?) or an Ethiopian. See, among many, Dennis T. Olson, *Numbers* (Interpretation; Louisville, KY: John Knox Press, 1996), p. 70. On the marriage as a mere excuse for the protest against Moses' unique position, see A. Noordtzij, *Numbers* (trans. Ed van der Maas, BSC; Grand Rapids: Zondervan, 1983), p. 107. If the wife in question is Zipporah the story acquires an added irony for it indirectly pits a foreigner who initiates a ceremony of male covenant (circumcision) (Exod. 4) against a female family member who defies Yahwist conventions.

72. The precise nature of the term (מצורעת, צרעת) is unclear since it covers a range of skin diseases; see Baruch A. Levine, *Leviticus* (JPS Torah Commentary; Philadelphia: Jewish Publication Society of America, 1989), pp. 75-76; Douglas, *Leviticus as Literature*, pp. 182-85, and below on leprosy as pollution; and Reuven Gafni, 'Leprosy as Penalty in the Bible and in Rabbinic Writings', *Megadim* 30 (1999), pp. 23-33 (Hebrew). On Miriam in general, see the various contributions in Brenner (ed.), *A Feminist Companion to Exodus–Deuteronomy*. For a detailed analysis of Num. 12, see Burns, *Has the Lord Indeed Spoken?*, pp. 48-55.

73. On the question of why Miriam alone is punished there are various opinions, summed up in Olson, *Numbers*, p. 74. She may have been the original instigator, or the author wanted to spare Aaron by making him forestall penalty through an early confession of sin.

rebellion, this time within Moses' own family.[74] But the initial subject of the controversy is drowned in an abrupt narrative transition. After Miriam and Aaron raise the topic of Moses' seemingly inappropriate wife, they challenge Moses' oracular authority, voicing reservations about Moses' prophetic voice.[75] Moses, 'the meekest of men' (Num. 12.3) maintains silence; Yahweh, Miriam and Aaron do all the talking.

Yahweh's intervention on Moses' behalf highlights the exclusive channels of communications to which Moses alone had been privy.[76] He alone can behold the 'picture' or 'image' of God (Num. 12.8), a gaze that had been withdrawn from every other Israelite and stigmatized through the Second Word. As soon as Yahweh concludes the speech of disapprobation outside the tent of the tabernacle, spectators realize that Miriam had turned white with 'leprosy'. She has thus become an alienated 'stranger' by virtue of her skin disease.[77] Aaron intercedes as though he had not been a party to the divine rebuke. Only then Moses raises his voice, briefly (with five words not exceeding two syllables each), and asks God to show mercy to his sister. In time of public affliction the family, or rather the brothers, align with the ailing sister. Alliances, however, have shifted. At the start of the story Miriam and Aaron unite in opposition to Moses' wife and to Moses' station; at the conclusion of the tale, Aaron and Moses combine to allay God's anger in defense of their sister.

Was the intent of the narrator to introduce the kind of internal rifts which exogamic or polytheistic marriage may cause? Sibling strife is hardly a novelty in biblical history. Yet, the combinations in Numbers 12 are exceptional. In Genesis' familial topographies, brothers covet fraternal space and privileges (Cain–Abel; Jacob–Esau; Jacob–brothers); sisters vie for the affection of their husband (Rachel–Leah–Jacob); and brothers ally against their sister's lover (Gen. 34). Nowhere, however, do a brother and a sister act in unison against another (male) sibling, nor is reconciliation enforced by direct divine intervention which espouses one side and penalizes another.[78]

74. In general, see George W. Coats, *Rebellion in the Wilderness* (Nashville: Abingdon Press, 1968).

75. Burns, *Has the Lord Indeed Spoken?*, p. 51, regards the crux of the controversy as Moses' singular oracular authority and Num. 12.6-8 as a component in a tradition that views this authority as unique and singular (p. 57). She relates Num. 12.2-9 to a conflict between priestly groups (Levites and Aaronic) over the question of oracular authority (p. 66). Wilson espouses the cause of prophecy (Robert R. Wilson, *Prophecy and Society in Ancient Israel* [Philadelphia: Fortress Press, 1980], pp. 155-56). Trible seems to support this assumption ('Bringing Miriam of the Shadows', p. 175). For Camp (*Wise*, pp. 191-99), the story embodies the erection of priestly boundaries in the post-exilic era.

76. See Num. 12.8's 'mouth to mouth', an expression that echoes 'face to face' of Exod. 33.11 and Deut. 34.10, and of 'eye to eye' (2 Kgs 10.21; 21.16; Exod. 9.11). See Noordtzij, *Numbers*, p. 109.

77. Camp, *Wise, Strange, and Holy*, p. 17 and *passim*.

78. I find the speculation (raised practically in all commentaries) about the alleged power of the unknown Cushite as an incitement to the siblings' quarrel unsubstantiated; see, for example Olson, *Numbers*, p. 71, with Renita Weems, *Just a Sister Away: A Womanist Vision of Women's Relationship in the Bible* (San Diego, CA: LuraMedia, 1988), pp. 72-74.

As events unfold, the sister is struck with 'leprosy'. The choice of the affliction seems deliberate.[79] Leviticus devotes two chapters (Lev. 13–14) to a discussion of 'leprosy' as a source of bodily impurity.[80] The 'Torah of the leper' (Lev. 14.1), like the 'Torah of jealousy' (Num. 5.29), features priests in a prominent position as arbiters of individual and collective states of purity and impurity. In Leviticus 13–14, these men have the authority to determine whether a member of the community is infected with 'leprosy', to send persons suspected of being infected to quarantine, and to supervise the rituals of purification. Within this Levitical context, where purity and impurity denote holiness and unholiness, ritual cleanness must be undefiled since it duplicates Yahweh's own purity (Lev. 11.44-45).[81]

Leviticus' focus on rituals revolves on the intertwining of holiness and cleanliness in order to ensure the removal of all defilement from the sacred precincts of the tabernacle (Lev. 15.31; 22.9; cf. Num. 5.1-4). It dwells on an elaborate classification of all living creatures who come into the domestic orbit of the Israelites, juxtaposing unclean creatures like lizards, moles and mice, with unclean humans, such as women after childbirth or sexual intercourse and men after an emission or intercourse (Lev. 11–12). The impurity of these categories is shared by 'lepers'. None of these three human categories is fit to be a part of the observances in the sanctuary. Neither are they deemed morally sinful, for Leviticus is uninterested in the causes of the disease.[82] 'Leprosy', like motherhood, is not generated by sin or guile. New mothers, like 'lepers', are ritually unclean and hence forbidden entry to the sanctuary and to the consumption of consecrated food. Expiation is made because a taboo had been broken.[83]

Yet, the very application of moral terminology (guilt, sin, expiation) to describe 'leprosy' suggests a connection between disease and sin, which Numbers 12 makes explicit. When Aaron realizes that his sister is infected, he 'translates' her 'leprosy' into terms of sin committed in folly (Num. 12.11), echoing Moses' appeal to Yahweh to forgive the sin of the gold calf (Exod. 32.31). In Aaron's gruesome words, the 'scaly' Miriam is like a walking dead: 'Let her not be like a dead whose flesh is half eaten upon emerging from a mother's womb' (Num. 12.12).[84] A process of

---

79. Trible, 'Miriam', p. 177, highlights the ironic color contrast between a dark-skinned wife and a 'white-skinned' sister, the former by nature, the latter by the 'culture' of penalty. For Camp, *Wise, Strange and Holy*, pp. 191-99, it is a means highlighting the strangeness of women even within the right genealogy.

80. On these chapters see B.A. Levine, *Leviticus*, pp. 75-77.

81. See Yehezkel Kaufmann, *The Religion of Israel: From its Beginnings to the Babylonian Exile* (trans. Moshe Greenberg; Chicago: Chicago University Press, 1960), pp. 447-48; and Roland de Vaux, *Ancient Israel: Its Life and Institutions* (trans. J. McHugh; London: Longman, 1961), pp. 460-64. See also the fascinating survey of medieval leprosy, Saul N. Brody, *The Disease of the Soul: Leprosy in Medieval Literature* (Ithaca, NY: Cornell University Press, 1974), *passim*, and esp. pp. 107-109, on biblical origins of the ecclesiastical tradition.

82. There is no attempt to identify a sin that causes the disease, Douglas, *Leviticus*, p. 185.

83. Brody, *Disease*, p. 112.

84. Saul M. Olyan, *Rites and Rank: Hierarchy in Biblical Representations of Cult* (Princeton, NJ: Princeton University Press, 2000), p. 45, with Tikva Frymer-Kensky, 'Pollution, Purification, and Purgation in Biblical Israel', in Carol L. Meyers and M. O'Connor (eds.), *The Word of the Lord*

purification follows. It has little to do with Levitical prescriptions. Moses asks Yahweh to cure his sister, and Yahweh responds with a question: 'had her father but spit in her face, should she not be shamed for seven days?' (Num. 12.14 RSV). Miriam's father materializes figuratively to cast her as a daughter rebelling against paternal authority. The metaphor transforms Miriam's opposition to her brother into a matter of unacceptable familial behavior, which deserves penalty.[85] It devalues her status, as does her temporary removal from the camp.

Miriam's 'leprosy', like apostasy, becomes a moral sin against Yahweh's idyllic cosmos, a defiance of Yahweh's supreme paternal authority. Numbers 12 prompts a double notion of irreverence, one introduced by challenging the choice of a partner made by Moses, the other by doubting Moses' subsequent status as God's preferred ambassador. The selection of Miriam as both the challenger and as the punished (or punishable) party highlights redactional policies which required the reinforcement of manhood through impugning agonistic womanhood. Such (re)shaping of the narrative outlines how a Hebrew-born woman, and specifically a member of Moses' own family, might become an agent of 'apostasy' within the Israelite family itself.

Numbers 12 proposes the extension of the ideology of the sin-bearing women from an anonymous and faceless crowd of women celebrating idolatry (Exod. 32) to a specific Israelite woman. In this, Numbers 12 comes close to the stories combined in Numbers 25 that, likewise, shift from the general to the particular, and from a mass of faceless Moabite women to a specific Midianite princess, in order to highlight the perilous link between all that is female and apostasy.[86] The Moabite temptresses of Numbers 25 entice their Israelite paramours to share their rituals, in addition to their sexual favors. The single Midianite in the same chapter appears in the company of a highly born Israelite at a sensitive time in the annals of the wilderness camp.[87] Her intrusion apparently induces a plague which decimates the Israelites. To appease the furious Yahweh, a grandson of Aaron murders her and her Israelite partner. The murderer is amply rewarded. Moses is seen here at his most helpless, becoming a silent witness of the events. The fate of the Moabite women, like that of the Israelite women in Exodus 32, remains outside the narrated or edited scope.

Both Numbers 12 and 25 explore the meaning of dissension by focusing on gender alliances. In ch. 12 Miriam must be brought to submission through collusion between males—Aaron who acknowledges Moses' authority by begging him to

Shall Go Forth: Essays in Honor of David Noel Freedman (Winona Lake, IN: Eisenbrauns, 1983), pp. 399-414 (400).

85. Jacob Milgrom, *Numbers* (JPS Torah Commentary; Philadelphia: Jewish Publication Society of America, 1990), p. 98, emphasizes the aspect of shame since her 'cure' has little to do with the Levitical laws of leprosy.

86. On Num. 25, see my 'The Rape of Cozbi', and below Chapter 6 §4. For another recent treatment, see Barbara E. Organ, 'Pursuing Phineas: A Synchronic Reading', *CBQ* 63 (2001), pp. 203-18 (204-10).

87. Cozbi's ethnic affiliation (Midianite) may be an indirect confirmation of the identity of Moses' unnamed wife in Num. 12; if so, this may support her identification with Zipporah the Midianite.

help her; Moses who begs Yahweh as he customarily does on behalf of Israel; a shadowy father who shames his daughter; and, of course, Yahweh. Yet, there is also a cure and reintegration. For the Israelite partners of foreign women in ch. 25, as for the noble Midianite and her Israelite partner of Numbers 25, there is neither expiation nor recovery.

At the start of the tale of liberation from Egyptian slavery, Yahweh introduces Moses to monotheism (Exod. 3). This initial introduction prefigures a moment of 'leprosy', imposed and withdrawn by Yahweh in a matter of minutes (4.6-7). Only Yahweh and Moses participate in these demonstrations of divine power. Miriam's 'leprosy' becomes a public matter. Her (and not Aaron's) doubting of Moses' spousal choice and unique relations with God engineers an intimate association between 'leprosy' and morality. In its pursuit of contrasting male and female notions of monotheistic piety, the text compromises its narrative integrity as it casts Miriam alone as the emblem of impiety.[88]

6. *Making Monotheists: Deuteronomy's Version*

A single letter (1, 'and/or') distinguishes the Deuteronomic opening of the Decalogue from its Exodus version.[89] It is a mere copulative vowel, but its omission from the Second Word in Deut. 5.4 seems to suggest that for the Deuteronomic redactor the prohibition on images was categorical and all-inclusive.[90] For some scholars, this tiny difference also indicates a chronological disparity between an older Deuteronomic Decalogue and a younger Exodus one.[91] It may further imply that, in this guise at least, the Word called for an exclusive worship of Yahweh, to the exclusion of even an admission of the existence of other gods. Deuteronomy 4.39 provides the first unambiguous attestation of what may, indeed, be termed exclusive monotheism.[92] But Deut. 10.17 ('This is Yahweh your Lord, God of gods, Lord of lords') hints at hierarchical rather than prohibitive or exclusive monotheism.

88.   Aaron may be a late redactional insertion.

89.   Rendering thus Exod. 5.4 as 'you shall not make a graven image nor a likeness', and Deut. 5.8 as 'you shall not make a graven image, any likeness…' (taking likeness in apposition to graven image).

90.   Whether this also implies that the Exodus formulation depends on that of Deuteronomy's *lectio difficilior*, as Frank-Lothar Hossfeld (*Der Dekalog: seine späten Fassung, die originale Komposition und seine Vorstufen* [Freiburg: Universitatverlag, 1982], pp. 21-31) argues, is less certain, although supported by Tryggve N.D. Mettinger, 'Israelite Aniconism: Developments and Origins', in van der Toorn (ed.), *The Image and the Book*, pp. 173-204 (176). See also Axel Graupner, 'Zum Verhältnis der beiden Dekalogfassungen Exod. 20 und Dtn 5', *ZAW* 99 (1987), pp. 311-15, and Halbertal and Margalit, *Idolatry*, pp. 37-66.

91.   Christoph Dohmen, *Das Bilderverbot: seine Entstehung und seine Entwicklung im Alten Testament* (Bonner biblische Beiträge, 62; Bonn: Hanstein, 2nd edn, 1987 [1985]), vs. Houtman, *Exodus*, p. 22.

92.   According to Jeffrey Tigay, *Deuteronomy* (JPS Torah Commentary; Philadelphia: Jewish Publication Society of America, 1996), p. 41, Deut. 4–11 serves as an expanded commentary on the first two Commandments. Thomas W. Mann, *Deuteronomy* (WBC, 5; Louisville, KY: John Knox Press, 1995), pp. 49-52, sees a more fragmentary structure with Deut. 5.6-7 and 6.1-25 focusing on the First Word, and Deut. 5.8-9a with 7.1-26 on the Second.

According to a fashionable terminology, Deuteronomy advances a theology of 'programmatic aniconism' which relies on name rather than on visual theology.[93] Using another word in vogue, if Genesis–Numbers espouses 'monolatry' in the sense of extolling one deity at the expense of other divinities or without denying their existence, Deuteronomy and its 'school' tenaciously promote 'monotheism' or the theosophy of the existence of one and only deity. But these, after all, may be mere semantics; and no chronology can be established for so complex a progress, if a progress it was.

In Moses' survey of the wilderness past, as recast in Deuteronomy, a full explication of the Second Word (Deut. 4.16-19) precedes the Decalogue itself (Deut. 5). The order is significant. Anticipating transgressions on the basis of the past, the man who destroyed the gold calf and who had guided, under Yahweh's auspices, the Israelites out of Egypt, injects a note of final separation at the very start of his resumptive narrative. The divine will, motivated by sentiments of a resentful God, decreed that he must end his life in no man's land (4.21-2). Moses' audience, by contrast, remains mobile. The 'divorce' between Moses and the promised land is as painful as that between Israel and Egypt had been. It is, however, just as imperative, for it engraves Israelite memory with the souvenir of Yahweh, and not of Moses, as the deliverer from Egypt, just as the First Word insists.[94] This Deuteronomic Yahweh, moreover, is a God of words and not of images:

> Therefore take good heed to yourselves. Since you saw no form on the day that the Lord spoke to you at Horeb out of the midst of the fire. Beware lest you act corruptly by making a graven image for yourselves, in the form of any figure, the likeness of male or female, the likeness of any beast that is on the earth, the likeness of any winged fowl that flies in the air, the likeness of anything that creeps on the ground, the likeness of any fish that is in the water under the earth. And beware lest you lift up your eyes to heaven, and when you see the sun, the moon and the stars, all the host of heaven, you will be drawn away and worship them and serve them, things which the Lord your God has allotted to all the peoples under the whole heaven. But the Lord has taken you and brought you forth out of the iron furnace, out of Egypt, to be a people of his own possession. (Deut. 4.15-20 RSV)

Invisibility is a key concept in this Deuteronomic 'preface' to the Decalogue. It provides an important compliment to the concept of 'Yahweh' as essentially a nameless or 'anonymous' divinity, an incorporeal essence which denies cosmic referentiality.[95] The 'I am who I am' of Exod. 3.14 becomes, in Moses' own words, a

---

93. For the expression, see Mettinger, 'Israelite Aniconism', p. 178, which he explains as a consciously anti-iconic stance (p. 202), vs. the mere absence of images. On name theology, see also Mettinger's *The Dethronement of Sabaoth: Studies in the Shem and Kabod Theologies* (Lund: Gleerup, 1982), and Martin Keller, *Untersuchungen zur deuteronomisch-deuteronomistischen Namenstheologie* (Weinheim: Beltz Athenaum, 1996).

94. Cf. the absence of Moses from the Passover haggada, as Assmann, *Moses the Egyptian*, p. 165, and others have remarked.

95. Assmann, *Moses the Egyptian*, p. 120. On the much-debated question of God in the Hebrew Bible see, among many, Otto Kaiser, *Der Gott des Alten Testament; Theologie des Alten*

script.[96] This is why Deut. 4.13 presents the tablets of the law *before* it actually un-folds the law itself. Monotheism, in Deuteronomy, is synonymous with law because, in the predicted absence of Moses the miracle maker, law is the only tangible and comprehensive means of translating the nascent religion into reality. At Sinai, communications were direct, through visions and voices which appealed to the senses; in the promised land, belief and body discipline become the only viable substitutes.[97]

A series of negatives frames Yahweh by a rigorous redrawing of a forbidden environment. The 'graven images' of the Second Word acquire specificity as they apply, in Deuteronomy 4, to every living creature and to every gender. Embedded in allusions to the writing of the law (4.13) and to Moses' own imminent departure, the species enumerated in 4.16-19 acquire distinction by this very proximity to the 'victory' of the written law (or a sacred text) over all mortal mediators.[98] This par-ticular (re)presentation of the Second Word, brushing away polytheism, limits 'monotheism' to a (written) bond between Yahweh and Israel based on 'laws' which accrue along the Exodus from Egypt.

Projecting a dim future paved with potential transgressions of Yahwist precepts, Moses' recapitulation of the recent past casts Yahweh's mercy and memory as instruments of salvation (Deut. 4.31). The Exodus becomes a proof of the inextri-cable tie between Yahweh and Israel—in spite of the former's propensity to sin and the latter's to wrath and revenge. Neither is likely to disappear. In a post-Decalogue summary of the 'future', Yahweh specifically warns the Israelites against forgetting the Egyptian 'past' (6.12) and against the idolatry that permeates their 'immediate' (Canaanite) surroundings (6.14).

Deuteronomy's preoccupation with the (vain) eradication of idolatry and with the establishment of Israelite monotheism crystallizes into the famed *Shema* (Deut. 6.4-9), which encapsulates the first two Commandments through an exclusive focus on Yahweh and on the behavior of the individual male.[99] Asserting the singularity of the divinity, the *Shema* demands Israel to 'love God with all one's heart, soul and might' (6.5). By positing love as the dominant form of bonding, the *Shema* questions the meaning of 'love' itself and the nature of relations among humans. It implies that this necessary attachment between God and the individual Israelite must be genuine and unconditional. Yet, the Decalogue itself does not mandate this

Testament. II. *Jahwe, de Gott Israels, Schöpfer der Welt und des Menschen* (Gottingen: Vanden-hoeck & Ruprecht, 1998), *passim*.

96. Michel de Certeau, *The Writing of History* (trans. Tom Conley; New York: Columbia University Press, 1988), p. 341 (on the tetragrammaton as inscribing what is being withdrawn—a trace of an evanescence), with Assmann, *Moses the Egyptian*, p. 122. See also, Michel Allard, 'Note sur la formule Ehyeh aser Ehyeh', *Recherches de science religieuse* 44 (1957), pp. 79-86, and Johannes C. de Moor, *The Rise of Yahwism* (Leuven: Peeters, 1990), pp. 175, 213 and *passim*.

97. Assmann, *Moses the Egyptian*, p. 124. Geller, 'God of the Covenant', p. 289, suggests that Deut. 4 even goes so far as to deny the theophany vision.

98. Cristiano Grottanelli, 'Making Room for the Written Law', *History of Religions* 34 (1994), pp. 246-64. Note also the indirect reference to the process of the creation itself.

99. Deut. 13.7-12, with Geller, 'God of the Covenant', p. 293 and *passim*.

kind of commitment, perhaps because law cannot 'buy' love. In the relational map
which the *Shema* outlines in Deuteronomy, the centrality of the individual's love
for God suggests that the covenant itself is both individualistic and collective,
applicable to every Israelite and, at the same time, to the whole of Israel.[100] And it
presupposes a total preoccupation with God at the expense of even the family and
one's own self.[101] In this web of powerful emotions, based on assumed reciprocity,
there is seemingly no room for love between the sexes.[102]

Because divine love is a conditioned state, it resembles the spiritual bond anchored in the social institution of friendship among males, so strikingly visualized
in Jonathan's gesture *vis-à-vis* David on whom he puts his robe, armor, belt and
sword (1 Sam. 18.4). Such love further presupposes a certain degree of equality and
interchange, wholly absent from male–female relations in the Bible. The friendship
between David and Jonathan is sealed by a 'covenant', precisely the term used to
describe the relations between Yahweh and Israel.[103] Operating in an agonistic
culture, men require close friends for moral, economic, social and physical support.
Such friendships ensure their own place in society as well as that of their allies and
supporters. In these constructs, the behavior of female relatives, free or bonded, and
indeed of women in general, has to be taken for granted as a predictable and
controllable factor. Any deviation runs the risk of fracturing the delicate human-
made balance between men. In the book of Exodus 'love' becomes an attribute of
slavery, expressing the emotion that a slave cherishes *vis-à-vis* his master or his
bonded wife. It is an unequal 'love' between two unequal individuals who differ
markedly either in status or in gender.

Deuteronomy's rules on slavery appear to promote an agenda of equality for
'Hebrew' slaves in 'Hebrew' households regardless of gender. Whether this is a
reflection of a vision of a reformed society rather than a rhetorical exercise is difficult to assess. In the Deuteronomic retelling of the gold calf episode, women (and
earrings) disappear altogether. This, too, may be taken as either a 'positive' or a
'negative' attitude on the part of redactors. The fact remains that the Dtr History
continues to generate unease and ambiguity. One tale (2 Kgs 11) casts a woman as
an epitome of impiety; another (2 Kgs 22) entrusts the authentication of the Torah
itself to a woman.

---

100.   Cf. the 'democratization' or the rise of personal religion in which the individual turns
directly to her/his own personal paternal deity, rather than through the medium of king or prophet,
as was the case in the late second millennium in the ancient Near East; see William H. Hallo, 'The
Birth of Kings', in Marks and Good (eds.), *Love and Death in the Ancient Near East*, pp. 45-52
(51).

101.   Geller, 'God of the Covenant', p. 295.

102.   This is, I suspect, why the scroll of Ruth is exceptional in its investigation of 'love'
between women; but this love is conditioned or generated by blood ties and hence cannot, ultimately, be compared with that among men.

103.   Only once does this term, in a metaphorical sense, apply to male–female relations, and
specifically to the marital bond with 'the wife of the covenant' (Mal. 2.14).

7. *Family and Female Slavery: Deuteronomy 15*

In a section which closely parallels Exod. 21.1-11 (above), Deut. 15.12-18 sets out to regulate relations among Israelites of unequal social standing. At first sight, an astonishing 'revolution' appears to have taken place some time between the Exodus and the Deuteronomic redacted texts.[104] While Exodus 21 distinguishes between male and female slaves, Deuteronomic law seemingly considers female slaves on exactly the same footing as male slaves, granting the former the same rights of manumission, and expecting their master to send them free and well equipped for their reintegration into their community of birth and faith:

> If your brother, a Hebrew man, or a Hebrew woman,[105] is sold to you, he shall serve you six years, and in the seventh year you shall let him go free from you. And when you let him go free from you, you shall not let him go empty handed. You shall furnish him liberally out of your flock, your threshing floor, and your wine press. As the Lord your God has blessed you, you shall give to him. You shall remember that you were a slave in the land of Egypt, and the Lord your god redeemed you. Therefore I command you this today.
>
> But if he says to you today: 'I will not go out from you' because he loves you and your household since he fares well with you, then you shall take an awl, and thrust it though his ear into the door, and he shall be your bondman forever. And to your bondwoman you shall do likewise. It shall not seem hard to you, when you let him go free from you. For at half of the cost of a hired servant he has served you six years. So the Lord your God will bless you in all that you do. (Deut. 15.12-18 RSV)

At the core of these rules are two entities, master and ear. Exodus 21 stipulates provisions only for a rejected slave-wife; Deuteronomy 15 prescribes a donation to any female slave who must be set free on the seventh year of her bondage. The Deuteronomic pericope on 'sabbatical' manumission links its regulations to the First Word by alluding to Egyptian slavery and to subsequent liberation. On a more concrete note, the passage justifies the allocation of goods to a manumitted slave by referring to the profit which had accrued to the master from the years of her/his bondage.

An allusion to the Egyptian experience, absent from the comparable rules of Exodus, is typical of Deuteronomy's preoccupation with the 'recent' past (seen most notably in the 'Egyptianization' of the Fourth Word on the Sabbath, below). Based on a tacit assumption of shared male/female bondage in Egypt, the Deuteronomic text on 'Hebrew' slaves draws a conclusion which presupposes an equal treatment of individual male and female slaves. Perhaps, as has been argued, the

---

104. I refrain from dealing with the perennial problem of whether Deuteronomy is a shortened version of the CC, and hence 'younger' in date, or the CC is an expanded one of Deuteronomy. Viberg, *Symbols of Law*, opts for the antiquity of Exod. 21; Van Seters, *A Law Book*, p. 89, prefers the antiquity of Deuteronomy.

105. On the term 'Hebrew slave' as an oxymoron, see Brueggemann, *Deuteronomy*, p. 166. On the inherent contradiction between the idea of slavery and the biblical ideology of freedom, see above (under the discussion of Exod. 21). On the passage's sexist language, see Phyllis A. Bird, 'Translating Sexist Language as a Theological and Cultural Problem', *Union Seminary Quarterly Review* 42 (1988), pp. 89-95 (92-93).

text represents a 'considerable advance' of 'Israel's social vision'.[106] The Deuteronomic pericope employs a masculine mode of address throughout, both with regards to the master and to the bonded. When dealing with voluntary rejection of manumission, Deuteronomy 15 omits love for one's family as a cause. Rather, it is love for the master and for the master's household in general that moves a man (and a woman?) to opt for perpetual slavery (Deut. 15.16).

Deuteronomy 15 presents Yahweh as an active partner in the transaction of liberation. The centrality of Yahweh contrasts with the concomitant absence of the 'gods' (or ancestors) from the ritual of the ear-branding. Instead, Yahweh reminds buyers of their duties toward slaves because Yahweh, and not the power of one individual over another, remains the source of all wealth. To entice potentially reluctant masters Yahweh uses memory as a weapon, assuring slave owners of future blessings and of remembrance. Here the experience of the Exodus is applied towards the education of Israelites who own other Israelites. In this context, the use of the extraordinary verb to 'ransom' (פדה, Deut. 15.15) in describing the Sinaitic experience of liberation accounts for the command to share one's wealth with one's former slave.[107]

Because forgetfulness of the overarching memory of Egypt can be fatal and can result in perpetual bonding of one Israelite to another, the Deuteronomic 'modification' of the Exodus' rules on self-willed retention in slavery is remarkable and tendentious. A slave who wishes to remain a slave, not out of love for his bonded family (Exod. 21.5) but rather out of love for his/her master and for the 'comforts' of the security which the master provides (Deut. 15.16), is a person guilty of a deluded emotional investment, like the Israelites who constantly missed the imaginary fleshpots of Egypt. Instead of directing her/his love to the liberating Yahweh, this wo/man illegally transfers their attachment to a mere human. Such 'love' reads as a travesty of the sentiment which prevails among men like Jonathan and David. It is unequal, misguided and consequently deserves to be branded.

8. *From Broken to Recovered Torah:*
A Calf of Gold, a Queen and a Prophetess

In the Deuteronomic version of the 'great sin' of apostasy as manifest in the erection of a gold calf (Deut. 9), gone are the earrings; gone are the women and children whose ears acted as bearers of idolatry; and gone are even the rituals, celebrations and orgies honoring the idol. Idolatry, it seems, no longer involves

---

106. As argued by Brueggemann, *Deuteronomy*, p. 168. Tigay, *Deuteronomy*, p. 149, argues that the text deals with a woman who, like the man, becomes indentured because of debt owed by herself, her husband or her brother. Hence, it represents an extension of Exod. 21.1-11 rather than new regulations which supersede it.

107. Note also the similarity in vocabulary between Deut. 15.13, which insists that slaves cannot be manumitted 'empty handed' (ריקם), and Exod. 3.21, which implies not an arbitrary appropriation of Egyptian property but a regular manumission according to law. See Roland Gradwohl, 'Nissal und hissil als Rechtsbegriffe im Sklavenrecht', *ZAW* 111 (1999), pp. 187-95.

sexual sinning. The crime in this recasting is the very making, rather than the vener-ating of a forbidden image. Deuteronomy 9 dispenses with a chain of material and men which leads from people to earrings, from assembled gold to Aaron, and from Aaron to an idol. Rather, all the Israelites are guilty of a collective sin, and Yah-weh's anger is directed at every single Israelite, including Aaron.[108] The calf meets the same fate as it does in Exodus 32, but the powdered metal is scattered down the river rather than fed to the worshippers (Deut. 9.21).[109] The ordeal of the drinking, with its adulterous connotations, is thus omitted. This is a selective account indeed, which emphasizes the essence of the Second Word by closely focusing on its wording. Here the interdiction on making images is at its most literal and, perhaps, the least convincing.

Deuteronomy's literalness seems deliberate. At the heart of its condensed narra-tive, Deuteronomy 9 positions not a golden calf as the chief if mute protagonist (as in Exod. 32) but two competing entities: Moses and the tablets, a man and a text.[110] Seemingly recounted by Moses himself, Deuteronomy 9 often refers to the 'tablets of the covenant' (Deut. 9.9). Designed to signify the apex of the bonding process between Yahweh and the chosen people, the tablets descend with Moses to en-counter a usurpation. Instead of waiting for a divinely inscribed text and a divinely chosen guide, the people turn to a human-made deity. Curiously, the tablets 'give up'. To be precise, Moses' instant and perhaps ill judged reaction is to shatter them in sight of the supporters of the usurping idol.

Marked by a series of tensions, the brief narrative of Deuteronomy 9 opposes the visible calf with a triangle made of invisible Yahweh, visible tablets, and visible Moses. The text further highlights a strain between the faithless Hebrews and their loyal leader on the one hand, and an *agon* between Moses with the text itself (= the oracular and the written) on the other. If the elimination of the divinely inscribed tablets symbolizes the expiration of the covenant, their fate also suggests the failure of Moses' monotheistic 'mission'. His Hebrews are simply not ready. By way of resolution, the redacted text sends Moses up the mountain once more in order to obtain (and write) another set of tablets (Deut. 10.4). This time the private process

108.   In general, on Deut. 9, see Robert H. O'Connell, 'Deut IX 7–X 7-11: Panelled Structure, Double Rehearsal and the Rhetoric of Covenant Rebuke', *VT* 42 (1992), pp. 492-509, and Moshe A. Zipor, 'The Deuteronomic Account of the Golden Calf and its Reverberation in Other Parts of the Book of Deuteronomy', *ZAW* 108 (1996), pp. 20-33. On the ideology of collective responsibil-ity, see Dale Patrick, 'The Rhetorical Collective Responsibility in Deuteronomic Law', in David P. Wright, David Noel Freedman and Avi Hurvitz (eds.), *Pomegranates and Golden Bells: Studies in Honor of Jacob Milgrom* (Winona Lake, IN: Eisenbrauns, 1995), pp. 421-36, who highlights Deuteronomy's original contribution to the collectivization of legal discourse. See also Eep Talstra, 'Deuteronomy 9 and 10: Synchronic and Diachronic Observations', in Johannes C. de Moor (ed.), *Synchronic or Diachronic? A Debate on Method in Old Testament Exegesis* (Oudtestamentische studiën, 34; Leiden: E.J. Brill, 1995), pp. 187-210, with delightful quotes from Potok's novels.

109.   Here, perhaps, Frankel's assumption ('Destruction') of pulverized tablets rather than calf makes more sense.

110.   On the centrality of the tablets, see Mann, *Deuteronomy*, p. 99, who regards these as a treaty document.

culminates not in usurpation but in perpetual concealment—the text must be sealed
in an ark specifically designed to house the tablets (10.1-2). In the Exodus version,
the making of the ark postdates that of the tablets by a significant temporal lag. In
Deuteronomy, the 'lost and found' tablets are immediately transformed into a
hidden object of veneration, a verbal 'image' of Yahweh. This is not, however, an
'image' in a forbidden sense but rather an imagination, since the text is to be read
but not seen.

Moses 'purges' idolatry and restores the balance between Yahweh and Israel
through prayer. The profaned space is 'cleansed' and reclaimed by Moses' self-
imposed asceticism. But he cannot reform the people who had been insubordinate
from the very day he had known them (Deut. 9.24). Such recalcitrance makes
Deuteronomy the history of a failed theodicy. Read against inveterate inability to
comprehend the greatness of Yahweh, Deuteronomy unfolds a story of a utopian
regime headed by an invisible divinity, presided over by a group of priests, and
exercised on a territorial unity which is imbued with diversity and idolatry. Shaped
by Moses' 'autobiography' and dominated by the Torah (31.9-13), Deuteronomy's
memorialization is patterned along the sins of the past and by those of the future
(31.16-20). Covenants are constantly broken and renewed. One palliative compromise (Deut. 17) projects kings, rather than prophets or texts, as the visible if not the
authoritative link between Yahweh and Israel. Yet, the royal annals of both Israel
and Judah are anything but the history of tranquil monotheism. Already the much
favored Solomon sows the seeds of destruction by granting freedom of worship to
his numerous foreign wives (1 Kgs 11.4-9) and by pandering to their desires.

In the recorded events which the book of Kings preserves, the redactor passes a
summary judgment based primarily on a simple criterion, namely whether a king
did the 'right' or 'wrong' in Yahweh's eyes. Verdict is determined on the basis of
royal comprehension of Yahwist 'monotheism' or according to a rate of idolatry and
the promotion of Yahweh's rivals, such as the Baal. To drive home the fullest ramifications of apostasy and of Yahwist piety, the Dtr historian(s) 'restore(s)' women
to center stage in two tales that deal with righteous kings and priests who either
oppose an impious queen (2 Kgs 11) or collaborate with a pious prophetess (2 Kgs
22–23). In one account of monarchic piety, a king turns to Yahweh after the finding
of a text and consultation with a prophetess; in another, a high priest king-maker
challenges the legitimacy of a ruling queen because of her idolatry and her sex.
Both tales resound with echoes of the episode of the gold calf.

Narrated like a parable on the theme of 'lost and found', the story of Athalia
(2 Kgs 11) encapsulates one strand of Deuteronomic comprehension of Decalogue's call to 'monotheism'.[111] The story begins on an ominous note. Often disrupted, royalty in Judah seems on the verge of an abrupt and sudden end when a
woman ascends the throne and sets out to eliminate all her male rivals. Like a witch
in a conventional fairytale, she is wicked by deed and by association. Her cruel

---

111.   What follows owes a great deal to the fine analysis of Grottanelli, 'Making Room for the
Written Law'. Similarities between Exod. 32, 2 Kgs 11 and 2 Kgs 22–23 have been noted by most
commentators.

scheme is checked not by a mighty general but by her own relative, another woman whose daring equals that of the queen, but who saves and conceals one little prince. One day a crafty priest brings the prince out of hiding, and with much fanfare celebrates his accession, not forgetting to execute the queen in the process. The new king rules to everyone's satisfaction for many years, doing what was 'right in the eyes of Yahweh' (2 Kgs 12.3).[112]

This, in very broad outline, is how the Dtr historian(s) edit(s) the story of queen Athalia, a woman of impeccable breed and genealogy, daughter of a king (Ahab of Israel, and of Jezebel?), wife of a king (Jehoram of Judah, 2 Kgs 8.18) and mother of a king (Ahaziah king of Judah, 8.26). Yet, even such triple distinction does not make her eligible to assume a Davidic diadem. Cast already by her very connection with Ahab as the epitome of impiety, Athalia is doomed to become the most derided of all royal usurpers. Her 'crimes' also highlight modes of correct manly behavior. As 8.27 insists, being an Omride entails an automatic estrangement from Yahweh, coupled with an inevitable promotion of Yahweh's mightiest rival, the Baal. Athalia is branded by infamy—both as a scion of a king who is not brought to proper burial, and as mother of a man who dies at the hand of a usurper (9.27). She cannot escape her fate, and even its postponement is a matter of divine plan.

Athalia comes to power in the wake of the sudden death of her son. Her brief reign in Judah coincides with that of Jehu whose sole claim to Israelite monarchy is based on a mission to eradicate the house of Ahab (2 Kgs 9.7-9). As a king, Jehu's first act is the elimination of potential rival claimants (10.7, 11, 17), including the brothers of the deceased king of Judah (10.14). In this, he and Athalia are worthy companions. To celebrate his victory, Jehu burns the Baal shrines (10.26-28), acquiring in the process the good opinion of the redactor: 'only the sins of Jeroboam son of Nebat who had caused Israel to sin Jehu did not shun, namely the golden calves that were in Bethel and in Dan' (10.29). Athalia's close relationship with the Baal is taken for granted.

Because Jehu had been anointed by Elisha (2 Kgs 9.2-3), or rather by one of the prophet's helpers, an otherwise dreary tale of conspiracy and murder is recast as a scene in the perennial theatre of the campaign between Yahweh and the Baal. Athalia, who starts as a perfectly legitimate ruler, ends as a 'usurper'. Read as a parable on 'monotheism', the tale of Athalia confirms the necessity to 'cut' a compromise, as well as a covenant. If Yahweh must tolerate other gods, these cannot include the Baal. Calves of gold, by contrast, prove more palatable to the divine taste.

Ironically, Jehu, killer of the Omrides, and Athalia the Omride, conspire to bring about the complete annihilation of the royal houses of both Israel and Judah. But just as Jehu cannot ultimately resist the allure of the gold calf or of the 'great sin' of the desert, Athalia's plan encounters an unexpected but fateful obstacle. In 2 Kings 11 the absence of male heir enables a woman to ascend the Davidic throne of Judah, although the text prudently avoids calling her a 'queen'. Like the calf, Athalia is a

---

112.   See also below Chapter 4 §6.

proscribed figure that desecrates a hallowed space.[113] The 'rediscovery' of a lost king in 2 Kings 11 ushers a new covenant and a new era, as does the reintroduction of a new set of tablets and the building of the ark in Deuteronomy. Lurking behind these two portrayals (of an inanimate and a human usurper) is a deliberate gender distinction.

At the beginning of Athalia's narrated history, a rivalry between two women, the mother (Athalia) and the sister (Jehosheva) of a diseased king, shape the fortunes of the kingdom. To the latter, 2 Chron. 22.11 joins in matrimony a priest named Jehoiada who emerges as Athalia's main opponent. The couple conspires to save the last male scion of the royal house. Affinities with Exodus 2, where a Hebrew male baby is saved by resourceful women, as well with the Deuteronomist's need to introduce a main male actor, are evident.

In the course of planning the usurpation of his royal protégé, Jehoiada 'cuts a covenant' (2 Kgs 11.4), imposing an oath of loyalty on those to whom he presents the child-king who had been hidden for six years in the temple.[114] He also unearths weapons belonging to David himself, as though the long dead king has lent a gracious assent to his male descendant. When Jehoiada shows the new king to the people, he dresses him with symbolic insignia of legitimacy, including a diadem and an elusive עֵדוּת (2 Kgs 11.12).[115] Such attention to ceremony also suggests that Athalia's regime would have been perceived as equally legitimate, but for her sex.

2 Kings 11 presents multiple conflicts: between a 'legitimate' male monarch and a 'usurping' female monarch, between Yahweh and the Baal, between sacred and profane space (temple and palace), and between countryside and town (or עַם הָאָרֶץ and urbanites).[116] To discredit all the 'negativities', the recorded annals of the monarchy invariably cast a woman (Jezebel, Athalia) as the Baal's most staunch supporter.[117] In their efforts to promote Mosaic monotheism, narrators and redactors of the history of Israel and of Judah conducted a concerted campaign against the Baal, perhaps the most pervasive of Yahweh's competitors. Cast in the shade of Deuteronomy 9 and 17, stories about impious queens delineate the threat of an ever lurking rupture of the orderly relations between Yahweh and Israel. In the hierarchy of Deuteronomy 17, monarchs, in general, are a choice between two evils, chaos and kings. No provisions are made for a female ruler, just as no room can be made for gods besides Yahweh.

113.   On spatial allocations and reversals in the narrative, see Burke O. Long, 'Sacred Geography as Narrative Structure in 2 Kings 11', in Wright, Freedman and Hurvitz (eds.), *Pomegranates and Golden Bells*, pp. 231-38.

114.   On Johoiada carefully planned conspiracy, see R.L. Cohn, *2 Kings* (Berit Olam; Collegeville, MN: Liturgical Press, 2000), p. 78.

115.   Usually translated as 'jewels' or some sort of royal insignia. But it may well be a text as well like a scroll which denotes legitimacy or divine election. See Norbert Lohfink, '*d(w)t* im Deuteronomium und in den Köngisbüchern', *BZ* 35 (1991), pp. 86-93, linking 2 Kgs 23.3 with Deut. 6.17, who sees עֵדוּת as pre-P.

116.   On the latter, see William M. Schniedewind, *Society and the Promise of David: The Reception History of 2 Samuel 7.1-17* (New York: Oxford University Press, 1999), pp. 72-80.

117.   I would further suggest that the episode with Athalia is a necessary counterpart to that of Jezebel; the one spreading impiety in Israel, the other in Judah.

Underlying Deuteronomy 9 and 2 Kings 11 is a clash between Yahwistic, or 'monotheistic' notions of legitimacy/illegitimacy and the inevitable violent resolution of tension. In Deuteronomy 9 Moses' smashing of the tablets encapsulates the breaking of the covenant, as well as the distancing of Yahweh from the faithless Israelites who had witnessed the theophany in Sinai. Athalia's version of 'monotheism' is, by its very inclusion of the Baal, unacceptable. Protagonists of the stories of the calf and of Athalia display unexpected commonalties of character. Equipped with the right text, Moses sets out to deal with the gold calf with the same thoroughness and determination which Athalia, equipped with royal blood and ingenuity, displays when she plans the elimination of the royal family. Moses realizes that neither the grinding of the calf nor the massacre of the sinners is likely to bring the desired eradication of idolatry. Athalia's actions do not cause the extinction of Davidic male monarchy. Two priests in these tales, Aaron and Jehoiada, manufacture images of impiety and piety respectively by constituting themselves as arbiters of legitimacy. Between women and calves, then, a vast and nebulous field breeds a harvest of transgressions. In Deuteronomy 9, as in 2 Kings 11, the *agon* between what is right and what is wrong is bound to be won by the 'rightful' man and the rightful text. In this particular map of Yahwist theological and social ideology women can only be the agents of sin and iniquity.

In 2 Kings 11 the transfer of the throne coincides with a restoration of the royal cult to Yahweh.[118] What takes place in 'Yahweh's house' determines what takes place in the royal palace. Athalia's murder, the purge of the Baal and the renewal of the ancient covenant redeem the territory of the palace as a seat of legitimate royal authority.[119] The entente, however, is short lived. Even a tale that begins with a king who 'does right in the eyes of Yahweh' (2 Kgs 22.20), like that of Josiah of Judah, carries its own seeds of destruction. In this story (2 Kgs 22), instead of unearthing a rightful king, the revealed 'find' is a book 'discovered' in the course of renovating the derelict 'house of Yahweh'. The 'finder' is, once more, a high priest.[120] The king's reaction upon hearing the news is peculiar: he rents his clothes (22.11, 19), as Athalia had done when confronted with conspiracy (11.14). Consultation follows. The ad hoc adviser turns out to be none other than the wife of the keeper of the royal wardrobe. Whatever the king might have sought to understand, Huldah (this woman) predicts doom and gloom for his kingdom and death for the king himself.[121]

---

118. Long, 'Sacred Geography', p. 231.

119. Long, 'Sacred Geography', p. 236.

120. It is interesting that the scribe and not the priest is charged with informing the king and with the reading of the text. Perhaps it is a hint of the superiority of the text *vis-à-vis* priestly claims.

121. The precise meaning of Huldah's oracle has been much debated. Some (like Steven L. McKenzie, *The Trouble with Kings: The Composition of the Books of Kings in the Deuteronomistic History* [Leiden: E.J. Brill, 1991], p. 111) see it as doom for Judah but a personal reprieve for Josiah; others (like Moshe Weinfeld, *From Joshua to Josiah: Turning Points in the History of Israel from the Conquest of the Land until the fall of Judah* [Jerusalem: Magnes Press, 1992], pp. 166-70 [Hebrew]), regard the entire discovery and its concomitant oracle as negative omens. On the differences, many and important, between the versions of 2 Kgs 22–23 and 2 Chron. 34–35, see

From the beginning, the 'find' in the temple is defined as 'a book of the Torah' (2 Kgs 22.8), a term that has generated lengthy scholarly debates. Be the precise nature of this book what it may (Deuteronomy?), what matters is the fact that the text entrusts its authentication or rather interpretation to a prophetess. In other words, in a context of demonstrable Yahwism and anti-Yahwism, Huldah the prophetess provides the antithesis of Athalia the queen. Deuteronomistic narrative politics of monotheism, as expressed in Deuteronomy 9, 2 Kings 11 and 2 Kings 22, excise and reinstate women as sources of illegitimacy and legitimacy and of exemplary impiety and piety.

According to 2 Kgs 23.25, the events 'on the eighteenth year of Josiah's reign' (22.3) also inaugurate a new era in the history of Judah, marked by a thoroughgoing purge of idols and their shrines, above all of the Asherah. Josiah treats the Asherah as Moses had treated the calf idol—expelling her from the temple in Jerusalem, he has her burnt and ground into dust (23.6). To mark Yahweh's victory over his mighty female antagonist, Josiah orders the Asherah's ashes to be scattered over graves in the Kidron Valley (23.6). The gesture recaptures the scattering of the calf ashes in Deut 9.21. At the conclusion of this 'battle' between divinities, the king 'cuts' a new covenant, precisely as had been done after Athalia's execution.[122] The timing of this covenant corresponds with the most memorable event in 'ancient' Israelite history, Passover, the very occasion that the First Word commemorates, namely the liberation from Egypt.

The figure of Huldah in this remarkable tale remains shadowy.[123] Speaking like a Delphic oracular priestess, Huldah's vocabulary recalls, significantly, moments from the gold calf episode as captured in Exodus 32, as well as the Decalogue itself. She addresses Josiah's emissaries with the words: 'Tell the man (אִישׁ) who had sent you to me, thus said the Lord...' (2 Kgs 22.15). Josiah is not a king but a 'man', like Moses 'the man' whose absence had induced the making of an idol (Exod. 32.1). Huldah invokes Yahweh's vindictive memory, as does the Second Word, and ensures her listeners that Yahweh's wrath will not be extinguished. In spite of Josiah's piety, then, the sins of his ancestors and of his people require the manifestation of divine revenge, tempered ever so slightly by a promise of a premature death for the pious king himself.

Huldah's address further suggests that genuine royal piety is measured primarily through an active interpretation of the Second Word. 2 Kings 23 provides a lengthy description of the demolition of idols, of shrines, altars and temples that encapsulate the very essence of transgressing the Commandment. Josiah's purge is so

David A. Glatt-Gilad, 'The Role of Huldah's Prophecy in the Chronicler's Portrayal of Josiah's Reform', *Bib* 77 (1996), pp. 16-31.

122.   Shigeyuki Nakanose, *Josiah's Passover: Sociology and the Liberating Bible* (Maryknoll, NY: Orbis Books, 1993).

123.   Cf. the medium of Ein Dor (1 Sam. 28), with Athalya Brenner, *The Israelite Woman: Social Role and Literary Type in Biblical Narrative* (The Biblical Seminar, 2; Sheffield: JSOT Press, 1985), and Claudia V. Camp, 'The Female Sage in Ancient Israel and in the Biblical Wisdom Literature', in John G. Gammie and Leo G. Purdue (eds.), *The Sage in Israel and in the Ancient Near East* (Winona Lake, IN: Eisenbrauns, 1990), pp. 185-203.

thorough that even Solomon's '*bamot*' and Jeroboam's altars do not escape the royal axe. Yet, this dramatic demise of 'paganism' does not entail a change of the divine mind bent, as ever, on punishing the rebellious Israelites (2 Kgs 23.26). The final message to the king, as that delivered by the medium of Ein Dor to his remote royal 'predecessor' Saul (1 Sam. 28), bears the tidings of premature death. Yet, Saul's death expresses divine disfavor while that of Josiah transmits Yahweh's favor. Does Huldah's announcement, then, hint at an altered view of manhood that rewards piety with death prior to destruction?

Shifting perceptions of Yahwist monotheism underlie the Deuteronomic and the two Dtr narratives about piety and apostasy (Deut. 9; 2 Kgs 11.22). Deuteronomy 9 employs a narrative strategy that excises elements, such as women, sex and ordeal potions, which feature prominently in the Exodus account of the same events. 2 Kings 11 restores a gendered ideology to the image of the forbidden by creating a murderous and impious queen, who remains true to the much maligned heritage of her Sidonian mother(?) Jezebel and her Omride father Ahab. Opposing this stereotypical depiction of a chaos created by a woman is the attempt of 2 Kings 22–23 to affect a reconciliation of polarized imageries by casting a woman (Huldah) in the venerable role of God's exclusive emissary.

Huldah confirms the superiority of the text. She expresses what scholars have regarded as the intimate link between 'Deuteronomic iconoclasm', and the promotion of the Book of the Law which provides Israel with a new identity.[124] She 'translates' the ban on images into a concrete language of another image, that of a book, thereby reinforcing the opening message of the First Word. But her brief appearance also introduces an ironic reflection on the history of Israel. In the Deuteronomic version of the gold calf affair, the Torah 'enters' the ark to accompany the Israelites to the battlefield (1 Sam. 4.1-11). In Josiah's tale, the Torah resurfaces in the temple itself where it had been apparently buried out of sight, just like Yahweh, during the reign of impious monarchs, such as Athalia. Like the forgotten past of liberation that the First Commandment memorializes, the Torah and Yahweh had been 'buried'. Looking into the 'future', Huldah contravenes and yet upholds the Torah.[125] Her dire prediction brings together Jerusalem, the temple, the calf and the goddess in a common fate.

The Second Word promises rewards and revenge, thus setting the divine within the perimeters of human experience.[126] It also makes men the explicit subject of Yahweh's favors and penalties. The First Word expects men to affirm that the Exodus had been an act of God. As the histories of Israel (Genesis–Numbers; Joshua–

124. Van der Toorn, 'The Iconic Book', pp. 240-41.

125. To echo Walter Benjamin, 'On the Concept of History', in *Selected Writings*. IV. *1938–1940* (trans. Edmund Jephcott *et al.*; eds. Howard Eiland and Michael W. Jennings; Cambridge, MA: Belknap, 2003), pp. 389-97 (396 [xvii], 597 [B]).

126. Nathan Rotenstreich, 'The Decalogue and Man as *Homo Vocatus*', in Ben-Zion Segal (ed.), *The Ten Commandments* (Jerusalem: Magnes Press/Hebrew University Press, 1990), pp. 247-59 (250).

2 Kings) set out to chart concrete expressions of such abstracts, narrators position women in the center stage of narratological etiologies. Women are routinely presented as agents of apostasy and as vehicles of male violation of monotheism's basic precepts. Thus the Moabite women of Numbers 25, faceless and nameless, and thus the numerous wives and concubines of Solomon whose polytheism leads this otherwise pious monarch astray.

To highlight the boundaries of moral transgression, the redactors of biblical annals single out individual women as indexes of impious behavior. Miriam, albeit a Levite, encapsulates defiance within the family. Her divergent behavior became a 'national' issue because its object is Yahweh's chosen leader.[127] In the royal houses of Israel and Judah women, like Athalia, hasten a crisis of Yahwist identity. The familial becomes national.

Because monotheism mirrors conjugality (or vice versa), the monochromatic casting of women (in Joshua–2 Kings) as either all good or all bad glosses over a huge embarrassment, namely the fact that copulation, sex and desire are guarantees of monotheism. Men are expected to exercise self-control in a territory governed by emotions and instincts. Recognizing the fickleness of human sentiments, laws interpreting liberty (Exod. 21; Deut. 15) attempt to regulate the social processes relating to freeing 'Hebrew' slaves. The voice of women remains mute. In households in which fathers can sell daughters and 'husbands' can expel unloved 'wives', the silence of these women is a double affirmation of their inferiority, as slaves and as females.

When women challenge the ideology of monotheism they emerge as icons of a chaotic order, conspicuously lacking Yahweh's guiding hand. Cozbi intrudes into an all-Israelite scene of mourning, thereby disrupting the course of divine determination. Athalia, a semi-foreigner, introduces confusion into royal genealogy. The very foreignness of these women threatens to destabilize the monotheistic establishment, although hardly any distinctions are drawn between Israelite and non-Israelite women whose experiences are captured in the biblical texts.

Perhaps the most singular distinction between the women of Genesis–Numbers on the one hand, and those of Joshua–2 Kings on the other hand, is the tongue. Miriam does not speak for herself, nor does Cozbi. But Athalia and Huldah are women of words. Occupying a space of resistance, the women who bear out the meaning of monotheism must do so in a way that ultimately reinscribes them into the system, with its hierarchies and oppression. In the end, these women are shown to be illegitimate constructs that, ironically, guarantee manhood.

9. Coda and 'Conversion'

The Hebrew Bible proposes specific venues of integration for non-Israelites. The very idea poses a paradox. How can a non-Israelite, whose ancestors had not been 'slaves in Egypt', fully share in the message of the First Word? There are, moreover,

---

127. Paradoxically, Zipporah, a foreign woman and her own sister-in-law, becomes an emblem of Yahwist piety in Exod. 4.

groups whose membership is forever proscribed. Thus the Ammonites; thus the Moabites (Deut. 23.4), descendants of forbidden unions (Gen. 19.36-37). Yet, the story of one Moabite woman, Ruth, points to a counter-interpretation of the First Commandment, as well as of Deuteronomic law.

Several links connect the tale of Ruth with Pentateuchal laws in general and Deuteronomy in particular.[128] None of these provides a 'positive' narrative exegesis. Rather, the scroll of Ruth appears not so much to address as to redress both the rationale and the principle of the law. Ruth 'rectifies' Deut. 23.4-7—the latter asserts Moabite exclusion on the basis of Moabite hostility and privation at a crucial moment in Israelite history; the former recounts Moabite hospitality *vis-à-vis* refugees from Judah in time of deprivation.[129] In Ruth, Moab is recast as the benevolent Egypt of Genesis. The story further suggests that changed circumstances call for an 'updating' of the law.[130]

Ruth's author 'pleads for differentiated judging of the criterion for admission to the congregation, which also includes a differentiated view of integrating alien women by marriage'.[131] In this it appears to respond to the ideology of Ezra–Nehemiah, which espouses a strict application of the very same laws.[132] Both narratives are carefully construed as re-enactments of the Exodus, each with its own comprehension of the meaning of this past. Ezra traces the footsteps of an exilic group on its journey of 'liberation' from Babylon to Persian Yehud, precisely as does the book of Exodus with the liberated tribes. Ruth focuses on the road of two women from widowhood to personal redemption, as though the Exodus had been a personal familial journey of individuals from an intolerable state of being to salvation. Both works share an extraordinary interest in the meaning of foreignness. In Ezra it is unclear who, precisely, are the 'foreigners' and who are the 'locals' because the exilic community, itself a stranger to the land, strains to forge boundaries between its members and everyone else, including their own non-exilic wives and children. Throughout the scroll, Ruth remains a 'Moabite' and a 'foreigner'; but the terms become honorary appellations designating exemplary Yahwism, if practiced by women.

Ezra–Nehemiah rejects 'conversion'. It suggests that to become a 'Jew' it is essential to separate from anything and anyone who does not share a common (exilic) past.[133] Ruth charts a path of 'conversion' that insists on precisely the

---

128. See Georg Braulik, 'Das Deuteronomium und die Bücher Ijob, Sprichwörter, Rut', in Erich Zenger (ed.), *Die Tora als Kanon für Juden und Christen* (Freiburg: Herder, 1996), pp. 61-138 (115-16); and Michael D. Goulder, 'Ruth: A Homily on Deuteronomy 22–25?', in Heather A. McKay and David J.A. Clines (eds.), *Of Prophets' Visions and the Wisdom of the Sages: Essays in Honor of R.N. Whybray* (JSOTSup, 162; Sheffield: JSOT Press, 1993), pp. 307-19.

129. Irmtraud Fischer, 'The Book of Ruth: A "Feminist" Commentary to the Torah?', in Brenner (ed.), *A Feminist Companion to Ruth and Esther*, pp. 24-49 (36).

130. Braulik, 'Das Deuteronomium', p. 116.

131. Fischer, 'Book of Ruth', p. 36.

132. The date of Ruth is hotly contested. It may be contemporaneous with Ezra–Nehemiah (c. 400 BCE?), earlier or later. This analysis assumes that it is a near contemporary.

133. See my 'The Silent Women of Yehud'.

opposite. In Ruth, voluntary joining of an Israelite community paves the way to integration and membership. But Ruth also requires an agent of 'conversion', a male in the shape of a distant relative of her deceased husband. The First and the Second Commandments insist on the exclusiveness of Yahwist monotheism. Ruth renounces her home and her family of origin, thereby abjuring her deities and accepting Naomi's God (Ruth 1.16). She seems a perfect convert who adopts the law and the lore of her chosen people. But her oath to Naomi is also personal, an expression of love and loyalty of one woman to another.

This is a problematic mold of monotheism out of love. The scroll blurs distinctions between family needs, religious identity and ethnic affiliation. In the process, Ruth confounds the most significant difference of all, that between men and women. In initially valuing both Naomi and monotheism, Ruth also honors the rights of the dead. She is in tune with the entire cultural order that the Hebrew Bible instills, paying homage to both the God as well as to Yahwist persons and to the collective. In leaving her idolatrous past behind, and in separating from family, Ruth observes the critical aspect that marks monotheism in the First Word, namely separation from the past and from 'Egypt'.

To Ruth, living with Naomi is the absolute principle to which she gives her undivided allegiance, privileging it to the extent of renouncing her home and her gods. The issue of explicit affinity with monotheism is only tangential to the fairy-tale which the scroll unfolds. But the symbolic value of Ruth's words and actions breeds problems of identifying the steps required to become a member of the covenant community. Because Deut. 23.2-9 prohibits Moabites from entering the congregation, the rabbis, for example, had to conclude that the ban applied only to males.[134] From this perspective, the monotheistic world constructed in the Hebrew Bible is a realm that obeys the law of Yahweh. Its history is supported by the paradigm of its founding myths as a point of origin which can be repeated, on a smaller and individual scale. Ruth's readiness to toe the line produces two positive patterns for the self—an imitation or doubling of a model of piety, and obedience to figures of authority.

Bethlehem becomes for Ruth what Moab had been for Naomi and her family. Except that Moab proved deadly, whereas Judean land, like Yahweh, provides life. Ultimately, Ruth is excised from the last scene of the scroll, her role minimized to maternity. The last word is Naomi's. Ruth is assimilated without a trace, yet her body produces David's ancestor. In this voyage into the biblical imaginary, Ruth's text begins as a quest of livelihood. It invents a fictional choice between two names, that of the covenant and that of Moab. But there is really no choice, because Naomi, Boaz and Bethlehem mean monotheism, while Moab stands for death, recalling the Moabite women of Numbers 25 whose allure engendered idolatry and disaster.

---

134. See *m. Yeb.* 8.3.

Chapter 3

OATH: DAUGHTER OF DISCORD?[*]
(WORD THREE; WORD NINE)

By God,
By Moses ben Amram,
By the light of my eyes,
By the life of my dear ones...

—An oath of a Jewish woman[1]

By Moses ben Amram, may I be sacrificed to his name, I have not done this!
By Aaron the priest, I have not done this!
By the life of my mother, I have not done this!
By the life of my father, I have not done this!
Now, if you believe you believe, if you don't, don't!

—An oath of a Jewish man?[2]

May God not forgive you, if you lie!
May a liar be given the water of Shema Yisrael and die!
May s/he not win (entry to) the world to come, s/he who lies.
May s/he hold a beggar's bowl in her/his hand if s/he does not tell the truth
May her/his child become an orphan...

—Traditional curse of Iranian Jews (modified)[3]

When one, knowingly, tells lies and swears an oath on it,
When he is so wild as to do incurable damage against justice,
This man is left a diminished generation hereafter,
But the generation of the true-sworn man grows stronger

—Hesiod, *Works/Days* 282-86[4]

He who has clean hands and a pure heart
Who does not lift up his soul to what is false,
And does not swear deceitfully,
He will receive blessings from the Lord
And vindication from the God of his salvation. (Ps. 24.4 RSV)

---

*   This chapter title echoes Nicole Loraux's 'son of discord', in her *The Divided City: On Memory and Forgetting in Ancient Athens* (trans. Corinne Pache and Jeff Fort; New York: Zone Books, 2002), p. 123.
    1.   Sorour S. Soroudi, 'Judeo-Persian Religious Oath Formulas as Compared with Non-Jewish Iranian Traditions', *Irano-Judaica* 2 (1990), p. 166-83 (170).
    2.   Soroudi, 'Judeo-Persian Religious Oath Formulas'.
    3.   Soroudi, 'Judeo-Persian Religious Oath Formulas', p. 179.
    4.   Quoted in Loraux, *Divided City*, pp. 132-23.

You shall not take the name of the Lord your God in vain because God will not exonerate the one who bears the name in vain. (Exod. 20.7)

You shall not bear false witness against your neighbor. (Exod. 20.16)

1. *Sins of Speaking*

Once upon a time there were twin sisters. One was married to a man in one city, the other to another man in another city. The husband of one woman wanted to submit her to his 'spirit of jealousy', and to make her drink the bitter water in Jerusalem.[5] The wife rushed to the city where her married sister lived. The sister asked: Why have you come? She answered: My husband wants to make me drink the bitter water. The sister said: I will go instead and drink it. She said: Go.

She wore her sister's cloths and went instead of her, drank the bitter water and was found pure. She went to tell her sister who came happily out of her home to meet her. She embraced and kissed her on the mouth. Because the sisters kissed each other, she inhaled the bitter water and died instantly.[6]

Rabbinic recasting of Num. 5.10-31 makes the sisters indistinguishable by birth and by insinuation. Suppressing names, either woman could have committed the suspected sin of adultery. Focusing on the deadly potion, the midrash further omits a crucial component of the biblical setting, namely words. According to the procedure relating to a *soṭah* (5.11-31), the priest who administers the husband's sacrifice and the bitter water also makes the woman swear an oath (5.19-21).[7] Water without words is powerless. If the woman is guilty, water and words will render her sterile, thus reinforcing her moral sterility. If vainly accused, she will be 'cleansed' or acquitted, ready to receive male semen and to engage in legitimate procreation (5.28). Whether guilty or innocent of perjury, the husband's sacrifice (albeit without oil and incense) 'cleanses' him, freeing him from punishment for false oath and for false accusation (5.31). Only readers' imagination can conjure up the post-ordeal atmosphere of a home inhabited by a man wreaked by 'a spirit of jealousy' and a woman who had been subjected, in vain, to public humiliation. Once exposed, even if found innocent, the woman was bound to carry the stain of social disapprobation for life.

In the make up 'court' of Yahweh's sanctuary, where priests and sacrifices determine the tenor of time, the spectacle of suspected adultery highlights a perennial problem. Although it takes three to commit adultery, the absence of a decisive proof, either in the shape of witnesses or the lover's testimony, means that God must become the ultimate arbitrator. Crime must be established through a ritual entailing the exposure of the body of an alleged adulteress, an oath and the drinking

---

5.   See Num. 5 and below, Chapter 7 §4.
6.   *Midrash Tanhuma* (*Numbers, Parasha* 2, *Naso* 10) (English trans. John T. Townsend; New York: Ktav, 2003), with Ruth Calderon, *The Market, the Home, the Heart* (Jerusalem: Keter, 2001 [Hebrew]), p. 21 (my translation).
7.   See below, Chapter 7.

of 'bitter water'. Of these inextricable three elements, the oath provides a verbal bridge between the body and potential sterility/fertility, depending on the outcome of the inhaling of the mixed potion.

Presiding over the proceedings is an invisible divinity who stands ready to avenge those who apply the divine name to undermine the familial and social appointed order. Nothing but the deepest belief in the efficacy of words and water accounts for the assumption of divine involvement, even in domestic matters. The *sotah*'s ritual of words illustrates the ubiquitous presence of oath in antiquity. Yahweh of Numbers 5, as well as of the Third Commandment, does not condone arbitrary and willful application of the divine name. Standing before Yahweh (Num. 5.30), wife and husband air a grievance which, if remained buried, can contaminate husbandly genealogy, in itself a major concern of husbands, priests and public. Defendant, accuser, viewers and participants share conviction in the potency of words, water and soil—vocal and visual representatives of divine justice. Bringing the nocturnal into the visible, rituals consisting of sacrifice, of gradual exposure of the female body, of oath and of bitter water combine to expose secret connections.

As though the oath's sole purpose is to punish its violators, the ritual of revealing concealed adultery highlights not only the violation of the bodily integrity of a married woman, but also of the assumed veracity of sworn words. Thus the oath which the priest utters and the woman confirms seems created solely to define offenders who become such by virtue of the oath itself, and who must be punished by the God whose name is thus implicated in perjury. Made to recite 'Amen, Amen' to an oath believed to have the potency of implicating her (Num. 5.21-22), the suspected adulteress is paradoxically entrusted with condemning herself. Oath and curses are committed to writing 'in a book' (5.23), a gesture that, together with sacrifice and potion, conspires to protect the husband and the order of the community from threats of tainted genealogy.

An oath, then, speaks of discord. Its contents aim at preventing, or at ending acts of rebellion and divergence. The priestly oath of Num. 5.21 invokes Yahweh as a witness who alone knows truth from falsity. Construed as a cornerstone of the entire ritual, Numbers 5 privileges oath (and water) as a communicator of an obscure 'prehistory', and as a metaphorical promissory note which acts to the detriment of a guilty party. To regulate the future, the oath also becomes a speech act. Hence, the procedure places the suspected adulteress in contact with 'sacred' substance (holy water and sanctuary soil), and with a tangible text of an oath (5.23), in order to elicit the 'truth'. The mouth of the suspected adulteress, through the tongue that enunciates words and the throat that inhales potion, becomes the sole witness of her own supposed misdemeanor or of her innocence. In this close complicity between oath and perjury, body and words, the essential is played out.

As the destiny of the woman is entrusted to a solemnly pronounced message, she forbids herself to go back on her word on pain of sterility. The concluding words of the ordeal state that any man touched by a spirit of jealousy has the right to make his wife stand before Yahweh, so that the priest will 'execute upon her this law (Torah)' (Num. 5.30 RSV). Yet, what if the ritual fails to uncover an adultery that had been committed? Does a silent and sinister pain gnaw at the oath breaker?[8]

Left to God, the sin of perjury becomes a matter 'not of the justice of man but of divine sanction'.[9] This is precisely what the Third Commandment implies, with its insistence on Yahweh's personal vengeance. In the theology of this precept, whoever bears in vain (or falsely or willfully) Yahweh's name is branded as a transgressor of divine law itself and as a human destined to be punished by a divine hand. Perjury, in this reading, is tantamount to disbelief and hence to idolatry.[10] Of the Ten Commandments only the Second and the Third carry a penalty devised and administered by Yahweh.[11] Both Commandments are decipherable in terms of reserving for God the task of sorting out offenders.[12]

Numbers 5 suggests that sins of speaking are akin to betraying the body. The Third Commandment implies that swearing misleadingly in God's name implicates the divine in the unforgivable, namely in upsetting the balance of social relations. The Word casts Yahweh as both a witness of violations and their avenger, conflating sanctions with the effectiveness of an all powerful imprecation. Yahweh's absence, by contrast, from the Ninth Commandment is as conspicuous because language remains at stake.

The Ninth Commandment makes perjury or willful lying a legally defined crime.[13] Wronged parties may call on Yahweh to disclose treachery. Mechanisms of court apply to false witnesses, if caught, but only the divine will can restrain the tongue. Appearances of veracity, either when swearing in God's name in general, or when abusing the trust invested in witnesses, are harmful precisely because they inspire confidence.

Modern analyses of the Ninth Commandment extend its scope to embrace the elevation of truth as a basic tenet in personal relations among covenant members.[14] Assuming truth, in principle, to be the matter at stake, it may be asked what, precisely, is the scope of the Third Commandment, which, likewise, shuns falsity and, implicitly, espouses veracity. Most scholars agree that by forbidding the frivolous

---

8.   As Louis Gernet, *Recherches sur le développement juridique et moral de la pensée grecque* (Paris: Leroux, 1917), p. 114, maintains.

9.   Emile Benveniste, *Problèmes de linguistique générale* (2 vols.; Paris: Gallimard, 1974), II, p. 256.

10.   On links between the Second and the Third Commandment, see Bernhard Lang, 'Das Verbot des Meineids im Dekalog', *Theologische Quartalschrift* 161 (1981), pp. 99-102; cf. Moshe Weinfeld, 'The Loyalty Oath in the Ancient Near East', *UF* 8 (1977), pp. 379-414. I have not seen Thomas R. Elssner, *Das Namensmissbrauch-Verbot: Bedeutung, Enstehung, und frühe Wirkungsgeschichte* (Leipzig: Benno, 1999).

11.   Allan M. Harman, 'The Interpretation of the Third Commandment', *The Reformed Theological Review* 47 (1988), pp. 1-7 (6).

12.   Both may have also outlawed 'magic' or unlawful means of divination.

13.   In ancient Greece perjury was not a legally defined crime, see Gustave Glotz, 'Le serment' in *Etudes sociales et juridique* (Paris: Hachette, 1906), p. 182; and Emile Benveniste, *Vocabulaire des institutions indo-européenes* (2 vols.; Paris: Minuit, 1969), II, p. 175.

14.   See practically all the standard commentaries.

association of Yahweh's name with mortal transactions, the Third Command-ment prohibits perjury, slander and defamation, and assures violators of divine punishment. The same contingency is surely imposed on any divergence of speech, particularly under oath, which entails the illegal serving of self interests and the undermining of the good name and social standing of another. Without going so far as to claim unwarranted duplication, both Commandments characterize the distor-tion of truth in terms of sins of speaking.

Difficulties associated with precise comprehension of either Commandment are reflected in the variety of existing translations. Literally translated, the Third Com-mandment asserts that 'the lifting up the name' of Yahweh in vain (frivolously or illegitimately) is a crime which merits divine penalty. The very prohibition appears to define the realm of naming of God, complementing the First Commandment, which defines Yahweh in terms of an act (liberation from Egypt), and the Second, which characterizes Yahwism in relations with other divinities.[15]

Conceptual varieties of an oath seem to motivate the Third and the Ninth Com-mandments as reflections of a social and legal system heavily reliant on the validity of oral evidence, both in court and outside it. Truth and falsity, as well as speaking and maintaining silence, express alignments of individuals and of groups. Leviticus 5.1 considers the suppression of evidence a grievous sin but leaves the sinner to his fate:

> If anyone sins in that he hears a public adjuration to testify, and though he is a wit-ness, whether he has seen or come to know the matter, yet does not speak, he shall bear his iniquity. (RSV)

The ability of a tongue sworn to God to inflict both incalculable damage, as well as to benefit, is clearly reflected in Leviticus' assumption of guilt, in the case of mind-less oaths:

> If any one utters with his lips a rash oath to do evil or to do good, any sort of rash oath that men swear, and it is hidden from him, when he comes to know it he shall in any of these be guilty. (Lev. 5.4)

Confession, however, can cleanse sinners (Lev. 5.5). Aided by a sacrifice and priestly mediation, it ensures Yahweh's forgiveness. Perhaps the publicity attendant on such a verbal admission is calculated to act as a deterrent. Leviticus is specific about sins committed 'in error' (בשגגה, 5.15) and those perpetrated 'knowingly' (ידע, 5.17). The text chastises the abuse of neighborly trust in matters of property deposited in good faith, but charts potential pardon by allocating substantial com-pensations and a sacrifice of atonement (5.20-26). For Leviticus, any such behavior is unsociable. It constitutes a breach of faith (מעל באדוני; חטא, 5.21) as does intercourse with a bonded woman who belongs to another man (19.20-22). Yet, both 'errors' of theft and of sex merit not death but pardon.

Denials of deposit, through a lying oath, suggests a violation of the Third Commandment, even before the matter gets to court. Levitical regulations on this

---

15.   Josiah Derby, 'The Third Commandment', *JBQ* 21 (1993), pp. 24-27 (26).

score assume individuals (males) can regulate their dealings with each other without resorting to mechanisms of formal justice. This is the opposite assumption of
Numbers 5, the ordeal of the *soṭah*, which invests the power to deal with the case of
suspected adultery in the priesthood. Especially striking is the common vocabulary
applied to theft of property and the 'stealing' of marital integrity. Both are depicted
an act of betrayal (מעל, Lev. 5.15, 21; Num. 5.12). Yet, the option of sacrifice of
atonement is only open to the suspecting husband, although potentially guilty of
perjury; the woman, if guilty, becomes a living 'curse' (אלה, Num. 5.27).

When Leviticus 19 recaptures the Decalogue, it enjoins Israel not to steal, nor to
deal falsely or to lie to one another (19.11). Leviticus 19.12 restates the Third Commandment as: 'You shall not swear by my name falsely, and so profane the name of
your Lord. I am Yahweh' (RSV). Such a reading suggests that the Third Commandment does not merely deal with ordinary profanities, whatever these may be, but
rather with any misappropriation or perversion of the divine name.[16] Intimately
entwined with the idea of 'truth', based on an oath, is the ideology of holiness, and
specifically of Israel as God's holy people. Leviticus 19 insists that sins of speaking
misuse Yahweh's name. Implicitly, the Ninth Commandment becomes the fountainhead of a judicial system which repeatedly calls for the execution of justice, not
only because of the divine approbation of rules and regulations, but also because
Yahweh led the Israelites out of Egypt (19.36), a land standing for iniquity and for
injustice. Perjury, then, become desecration of the divine.

Perjurers elicit multiplicity of portraits. In Exod. 20.16 a perjurer is a promoter
of lies; in Exod. 23.1 perjury entails violence and maliciousness (cf. Deut. 19.16);
and in Deut. 5.20 a perjurer is one who speaks vainly and inanely to damage others.
None of these texts provides a procedure to deal with false witnesses.[17] Exodus
23.1 ('You shall not bear slander [or: idle report], nor should you join hands with
an evil man to become a witness of violence [or: "of promoting wrong or perver-
sity"]'), reflects on the inextricability of the two types of language abuse that the
Third and the Ninth Commandment incorporate.[18] But it fails to reveal how a conspiracy of perverting justice is to be detected in the first place. Its prohibition
combines a straightforward 'exegesis' of the Ninth Commandment within a court
setting and, potentially, lying witnesses, with a general ban on bearing slanderous
reports. The former hurts human justice; the latter is an explicit offense against
Yahweh.

By positing an individual *vis-à-vis* Yahweh on the one hand, and individuals
among themselves on the other hand, the two Commandments embody the verbal
bonds that bind society together. They envision modalities of enunciating solemni-
ties by outlining a domain of words. And they implicitly conjure up the catastrophe

---

16. Marvin E. Tate, 'The Legal Traditions of the Book of Exodus', *Review and Expositor* 74
(1977), pp. 483-509 (490).

17. Van Seters (*Law Book*), assumes that Exod. 23.1 deals with two false witnesses, thus
complimenting Deut. 19.15-19 and enlarging the scope of the Ninth Commandment.

18. Another possibility is: 'you are not to start a false rumor. You are not to conspire with an
evil person to be a malicious witness', *pace* Van Seters, *Law Book*, p. 135.

of a violated oath, an eventuality that bears witness to the eminent value of the sworn word. The focus of the Third Commandment is on the idle and empty use of the divine name; the Ninth focuses on the negativity of perjury. Both highlight the misuse of speech, a form of the original sin itself.

In Paradise the serpent 'discusses' the validity of divine threats, advising the dissolution of the verbal contract (or 'oath' or 'covenant') between Yahweh and humans (Gen. 3). In the Hebrew Bible, the whole set of relationships between Yahweh and Israel is grounded in a 'covenant', a treaty-type commitment based on stipulations, and anchored in oaths which are violated as often as they are renewed. Genesis' diction defines the consumption of prohibited 'food' as a violation of trust, which is precisely the essence of oath breaking. It depicts humans (and reptiles) as a group potentially prone to perjury, in its widest sense. God's curse consigns serpents to the soil and introduces generational enmity with humans. Such is the penalty of perjurers who, paradoxically, tell the truth. Woman is hit at her most vulnerable, her womb, precisely like the *soṭah*, another potential perjurer. All three, serpent, woman, man, are deemed oath breakers, although none had actually taken an oath. Such is the inverse logic that makes Eve a plague for humanity, even before evoking the existence of either oath or of oath breaking.

In cultures where the spoken word carried as much, if not greater weight than the written word, 'acting and listening' provided a verbal seal of the most important transactions. Thus the Israelites in the Sinai (Exod. 19.8; 24.7; Josh. 24.24), and thus, inversely, definitions of sin in prophetic parlance (i.e. 'deafness' and deliberate transgressions). Yet, the weaving together of doing and of hearing, or their opposite, does not ensure concord or harmony. Actions and words engage but also disengage. A covenant can bond and dissolve. Speaking truthfully in God's name can make a truce; speaking falsely can put an end to one. Because the negative is so closely intertwined with the positive, the question of whether words are more binding than socially accepted values is constantly raised in narratives.

2. *Harmony and Matrimony*

> And Abraham was growing old and Yahweh had blessed Abraham with everything. And Abraham said to his slave, the oldest in his household and the one who had charge of all his possessions: Put your hand under my thigh and I will make you swear by Yahweh, the God of heaven and God of earth, that you will not take for my son a wife from among the daughters of the Canaanites among whom I dwell. To my home country and my kindred you will go and you will take there a wife for my son Isaac. (Gen. 24.1-3)

What one has by way of valuables constitutes an extension of the self. Yet, one exists only insofar as one will be alive after death, through a son and through a grandson. A familial paradigm of this sort is vulnerable when a bride must be sought from a specific lineage and a specific location. In Genesis 24 matchmaking is a male occupation, with father and trusted male slave collaborating over a carefully planned extension of the family. The slave puts his hand 'under Abraham's thigh', the seat of male procreative organs, becoming a participant in a process which is calculated to promise continuity. But he also threatens the future of his master's name, his house and his offspring, if he fails.[19] Because miscarriage of instructions entails the demise of divine promises, the slave must anticipate success. The prospect, too, of not abiding by an oath is too terrible to contemplate. Only if the woman herself refuses can the emissary be released from his pledge (Gen. 24.8).

This is, perhaps, a peculiar prelude to the most famous biblical tale of wooing a woman, but not as strange as the appearance of a sworn slave in the role of a bridegroom's proxy.[20] The slave's story, as recounted by himself to the family of the prospective bride, recaptures the events nearly verbatim. But he adds an important item: 'Abraham said to me: Yahweh, before whom I walk, will send an angel with you so as to make your mission a success' (Gen. 24.40).[21] The issue of oath-release becomes, in the retelling, a matter not between intended bride and Abraham's representative but between the family and the slave. Listeners become sharers in the oath and in its repercussions.

An oath, in this narrative, emerges as an effective prevention against oath breaking and failure. By narrating the ritual in the first person singular, the slave paves the way to the desirable alliance. The 'I' becomes an expression of collectivity, combining the sum total of its members' commitment, Abraham's to endogamy, the slave to his master, and the hosts to oblige a guest. In the absence of a 'law' that prescribes exogamy or intermarriage, an oath, even when related, confirms the slave's veracity. With the oath, those who swear and those who hear shoulder responsibilities to make a decision according to truth and justice. Such a conceptual

---

19.   On the crucial role of the anonymous slave and confidant, see Wolfgang M.W. Roth, 'The Wooing of Rebekah: A Tradition-Critical Study of Genesis 24', *CBQ* 34 (1972), pp. 177-87; Kenneth T. Aitken, 'The Wooing of Rebekah: A Study in the Development of the Tradition', *JSOT* 30 (1984), pp. 3-23; Sternberg, *The Poetics of Biblical Narrative*, pp. 129-52; P. Mandel, 'The Servant, the Man, and the Master: An Inquiry into the Rhetoric of Genesis 24', *Jerusalem Studies in Hebrew Literature* (= *Mehkarei Yerushalayim beSifrut Ivrit*) 10-11 (1988), pp. 613-27 (Hebrew); Lieve Teugels, 'The Anonymous Matchmaker: An Inquiry into the Characterization of the Servant in Genesis 24', *JSOT* 65 (1995), pp. 12-23; Susanne Gillmayr-Bucher, 'The Woman of Their Dreams: The Image of Rebekah in Genesis 24', in Philip R. Davies and David J.A. Clines (eds.), *World of Genesis* (JSOTSup, 257; Sheffield: Sheffield Academic Press, 1998), pp. 90-101. On the theme of oath in Genesis, in general, see Richard S. Hess, Gordon J. Wenham and Philip E. Satterthwaite (eds.), *He Swore an Oath: Biblical Themes from Genesis 12–50* (Carlisle: Paternoster Press, 1994).

20.   Cf. *Digest* 23.2.5 (Pomponius): 'A woman can be married to a man who is not present by means of his letter or a slave messenger, if she is brought to the messenger's master', quoted in Jane F. Gardner and Thomas Wiedeman, *The Roman Household: A Sourcebook* (London: Routledge, 1991), p. 17. On structure and characterization in Gen. 24, see Lieve Teugels, 'A Strong Woman, Who Can Find? A Study of the Characterization in Genesis 24, with some Perspectives on the General Presentation of Isaac and Rebekah in the Genesis Narratives', *JSOT* 63 (1994), pp. 89-104. On Rebecca, see Mary D. Turner, 'Rebekah: Ancestor of Faith', *Lexington Theological Quarterly* 20 (1985), pp. 42-50. In general, on Gen. 24, see Fèlix García López, 'Del "Yavista" al "Deuteronomista": Estudio critico de Genesis 24', *RB* 87 (1980), pp. 242-73.

21.   Ellen J. van Wolde, 'Telling and Retelling: The Words of the Servant in Genesis 24', in de Moor (ed.), *Synchronic or Diachronic?*, pp. 227-44.

framework ensures that both slave and hosts 'deal loyally and truthfully' (Gen. 24.49) with the issue at hand.

Rebecca's sole word, 'I will go' (Gen. 24.58), in response to the urging of Abraham's slave to leave, confirms the solemnity of the speech-act that is the oath. But it also questions just who has the complete power over decisions relating to marital alliances, as well as to the separation of the bride from her home and family. From the start, Rebecca acts in a complementary fashion to her environment— her gestures, first quenching the thirst of a stranger and of his animals, then inviting him to stay with her family (24.18-20, 25), underscore the unity of a male formula of hospitality that is one and the same for all.

Boasting a lineage that harks back to a specific man (Nahor) through a specific woman (Milka), Rebecca reveals her ancestry (Gen. 24.24), a fact that remains singular in the face of the guest's striking anonymity. Yet, this is hardly a one-sided exchange. Before asking her to identify herself, Abraham's slave had presented Rebecca with expensive gold jewelry. The presents, ostensibly calculated to reward the woman for her exceptional consideration of a stranger's needs, prompt a revelation of familial ties. The disclosure empowers Rebecca to act in the name of her ancestors and relatives, anticipating her own importance in the chain of generations.

Abraham's confidant reacts to Rebecca's hospitality with a brief prayer to God (Gen. 24.26-27). Based on verbal gestures, and closely linked with oaths, formulas of hospitality bind together families and 'strangers' within institutional structures that ensure safety and orderliness. Laban addresses his guest with a welcoming speech that amounts to a hospitality oath which contains a reference to God: 'Come in, O blessed of Yahweh' (24.31). His words echo the servant's own prayer which acknowledges Yahweh's guiding mercy and hand (24.27).

Genesis 24 is exceptional in according the daughter of the house an instrumental and active role in an all-male scheme of hospitality. With the exception of Genesis 29 (Rachel/Jacob), other biblical tales of hospitality, such as Genesis 19 and Judges 19, cast daughters and wives as victims of violated trust, and hence as the price that oath breakers charge.[22] In each of these cases the punishment for transgressing oaths is a general massacre of both law breakers and their co-patriots. And although such a penalty may seem out of proportion to the crime itself, its harshness is embedded in rules which upheld the binding nature of oaths, especially in implied contracts of hospitality. In Genesis 24 the presence of a guest acts as a source of familial accord; in Genesis 19 and Judges 19 it ushers discord and division of sexual entertainment.

If interpreted in the light of the Third Commandment, Genesis 24 suggests that words uttered in God's name, regardless of gender, status and circumstances, are binding. Genesis 24 effectively covers all three—it begins with a verbal exchange between two men of unequal status (Abraham/slave), continues with an interchange of gold and words between a woman and a slave (Rebecca/Abraham's man), and ends with a conversation and interchange among men. It may be asked, therefore,

22. See below, Chapter 6 §9.

whether women become a part of the male orbit of sworn oaths only upon specific 'initiation' through an exchange of goods.

Cast as a fairytale with Yahweh as an invisible matchmaker, Genesis 24 has the aura of a fantasy with a twist. It puts on stage a beautiful and providentially un-betrothed young woman who appears an answer to paternal prayers. It presents a hospitable family happy to comply with a stranger's needs and request. Indeed, only the future groom is missing. With so promising a beginning, based on oaths that induce harmony and matrimony, a happy end is bound to follow. Or does it?

The first meeting between Rebecca and Isaac generates a ruse. She covers herself with a veil (Gen. 24.65), although the chances of Isaac recognizing her are, to say the least, slim. According to narratological sequence, Isaac brings the veiled woman to his mother's tent (who had been all but dead, 23.2), presumably unveils her, and certainly falls in love with her (24.67). She is the consolation prize who substitutes mother's love. Strangely, her veil (of modesty?) recalls Tamar's veil of prostitution (Gen. 38) which plays a prominent role in a failed matrimonial scheme. Tamar's anonymous 'hospitality' highlights the exclusion, rather than inclusion, of women from the charmed circle of male oath-hospitality. Taken as a commentary on Genesis 24 idyllic image of an all-embracing oath- hospitality, Genesis 38, by strik-ing contrast, betrays hostility towards the spoken word.

Women, in Genesis–Numbers, do not feature as oath-breakers but they cause men to assume this role. When Yahweh orders the Israelites to wage war against Midian, the command renders the war holy (Num. 31.1-2). When the Israelites spare Midianite women and children (31.9), Moses is furious. His anger is directed, primarily, to the sparing of women (31.15). Only the execution of married women (and children) can purify the Israelite males who had unlawfully appropriated females, infants and property (31.19-20). Rituals of cleansing are conducted through the purification of both metals and men with fire, as well as with 'waters of im-purity' (מֵי נִידָה, Num. 31.23). These waters hint at another type of 'impurity', namely the one associated with emissions through intercourse, parturition and menstruation. Both Leviticus 12 and 15.18-33 deal with procedures of 'purifying' women. In all such cases the law prescribes a ritual of purification (washing cloths and self in clean water) and, for women, an additional sacrifice of atonement. The verbal association between the narrative in Numbers 31 and the Levitical rules casts women, as well as metals belonging to foreigners, as metaphorical sources of impurity and of communal discord.

The equation of women (Israelite or Midianite) with material goods in contexts of oath-actions suggests an analogy aimed at reconciling friction. Both become constituents of verbal agreements that regulate the environment of men. The har-mony that the Decalogue projects as a result of compliance requires periodic exhi-bitions of divine power and of human authority (i.e. laws). When the two clash, the judicial basis by which males abrogate or follow the law sows discord and dis-enchantment. Genesis 24 shifts familial alliances by 'naturalizing' the transferred object (woman) through a series of oaths; in Genesis 19 and Judges 19 protagonists cross the boundary of swearing that marks the eternal return of the patterns of hospitality, beyond the narratives of family history and into a new zone where no one has ventured before. And it is precisely on the terms of making and breaking an oath, of being true to others, to God, and to oneself, that the Third and the Ninth Commandments claim the right to limit spatial interactions between males.

3. *Deuteronomy on Justice*

You shall not take the name of Yahweh your God in vain (לשוא), because Yahweh will not acquit the one who will take the name in vain. (Deut. 5.11)

You will not bear false witness (עד שוא) against your neighbor. (Deut. 5.20)

If a malicious witness rises against any man to accuse him of wrongdoing, then both parties to the dispute shall appear before Yahweh, before the priests and the judges who are in office in those days. The judges shall inquire diligently, and if the witness is a false witness and has accused his brother falsely, then you shall do to him as he had meant to do to his brother, thus purging the evil from the midst of you. And the rest shall hear, and fear, and shall never again commit any such evil among you. (Deut. 19.16-20)

Justice, justice you shall pursue. (Deut. 16.20)

Deuteronomy betrays deep concern for the kind of harmony generated by the certainty of justice.[23] In Deuteronomy 19 (quoted above), priests and judges set out to settle disputes and to mete out exemplary punishment to law breakers. Deuteronomy's Ninth Commandment brings the covenant into an institutional setting which operates under divine auspices in a public forum and format. Yet, there is no precise procedure of investigation, nor is it clear how either judges or priests are to detect either falsity or false witnesses. Laying the contested matter 'before Yahweh' invests the judges' decision with an authority in cases in which there are, in fact, no external witnesses. By dividing society into priests, judges and witnesses, Deuteronomy makes the public a symbolic arbitrator of itself. The emphasis on 'brotherhood' (אחיו, Deut. 19.19) translates the issue into a fraternal theme, well beyond the immediate subject of lying and harming. The paradigm of a lying witness incorporates fraternal discord which the legislation of the law courts sets out to excise in the name of cohesion.

Yet, it may be asked how the community of property and wives that characterizes the guardians of justice functions in an ideal covenant society. How can the covenant itself ensure that they are free from accusation against one another? In the age of the Genesis community, the group's unanimity rendered a judicial system superfluous. Ancestral narratives portray a blessed age in which even harsh decisions, such as Sarah's engineering of Hagar's removal, as well as the infliction of wrong and injury, are invariably directly conceived and directed by Yahweh, each enacted in order to preserve the integrity of the original promise of land and progeny. In the world which Deuteronomy depicts, an iniquity or crime must be

---

23. On the notions of justice vs. righteousness in the context of paternalism, see Bernard S. Jackson, 'Justice or Righteousness in the Bible: Rule of law or Royal Paternalism', *ZABR* 4 (1998), pp. 218-62.

substantiated by at least two witnesses (Deut. 19.15), although one of these may prove false. Little, besides fear of revelation and of retribution, can prevent the corruption of the system. Ideal justice remains an internal system of checks and balances which operates on its own. In its most complete form it does not require prohibitions.

In Deuteronomy, inner voice and external necessity converge to sanction whatever form of justice is demanded for covenant fulfillment. The nature of Deuteronomic justice seems defined by the simultaneous presence of a self and the immanence of the divine. The Third Commandment appoints Yahweh as judge; the Ninth alludes to court judgment. Both are set in a context of oaths and swearers, and both envision the tongue as a weapon of discord. Such perceptions are strikingly illustrated in the procedure surrounding the 'slandered bride' (Deut. 22.13-21) which reflects, most suggestively, Deuteronomy's understanding of the two Commandments.[24] The woman whose integrity is at stake is not allowed to speak. She cannot be a witness, because there is no elaborate inquiry into the complexities of the case. The public trial takes place between her parents, or rather father, and her husband. Parental defense 'rests' its case on a public display of the woman's 'tokens of virginity' (22.17). These provide proof of her eligibility at time of betrothal, as well as of complete paternal control over the daughter's body prior to marriage. Only males engage in a judicial rhetoric which can turn deadly. Illusion and reality engage in paradoxical crossing, itself a reflection of the ontological status of the feminine. There are really two women at stake in Deuteronomy 22: one is an ideal image of a chaste bride, in this case perhaps an illusion; another is the adulterous wife who may turn out to be a phantom.

Such double vision of femininity rules the procedure and, at the same time, serves as an objective referent through which men must question their previous perceptions of the world and of women. The essential strategy for ensuring the 'success' of the agonistic operation in Deuteronomy 22 requires that the woman be sacrificed. When the father accuses the husband of hating the daughter and of bringing 'shameful or defaming charges' (עלילת דברים, Deut. 22.16-17), both accusations are, at that point, paradoxically irrefutable. Wrangling about the justice of respective claims, litigants quarrel about a past without questioning the woman herself. The trial becomes a masculine *agon* whose 'winner' is hailed by a tribunal of local 'elders'. The hideous specter of execution of the woman lends the proceedings a concrete sense of a 'trial' which is, in fact, a spectacle calculated to instill fear in women and to promote the social status of the 'elders'.

Conspicuously absent from the scene of judgment in Deuteronomy 22 is the ideology of *quid pro quo* that concludes the exegetical pericope of 19.16-20. If found guilty of a lie, the husband is not executed. Yet, this is the penalty that his wife, if found guilty, has to face, not to mention the loss of status and social respectability for her parents. Her execution takes place at the gate to her father's house, a symbolic passage from virginity to marriage and from life to death. Both

---

24.   See also Chapter 5 §5 and Chapter 6 §5.

trial and execution are public, highlighting the communal dimension/public extension of the Third and the Ninth Commandments. The adversaries must plead the
cause in person, posing as both litigants and witnesses. The judgment amounts to
arbitration between two families, previously linked through marriage which is
under threat of dissolution. The judges' main function is to listen and, implicitly, to
decide the veracity of one side or the other. There is no appeal.

Deuteronomy knows the value of veracity. Deuteronomy 10.20 encourages not
only complete belief in Yahweh but also oaths in Yahweh's name. The distribution
of attributes, negative and positive, of the Third Commandment, contributes to the
make up of a covenant profile. Deuteronomy 10 links love and worship of Yahweh
with Yahweh's indefatigable pursuit of justice, and Yahweh's extraordinary favor.
The vocabulary of choosing Israel as a holy nation occurs frequently with allusions
to justice in which the function of injustice is to alienate God from Israel. This is
why Deuteronomy 27 and 29 include both curses and blessings, as though their
contradictory nature is intensified by a rhetorical juxtaposition which, in turn, is in
itself framed in Decalogue's references.

The agonistic character implied in the Third and the Ninth Commandments becomes a structural element of the society which Deuteronomy's Decalogue aspires
to regulate. Vain swearing and perjury undermine the all-male bond which covenant regulations promote and enforce. In this covenantal typology the ways in which
humans uphold or violate the Commandments prompt retribution of tragic justice.
This is the message of Dtr narratives, such as Judges 11, which explores not the
breaking but the maintenance of a sacred oath, and of stories like 1 Kgs 2.13-25 that
investigates domestic disputes with national repercussions. Oath and perjury sow
dissension, as 1 Kings 21 strikingly demonstrates: when the feminine self equals
the male, Jezebel reverses male conventions and entitlements.[25]

4. *Vows, Virginity and Parenthood*

The tale of Jephthah's daughter (Judg. 11) is precariously balanced. It features a
(male) 'hero' and a hero's daughter caught together in a deadly game of words. The
daughter's death is required to ensure her father's compliance with the Third Commandment.[26] With her demise, still a virgin, the line of women that had begun, in

25. See below, Chapter 6 §8.
26. Among many, see Phyllis Trible, 'The Daughter of Jephthah: An Inhuman Sacrifice', in
idem, Texts of Terror: Literary-Feminist Readings of Biblical Narratives (Philadelphia: Fortress
Press, 1984), pp. 92-116; J. Cheryl Exum, 'The Tragic Vision and Biblical Narratives: The Case
of Jephthah', in *idem* (ed.), *Signs and Wonders: Biblical Texts in Literary Focus* (Atlanta: SBL,
1989), pp. 59-83, and W. Lee Humphreys, 'The Story of Jephthah and the Tragic Vision: A Reply
to J. Cheryl Exum', pp. 85-96 of the same volume; Peggy L. Day, 'From the Child is Born the
Woman: The Story of Jephthah's Daughter', in *idem* (ed.), *Gender and Difference in Ancient Israel*,
pp. 58-74; Heinz D. Neef, 'Jephta und seine Tochter (Jbc XI 29-40)', *VT* 49 (1999), pp. 206-17.
Especially interesting is Mieke Bal's analysis in her *Death and Dissymetry*. On Judg. 11 as a late
(Persian or Hellenistic) insertion, see Thomas Römer, 'Why Would the Deuteronomists Tell about
the Sacrifice of Jephthah's Daughter?', *JSOT* 77 (1998), pp. 27-38.

the recorded annals, with a 'harlot', comes to an abrupt and untimely end. Briefly recaptured, the story narrates how on the eve of a crucial battle Jephthah undertakes a vow in Yahweh's name. The vow constitutes what he considers a fair exchange— victory on the battlefield in return for an appropriate sacrifice. Yahweh seemingly enters the pact. Jephthah wins the desired triumph. When he returns from the battlefield his daughter (= the Gileadite) greets him.

The plot revolves on an ironic twist of a familiar motif which calls for the sacrifice of daughters. The myth of Iphigenaia, for example, relinquishes the daughter before the battle; that of the Gileadite depicts Yahweh as a trusting divinity, willing to grant victory first and to exact payment later. A complex interplay between ignorance and knowledge guides the plot throughout. Daughter is ignorant of father's vows; father is ignorant of the fatal consequences of the oath; daughter is fully aware of the power of an oath to God; father knows that his part of the 'pact' must be fulfilled. Using the Decalogue as a decoding key, the text insists on unconditional and unilateral respect for parents as it explores the extent and the cost of filial duty. By focusing solely on father and daughter, Judges 11 exposes the hazards of parenthood and the dangers that a child may face as a result of unilateral parental vows. In this setting, the uncompromising requirements of both the Third and the Fifth Commandments bring tragedy rather than rewards.

Two patterns of behavior underlie the final outcome. Jephthah implicates the domicile in a decision that involves the fate of all the Israelites. His vow reflects the sharing of destinies between the people, as a whole, and individual households. The issue at stake is not only the viability of Jephthah's vow, but also the unlimited power that fathers exercise over the lives of their children. Jephthah's general authority, an asset on the battlefield, is logically, if tragically extended to his own home. But the story also questions this manifestation of parental power and ostensibly leaves the daughter, rather than the father, to decide the outcome. Unquestioned obedience, rather than contempt and disregard, then, can turn into a deadly parental asset.

The text seems to suggest that the daughter was endowed with a surprising scope of free choice. Her insistence on parental compliance with a vow emphasizes her potential to undermine the special bond between humans and the divine that an oath engenders. The tale also raises a crucial issue: What do parents owe their children if not the preservation of their bodily integrity? Jephthah fails this basic test of fatherhood. Driving home the ideology of the irreversibility of oaths, the subtlety of the story resides in its notion of human subordination not to another human's will, but to an alleged divine desire. Fathers, loving as they may be, cannot foresee that they may become the instruments of their children's destruction. When they do realize the extent of the calamity, daughters become an enemy. Jephthah's vow, the need for compliance and her determination to abide by it, usher a rupture for which there is no remedy.

Dying a virgin, the Gileadite also dies as a sacrifice. Virginity, sacrifice and marriage appear inextricably joined, as they are in Samson's 'folk' tale (Judg. 13–16), which outlines how a son's matrimonial and amorous choices infringe parental authority.[27] In Judges 11 a father is 'vanquished' by a daughter whose appearance signals not the celebration that he richly deserves, but mourning (Judg. 11.35). She is a 'winner' in a rhetorical debate that, like Samson's argument with his parents over his proposed marriage with a Philistine woman, extols the free choice of sons and of daughters. Winning a battle of words, the Gileadite woman is preparing for the final triumph—not a nuptial celebration but a demonstration of filial piety and death. For Samson, the wedding celebration is only the beginning.

Samson celebrates his approaching nuptials with a group of male friends; Jephthah's daughter laments the approaching 'loss' of virginity and the concomitant deprivation of matrimony with her female friends. Leaving home for the mountains she reverses the metaphor of marriage by a voluntary severance, and by departing not for the house of a husband but for the wilderness. Her gesture becomes 'law', to be observed, by women only, once a year. Paternal oath turns into a 'torah' of women, both inviolable.

In commemorating virginal mourning Judges 11 reveals two strands of familial ideology, one that stakes survival on conventional means of procreation; and another that espouses the perpetuation of memory through outstanding and unconventional deeds. A vocabulary of division dominates the narrative: first among Jephthah's own siblings; then among Israelites and Ammonites; Gilead and Ephraim; between father and daughter; and, finally, between God's right to exact the execution of an oath and human's right to live. The word for decision becomes a choice and an action—both woman and narrator repeatedly resort to the verb 'to do' or 'carry out' (עשׂה, 11.36, 37, 39). Such an emphasis, on doing rather than talking, highlights the enormity of an act that must follow words which turn out to be both rash and deadly.

A redistribution of roles, with the Gileadite standing firm and the father irresolute, suggests that legal realities of a court scene, as anticipated in the Ninth Commandment, are exhausted by the idea of latent struggle. There is no formal court procedure in Judges 11 because from the very start the story informs its readers of the reason for the ultimate verdict. Nor is there need for either proof or witnesses. Even the punishment is fixed in advance. What remains paradoxical is the acquiescence of the victim in the verdict, and the implication that to keep an oath entails a penalty potentially much greater than the one meted by law to oathbreakers or to perjurers.

The Gileadite story challenges the meaning of both the Third and the Ninth Commandments by probing the aftermath of a manly vow to win. Because she makes her choice public, Jephthah's passivity vividly illustrates the constraints of the Third Commandment. He must accept the sacrifice because in this domestic contest she is the 'winner' (Judg. 11.35). Without passing concrete judgment, the narrative examines the ethics of practices that originate in 'legal' rules. Dwelling on postulates of the Decalogue, Judges 11 insists that the only way to decide, without trial, is to choose one or the other of the parties. The text also advances its own

27. See below, Chapter 5 §6.

choice, albeit implicitly, by duly recording a single aspect of the judgeship of
Jephthah's successor, Ibtzan of Bethlehem. Known neither for prowess in battle nor
for any other achievement that would rank him among heroes, this man is accred-
ited with fathering no less than thirty sons and thirty daughters (12.8-9), all living,
and with finding mates for all of them. This, the narrative suggests, is a feat equal
to victory in war, as well as a rebuttal of the ideology that drives Jephthah to
challenge family, tribe and Yahweh, and drives daughters to death.

Scenes of domestic strife, however, need not end in tragedy. The scroll of Esther
explores the meaning of justice in familial realms in which husbands, if royal, dis-
miss wives for alleged insubordination; and wives, if queens, are invested with
authority to exact national vengeance for a private insult. In Esther's rigmarole,
women are catalysts of words as actions. They must navigate amid male antagonism and between oaths made by men.[28] Linking the law of the land with domestic
dissension, Esther's narrator implies that the existence of positive justice is closely
correlated with negative justice—there is no oath without the possibility of perjury,
nor perjury without an oath.

Justice, in Esther, is characterized by activities. The supreme judge is the king,
and his words and desires are 'translated' into 'realities' by his subordinates. There
is no denunciation of the process of deliberation, nor a discussion of the implementation of justice in the kingdom. Vashti is not called upon to account for her refusal
to join the royal banquet. In order to elevate another woman to her position an
arbitrary process of selection takes place. The appearance of Esther is anchored
in domestic strife (between Ahasuerus and Vashti), and in personal antagonism
(between Haman and Mordechai), in both of which she plays no role. Yet, both
situations generate laws that converge to highlight the tragic ambiguity of the
female protagonist. In Judges 11 the Gileadite must pay with her life to ensure her
father's compliance with the Third Commandment. Esther must pay, potentially
also with her life, to change a law that is unacceptable to her 'father'.

Whether the scroll of Esther mocks such heavy-handed legal procedures is
difficult to determine. In its effort to achieve a reconciliation between Jewish need
to survive and the kingdom's need to abide by royal rules, the story progresses
along a path of rapidly changing rules. It begins with a law which ordains the dismissal of a royal wife; continues with one which makes men masters of language in
their households; and with another that gathers women in the harem to be periodi-
cally displayed according to the 'law of women' (דת הנשים, Est. 2.12).[29] The royal
annals duly record an act of loyalty to the king (2.23), as well as a law which orders
the annihilation of the Jews (3.13), and another which calls for the death of anyone
who enters the royal court without summons (4.11). Disrupting this erratic legal
progression, Mordechai, a law breaker (3.2; 4.2), orders Esther to become one
herself (4.8).

---

28. See my *Dinah's Daughters*, Chapter 3.
29. All apparently in writing. On the importance of the written Word in Esther, see Mieke Bal,
'Lots of Writing', in Brenner (ed.), *A Feminist Companion to Ruth and Esther*, pp. 212-38.

Rooted in a basic disagreement over male honor, the battle between Mordechai and Haman which had begun with Haman's vow to avenge a dishonor, shifts to the inner court where Esther must confront the powerful minister on her own, as the Gileadite had to come to terms with her imminent death far from home. Justice for the Jews, in Esther, is potentially injustice for Esther herself. The rivalry that pitted Haman and Mordechai against each other is channeled through Esther who must attempt the improbable, namely changing the law of the land. Mordechai enjoins Esther to 'remember' why she had been made queen (Est. 14.4), but knowledge, like God, is absent from the scroll.

In Haman the narrative recognizes a bad man who brings disaster. But Ahasuerus is a bad king, a tyrant, and Mordechai rules his own household like a tyrant. Each of these man is sworn to a cause, Haman to kill the Jews, Mordechai to save them, and the king to remove unpleasantness from his life. Collectively they are the same, the products of a similar logic. Judges 11 shows Jephthah as directing the impreca- tion against himself alone; Mordechai distinguishes between his own person and Esther whom he orders to sacrifice herself. He had pledged to save the Jews, but his vow can only be fulfilled through Esther's action. The absence of Yahweh means that the protagonists must engage in strategies of currying royal favor because in the battlefield of vows in Esther's Persia only the king has the last word.

When Esther becomes a designated sacrifice, the Third Commandment becomes a gesture dissociated from fertility and military victory, as it had been with Jeph- thah and his virgin daughter. In Esther's Persia, a chaotic realm, the fate of Haman, an oath taker, provides an ironic illustration of the power of self annihilation of the Third Commandment. To obliterate the oath, the oath-taker must die. Haman be- comes a personified imprecation whose role is to usher the reversal of the laws through a complete reversal of his own being. Esther is turned into a blessing. The community's future is no longer at risk. Haman is eliminated. A happy end stands in a jarring contrast with the untimely and gruesome death of the Gileadite. Only in Esther, human encounters with intractable laws result in reconciliation between king and Jewish subjects, in spite of Yahweh's silence and remoteness.

5. *Tongues of Duplicity? Rahab and Jael*

In the annals of ancient Israel the fortunes of two wars revolve on the actions of two foreign women. One, Rahab, shields the enemy and changes sides to win life (Josh. 2); the other, Jael, proffers protection to a 'friend' and ends by killing him (Judg. 4).[30] In Joshua 2, Rahab, who lives in a dwelling adjacent to the walls of Jericho, negotiates an exchange of commitments with two 'guests'. Resorting to an unspoken oath of hospitality, she provides shelter and safe passage in return for future securities. In Judges 4, Sisera presumes on Jael's hospitality to elicit an ex- pressed oath of allegiance: if asked, Jael is to lie and to deny his presence. Jael, who lives in a tent on the border between Israelites and Canaanites, switches sides in the

---

30. On Rahab see also below, Chapter 4 §6; on Jael, see Chapter 6 §8.

war between Israel and Canaan, fetching a high price for acceptance. The serenity of Jael's tent contrasts with the uncertainty that envelopes Rahab's home near the wall. Yet, when Jericho erupts, Rahab's home becomes the only 'safe' place, a 'womb' that gives life in the midst of gore and demolition.

A comparison between the two women must take into account the literary and the 'civic' dimensions of the narratives. Rahab is a member of the Jericho community, but her profession and location locate her in the social and physical margins of society. Jael lives in no man's land, belonging to neither Israelites not Canaanites. Both women are liminal, and both highlight the liminality of the Third and Ninth Commandments. It seems hardly an accident that these female catalysts of spoken and unspoken oaths are foreign women whose fate is closely intertwined, by choice, with that of Israel. Their words and gestures, enacted within the space of their domicile, form a counter-embodiment of an all-male battlefield where the fate of Israelite men determines that of women.

Justice, in either Joshua 2 or Judges 4, is a product of neither war nor court, two masculine arenas where triumph and defeat equal truth and falsity. Rather, the justice of these two narratives is an outcome of women's ostensible lies and decisive actions. In the 'reality' of social practices, the behavior of Rahab emphasizes the temporary sexual bonding that unites a prostitute with her clients, while Jael's invitation to Sisera turns norms of male hospitality into an exchange between a woman and a man. The two scenes deal with issues that are ordinarily rejected or ignored. The fact that one takes place in Jericho and the other in Kenite land inserts them into a specific biblical reorganization of space in which crucial moments for Israel in general occur away from Israelite camp and land.

Jael is eager to disclose her action (i.e. killing Sisera); Rahab is anxious to cover up her interaction with the spies. Both welcome their 'guests' in order to give more effective power to their own actions, and both use words to lull men into reassurance. Rahab's accommodation is laden with moral and political symbols—she shares her home as a prelude to her own integration into the Israelite camp. Jael pretends solidarity with Sisera as a prelude to sharing her tent. Ironically, one sequence results in solidarity, the other in separation. Jael speaks to Sisera in an appropriate manner; he demands specifics of hospitality, such as shelter and drinks. However, in commanding her to deny his presence, Sisera makes Jael a lying witness and anticipates his own end which is, after all, what he himself had insisted upon. Rahab volunteers a denial but exacts a true oath and tokens of enforcement. The basic binary opposition between men and women is both confirmed and undermined through these diagnoses of oath.

The spies swear in Yahweh's name to save Rahab. Both sides appeal to Yahweh, as though conforming to a ceremony or tradition. As the drama around Jericho is drawn to an end, the validity of the oath is tested. No violation is allowed. Rahab's story, with its happy end, for Rahab's family, becomes a perfect foil of a political discourse that is also the keeper of memory. Here, the narrative provides a radical perspective, precisely because the vows in Yahweh's name occur outside the prescribed orbit of the Third Commandment, and their object is not Israelite males but a foreign woman and her clan. Rejecting her town and her people, Rahab becomes worthy of inclusion in an all-male ideology that seems to have little else in common when it deals with foreign women.

Crushing Sisera with impunity, Jael first speaks to him as a 'friend'. Her incarnation of hospitality provides ideological justification for both his assumed trust and her ultimate betrayal. He deems her spontaneity as sympathy, disregarding the potential danger, or rather believing it to be outside Jael's tent. Proximity generates both trust and danger. In Joshua 2 the use of Yahweh's name provides corollary and compatibility. In Judges 4 the traditional exchange of polite words acquires an added edge, because the supplier of shelter is a woman whose husband had been in the power of her 'guest'.

Jael disavows Sisera. She proclaims his vulnerability by successfully applying violence. In the seemingly pacific but, in fact, intensely violent tent, when the text juxtaposes a man of war with a woman of words, incompatible formulas are condensed into an oxymoron. The ultimate tragic figure may be Sisera, a point of view confirmed by the image of his mother in the window, expecting his return, in vain. In Judges 4, Jael's silent response and seeming compliance with Sisera's demands promotes a misunderstanding of complicity. She articulates, in action, her reaction to becoming a 'false witness' against her own will and judgment. When Barak arrives she greets him with the words which she had been asked to suppress.

Foreign women, in these two cases, do not need an interpreter. The spectrum of discursive modes is set forth in the episodes that feature Rahab's disclaimer of the spies' whereabouts, and Jael's divulgence of Sisera's presence at her home. In Joshua 2 the discourse testifies to the all-embracing orbit of the taking of Yahweh's name in earnest. Balancing the rules of hospitality with a specific Israelite need, Judges 4 produces a discourse of imbalanced justice. The crowning moment in a war engineered by Yahweh (4.6) is a victory of woman at home, made all the more ironic by a promise to deliver the enemy's general into man's, and not woman's hands (4.14).

6. *On Witches and Wives: From Ein Dor to Jezebel*

On the eve of a crucial battle with the Philistines, King Saul, whose appeal to Yahweh fails to elicit response, turns to consult a 'medium', a woman who is 'a mistress of magic' (בעלת אוב, 1 Sam. 28.7). Initially, she refuses to comply. He then swears 'in Yahweh's name'. His oath, seemingly in perfect accordance with the Third Commandment, violates his own law that had outlawed any but Yahwist forms of divination. The textual juxtaposition of king, an embodiment of the law, with proscribed woman, an incarnation of illegalities, confounds cast stereotypes. The king is in also need and is willing to break the law; the woman is afraid but she is persuaded to provide the information which he so desperately seeks. His fear of the unknown is greater than her apprehension of legal penalties (28.12, 21).

Saul's oath changes everything, enabling the woman to exercise her profession with impunity. It further puts him in a position of dependency on her skills. She brings Samuel out of the dead, transforming the prophet in the process into 'a god' (אלהים, 1 Sam. 28.13). He is an 'old man' (28.14), but his words replicate the rhetoric of his fiery self and the pronouncement of the grim fate which awaits Saul and his dynasty (15.16-35). The dualities in the episode (king–'witch'; king–prophet; man–woman; living–dead), furnish endorsements of oaths and become producers of tragedy. Considering the connotations, Saul and the woman become identical in their quest of knowledge beyond the perimeters of the permissible in Yahwist society. We may wonder about Yahweh's presence in the realm of divination where women and men operate on equal grounds.

Saul is in disguise; the medium is herself. He lies about his identity but employs the 'positive' inference of the Third Commandment to inspire confidence. She confronts him, first with a 'historical' truth (his edict against practitioners of divination), and then with his own self. She also remakes Samuel, enrolling his ghost in a divine pantheon. Her reactions shed light on the meaning of mediation between the world of the dead and of the living, which she sets in motion as a result of a royal oath of protection. When Saul's true identity emerges, she feels cheated; the prophet is angry; Saul is desperate. The distinctions operating between legal and illegal means of 'knowing' God's will have become blurred. As king confronts the 'medium', the prophet and his own imminent end, the only constant remains the power of the oath taken. The rest is transient and ultimately as 'alien' as is the woman, and even as is the king.

Saul dies fighting in Jezreel, a locality which features recurrently on the mapping of a biblical topography whose zones revolve around alien, alienating and alienated figures. In the valley of Jezreel, voices of women, murderous and murdered, like Jezebel, fearful and compassionate, like the 'witch' of Ein Dor, or lamenting the fallen followers of Saul, like the daughters of Israel (2 Sam. 1.24), register words and actions in contexts that measure the breadth and depth of the Decalogue's Commandments. In this geography Saul's demise is the fulfillment of a prophecy which a woman had mediated; the death of Naboth, Ahab and Jezebel inscribe another bloody chapter in Israelite spatial annals into the soil.[31]

The narrative of the vineyard of the Jezeraelite Naboth (1 Kgs 21) provides proof, if proof is needed, of the way in which the text forges intricate and inextricable connections between spatial and social plains; and between the ideal Israelite society that Yahweh's law organizes and the behavioral realm of 'reality'. When Ahab confronts the king of Aram on the battlefield in Jezreel, the king of Israel is in disguise (22.29), as Saul had been when he sought the help of the medium. In both cases, the future had been already foretold—Yahweh's prophet had proclaimed the demise of the Omrides dynasty (21.19-26). The end is inevitable, in spite of uncertain beginnings.

Jezebel's orchestration of a mock trial, with two false witnesses, provides a striking illustration of the disastrous consequences of transgressing the Ninth Commandment, at least when at stake is coveted property adjacent to the royal palace. Yet, the exceedingly disproportionate 'revenge' which Yahweh prepares for Ahab

---

31.   See also below, Chapter 6 §8, with my 'From Jezebel to Esther: Fashioning Images of Queenship in the Hebrew Bible', *Bib* 82 (2001), pp. 477-95.

and for Jezebel prompts questions about narratological tension in stories in which the end can be foreseen from the start. How compatible are these with the basic import of the Decalogue? The Third Commandment assures divine intervention for the misuse of the divine name. The bleak prospect of transgression unfolds, however, when a king (Saul) swears an oath in Yahweh's name to a female 'seer' in order to elicit the truth which Yahweh had denied him. The Ninth Commandment proscribes the abuse of court proceedings; its fullest illustration is enacted through a strategy that implicitly embraces women as promoters of illegalities.

The figure of the 'witch' of Ein Dor is invested with power and pity, two attributes that mingle modalities of speech, namely words spoken by the living with those spoken from the grave. She speaks constantly but is uncertain. Her wordiness contrasts with Jezebel's brevity and decisiveness. Both women engage in multiple forms of counter-Yahwism. The medium of Ein Dor pursues foreign forms of divination. Jezebel is a foreigner but also an astute interpreter of situations. Because the narrative puts an inordinate stress on Jezebel's alien background and on her alienation from Yahweh, one is entitled to ask whether she was at all bound by Yahweh's laws. In 1 Kings 21 Elijah addresses his remonstrance to Ahab alone. But his censure implicitly targets Jezebel in an entanglement of guilt. Her invisibility renders her initiative all the more sinister. It marks her prompting of perjury at court as more grievous than the actual false witnessing. The fate of the men she had allegedly set up to implicate Naboth in crime is never disclosed.

To grasp the full range of Jezebel's transgression of both the Third and the Ninth Commandments, the trial in Jezreel makes Naboth a violator of the former, and Jezebel of the latter. Yet, neither is guilty as charged. Readers know that Naboth had been falsely accused of a curse. Jezebel does not even appear at the court in Jezreel. To Naboth, the indictment poses an enigma; to readers, Jezebel remain undecipherable. Because language initiates a world of images, the stories that illustrate transgressions use women, although women are as ambiguous as the message that the texts convey.

Decoding the Third and the Ninth Commandments in terms of narratives and negativities breeds descriptions that communicate lugubrious scenes in which blood replaces words. In spite of divergences of detail, the events in Jezreel (in 1 Kgs 21), and Saul's fatal and final clash with the Philistines, present a logic that demands the casting of women, 'foreign' by ethnicity, by profession and indeed by nature, as catalysts. Yet, the Bible also conjures female images of foreignness to state, with perfect clarity, that there are differences within likeness. In the scroll of Ruth, the Moabite female protagonist openly makes use of oath formulae that range Yahweh on her side. The scroll's male protagonist, an Israelite, uses a 'court' to test the limits of the Ninth Commandment.

7. *Coda: Ruth and Redemption*

In the beginning there were three deaths, all of men, and three widows. Such is the lugubrious launching of the narrative that bears the name of Ruth, a classic 'fairytale' (from male point of view), that ends with marriage and birth of a male heir.[32] The map of Ruth is circular—its two poles are firmly fixed in Bethlehem, with a brief excursion to the land of Moab. It is woven with threads which, when mingled, produce a reconciliation of contradictory elements, replacing hunger with plenty, widowhood with marriage, and one husband with another.

Orpah and Ruth confront the dismantling of their household. The sisters adopt antagonistic stands, one returning to her maternal home and gods, the other following her mother-in-law. In this alchemy of new alignments, sisters are separated by a vow. Ruth's emotional response to Naomi's imminent return recasts the two women as symbolic sisters, linked by their common past, by need and by word. They refute the biblical model of blood kinship by forging a bond based on an oath, and modeled after the Third Commandment.[33] And they constitute a new pattern of fictitious blood relations that must survive through the mediation of man. Within a 'reality' of an institutional strategy of levirate marriage, Naomi and Ruth provide an imaginary mode of operation that seems to subvert, yet to uphold the law. Naomi grooms Ruth, as the eunuchs groom Esther, in order to exit a quandary by dangling the specter of female beauty and sex.

In the paradigm of justice that the scroll of Ruth espouses, irreconcilable pairs overcome conflicts by resorting to law. Boaz' contends that the 'redeemer' (גּוֹאֵל) must acquire the widow together with the widow's land. Whether or not this is a correct reflection of the law of levirate marriage, and whether the designated 'redeemer' is right in fearing damage to his own inheritance, this theatrical trial at Bethlehem's gate plays on male emotions in order to accomplish a double operation—the invalidation of a legal claim to redemption, and the legalization of another's claim to assume the very same function.[34] Potentially leading to discord, not to mention penury, Ruth's vow to remain by Naomi's side dissolves in a near comic manner. Male relatives confront each other, the one forearmed with knowledge of the widow's beauty, the other ignorant of pre-trial negotiations. The ten elders chosen by Boaz to 'judge' the case appear as ignorant as the unnamed 'redeemer', who happened to be passing by the gate when cornered by Boaz. Boaz himself becomes a witness to a transaction that he himself desires to execute. In a less benign context, he would have been suspected of perjury.

Male and female ruses, balanced by female beauty, innocence and youth, resolve, or rather dissolve potential crises. They clarify contradictory configurations and reinstate relationships between males and females, always asymmetrical and non-reciprocal. Ruth delivers a son; Naomi and her female neighbors name the child. The narrator cleverly links that event with 'history' by resurrecting Tamar as a

---

32. Above, Chapter 2 §9. On parallels with Gen. 38, see Ellen J. van Wolde, 'Texts in Dialogue with Texts: Intertextuality in the Ruth and Tamar Narratives', *BibInt* 5 (1997), pp. 1-28; I would add to her list the theme of 'redemption'.

33. Cf. the oath of friendship between David and Jonathan.

34. Dale W. Manor, 'A Brief History of Levirate Marriage as it Relates to the Bible', *Restoration Quarterly* 27 (1984), pp. 129-42.

model of fertility, and by designating Boaz as the ancestor of the greatest king of ancient Israel.[35]

Thinking in terms of organic divisions between males and females is difficult when the two range around a single law. Imperatives of mutual aid and the perpetuation of the family's (father's) name engender an ambiguity that obscures the distinction of boundaries between the reciprocal and the unilateral. Boaz and the unnamed redeemer are not simply the closest of relatives who owe the women support and help. They are also doubles. The denial of one assists the affirmation of the other just as, inversely, Ruth's denial of her parentage affirms her new Israelite identity.

Through a display of solidarity the scroll depicts a woman assisting another, because in the 'time of the judges', when the tale allegedly takes place, these personal relations act as adhesives in a loosely bonded society. From the moment Ruth undertakes a vow of loyalty everything progresses according to a plan which seems carefully orchestrated by an invisible divine hand. This amounts to saying that, collectively, all the actors in the scroll, males inclusive, are by definition unfree. Symbolic or ideal sisterhood, an essential bond between women, must ensure the community's well-being by conforming to male-appointed traditional roles. In this specific conceptual rendering of the Decalogue's Commandments, women are interchangeable, or as least supposed to be so.

In Ruth's epic of mythic perspectives, everything appears perfectly simple. Ruth swears by Yahweh and admirably adheres to her vow; Boaz keeps his promise and marries the beauty; Naomi witnesses the fulfillment of her desires and designs. Orthodoxy prevails, but it entails a definition of 'citizenship' that amalgamates, rather than rejects foreigners. By marrying Ruth, Boaz seemingly solves everything. Yet, even then, one cannot be sure that the acquisition of Ruth resolves all difficulties. Deuteronomy 23.4 relegates Moabites to the margins of bastardy. Ruth turns out to be a bearer of legitimacy and ancestress of the longest living dynasty in Israel's history. In extremis, then, the dilemma is determined, as it is in Tamar's case (Gen. 38), in a manner that deliberately links the remote past with the 'present reality' of legal institutions. Ruth's descendants will be kings, and Israelites. Tragedy dissolves in this 'comeback', reminding us that it introduces one orthodoxy only to confront it with a superior one.

---

35. Gary N. Knoppers, 'Intermarriage, Social Complexity, and Ethnic Diversity in the Genealogy of Judah', *JBL* 120 (2001), pp. 15-30, and above, Chapter 7 §3.

Chapter 4

THE SABBATH:
INVOKING LIBERATION? REVOKING CREATION?
(WORD FOUR)

Remember to sanctify the day of the Sabbath. Six days you shall labor and do every type of work. But the seventh day is a Sabbath to the Lord your God. In it you shall not do any work, you or your son, your daughter, your slave, maid, animal or the alien within your gates. For in six days Yahweh made the heaven and earth, and the sea and all that there is in them, resting on the seventh day. For this reason Yahweh blessed and sanctified the day of the Sabbath. (Exod. 20.8-11)

Observe the Sabbath day and keep it holy as the Lord your God has commanded you. For six days you shall labor and do all every kind of work. But the seventh day is a Sabbath to the Lord your God. In it you shall not do any work, you, your son, your daughter, your slave, your maid, your ox, ass, or any of your cattle or the sojourner who is within your gates, so that your slave and your maids will rest as you do. Thus you shall remember that you yourself was a slave in the land of Egypt and that Yahweh your Lord brought you out with a mighty hand and an outstretched arm. For this reason Yahweh your Lord ordered you to celebrate the day of the Sabbath. (Deut. 5.12-15)

1. *The Sabbath: Biblical and Modern Interpretations*

In a public assembly in Jerusalem in the days of Nehemiah a public prayer and confession were heard.[1] The prayer provided a prelude to a new covenant between Yahweh and a group of exiles who had returned to Judea/Yehud with Persian consent.[2] 'Recalling' the history of Israel from creation to restoration the praying people appealed to Yahweh to sanctify a new covenant. Their commemorative recollection was selective. Beginning with an invocation to Yahweh as the Creator of all things, they asserted that:

---

1.   See Neh. 9, with Judith H. Newman, 'Nehemiah 9 and the Scripturalization of Prayer in the Second Temple Period', in Evans and Sanders (eds.), *The Function of Scripture in Early Jewish and Christian Tradition*, pp. 112-23; Mark J. Boda, *Praying the Tradition: The Origin, and Use of Tradition in Nehemiah 9* (Berlin: W. de Gruyter, 1999); and Tamara C. Eskenazi, 'Nehemiah 9–10: Structure and Significance', *Journal of Hebrew Scriptures* 3 (2000–2001), available online at <http://www.arts.ualberta.ca/JHS/Articles/article_21.htm>.

2.   See my 'The Silent Women of Yehud', for what follows.

You, alone, are Yahweh who made heaven… You are Yahweh the Lord who had chosen Abram to lead him out of Ur of the Chaldeans and to rename him Abraham… (Neh. 9.6-7)

In this reading of the past, the opening statement, with its insistence on Yahweh as the sole creative God and as the guiding divinity of the first Hebrew, bears unmistakable echoes of the First Word. Donning sack cloths and soil, the repentant exiles recreate biblical history as a tissue of highlights abstracted from Genesis and Exodus. With the Sinaitic theophany, the prayer reaches a crescendo:

On Mt Sinai you came down and you talked to them from heaven and you gave them just precepts and true laws, good statutes and commandments. And you informed them of your holy Sabbath and bade them commandments, ordinances and a law through Moses your servant. (Neh. 9.13-14)

Of the Ten Commandments Nehemiah specifically alludes only to the Sabbath and to its sanctity. The rest of the Ten he 'canonizes' as 'straight laws, true Torah, rules and good precepts' (Neh. 9.15).[3] This exilic exaltation of the Sabbath ultimately leads to a vow of separation from the local inhabitants, including a ban on intermarriage, on commercial transactions with 'locals' on the Sabbath, and on tilling the land during sabbatical years (10.31-32).[4] In exilic interpretation of the Fourth Commandment, celebrating the Sabbath as a major covenant tenet erects specific familial and 'national' zones. Its strict observance and enforcement acts as a reminder of the uniqueness of the covenant community and of the urgent need to maintain separate existence within rigid sectarian boundaries.

The centrality of the Sabbath in the creation of Nehemiah's Yehud reflects its pivotal place within the Decalogues of the Pentateuch.[5] Measured by length alone, the Fourth Word is the longest, most comprehensive and most detailed of all the Commandments. It is also the one Commandment that has two strikingly different textual versions. And it is the one tenet which characterizes Israel even before the Sinaitic theophany and the issuance of the Decalogue itself. Already Exodus 16 provides a cautionary tale regarding the function of the Sabbath as a day of 'rest' and as a measure of bonding between Yahweh and Israel. By the time the Israelites 'receive' the Sinaitic Sabbath in Exodus 20, the mandatory day has become a Commandment to be 'remembered' (20.8). Yet, the Fourth Commandment, perhaps the most distinctly Israelite/Jewish of all the Decalogue, enjoins compliance, at least in Exodus 20, not on the basis of recent events but on account of the creation of the entire universe.

---

3. The term 'holy or sanctified Sabbath' itself is found only in Neh. 9.14 and Exod. 16.23. The consecration of the Sabbath is mentioned elsewhere, Exod. 20.8 and 31.12-18; see Newman, 'Nehemiah 9', p. 115.

4. On intermarriage, cf. Exod. 34.15-16 and Deut. 7.3-4.

5. Cf. Neh. 13.15-18 on desecrating the Sabbath and Neh. 13.19-21 on Nehemiah's measures to prevent trading on the Sabbath in Jerusalem. According to Mayes, 'Deuteronomy 5 and the Decalogue', pp. 68-83 (75), the Deuteronomy Decalogue lays chief emphasis not on the First Commandment but rather on the one to observe the Sabbath which becomes a central demand as it is thrust into prominence by a number of literary devices. But this can also be said of the Fourth Commandment in the Exodus Decalogue as well.

In Deuteronomy the Sabbath becomes a law to be carefully observed rather than remembered, simply because God had so willed. No longer inspiring recollections of universal beginnings, the Deuteronomic Sabbath is firmly anchored in a specific Israelite past of liberation from Egypt. Deuteronomy even omits the story of the manna (Exod. 16) which accounts for the very first appearance of the Sabbath in the wilderness. Thus (re)cast, the Sabbath of Deuteronomy ceases to be a universal manifestation of God's relations with the cosmos. It signals instead a particular covenant between Yahweh and a chosen people. 'Remembering' the Sabbath becomes, in Deuteronomy, an action generated by the day itself (Deut. 5.15).

Scholarly discussions of the Sabbath have, nearly exclusively, focused on attempts to elucidate its etymology, origins and history.[6] Scholars have explored the connections, if any, between the Sabbath and its ideology of resting or 'ceasing' from work;[7] and the chronology of the Sabbath—when, how and why it was introduced into the fabric of the Israelite/Jewish week—exilic or post exilic;[8] other questions posed relate to the scope and nature of Sabbath's liturgical activities, and whether these included public assemblies, as Isa. 1.13 suggests.[9] Yet more queries have been directed at the issue of the links between manumission and a specific Hebrew calendar on the one hand, and the Sabbath and the observance of the sabbatical year on the other hand.[10] The latter is especially interesting because it points

6. The bibliography is substantial. Among many, see Gnana Robinson, *The Origin and Development of the Old Testament Sabbath: A Comparative Exegetical Approach* (Bern: Peter Lang, 1988). For a useful overview, see Gerhard F. Hasel, 'The Sabbath in the Pentateuch', in Kenneth A. Strand (ed.), *The Sabbath in Scripture and History* (Washington, DC: Review and Herald Publishing Association, 1982), pp. 21-43; *idem*, 'Sabbath', in *ABD*, V, pp. 849-56; Moira J. Dawn, *Keeping the Sabbath Wholly: Ceasing, Resting, Embracing, Feasting* (Grand Rapids: Eerdmans, 1989); and Leo Laberge, 'Sabbat: étymologie et origines', *Science et esprit* 44 (1992), pp. 185-204.

7. Matitiahu Tsevat, 'The Basic Meaning of the Biblical Sabbath', *ZAW* 84 (1972), pp. 447-59.

8. Heather A. McKay, 'New Moon or Sabbath?', in Tamara C. Eskenazi, Daniel J. Herrington and William H. Shea (eds.), *The Sabbath in Jewish and Christian Traditions* (New York: Crossroad, 1991), pp. 12-27 (19-22), argues for a late (post exilic) introduction of the Sabbath as a holy day and one of communal worship on the basis of few biblical references to terms of actual worship.

9. Ian Hart, 'Genesis 1.1–2.3 as a Prologue to the Book of Genesis', *TynBul* 46 (1995), pp. 326-67. On the seven-day week as a cycle of purification with the 'Sabbath' marking a moment of reintegration into the community, see S.A. Meier, 'The Sabbath and Purification Cycles', in Eskenazi, Herrington and Shea (eds.), *The Sabbath in Jewish and Christian Tradition*, pp. 3-11, based on seven days maternal impurity period after birth of a male child (Lev. 12.2); fourteen after the birth of daughter (12.5); seven days of purification for leprosy (15.13) but with the eighth day as one of re-entry; seven days menstruation impurity period (15.19, 28) once more with the eighth day as the critical moment of shedding the 'pollution'.

10. William W. Hallo, 'New Moons and Sabbaths: A Case Study in the Contrastive Approach', *HUCA* 48 (1977), pp. 1-18, claims that already in biblical times the sabbatical concept was extended beyond its ritual applications to the week (p. 11); see also Moshe Weinfeld, 'Sabbatical Year and Jubilee in the Pentateuchal Laws and their Ancient Near Eastern Background', in Timo Veijola (ed.), *The Law in the Bible and in its Environment* (Göttingen: Vandenhoeck & Ruprecht, 1990), pp. 39-62; and Niels P. Lemche, 'Manumission of Slaves—the Fallow Year—the Sabbatical Year—the Jubilee Year', *VT* 26 (1976), pp. 38-59.

to an effort to incorporate the land itself in a visible confession of faith which, like the Sabbath, demonstrates Yahweh's original right and absolute sovereignty over humans and soil alike.[11] Sabbaticals, like Sabbaths, also postulate polemics since both represent a conscious repudiation of other gods.[12]

Leaving aside such important investigative strands, there is hardly a doubt that, regardless of its introductory period, the combination of a 'Sabbath' and weekly rest is original to the Bible. The biblical Sabbath endows an otherwise ordinary day with sanctity, forging an intimate and inextricable connection with Yahweh and Yahweh's own historical imprint.[13] Because the Sabbath denotes both the creative impulse of the divine (Exod. 20) and the freedom that Yahweh's covenant bestows on its (male) members (Deut. 5), the Commandment of the Sabbath seems self explanatory. Yet, its connotations are contentious. What, exactly, is the meaning of 'rest', of 'liberty' and of 'creation' in the Sabbath context? Why are women *qua* wives and mothers omitted from the orbit of rest?

2. *Exodus and the Sabbath: Labor and Leisure on the Seventh Day*

In the redacted Exodus narrative, the sanctification of the Sabbath precedes even the issuance of the Decalogue itself. This is a curious and important exception—no other Commandment is specifically couched, either as a succinct prohibition or as an injunction, prior to its incorporation in the code. The Sabbath's historical or narratological etymology brings together the idea of rest with divinely appointed food provisions. Yet, the account (Exod. 16) of how the Israelite Sabbath came into being, a component of the wilderness record of the liberated Israelites, depicts the people as desiring neither rest nor complying with divine instructions.

As it stands, the narrative of the first wilderness Sabbath (Exod. 16) opens with complaint about food scarcity which engenders memories of Egyptian abundance. In response, God showers manna from heaven. But the celestial food lacks preservatives—it grows moldy within a day, necessitating repeated labor of gathering on a regular daily basis. On a 'Friday', however, God allows the Israelites to amass a double quantity of manna in order to stay put on a 'Saturday'. Disobeying, Israelites nevertheless scavenge the desert on a 'Sabbath', looking for fresh manna. There is none.

Such are the turbulent annals of the first recorded 'Sabbath' of liberation. It is a day that marks not freedom from Egyptian slavery but rather Yahweh's capacity to provide for the recalcitrant Israelites just as well as the Pharaoh had done. The 'Sabbath' of Exodus 16 is a day of competing diet. In Egypt, nourishment depended on slavery and on continuous bondage; in the desert, it depends on believing in God's

11. See Lev. 25.23, with Gerhard von Rad, *Genesis* (trans. John H. Marks; Philadelphia: Fortress Press, 1961), p. 16, echoed by Martin Noth, *Leviticus* (trans. J.E. Anderson; London: SCM Press, 1965), p. 166.

12. Hans-Joachim Kraus, *Worship in Israel: A Cultic History of the Old Testament* (trans. Geoffrey Buswell; Oxford: Basil Blackwell, 1966), p. 72.

13. Martin Buber, *Moses* (Tel Aviv: Schocken Books, 2nd edn, 1963 [Hebrew]), p. 81.

care, and on comprehending the meaning of liberty. As is turns out, the liberated generation fails both tests.

Divinely ordained, the text gives no other reason to account for either 'sitting' on the seventh day or for the Sabbath's sanctity. It suggests that to do nothing on the seventh day reflects an unquestioned obedience to God's will. In Exodus 16, the Sabbath designates the end of a six-day period of divine bonus characterized by continuous harvesting of an alimentary product which the Israelites had not sown.[14] It is a day of 'rest', both for humans and for nature; and it is also a feast of honeyed edibles. The Sabbath's main purpose, it seems, is to remind future generations of Yahweh's inimitable abundant generosity. To preserve the memory of the miraculous desert nutrition which nurtured the Israelites during forty years, Moses instructs Aaron to conserve a sample in a jar (Exod 16.32-35).[15]

Within a context of constant nourishing needs, the Sabbath of Exodus 16 emerges as a test of trust between Israel and Yahweh, as well as a contest between the earthly ruler of the fertile land of Egypt and the divine patron of the wilderness.[16] Yahweh's bounty, especially on a 'Sabbath', aims at erasing a specific mirage of the Egyptian past which hunger has conjured in the minds (and stomachs) of the starving Israelites. This is a peculiar prelude to the Decalogue's Sabbath Commandment which ordains 'remembrance'.[17] Nor does Exodus 16 anticipate the insistence of Exod. 20.11 on the Sabbath as a link between a pattern of universal creation and an individual cessation of labor.

The actual Decalogue 'law' of the Sabbath resides in a demand to 'sanctify' the seventh day (Exod. 20.8).[18] The Commandment enjoins Israelites to complete their work within six days and to cease from laboring on the seventh.[19] The observance, ostensibly entrusted into the hands of individual male heads of households, extends to members of the younger generation (sons and daughters), to bonded dependents (male and female slaves), to animals and to the *gerim* who inhabit Israelite space. A notable omission is that of a wife/mother.

Equally striking is the justification which the Fourth Commandment provides to account for the rhythm of repeated remembrance and observance of the Sabbath.

---

14. Here I follow Hasel, 'The Sabbath', p. 27.

15. Jan A. Wagenaar, 'The Cessation of Manna: Editorial Frames for the Wilderness Wandering in Exodus 16.35 and Joshua 5.10-12', *ZAW* 112 (2000), pp. 192-209.

16. See Hasel, 'The Sabbath', pp. 26-27, on the terminology and theology of the Sabbath in the manna narrative.

17. The root of the First word of the Fourth Commandment, זכר, suggests a retrospective and prospective angle, simultaneously harking back to any past as well as to a future of continuous observance; see Brevard S. Childs, *Memory and Tradition in Israel* (London: SCM Press, 1962), *passim*; and Willy Schottroff, *Gedenken im Alten Orient und im Alten Testament: die Wurzel Zakar im seminitischen Sprachkreis* (Neukirchen–Vluyn: Neukirchener Verlag, 1964), *passim*.

18. On the 'ring' structure of the Fourth Commandment (introduction–command–motivation–command–motivation–conclusion), see Hasel, 'The Sabbath', p. 29.

19. On the terms employed to designate 'work', מלאכה and עבודה, as distinct rather than overlapping, see A. Graeme Auld, 'Sabbath, Work and Creation: מלאכה Reconsidered', *Henoch* 8 (1986), pp. 273-79.

Exodus 20 holds the creation as a mirror in which the weekly human Sabbath reflects the divine design of the primordial cosmos. The text thus suggests that the Sabbath, although first enunciated to Israel in the wilderness, has its roots in an ancient (and non-Israelite) history. 'Resurrected' for the benefit of the liberated Israelites, the Sabbath of the Exodus occupies a space which designates a meeting-ground between divine and Israelite time (Gen. 2.3; Exod. 16; 20.11). The Sabbath, a seventh-day break from the weekly pattern of labor, provides a tangible token of contractual obligation and of contractual creation.[20]

An all-inclusive mandate, the Sabbath implies that Yahweh is a source of Israel's uniqueness, reinforcing the exclusive claim of Yahwist brand of monotheism which the First and the Second Word formulate. Other texts directly express the connection between the Sabbath and campaigns against idolatry.[21] The 'Covenant Code' refers in one breath to the Sabbath and to the banning of other gods (Exod. 23.12); the so-called 'cultic Decalogue' embeds the Sabbath and other festivals in a context which calls for the banning of intermarriage and other gods (34.21); and Lev. 26.1-2 condenses the Decalogue into two basic precepts: one which proscribes idolatry and another which preserves Yahweh's Sabbaths [*sic*] and Yahweh's temple(s).

Exodus' most expansive exegesis of the Sabbath Word (Exod. 31.12-17) is especially illuminating:

> Tell the sons of Israel the following: My Sabbaths you shall keep because this is a sign (אות) between me and you for generations (to come) to know that I am Yahweh who is sanctifying you. And you shall keep the Sabbath because it is sacred to you. Its violators will die because whoever works on that day will be cut off from among the people. For six days work will be done but on the seventh [none] as it is a Sabbath, a non-working day [sabbatical] sacred to Yahweh. Whoever does work on the day of the Sabbath will die. Therefore the sons of Israel will keep the Sabbath, observing the Sabbath throughout their generations as a perpetual covenant. Between me and the sons of Israel it is a sign forever, because Yahweh made the heaven and earth in six days and on the seventh he ceased and took respite.

The Sabbath exegesis of Exodus 31 comes at a juncture which bridges a series of cultic instructions (chs. 25–30) with an illustrative sample of a disastrous transgression (ch. 32).[22] Its textual position suggests that the Sabbath, in this context, highlights the benefits of compliance and conformity, as well as the penalties in store for violators. While dispensing with a list of Sabbath beneficiaries, Exodus 31 insists on capital punishment for breaking the Sabbath law. Activities that constitute Sabbath violations include the types of labor that involve food production, namely baking and cooking (16.23), plowing and harvesting (34.16), and the kindling of fire (35.3). The punishment for breaking the Sabbath rest is exemplary and,

---

20. On this passage as a reminder of the sanctity of the Sabbath even over the building of the tabernacle, see Ralph L. Smith, 'Covenant and Law in Exodus', *Southwestern Journal of Theology* 20 (1977), pp. 39-40.

21. Hart, 'Genesis 1.1–2.3 as a Prologue', p. 328.

22. On Exod. 32, above Chapter 2 §4.

as the case of the Sabbath wood gatherer shows (Num. 15.32-36), is to be administered by the community through public execution. Because the Sabbath is a communal feast that reflects Israel's homogeneity, 'working' during the day reflects
poorly on the entire covenant group.

Like the Fourth Word itself, Exodus 31 holds the Sabbath as a temporal plain
that merges two distinct chronologies, universal and Israelite, into a new historical
scheme which obliterates distance and time. By casting the Sabbath as a 'sign'
(אות) of the covenant, Exodus 31 incorporates souvenirs not only of the creation of
Genesis 1, but also of the primordial flood, a cataclysmic event that generated
another 'creation'.[23] In Gen. 9.12, a divine 'sign' in the shape of a rainbow, guarantees God's memory and perpetual mercy for the new post-fluvial order.[24] It ensures
that God will not inflict another flood, nor will there be need to recreate the world.
Embedded in this pattern of creation–destruction–creation, Exodus 31 explicit
threat of death for transgressing the Sabbath rules provides a powerful testimony of
human frailty and mortality, and of humans' ultimate impotence *vis-à-vis* Yahweh.

The Sabbath of creation devises a textual transit between the primordial era of
creation, as described in Genesis 1–2, and the wilderness period, as outlined in
Exodus. Both the Fourth Commandment and Exodus' exegesis on the Sabbath
suggest that its regular enactment forms an external, visible and perpetual marker of
the bond between God and Israel based, ironically, on a past that excluded Israel
itself. On a weekly basis, the horizons of Exodus Sabbath reinstate Yahweh as the
ubiquitous creator of an entire cosmos and Israel as an emblem of humanity. To
read Exodus 31 as hermeneutic of the Fourth Word suggests a perspective of 'reception' which situates Israel, as a distant reflection of *adam*, in the continual process
of generation which makes up universal history.

Genesis 1 depicts *adam* as an artifact. Endowed with divine blessings, this *adam*
is nevertheless invested with power to control, to consume and to procreate. In
other words, the productive outcome of the sixth day of creation (in Gen. 1) is vital
for the maintenance of order and for its future viability. Implicitly, this same creature, the last in an effervescent divine manufacturing line, also has the power to
destroy. The six-day creation scheme represents, therefore, a smooth process but
also a trauma. *Adam* is a pure imitation of God, but if it fails to procreate, God's
creation remains empty and meaningless. After *adam* comes the Sabbath (Gen.
2.1-3).

The Sabbath introduces the ultimate division between humankind and God, and
between divine and mortal types of labor. In Genesis 2, however, it is woman who
signifies the ultimate separation between God and humans, and between divine and
mortal space.[25] The Sabbath problematizes woman just as woman problematizes the
Sabbath. In Genesis 2 creation, *adam* acquires sexual identity only with the advent

---

23. On the meaning of אות, Carl A. Keller, *Das Wort OTH als offenbarungszeichen Gottes*
(Basel: Buchdruckerei Hoenen, 1946).

24. The tale of Noah is also replete with number symbolism, most notably of the number '7'
(Gen. 7.4, 10; 8.4, 10, 12, 14).

25. See below, Chapter 5 §3.

of 'woman'. To temper the dilemma of categorization, Genesis 2 casts 'woman' as the second *adam*. She is not the first human being but the first woman. But, like the Sabbath itself, she is also the last in a narrated order of creation that leads, in the first round, to God's own choicest day, and in the second, to woman.

3. *Eve: A Gift of the Sabbath?*

Scholars have long been aware that the Exodus' casting the Sabbath in terms of the story of the creation makes Genesis 1–2 a functional foil in terms of intertextuality.[26] No one, to my knowledge, has extended either comparison or interpretation to the problems that underlie the literary paradigms of Genesis 1 and Genesis 2, and how these reflect on the formulation of the Sabbath in Exodus. Genesis 1.27 records the making of a double gendered *adam* on the sixth day. This 'androgynous' is expected to uphold indefinitely the structure of the creation itself and to bring it to maturity and perpetuity. Specifically, the sixth day *adam* is to 'procreate and multiply, to fill the land and to conquer it' (Gen. 1.28). But no strategies are delineated, nor is it clear how this order is to be fulfilled. As it turns out, there is no sex or procreation in Paradise.

Genesis 2 casts *adam* as a creature created, or recreated, from dust (2.7). In this 'latter' version of the creation, 'he' is appointed a gardener for a well-laid Paradise. 'His' task is specifically defined as 'tilling' (עבד) and 'preserving' (שׁמר) the divine artwork (2.16). There is no anticipated cessation from labor for this creature, because work is man's fundamental purpose.[27] This is why *adam* is created in 1.28, recreated in 2.5, 15, and joined by woman in Gen. 2.18, 20. The Sabbath is God's day of appointed rest. There is no indication whatsoever that it is *adam*'s day of repose as well. The opposite is more likely. It is not designated as leisure time for any of God's creatures. Rather, incessant human toil is the only guarantee of the preservation and perpetuation of the divine creation. God's rest marks the first day of humanity's labor.[28]

Once only does *adam* enjoy a brief respite. The break takes place when God induces somnolence in order to effect a surgery under anesthetic (Gen. 2.21). Woman materializes. The time of this divine accomplishment is not specified. But *adam*'s temporary rest from toil, and the ideology of the Sabbath in Exodus, suggest that the coming of woman coincided with the earliest recorded respite of humans.

26. Cf. Hart, 'Genesis 1.1–2.2', pp. 315-36; and J. Severino Croatto, '¿Como releer la Biblia desde su contexto socio-politico? Ejercicio sobre algunas temas del Pentateuco', *Rivista Biblica* 53 (1991), pp. 193-212 (196-209), for recent rapprochement. The bibliography on Genesis, especially on the first three chapters is vast. The ATLA electronic database index supplies a useful point of departure. Textual problems are perused in Ronald S. Hendel, *The Text of Genesis I–II: Textual Studies and Critical Edition* (New York: Oxford University Press, 1998). In what follows I deliberately avoid questions of authorship, redaction and date. My focus, as elsewhere, is on the 'final' redacted version as it now stands.

27. Hart, 'Genesis 1.1–2.2', p. 333.

28. Meier, 'The Sabbath and Purification Cycles', pp. 4-5.

According to the first round of creation, God created animals on the fifth day of the weekly cycle (Gen. 1.20-23). Not all living creatures, however, materialized then. On the sixth day God was still preoccupied with fashioning animals, including an *adam* (1.24-31). In the second version of the creation (ch. 2), animals were (re)created *after* the making of Adam, specifically to keep the gardener company and to provide assistance (2.18). In this articulation of beginnings, the order contradicts, as well as reinforces the chronological scheme of Genesis 1. Woman now comes at the very end, as 'she' does in Genesis 1, but this time she appears in splendid isolation, as does the Sabbath. Her ingress highlights the disjuncture of genders, just as the Sabbath accentuates distinctions between 'work' and 'rest', creation and chaos.

Underlying the 'first' creation is a logic of a cosmic order which confers membership on humans by virtue of procreation and superiority (Gen. 1.28). In the Genesis 1 heterosexual pattern of reproduction, a harmony exists between all of God's products, motivated and monitored by an *adam* as the chief consumer of agricultural wealth. With the Genesis 2 unfolding of the 'history' of heaven and earth, the text stops at a crucial moment. It introduces an *adam*, but this creature is as yet incomplete (2.7). When the text (re)introduces woman, she must now be integrated into a space of vital continuation. Her arrival is hailed as a fitting conclusion to a process which had been, thus far, unachieved.

Neither the first woman nor the Sabbath are 'natural'. She is made out of *adam*'s body, with flesh and bones originally derived from clay. The Sabbath simply signifies the end of God's work, a temporal unit which God sanctifies, although nothing in the course of creation indicates a need for either rest or completion. Genesis' seventh day provides a striking contrast to the process that engenders the entire universe. Like woman, the seventh day 'wins' its rightful place in the cosmos after a series of divine labors. And both suggest an end as well as renewal.

Paradoxically, the very manufacturing of woman during a divinely imposed 'rest' constitutes a violation of the seventh day's rule of inaction. Genesis resolves this potential conflict by removing humans from the immediate sphere of the divine. In the book of Exodus the proximity which the wilderness breeds between God and Israel generates a pattern of conformity and transgression, echoing the ecology of Paradise. The establishment of the Sabbath soon after the departure from Egypt (Exod. 16), allows for a necessary integration of the Israelites into a Yahwist desert. Framed in a mythic context of creation, the codification of the Sabbath in the Exodus Decalogue positions the seventh day of Israel between the celebration of God (Gen. 1) and the installation of the first woman in Paradise (Gen. 2).

In evoking patterns of primordial creation, the Fourth Commandment constructs the same types of continuity and diversity which Genesis 1–3 advances. Challenging, however, Genesis' call to human toil, the Commandment allows the Israelites to partake in God's own temporal ideology. At the same time, the Sabbath Commandment restores the identity of Israel as Yahweh's own people, thus becoming a double signifier—of God's creation and of Israel's distinction. Since the Commandment is the only one which requires observance on a regular basis, its fulfillment induces harmony between Yahweh and Israel just as the insertion of woman into the fabric of creation conferred unity on the mythical complex of the textual Paradise of Genesis. Without woman, the very balance of the creative impulse remains precarious, if not altogether unachievable. Without the Sabbath, Yahweh's conceptual framework for Israel is meaningless.

Unlike the first 'Sabbath', however, Eve continues to occupy the story of the start. In Genesis 3.20 she becomes the 'mother of all beings', a giver of life, not unlike God. In the Israelite tale of beginnings (Exod. 1–2), the recreation of Israel is inextricably linked with women, once more as life givers. Besides mothers and presumptive mothers, the narrative introduces sisters and midwives, all of whom conspire to save Israelite males. Genesis suggests that without Eve there is no humanity; Exodus insists that without women there is no Israel. The Decalogue postulates that without the Sabbath of creation there is no Israelite identity. In spite of obvious parallels, the Fourth Word excises women *qua* mothers and wives from the orbit of the Sabbath.

Exodus 20.10 casts the direct recipients of the Sabbath law as men in control of a household full of dependents. There is no reference to either wives or mothers. Has woman been 'naturalized' to the point of omission? The canonical image of the Sabbath as an Israelite time par excellence, and God's own measure of labor, necessitated a simultaneous induction and excision of woman. Within the religious space of ancient Israel the time of the Sabbath indicates, therefore, an imbalance. In the beginning God celebrated the remarkable birth of the universe; in Paradise, the making of man and the advent of woman were both placed under God's patronage. In the Exodus, the Sabbath makes the meaning of Israel specific. After a series of reductions, the Sabbath once more came to symbolize the entire creative process. Blending the recent past into a mythic discourse, the formula of the Exodus Sabbath is charge with significance and with contradiction.

4. *Deuteronomy's Sabbath of Liberation*

In its two versions, the Fourth Commandment emphasizes the universality of the Sabbath. It is a day to be shared by the free, the bonded and even by the animals of every Israelite household. This is the liberating sense which the Deuteronomic Decalogue emphasizes. Moreover, in what constitutes a radical alteration of the text, Deuteronomy 5 presents the Fourth Word as a re-enactment of the Exodus, rather than of Genesis. The Sabbath in Deuteronomy introduces not so much a rest as a temporary equality of liberty into the lives of all human and animal members of the Israelite 'family'. This unusual measure is designed to recall the formative past of Israel with its Egyptian bondage and its miraculous liberation. To echo this crucial passage from slavery to liberty the redactor placed the Fourth Commandment at the heart of the Decalogue, as though to provide a verbal bridge between the First and the Tenth Commandments, two statements of unique Israelite identity.

Appealing to liberation rather than creation, the Deuteronomic Sabbath erases the souvenirs of a pre-Israelite past in favor of a specifically Israelite event. It represents a perception that favors a transition from the universal to the particular, and from a potentially universally applicable code to a specific Israelite one, as Nehemiah's words fully illustrate (above). The Sabbath of the Deuteronomy's Decalogue becomes an act, a gesture and a motive to recall a period of slavery and the tribulations of liberation. Sabbath and freedom from human oppression, in this version, are components of a recent past which the Decalogue reduces to its essence, independent of all temporality and the effective conditions of its fulfillment.

So solicitous is the Deuteronomic redactor to embed the memory of Egypt in the preservation of the Sabbath that slaves are mentioned twice, both times with an emphasis on their right to enjoy the same respite as that of their free masters (Deut. 5.14). Yet, Sabbath and slavery project an artificial, chronologically based bond, rather than cause and effect. The space allotted to dependents diverts the reader from the text's conspicuous omission of women as wives and mothers.

Wielding a mighty hand, Yahweh introduces the Israelites to freedom and to Sabbath. Both are cornerstones of collective Israelite memory, to be transmitted from one generation to another. No recollection of either creation or of other gods is present. Eve is excised. The stage is set for Yahweh alone, removed from primordial scenes and from woman. The essential becomes a relationship between two entities, Israel and Yahweh, in which divine patronage is a pivotal part of the machinery of the all-powerful God.[29] There is no room for women, collectively or individually, implicitly or explicitly. Nor is there space for memories of the mothers and midwives of Exodus 1–2 in this carefully laid invocation of the past. The only women which the Sabbath Commandment categorically embraces are servile, maids and daughters, dependent and/or blood relations. The Sabbath text trivializes marriage and motherhood through a tacit assumption that 'daughters' ultimately become wives and mothers of other men.

The Yahweh of Deuteronomy's Sabbath is no longer a creator but a warrior. In Deuteronomic imagination the divinity's fighting attributes become a mechanical exaltation of imaginary male virtues. The Sabbath Commandment, like the rest of Deuteronomy, becomes an all-male discourse which suppresses the gender polarity that may have been at the heart of the Exodus' Sabbath discourse. Even the Sabbath itself disappears into the legal maze of Deuteronomy which, strikingly, fails to include a single interpretative injunction on this crucial day of 'rest'.

5. *'Is it a Sabbath or New Moon Today?'*
Maternity, Sabbath and 'Creation'

In the royal annals of ancient Israel prophets often succeed where kings fail. One area of competition relates to nourishment. 'Bad' kings, like Jehoram, usually prove incapable of providing for their people, especially for helpless mothers and

---

29. Cf. the repeated use of 'as the Lord has ordained' (Deut 5.12), and 'hence the Lord ordains' (5.15) with the absence of comparable formulae from the Exodus Sabbath, as observed by Bernhard Lang, 'The Decalogue in the Light of a Newly Published Palaeo-Hebrew Inscription (Hebrew Ostracon Moussaieff no. 1)', *JSOT* 77 (1998), pp. 21-25.

children in distress (2 Kgs 4.1-7).[30] Prophets, like Elisha, manage, miraculously, to generate abundance in households of destitute widows (4.1-7).[31] Kings drive mothers to feast on their own children; prophets empower mothers to become providers for their family. Once only does the link between prophets and people prove unpredictable. The tale of the great woman of Shunem (4.8-37) brings together, in the woman's own home, a rich married lady and a wandering prophet whose connection with each other transcends food, the feminine and the Sabbath.

The narrative, an object of several recent feminist analyses, centers on matters of procreation, underlined by competition between mothers and Yahweh's prophets as givers of life.[32] It presents Elisha as a frequent guest in Shunem, in the house of an unnamed woman who providentially provides the prophet with food and shelter. The story follows another episode which involves the same prophet but another woman, a widow who had not been able to feed her children. In the 'early' narrative, Elisha is the benefactor; in Shunem, however, he is the recipient of favors dispensed by a woman.

Masculine perspectives of hospitality dictate forms of exchange which breed due reciprocity. To regulate the relationship, Elisha offers the woman his services as a mediator between herself and the authorities. She defies expectations, declining the prophetic 'gift'. Secure in her home, her environment and her social status, the Shunammite needs nothing, least of all the prophet's proffered mediation. Her rejection of Elisha's 'favor' implies that he is an alien and hardly a man in a

30. Laurel Lanner, 'Cannibal Mothers and Me: A Mother's Reading of 2 Kings 6.24–7.20', *JSOT* 85 (1999), pp. 107-16.

31. See Stuart Lasine, 'Jehoram and the Cannibal Mothers (2 Kgs 6.24-33): Solomon's Judgment in an Inverted World', *JSOT* 50 (1991), pp. 27-53, also on the identification of the king as Jehoram of Israel.

32. The bibliography is growing. See Burke O. Long, 'The Shunammite Woman: In the Shadow of the Prophet?', *BR* 7 (1991), pp. 12-25; Mary E. Shields, 'Subverting a Man of God, Elevating a Woman: Role and Power Reversals in 2 Kings 4', *JSOT* 58 (1993), pp. 59-69, with an emphasis on undermining predictable male–female typology; Fokkelien van Dijk-Hemmes, 'The Great Woman of Shunem and the Man of God: A Dual Interpretation of 2 Kings 4.8-37', in Athalya Brenner (ed.), *A Feminist Companion to Samuel and Kings* (The Feminist Companion to the Bible, 5; Sheffield: Sheffield Academic Press, 1994), pp. 218-30; Joppie Siebert-Hommes, 'The Widow of Zarephath and the Great Woman of Shunem: A Comparative Analysis of Two Stories', in Bob Becking and Meindert Dijkstra (eds.), *On Reading Prophetic Texts: Gender-Specific and Related Studies in Memory of Fokkelien van Dijk-Hemmes* (Leiden: E.J. Brill, 1996), pp. 231-50; David Jobbling, 'A Bettered Woman: Elisha and the Shunammite in the Deuteronomic Work', in Fiona C. Black, Roland Boer and Erin Runions (eds.), *The Labour of Reading: Desire, Alienation and Biblical Interpretation* (Atlanta: SBL, 1999), pp. 177-92; S. Brent Plate and Edna M. Rodríguez Mangual, 'The Gift that Stops Giving: Hélène Cixous's "Gift" and the Shunamite Woman', *BibInt* 7 (1999), pp. 113-32; Danna N. Fewell, 'The Gift: World Alteration and Obligation in 2 Kings 4:8-37', in Saul M. Olyan and Robert C. Culley (eds.), *Wise and Discerning Mind: Essays in Honor of Burke O. Lang* (Providence: Brown University Press, 2000), pp. 109-23; Mark Roncace, 'Elisha and the Woman of Shunem: 2 Kings 4.8-37 and 8.1-6 Read in Conjunction', *JSOT* 91 (2000), pp. 109-27; and, less directly on the biblical tale but instructively on modern reactions and political appropriation in contemporary Israel, see Yaira Amit, 'The Shunammite, the Shulamite, and the Professor between Midrash and Midrash', *JSOT* 93 (2001), pp. 77-91.

position to give gifts. It further suggests that the prophet is an alienated man who does not know himself. When Elisha announces the forthcoming birth of a son the woman is incredulous. Her reaction does not stem from lack of trust in her own procreative capacity. Rather, she suspects the 'man of God' of concocting a pleasurable lie so as not to be outdone by generosity. She is also a realist—her husband had long passed the age of insemination. Above all, she has not asked for an offspring.[33] Nevertheless, a son is born. All seems well for a moment—prophets, structures of hospitality and elderly husbands are all vindicated.

When the son first ventures away from home, he joins his father in the open field only to be seized by a mysterious ailment (sunstroke?). The father instructs his workers to carry the child back home to his mother. He dies in his mother's lap. His demise implies that Elisha is not merely a false prophet but also a false guest. Delivering a promise of birth is insufficient as far as the woman is concerned. In her attempt to save her son she exposes paternal helplessness and prophetic limitations. She demonstrates that 'liberation' from maternal womb, especially through prophetic rhetoric, does not guarantee life.

Initially, the wife–husband–prophet triad at Shunem appears to lead a precariously balanced mode of life: husband is old and deferential; wife is younger, wiser and strong-minded; prophet is needy, requiring shelter and sustenance. The husband does not interfere with his wife's relations with the prophet; she conducts herself admirably, as any man in her superior position would. Yet, husband and wife are never drawn together into an intimate association. The drama essentially unfolds between wife/mother and prophet, with husband and son limited to brief yet crucial utterances.

At a promising moment in his Shunem sojourn, the prophetic annunciation unsettles this seemingly harmonious domestic stage. The announcement of imminent pregnancy, ostensibly every wife's greatest craving, is nevertheless carefully calculated to subvert the double anomaly that exists, at least in the eyes of prophet and narrator, in a house of hospitality where a woman acts for a man, and where a woman rejects a guest's good will. By reducing the Shunammite woman to a stereotype of a barren wife and, implicitly, by restoring to her husband his status as master of his household through projected paternity, the narrative 'redresses' the blatant gender imbalance that mars the standing of Elisha in this community. As the prophet leaves, a son appears.

Elisha's reading of the Shunem situation dictates that the woman must become an agent designated to fulfill an oracle predicting pregnancy. His 'gift', a donation which she had not solicited, becomes, in male terms, a reminder of women's idealized position as mothers in a society whose survival depends on reproduction. When the death of the child interrupts the principle of procreation and deprives the father of the hope of posterity, the latter resorts to the letter of the 'law' (below). By contrast, the mother, a woman who had previously never perceived posterity as her destiny nor barrenness as ruin, plunges into acts of salvation. With prophetic words

33. On the conventionality of this annunciation scene, see Shields, 'Subverting'; also Plate and Mangual, 'Gift', p. 124, especially on similarities with the Sarah's conception scene.

she had given birth and with prophetic words she hopes to effect a rebirth. Her appeal to the prophet implies that Elisha is required to imitate divine creativity.

The Shunammanite is galvanized into acts that bespeak of subversive piety. She places the corpse of the child in the bed designated for the sole use of the prophet. She summons her husband and asks, or rather commands him, to prepare an escort for a journey to visit the prophet. She fails to invite the husband to join her on this fatal quest, nor does she share with him its reason. And she shuns his single reservation, encapsulated in a crucial question: 'Why do you go to him (i.e. to Elisha) today, seeing that it is neither a new moon nor a Sabbath' (2 Kgs 4.23)? Why indeed?

Without exception, modern readers of the tale have invariably inferred from the man's comment that the Sabbath was a day of traveling, namely of taking away from work.[34] The new moon and the Sabbath, it is often stated, entailed a suspension of normal business because a regular working day did not allow for time for travel. All this is fine but much too simplistic. Such observations fail to explain the nature of this rare utterance which the narrator places in the mouth of a man who remains singularly taciturn throughout. Nor do they account for the seemingly irrelevant answer of the wife: 'Shalom' (2 Kgs 4.23), a term that covers much territory, ranging from 'peace' to 'God bless you' and to 'all is well', all of which hardly reflecting either her state of mind or the child's well-being. Even less does the modern dismissal of the brief spousal exchange illuminate its central position in the narrative, in spite of its apparent irrelevance.

At first glance, then, the curt 'conversation' of 2 Kgs 4.23 appears to contribute little or nothing to the ensemble of life and death which punctuates this once happy domicile. Yet, these words, and especially the emphasis on Sabbath and on 'shalom' (a nice alliteration in Hebrew), infuse the drama of the mother's imminent departure with meaning far beyond the action itself. In particular, they articulate the complex position occupied by the feminine 'other' in the household.

The Shunammite's prompt venturing out, so soon after the trauma, shows her a woman who insists on the binding nature of her contract with a man who had been a frequent guest at her home. She thus acts according to a male code, reversing a predictably cultural flow and establishing her own conventions and entitlements. When she leaves home on a day that is neither Sabbath nor a new moon, the selection of date signals her continuing independence. It also generates a deceptively stylized exchange of spousal dialogue which focuses not on the recent death but on the timing of female activities.

I suggest that in this narrative the Sabbath performs the task of a radical cultural referent in the traits and aspects that society most associates with the masculine domains within the context of the domicile and the feminine. In the fast changing contexts which shift the story from birth to death, from house to field, and from the woman's domain at Shunem to the prophet's stronghold on Carmel, the husband/ father, having lost paternity, has one chance to assert his precarious position. He

---

34. See J. Gray, *I and II Kings* (OTL; London: SCM Press, 1970), p. 497, and other standard commentaries.

appeals to a temporal rhythm, based on Sabbaths (and new moons), that had been established by male authority to demonstrate, on a weekly basis, the power of males in their own homes. In 2 Kings 4 this power is regularly challenged by the wife/mother. The husband's attempt to interfere in his wife's travel plans neatly parallels Elisha's endeavor to reinstate the balance of power in the woman's household by 'impregnating' her.[35]

In her eyes, the Sabbath, a day ordinarily signifying closure and completion, fails to provide a context for maternal movements. She is seeking not rest but (re)creation or rebirth, in a sense the original Genesis meaning of the day. The Deuteronomic Sabbath of freedom from slavery has no relevance to a narrative in which a promise of life vs. the facts of death are at stake. Seeing through the true meaning of her husband's query, she responds with an equally innocuous answer which posits a wishful thinking with grim reality. She knows well that there is no 'shalom' at home; but her husband shares with the prophet a nescience of the true state of affairs. Neither husband nor prophet comprehends her urgency. God had withdrawn knowledge from the prophet (2 Kgs 4.27); the husband never possessed one.

In 2 Kings 4, the father 'exposes' the child to maternal mercy. This is an action which, in the Bible, men often perform, as the case of Jeroboam and Avia shows (1 Kgs 14.1-13). The strategy may be read as a denial of legitimacy and paternity. In Shumen, the woman must decide whether to affirm or deny this paternal acceptance of death. Shifting the scene to mount Carmel, she leaves husband behind to bring back the prophet to the scene of death and disillusion. The second confrontation between woman and prophet, so different from the first one, hinges on the meaning of matrilineal and patrilineal filiation as interwoven around the concept of the (male) Sabbath. Both encounters zoom on the Shunammite woman in her equivocal position as a woman acting in the place of man, and as a mother standing in for a father.

Challenging the dominance of the paternal principle which women often reinforce, the Shunammite diverges at a strategic point from biblical conventions. Having dismissed the husband/father's question with an assertion of 'peace' and 'wellbeing', she seemingly helps to reinstate paternal authority. Between woman and prophet, however, there is no balance. The mother's arms prove no refuge for a dying child; the prophet's words appear meaningless. When the figure of the woman is becoming dangerously dominant in the discourse because she commands the truth, the prophet avoids direct confrontation by delegating the talking and acting to his assistant.

Caught up in the dilemma of the Sabbath's etymology which the shapers of the Fourth Word had confronted, Elisha returns to the original sense and scene of 'creation' and birth, but this time as a giver of life rather than of words. He 'recreates' the child through his own body, as God had shaped woman through man's body. To drive home more banal parallels between creation and resurrection, the redactor makes the child sneeze seven times (2 Kgs 4.35). Orthodoxy is reintroduced.

---

35.   Plate and Mangual, 'Gift', pp. 126-32, read this as (metaphorical?) rape.

Prophetic power reasserted. But the tragic distortion of the Shunammite's life, allied to a man incapable of procreation or protection, and hostess to a prophet who appears equally helpless, remains unresolved. The child comes back to life, but for how long? Sabbath is cyclical, as is human life. Themes and time of the seventh day constantly intersect with its two Decalogue images, the one harking back to creation, the other to liberation.

The narrative in 2 Kings 4, then, comes to an end without ending. Figurations and protagonists of 'miracles', birth and resurrection, prophet and woman, appear paradoxically interchangeable, in spite of differences of emphasis and gender. Each is engaged in battles on two fronts, the woman with an outside 'enemy', namely death and nature; the prophet with 'culture', namely royalty. Both woman and prophet are products of perceptions of gender which remain hostile to women who escape their domestic roles into public places controlled by men. Both exhibit aberrant forms of conduct and their behavior triggers intemperate reactions that shift the issue of control over the self and over the other. Even the seemingly happy conclusion of 2 Kings 4, with the child safely deposited into his mother's lap, does not resolve this tension between the two protagonists. This is why the story must continue. The sequel resorts to a banal temporal scheme which reflects the centrality of the Sabbath/seventh chronology.

Years later, at an unspecified time, the Shunammite, perhaps by then widowed, leaves home, on the advice of Elisha, to avoid hunger and starvation (2 Kgs 8.1-6). She settles in Philistine land. On the seventh year she returns home to find her home and field gone. She appeals to the king (of Israel, implicitly). The appeal is timed to coincide with a remarkable, if somewhat implausible scene which features the monarch entertained by a recital of Elisha's miracles as recounted by none other than the useless disciple of 2 Kings 4. Uncannily, the very appearance of the woman at this juncture proves the disciple's veracity. Needless to say, the king grants the woman her request and property is restored to its rightful owner.

In spite of obvious clichés, not the least the number seven symbolism, bolstered by the woman's anonymity and by the equal anonymity of the royal protagonist, the renewed focus on the Shunammite woman suggests that the intertwining of 'sabbatical chronology' and subject matter (life–death/starvation–nourishment) has been carefully plotted. The narrative distinguishes between the time of the land, namely seven years of hunger, which is repetitious and timeless, just like the Sabbath itself, and human time which is subject of royal whims and devoid of deeper meaning. Subject to the timelessness of eternal return, the specific period of the Shunammite in Philistine territory reflects time in its purely human dimension of flux and reversal. It also designates the final closure of her relations with the prophet because her return, on the seventh year, brings with it a fulfillment of Elisha's original proposition of mediation and reinforces the prophetic function of providing sustenance for the needy.

Although absent, Elisha is in a position to stand between the woman and the king, not with the ambiguity of a guest but with the assuredness of an intermediary who bridges between the mortal and the immortal. 2 Kings 8 returns the protagonists of

2 Kings 4 to the past. Metaphors of time and mediation invest the language, and especially the appeal to the Sabbath in 2 Kings 4 and to a seven-year cycle in 2 Kings 8, with its fullest resonance. The rule of reversal, which governs the structure of gender relations in the Bible, is also the principle that rules the structure of the Shunammite's life. It accompanies her as she undergoes the full round of a process from high to low and then again from low to high. Underlying the schemes of Sabbath and seven is a view of time that reaches out far beyond a single lifetime or a single female protagonist, and beyond the span of generational time.

The significance of the husband's few words in 2 Kings 4, as their relations to the events and the notions of time, sharpen the dialectic between the woman and the prophet, as do the meager words of the prophet in 2 Kings 8. The Sabbath invokes stages of the life cycle that integrate the family with male values. The seven-year cycle reflects the undulation of the land which, in the Bible, remains an object of divine dictation. The substance of the 'message' of the tales of the Shunammite is, ultimately, to 'naturalize' women by coordinating space and time in a characteristically male way. The seven-year bareness of the land, followed by renewed prosperity, restores normative linear male time which the Sabbath punctuates and reinstates on a regular weekly basis.

6. *From Jericho to Jerusalem: Rahab, Athalia and the Meaning of Sabbatical 'Liberation'*

When asked for her reason for traveling, the Shunammite responds with one word, 'shalom'. The term forms a vocal thread throughout the story (2 Kgs 4.23, 26). It constitutes a barrier of misunderstanding between husband and wife, father and mother, woman and prophet. Borrowed from masculine vocabulary of war, victory and prosperity, the word designates an idyll. Echoing the ideology of restoration after creation, 'peace' or 'wellbeing' suggests a post-paradisiacal order that hinges on the actions of humans within a well-ordered universe created by God. In the tale of the Shunammite 'shalom' it is an ironic term, expressing expectations but denoting the opposite. It also suggests that men accept 'reality' without investigation and that women depict the desirable by delineating, verbally, an unreal existence.

Dying 'in peace' is a sought-after asset. It reflects divine favor and lifetime achievements. God's favorite patriarchs and monarchs die in their beds, in peace and in old age. Thus Jacob and thus David; thus Sarah, Rebecca and Leah. Timely death is, then, an extension of the Sabbatical rest, a permanent release from toil and tribulation. Symbolically, the Shunammite's child regains life on the seventh sneeze. In the stories of Rahab, a whore, and Athalia, a queen, Sabbath's chief signifiers, namely the figure of 'seven' and the ideology of creation/liberation, combine to explore the meaning of belonging to the covenant community of 'peace' (Num. 25.12).

In the narrated order of the book of Joshua, the appearance of Rahab, a prostitute practicing in Jericho, hails the first war conducted on the territory of the promised land.[36] Yet, her place is the narrative is baffling.[37] The information that Joshua's spies gain with her help appears superfluous.[38] The battle over Jericho is not conducted along precepts of conventional warfare but through pomp and ceremony orchestrated by Yahweh. Jericho's walls tumble on the seventh day of a 'siege' consisting of circular marches of an army which, instead of engaging in a fight, is accompanied by seven priests blowing seven horns (Josh. 6). What, then, does Rahab have to do with this sevenfold scheme of the victory over Jericho?

In the intimacy of her room, Rahab enacts a private covenant with Joshua's representatives.[39] She is in a position of power and mercy, not unlike Yahweh *vis-à-vis* Israel in Egypt. Employing Decalogue concepts and, astonishingly, counter-Deuteronomic theology, she enjoins her 'guests' to swear in Yahweh's name to preserve her clan (אב בית).[40] If violated, the spies would be deemed guilty of transgressing the Third Commandment.[41] Rahab also demands 'a true sign' (אות) or a pledge of their word (Josh. 2.12), a term that in Exod. 31.13 signals the significance of the Sabbath as a visual bond between Yahweh and Israel. Another Exodus 'reminiscence' is the token of recognition (a scarlet thread) which is designed to spare Rahab's house from annihilation, just as the brush of blood in Egypt (Exod. 12.22-23) marked homes destined to be spared from Yahweh's tenth plague. Ironically, Rahab's words, a perfect sample of male covenant rhetoric, also constitute

---

36. On Athalia, see above, Chapter 2. On Rahab, see Phyllis Bird, 'The Harlot as a Heroine: Narrative Art and Social Presuppositions in Three Old Testament Texts', *Semeia* 46 (1989), pp. 119-39; Yair Zakovitch, 'Humor and Theology or the Successful Failure of Israelite Intelligence: A Literary-Folkloric Approach to Joshua 2', and Frank Moore Cross, 'A Response to Zakovitch's "Successful Failure of Israelite Intelligence"', both in Susan Niditch (ed.), *Text and Tradition: The Hebrew Bible and Folklore* (Atlanta: Scholars Press, 1990), pp. 75-98 and pp. 99-104 respectively; Gordon H. Matties, 'Reading Rahab's Story beyond the Moral of the Story', *Direction* 24 (1995), pp. 59-62; Tikva Frymer-Kensky, 'Reading Rahab', in Mordechai Cogan, Barry L. Eichler and Jeffrey H. Tigay (eds.), *Tehilla LeMoshe: Biblical and Judaic Studies in Honor of Moshe Greenberg* (Winona Lake, IN: Eisenbrauns, 1997), pp. 57-72; Judith E. McKinlay, 'Rahab: A Hero/ine', *BibInt* 7 (1999), pp. 44-57.

37. As is her name, which may indicate a generic prostitute rather than a name of an individual, McKinlay, 'Rahab', p. 45 n. 6. The message of this name is to highlight the land as seductress, according to Daniel L. Hawk, *Every Promise Fulfilled: Contesting Plots in Joshua* (Louisville, KY: Westminster/John Knox Press, 1991), p. 62, and to emphasize the sexual availability of foreign women whose bodies, like their land, lies there for the taking, so McKinlay, 'Rahab', p. 53.

38. The mission itself seems to betray a lack of faith in God's promise; see McKinlay, 'Rahab', p. 52.

39. Cf. the language of pledges used in Gen. 38, first in direct exchange, verbal and physical between Tamar and Judah, then as a testimony.

40. See McKinlay, 'Rahab', p. 47, citing Deut. 7.2; 20.16-18, which prescribes utter annihilation of humans and of inanimate objects in a holy war, and pp. 50-51 on Rahab's Deuteronomic language. See also John L. McKenzie, *The World of the Judges* (Englewood Cliffs: Prentice Hall, 1966), p. 48; and Gene M. Tucker, 'The Rahab Saga', in James M. Efird (ed.), *The Use of the Old Testament in the New and Other Essays: Studies in Honor of W.G. Stinespring* (Durham: Duke University Press, 1972), pp. 66-86.

41. The fact that the verbal exchange and her actions casts Rahab as a traitor to her own people is happily ignored; see Fewell and Gunn, *Gender, Power and Promise*, p. 120.

a striking example of a discourse of liberty which forms the core of the Deuteronomic concept of the Sabbath.

Rahab informs the spies of the fear which has pervaded her city. She also provides the two men with shelter. Reversing the process of birth, she hides them in the safety of her attic, for three days, in a gesture reminiscent of Elisha's birth miracle in the Shunammite's attic. Number symbolism is rife—Moses' own mother had hidden the newly born for three months before she let go.[42] Yet, contrary to Rahab's image of the frightened Jericho, the city does not surrender as the Israelites appear on the scene. No resistance, however, is recorded to the Israelite onslaught when the walls tumble noisily on the seventh day (= a Sabbath?). Nor is there an explicit allusion to the scarlet thread that was to mark Rahab's home from the rest of the Jericho dwellings. But there are no less than three references to Rahab herself (Josh. 6.17, 22, 25), because the survival of her family provides a lively illustration of the validity of Third Commandment within a context that celebrates the power of 'seven'.

Within a narrative that purports to vindicate the conquest of the land, Rahab becomes the catalyst of the ability/inability of the Canaanite inhabitants to accept/ reject Yahweh's divinely dictated course of events. She is also the very first 'local' who enters the annals of the Israelite presence in Canaan. In a tale so singularly replete with number symbolism, the singularity of her knowledge of Yahweh stands out in the midst of general ignorance.[43] Her primacy in the narrative suggests an association with Eve, another woman whose appearance (in Gen. 2) signals the end of one era and the beginning of another.

When the Israelites cross the Jordan, the last visible fluid barrier between the past and the present, they come face to face with their future, a space filled with non-Israelite neighbors whose presence threatens to subvert Israelite identity. Rahab is the exception that confirms this rule. Joshua 2 reveals the possibility of a fruitful exchange of sex and favors between Israelite (males) and gentile (females). This, in itself, runs counter to Pentateuchal ideology which opposes sexual relations with locals (Exod. 34.15-16; Deut. 7.3-4), and to narratives, such as Numbers 25, which explore the disastrous consequences of transgressing boundaries of sect and sex.

Yet, Rahab's foreignness also highlights the foreignness of all women, Israelites and otherwise, from the very 'creation' of Eve and throughout biblical annals. Eve and Rahab are as 'foreign' as is the city of Jericho. The city must be erased; Rahab must 'disappear' into Israel. Because both women are also givers of life, both must be 'naturalized'. Beginning as a triply marginalized figure, a Canaanite, a woman and a prostitute, Rahab nevertheless becomes an 'oracle of Israel's occupation of the land'.[44] Her survival, after six days of 'warfare' (Josh. 6.3), lends meaning to

---

42.   Exod. 2.2, again a play with number symbolism, this time of the figure of three. Cf. the three days of sexual abstinence prior to the theophany in the Sinai in Exod. 19.15; and see above, Chapter 2.

43.   On 'knowing' as a running motif and on Rahab as echoing Miriam (in Exod. 15), see Zakovitch, 'Humor and Theology', p. 89; and McKinlay, 'Rahab', p. 47.

44.   Frymer-Kensky, 'Rahab', in Meyers *et al.* (eds.), *Women in Scripture*, p. 141.

the very existence of Israel in its land. She represents a 'race' of women who, like the pious midwives of Exodus 1, somehow receive divine illumination and follow Yahwist precepts without direct orders from God. Their very being rejects attempts to feminize all types of behavior that can be expressed by an essentially masculine model, like fear, treachery and distrust.

That the fall of Jericho on a 'Sabbath' is ultimately achieved solely by divine design, unaided by either Rahab's generosity or the information gathering mission which she rescued, poses an ambiguity that may mask a profound anti-feminine agenda. Such an agenda becomes clear in the case of Athalia, the queen whose murder is carefully scheduled to fall on the Sabbath.[45] Nor is this a mere play of numbers. Rather, the text projects a play of war, gender and politics.

In the background to Athalia's tale there are the Judean kingdom, Jerusalem and a latent power struggle within the royal family itself (2 Kgs 11). For six years, while the sole surviving male heir is hidden in the temple, Athalia, daughter of King Ahab and Queen Jezebel(?), reigns without visible opposition. On the seventh year, and on a Sabbath, the child prince is brought out of temple hiding to be displayed by the man behind the throne, the priest Jehoiada. Surrounded by guards of the Sabbath, the boy is hailed king. The queen decries the conspiracy but, upon the priest's orders, is executed. This one fateful Sabbath, then, witnesses the untimely demise of one monarch and the elevation of another at a record young age. Athalia's death serves as a spur to a feast of iconoclasm (11.18) and to a new covenant.

That this all takes place on a Sabbath can hardly be a mere coincidence. In a familial context in which private interests intersect with national concerns, the six years 'incubation' period of the future king, equaling six years of queenly 'usurpation', signal a rupture in time. To bridge between the past and the present, the Sabbath becomes a protagonist entrusted with a crucial role reversal. It ensures continuity of creation and the enshrining of a permanent memory of liberation. In the story of Rahab, the identity of the female actor is calculated to carry the meaning of the Sabbath as a celebration of liberation; in Athalia's tale, the identity of the queen carries the meaning of the Sabbath as souvenir of creation and recreation.

Symbolic scenes of walls crashing to the ground on the seventh day, and of queens executed on the Sabbath, recognize the fragility of the edifice of creation. Torn away from the bonds of her city, Rahab establishes a new genealogy which floats in a sort of eternal presence. As a political figure, Athalia is removed from both temple and Sabbath to become doubly abstracted. Because queenship must invariably remain an abstract concept, and because the pattern of Israelite history demands that men become the guardians of the Sabbath and of legitimacy, there is no room for a queen, least of all on a Sabbath.

Endowed with rich lineage, Athalia is stripped of life; Rahab endows a line without being subject of procreation. Is the Sabbath, then, a day sanctified for killing of women and for war against Israel's declared enemies? Is it a holy day displaced by gender symbols? Hiding a profusion of rival identities, the Sabbath erects

---

45. See above, Chapter 2 §8.

domestic barriers and legitimizes usurpation against a female royal. It also conceals a discourse about the structure of parentage that penetrates the entire sequence of biblical 'history', from the very opening of Genesis. The Sabbath, both of creation and of liberation, endeavors to reaffirm males in power and to authorize a version of history that expresses what male members of society want or imagine themselves to be.

Chapter 5

THE BURDEN OF BIRTH AND THE POLITICS OF MOTHERHOOD
(WORD FIVE)

Miles of shore
I walk alongside my son who faces war...
Let my child get aware of uncertain security
Life perpetuates
Now he is at the border of doom
Whereas I ought
To withdraw into solitude
Of tormented motherhood.

> —Ava Kadishson Schieber, *Selected Unpublished Poems*
> (courtesy of author)

Honor your father and your mother so that your days on the earth that the Lord God has given you will last longer. (Exod. 20.12)

1. *Motherhood and Deference*

Three partners unite to produce every newly born: God, the child's father and the child's mother. From the father [the child inherits] brains, bones, veins, nails, and the whiteness of the eye. From the mother, the flesh, the skin, the black in the eye and blood. God infuses the newly born with spirit, soul, knowledge, wisdom and discernment. When a person dies, God takes back the divine investment, leaving behind that of the parents. If God sees that the deceased had honored his/her father and his/her mother, their years are lengthened. But the one who holds own parents in contempt will be hanged from a tree and stoned to death, as happened to Abshalom, son of Maacha, who disrespected David, and who was hung on a tree and thrown to the threshing floor where they threw a pile of stones over him. God ensures that everyone who respects own parents gains in this world and in the world to come.[1]

Rabbinic contemplation of the Fifth Word, as reflected in this popular midrash, delineates the distinct contribution of each member of a parental triad to the shaping of a child. In this reading, full membership in the covenant community

---

1.   *Midrash Decalogue* (= מדרש עשרת הדברות) (Jellinek, *Bet ha-Midrasch*, I, pp. 76-77) (slightly modified). Cf. the Pre-Socratic ideas of conception and regarding the nature of the male and female contribution to the child in Jan Blayney, 'Theories of Conception in the Ancient Roman World', in Beryl Rawson (ed.), *The Family in Ancient Rome: New Perspectives* (London: Routledge, 1992), pp. 230-36.

depends on the generic identity/genetic composition of the parental couple, and on Yahweh's contribution. Stated otherwise, an Israelite is an Israelite by virtue of being born to an Israelite father and an Israelite mother. In this variant, the link forged at birth must be continuously nurtured, precisely as projected in the Fifth Word. This specific scheme of creation accounts for the inclusion of a tenet that, at first reading, appears exceptional within a set of rules that refer to the behavior of (male) individuals *vis-à-vis* God, other Israelites and one's own household members.

Requirements to respect the Sabbath (Word Four) focus on the male Israelite as *paterfamilias*, a man in charge of an entire household—father, slave owner—a master in his micro universe. The demand to honor parents (Word Five) falls, primarily, on sons and on daughters(?) who are in obligatory relationship to 'fathers and to mothers'. Encoding birth, the Fifth Commandment provides unique, if perfunctory recognition of the role of both parents in the process of engendering humans. But the birth itself, that crucial moment in the life of an Israelite, is entrusted into a past that falls outside the text. Only the consequences are contemplated. Linking maturation with death, implicitly, the Word insists on conditional longevity, dependent on the discharge of filial duties towards parents. The glorification of parenthood, then, is anchored twice, once in the text itself by its very inclusion in so basic a code, and once by the intimate tie which it forges between parents and children through unilateral respect.

The Fifth Commandment imaginatively ranges the parental couple on the one hand, and their offspring on the other hand, along specific lines of behavior. Not affection but, to use a Roman expression, *pietas*, a deep sense of obligation to a parent *qua* parent dominates domestic relationship. This, like love, is ambiguous. Already Gen. 2.24 calls for separation from the parental home in order to establish marital habitation. Ancestral stories repeatedly feature protagonists, female and male alike, leaving either a בֵית אָב (literally 'the paternal home') or בֵית אֵם ('maternal home', Gen. 24.28; Ruth 1.8) to join a new patriarchal establishment through marriage (Rebecca and Ruth) or through displacement (Abraham). The Fifth Word reinstates the self as an entity inextricably bound with precisely such familial forms.

In Decalogue discourse the Fifth Commandment shifts the focus from the collectivity and the paternal household unto a narrow circle of father–mother–offspring. Modern readings have interpreted the Word as a tenet aspiring to regulate familial structures by instilling discipline among the younger generation.[2] The Commandment, then, deals not with infants but with mature sons and daughters(?) for whom parents, much like the Sabbath, become a sanctified module of covenantal operation. The very existence of the parental couple, and the act of procreation, cast 'father' and 'mother', in a perpetual role of venerable patriarchs and matriarchs.

---

2.   Phillips, *Ancient Israel's Criminal Law*, p. 82, on addressees as 'younger adult members of society capable of committing any of the crimes set out in the Sinai Decalogue', limiting membership, however, 'originally' to sons only.

The selection of the term 'respect/honor/weight' (כבד) to define parental–youth relations further inscribes the Fifth Word in a unique chronological scheme. The narrative of the Exodus itself begins with a singular lack of (monarchic/Pharaonic) respect for (Hebrew) parents, continues with Yahweh rendering Pharaoh's heart 'heavy' (כבד) and unresponsive (Exod. 10.1), and ends with Yahweh's visible 'honor' which becomes proof of continuing divine favor (Exod. 33.19: 'show me your honor'). This is a 'history' cast as a fatal intertwining of manifestations of respect and disrespect.

'Respect' or 'giving weight', the expression which the Fifth Word uses to denote desirable attitudes on the part of 'children', is borrowed from a masculine language of war and politics. It is also a theologically loaded term.[3] In Judg. 20.34, for example, the term 'heavy' or 'intense' describes a devastating civil war between the tribes of Israel and of Benjamin. More often it relates to male social status and to what men expect of other men by virtue of their place in society. The term further describes specific physical conditions of bodily parts, primarily the heart, the ears and the eyes. It is notably absent from descriptions which touch on relations between the sexes in general, and between mothers and 'children' in particular. The omission may have led 'Malachi' to paraphrase the Fifth Word by positing not the parental couple in apposition with Yahweh but only the father:

A son respects his father, a slave his master
If a father I am, where is my honor?
If a master I am, where is the fear [due to me]? (Mal. 1.6)

As though to confirm the indelible role of paternity, the Fifth Word registers fathers before mothers. Promising (in Exod. 21.12) longevity on the 'earth' (אדמה), the Commandment 'recalls' the very matter that Yahweh had used to mold man during a 'creation' process that had reached maturity outside the maternal womb (Gen. 2.7, 19). This linguistic bond between the Fifth Word and Genesis 2 suggests that the subject of the Fifth Word shares the particular idea of the conditions of masculinity and of femininity with one parent only, the father. Juxtaposing 'father', 'mother' and, implicitly, Yahweh, with an adult child, the Fifth Word de-naturalizes the process of birth by conceptualizing origins in which parents have a limited role and Yahweh a crucial one, as the rabbis shrewdly observed.

'Father and mother' (Exod. 20.12) is an idiomatic expression representing the basic familial unit. Parents are producers of genealogy, and genealogy is a pivotal theory in the Hebrew Bible. Within this narrow configuration, the son of the family is the direct heir not only of the family's property but also of its genealogical heritage. Parental reverence, according to the Fifth Commandment, becomes an essential cornerstone of familial relations already dominated, according to the Fourth Word, by a benevolent and punctilious paternal power. Extending the

---

3. Claus Westermann, 'כבד', in *THAT*, I, pp. 794-812 (English translation = *TLOT*, II, pp. 590-602); Christoph H. Dohmen, 'כבד, כבודה,כבד', in *ThWAT*, IV, pp. 13-40 (English translation = *TDOT*, VII, pp. 13-38); Elizabeth Bellefontaine, 'Deuteronomy 21:18-21: Reviewing the Case of the Rebellious Son', *JSOT* 13 (1979), pp. 13-31 (15); Julian Carrón, 'Honor your Father and your Mother', *Communio* 22 (1995), pp. 28-43 (31-34).

foundation of the Fifth Commandment beyond the purview of the human family, parental metaphors of Yahweh emphasize the unique nature of filial obligation and responsibilities.[4] Underlying the faith of Yahweh is a theological scheme in which the bond between parent and child cannot be sundered.[5]

To drive home the meaning of a rather banal precept, Yahweh links 'honoring parents' with longevity.[6] No penalty for violation is provided but rather a reward for abiding by what may appear as a 'natural' or inborn proclivity. The promise is unique.[7] Decalogue Commandments either prohibit or prescribe. They offer neither consolation nor compensation. They remind the Israelites of Yahweh's implacable anger and generational memory. By extension, the Fifth Word, too, implies that its transgression entails short life and dispossession.

Inserting Yahweh as a guarantor of longevity, the Fifth Word serves to remind the community of the indispensable place that Yahweh must occupy not only in the life of the community in general, but also in the lives of individuals. As an arbiter of familial relations Yahweh stands resolutely by the parents. As a promoter of procreation, Yahweh also mediates sterility, the prospect of horror that haunts the existence of women in the Hebrew Bible. In the biblical archaeology of generation the womb is secondary to the will of Yahweh. Fertilized by the masculine principle of the engenderer, female maternity remains passive. And although motherhood ordinarily implies beginnings, the Decalogue begins with Yahweh and with Egypt, as does Genesis itself (with Yahweh alone in Paradise).

Selecting a god who is predominantly male obliged the makers of the Hebrew Bible to come to terms with the limits of human understanding of gender. In the biblical discourse of birth, Yahweh often assumes the role of nurse, father and mother. Maternity is suspended. People (male citizens) and God remain connected through God's appropriation of a state of existence that mortal women share. Language and the politics of kinship are crucial. In spite of a creation narrative that casts Yahweh as the genitor of all humans, the selection of a specific individual (Abraham) as the stereotypical 'Hebrew' entails a specific bond with a specific people. But in the 'creation' of Israel as a favored nation or child, the narrative excludes women altogether. The myths of the creation and of the selection in Genesis present two alternatives of the relations between God and humans: one embracing women (Gen. 1–3) as an integral part of the process; the other focusing on patriarchal transmission from a God-father to a favored male (Abraham, Isaac, Jacob).

Tales of nativity in the Hebrew Bible vacillate between extolling the role of the mother or of the father. The parental couple, even when appearing in tandem,

---

4.   Don C. Benjamin, 'Israel's God: Mother and Midwife', *Biblical Theology Bulletin* 19 (1989), pp. 115-20; see also Frymer-Kensky, *In the Wake of the Goddesses*, Chapter 14, on parental metaphors.

5.   Carrón, 'Honor', pp. 28-40, emphasizes the role of parents as transmitters of covenantal traditions.

6.   Cf. the Athenian laws on maltreatment of parents which could result in disqualifying the offender from public life, in I. Arnaoutoglou, *Ancient Greek Laws: A Sourcebook* (London: Routledge, 1998), pp. 62-63.

7.   Jacque Briend, 'Honore ton père et ta mère', *Christus* 122 (1984), p. 204.

hardly ever acts in harmony. At moments of annunciation, either future mother or future father appears incredulous. At scenes of birth, future mothers are attended solely by midwives. Such an unequal arrangement anticipates the extraordinary emphasis that narratives place on father–son relations, at the expense of mother–son intimacy. Rare insights into the latter reinforce an opposition between the masculine and the feminine as the family realigns to protect or subvert the principle of primogeniture. There are no narratives that probe mother–daughter networks, although a few deal with father–daughter troublesome interaction.

Often omitting mothers, as well as children, the Hebrew Bible rarely elaborates upon terms of reciprocity of respect. What is due from 'child' to parents is made clear, at least in Exod. 20.12. But what do parents owe to their children beyond the moment of insemination, pregnancy and birth? Biblical law and lore on relations between children and adults assume that 'children' are miniature adults shaped by family and society for their future roles.[8] Such a module generates the proverbial 'like mother, like daughter' perceptions. Yet, in Genesis sons behave like mothers (Jacob–Rebecca), while in the Dtr History, by insinuation at least, a daughter becomes the spitting image of her mother (Jezebel–Athalia).[9] Absalom's mother, Maacha, is altogether absent from the iconic tale of the 'rebellious' son who is also, ironically, an ideal brother of a compromised sister. And in the most detailed biography in the Hebrew Bible, that of Moses, the parental duo disappears right at the start of the narrative. Instead, family bonds are forged through sibling attachments. When biblical narratological exegesis of the Fifth Word penetrates domiciles inhabited by 'children', young women and men learn the meaning of the Commandment by shouldering the results of parental decisions and proclivities, as does the unnamed daughter of Jephthah.

An imbalance emerges. 'Fathers and mothers' hardly ever appear as a unity that aspires to elicit their offspring's 'respect'. In spite of a rhetoric of parental equality, the image of the mother, even of motherhood itself, remains a dubious proposition, at best, and a necessary evil at worst. Genesis sets out to define 'Hebrew' identity on the basis of a single lineage. As a result, Genesis' dominant pattern is that of familial endogamy. But beyond the ancestral clan, marriages ordinarily incorporate women of distinct lineage into paternal households. Since the myth of equality of origins had to be maintained, it required a paradigm that demanded repetition. This repetition, or imitation, became an essential rule of Israel which allowed the intermingling of the past and the present, not in order to confuse temporality, but to set up a system of echoes in which patterns played on themselves.

Procreation of legitimate children is at the heart of Israelite self-definition. Since humans cannot reproduce the divine process of creation, they engage in sex in order to become parents, becoming thus objects of a core Commandment. The Hebrew

---

8. Charles M. Radding, *A World Made by Men: Cognition and Society 400–1200* (Chapel Hill: University of North Carolina Press, 1985), p. 26, summarizing Jean Piaget; cf. Philip Ariès, *Centuries of Childhood: A Social History of Family Life* (trans. Robert Baldick; New York: Knopf, 1962), *passim*.

9. Above, Chapters 2 §8; 4 §6; and 6 §8.

Bible does not allow the feminine to challenge the dominance of the paternal principle. Yet, the very reinforcement of this axiom also engenders divergence at certain strategic points. Daughters do not always dutifully become wives of men chosen by fathers. Sons do not always adopt the path charted by their parents. When a mother stands in for a father, her equivocal position is insisted upon. To understand, therefore, the parameters of the Fifth Word it is vital to explore narratives that deal with the least representative member of the family unit, namely the mother.

2. *The Name of the Father:*
From Leviticus to the Daughters of Zelophehad

Whoever beats his father or his mother shall die. (Exod. 21.15)

Whoever curses his father or mother shall die. (Exod. 21.17)

You shall each revere his mother and his father and keep my Sabbaths. (Lev. 19.3)

Already the 'Covenant Code' outlines two forms of violating the Fifth Word: (1) beating parents, a crime that merits death (Exod. 21.15); (2) cursing parents, a sin that likewise merits capital punishment (Exod. 21.17). The first injunction is inscribed into a series of brief regulations regarding murder; the second follows a rule about the sale of an abducted person into slavery.[10] The juxtaposition suggests that any harm inflicted on parents, physical or verbal, is deemed as severely as is the deprivation of life or liberty.

Leviticus 19.3 succinctly restates the Fifth Word in slightly different terms. The statement enjoining respect is inserted into Leviticus' own abbreviated version of the Decalogue (19.1-4) which begins with a declaration of Yahweh's sanctity and the concomitant sanctity of Israel, continues with the demand to honor parents and the Sabbath, and ends with a ban on idols and idol worship. Parental reverence, in this Levitical reading, is a reflection of the correct deportment of the individual *vis-à-vis* Yahweh, implying fear and awe. A man who 'fears' his parents assumes thereby an appropriate attitude which duplicates the sentiment that Yahweh commands. In Leviticus 19, recapturing of the Decalogue, Yahweh is no longer a liberator with a historical identity and a common past with Israel, but a demanding deity with an exclusive claim over Israel. Israel is no longer Yahweh's community, tied to the divinity through a specific event, but a congregation linked by commonality of sanctity, regardless of temporality. This is why in Leviticus 19 the Fifth Word (together with the Fourth) precedes even the First and the Second, as though parental reverence and Sabbath preservation embody the very sanctity of the people.

To drive home the essence of transgression, Lev. 20.9 repeats Exod. 21.17 with a twist: 'Anyone who curses (or: makes light of) his father or his mother shall be put to death; his father and/or his mother he has cursed. Their blood is upon him.' An

---

10.   On this pericope, see Van Seters, *Law Book for the Diaspora*, pp. 99-108. On abduction see below, Chapter 8 §2.

ultimate penalty acts as a deterrent, complementing the Commandment's concept of the rewards of longevity attendant on compliance. Since death sentences are, in all likelihood, to be carried out by the community, a cursing son becomes a liability to both parents and the public. Leviticus' basic assumption infers that if one does not behave in the correct manner toward own parents, this person can hardly become a responsible member of the congregation, all the more so since familial relations mirror a divinely created hierarchy and order.

None of these rules reflects on parental roles. None proposes to examine the specific contribution that each parent makes to the elevation of a future member of the community. Like the Fifth Word, the laws which punish the beating and the cursing of parents envision a familial unit (father–mother–'child') as one ultimately conditioned by Yahweh's will. This is why the beating of parents is deemed as serious as killing, and this is why the 'cursing' of parents, as well as of kings and of Yahweh is punishable by death. Genesis–Numbers narratives, although delving into episodes of lying sons and thieving daughters, never record murderous or physically aggressive 'children' *vis-à-vis* their parents. Rather, narratives commemorate how fathers are willing to sacrifice sons, and how mothers must bow to divine orders to expose their children to potential death.

Because the masculine element dominates the discourse of parenthood, the perpetuation of the name of the father becomes an overriding concern. This is the message of the closing episode of the book of Numbers which unfolds the case of the daughters of Zelophehad. The narrative spans an astonishing length, beginning with a post-plague census (Num. 26.33) which, exceptionally, refers to a family of five women; continuing with a legal suit that these women initiate regarding their paternal inheritance (27.1-11); and ending with a judgment aimed at balancing the clan's claim to the property with the women's desire to preserve paternal name (36.1-12). As far as the narrator is concerned, this is a happy end. The orphaned daughters are married off to male relatives and the collective possessions of the clan remain intact.

From the daughters' point of view, the 'respect' that the Decalogue enjoins on 'children' *vis-à-vis* parents calls, primarily, for the preservation of the father's name through a gender-inclusive pattern of inheritance. From the male point of view, however, the prospect of 'exogamic' marriage, with its attendant alienation of the clan's property, constitutes a distinct disadvantage *vis-à-vis* the rest of Israel. Clearly the daughters of Zelophehad must marry. But the choice of bridegrooms becomes critical, not only because of the absence of a father's monitoring hand (there is no reference to a mother), but also because of fears of diminishing the allotted tribal lands. The twin matters of paternity and property/prosperity, absent from Exodus' formulation of the Fifth Word, become central in the Deuteronomic casting of the same Commandment (below).

The five daughters of Zelophehad advance a principle of filiation based on blood. In response to their appeal, Moses decrees that a man's property is to be passed on to the nearest blood relatives in descending order, first sons, then daughters, then brothers, uncles, and so on (Num. 27.7-11). In their public presentation of the case, the elders of Manassan Gilead, who are the remaining relatives of Zelophehad, range the tribe against the collectivity, and their potential loss of land as a potential gain for other tribes. They further present the five women as a potential source of damage and diminution to the tribe. Two antagonistic principles are, therefore, at stake in this case: the tribal vs. the people; and the feminine vs. the masculine. The solution that Moses advocates in Numbers 36 subjects the feminine to the masculine, predictably, and the general to the particular. The five daughters of Zelophehad must marry, even to men of their choice (Num. 36.6), but the marriage partners must belong to their own clan. Had Zelophehad been alive, the solution might have been different.

Israel's 'primordial' history, unfolded in Genesis–Numbers, ends thus on an intimate note, with the recording of the marriage of the five daughters of Zelophehad, all named, with their own five cousins, all unnamed (Num. 36.12). The role of women as wives and mothers, as well as transmitters of paternal property, is thus affirmed. The ultimate story of Israel in the wilderness comes to an end with the domestication of women by law. The 'state' steps in for a father, and male relatives appropriate paternal rights. With this reassuring touch of reasserted masculine values, the law curbs justice. The familial 'respect' which the five women had demonstrated is used as a weapon to curtail their independence. 'Balance' returns.

The necessity to incorporate women into schemes of patrilineal descent engineers unsolved tension between the need to determine Israel's identity through paternity, and to affirm the importance of descent from the right mother.[11] Endogamous marriage ensures patrilineal membership. The right wife must also be the right mother. Initially, the very inclusion of the five women, daughters of Zelophehad, in the tribal genealogical list (Num. 26.33) is exceptional because women are hardly ever present in this important indication of an all-male affiliation.[12] Until its very resolution in the last page of Numbers, the case resists classification. The absence of a direct male heir, coupled with basic male anxiety to perpetuate the father's name and to retain the family's property, generates temporary genealogical confusion. What is due to fathers, as well as to other paternal figures, is made abundantly clear. The absence of a mother is as striking as is the vocal presence of the daughters.

Looked at differently, the history of Israel from creation to wilderness maturation (Genesis–Numbers), can be unraveled as a braided tissue of parables of the theme of the family.[13] But Genesis' tales never feature a Decalogue triad of 'father–mother–child'. Rather, they record familial feuds in which fathers side with their eldest born, and mothers muddle genealogy. The book of Exodus opens with a patrilineal tribute (Exod. 1.1-5). But it proceeds to narrate how women saved Israel from extinction. Such plots leave open the question to which parent a 'child' must 'give weight'. And with what results and repercussions? The Fifth Commandment

11. Exum, *Fragmented Women*, pp. 107-10.

12. Robert R. Wilson, *Genealogy and History in the Biblical World* (New Haven: Yale University Press, 1977); Exum, *Fragmented Women*, p. 112.

13. The term 'family' is equally ambiguous, at least to our modern eyes, as Ariès as shown in his *Centuries of Childhood*, p. 365 and *passim*. See also the articles in Perdue *et al.* (eds.), *Families in Ancient Israel*.

itself endeavors to present parents as a unified entity, 'a father and a mother', but narratives of familial relations, calling into question the very essence of motherhood and of fatherhood, show the pliability of such configurations.

3. *The Meaning(s) of Motherhood: Genesis Variations*

Motherhood ordinarily implies beginnings, but of what?[14] The book of Genesis provides two codes of creation, one in which Yahweh is the 'mother' or sole engenderer (Gen. 1); the other in which maternity is male and God is the midwife (Gen. 2).[15] In the first scheme a promise of de-genderized multiplication seems to lead nowhere: Gen. 1.28 issues a call for procreation and multiplication whose addressees consist of 'a male' and 'a female', each casts in the 'image of God'. Neither is assigned a precise role in the process. Nor is the outcome clear.[16] In the second creative order, procreation comes only with the exile from Paradise. By separating from it, Adam and Eve become subjected to mortality, to parenthood and, above all, in woman's case, to maternity. In both versions of beginnings, human condition is 'created' only when the cycles of divine creations are complete, as though enabling human procreation to find its own rhythm.

The tales of creation in Genesis 1–2 do not directly deal with either motherhood or with fatherhood. In the garden of Eden there is no room for procreation. But in one version, Genesis 1, the two first humans are both children of God, worthy supplements of the 'animals of the land' and of 'all crawling creatures of the earth' (1.25), regardless of sex and gender. In the other version, Genesis 2, man, made of earth, appropriates reproduction and produces woman. Does human birth, then, involve female maternity if sexual reproduction is not considered the point of true origin?

Genesis 1 uses the verb 'create' (ברא) as a term for engendering, thereby incorporating a notion of bringing something into being from a beginning nowhere. In Genesis 2, man is 'fashioned' out of earth (2.7, 19), but woman is 'constructed' (בנה) out of man's rib as an artificial creation. Adam the sower is a name giver, but the 'birth' of woman is not an act of sowing. In primordial existence, woman comes in a restful dream and as a supplement fleshed out by God. The divinely created matter and marrow, man and woman, are endowed with powers of procreation. Fulfillment, however, is postponed till it is linked with sex and preceded by severance and by commination. Because humans acquire 'knowledge' in Paradise,

14. The following remarks are inspired by Nicole Loraux, *Born of the Earth: Myth and Politics in Athens* (trans. Selina Stewart; Ithaca, NY: Cornell University Press, 2000), *passim*, and *The Children of Athena*, *passim*.

15. In general, see Mayer I. Gruber, *The Motherhood of God and Other Studies* (Atlanta: Scholars Press, 1992). On feminine and maternal attributes of God, see Phyllis Trible, *God and the Rhetoric of Sexuality* (Philadelphia: Fortress Press, 1978).

16. This is exactly where Gen. 5.1 picks up the narrative that Gen. 2.4–4.26 interrupted. See the magnificent exposition of Jeremy Cohen, *'Be Fertile and Increase, Fill the Earth and Master It': The Ancient and Medieval Career of a Biblical Text* (Ithaca, NY: Cornell University Press, 1989), *passim*.

man is cursed with perpetual tilling of the land, and woman with constantly painful pregnancies. The seed of humans and of serpents become enemies forever. Read otherwise, in the post-paradisiacal environment, earth produces nourishment and woman produces children, but neither can reach its purpose without the mediation of males.

Cast in slightly different terms—just as the earth produces vital foods, women engender men, the vital ingredients of humanity. Wombs become furrows or vineyards, domesticated and civilized by the agriculture of marriage.[17] The 'curse' of knowledge ushers a new age which valorizes the role of the mother, but also signifies 'the sad and troublesome coming of age of humanity'.[18] Ambiguity lingers. In Genesis 2, Adam is made of earth, as though his material body enshrines a permanent link with everything that is below. Woman is made of marrow, a secondary substance, as though to ensure her secondary place in the order of the (second) creation. But she is also the receptacle of the productive energy that guarantees perpetuation, since conceptualizing origin without women is simply unthinkable. Even in the divine schemes of hierarchical creation in Paradise a female must be included, one with a clearly definable role of wife (2.23-24), who only later becomes 'the mother of all living' (3.20), destined to produce sons on earth (3.16; 4.1-2).

In post-primordial chronology, the collaboration of God and earth over the production of man becomes, in 'reality', a contest between man's ability to tease nourishment out of seeds planted in the earth and to produce sons out of seeds planted in the womb. In the process, earth-woman's own needs and desires become secondary, for Yahweh stands on the side of man. Both 'females', woman and earth, are static, passive matters waiting for implantation.

Motherhood, then, seems to have been established outside itself, a subject of erasures and of super-impositions, as though it cannot confirm to any social code.[19] But it also remains a central theme in the elaboration of female identity, a producer and projector of images and signs that contribute to a universal cultural dialogue.[20] Because the knowledge of the self is rooted in gendered unconscious, the maternal body is a semiotic reality that creates meaning only indirectly, and in relation to others. Imagination, rather than anatomy, has constructed sexual identity and motherhood.[21]

Procreation and maternity are seemingly unnecessary in paradisiacal existence. Posterity in this golden age is the job of the divinity. After all, the earth has an unlimited supply of matter, and every man has several ribs. Neither pregnancy nor

17. Ps. 127.3; 128.3; Judg. 14.18 apply agricultural imagery to mothers/wives. See also Phyllis A. Bird, 'Images of Women in the Old Testament', in Rosemary R. Ruether (ed.), *Religion and Sexism: Images of Women in the Jewish and Christian Traditions* (New York: Simon & Schuster, 1974), pp. 41-88; and Marc-Zvi Brettler, 'Women and Psalms: Toward an Understanding of the Role of Women's Prayer in the Israelite Cult', in Matthews, Levinson and Frymer-Kensky (eds.), *Gender and Law*, pp. 25-56 (29-41).

18. Loraux, *Born of the Earth*, p. 85, for the expression.

19. Silvia Finzi Vegetti, *Mothering: Toward a New Psychoanalytic Construction* (New York: Guilford, 1996), p. 145.

20. Vegetti, *Mothering*, p. 146.

21. Vegetti, *Mothering*.

reproduction has a place. But in the process of separation from origins both appear to become duties, the 'natural' obligation of women. Based on an assumption of the maternal nature of mothers, this ascribed 'nature' further implies a 'natural' bond between mother and children, an attachment that is not always born out. For mothers can 'devour' their own children, bringing them 'back' into the womb from which they had emerged.[22]

Yet, as long as the all too fragile title of 'mother' is based on the repetitious act of birth it has, and will, persist. As progenitor of male children, woman provides her husband with sons to perpetuate his family and to secure the future of the commonwealth by producing 'citizens'. Without her there is no covenant, because there is no transmission from the same to the same, from male to male directly.[23] Coming to terms with facts of life, men have elected to focus with vengeance, and with endless repetition, on the most conspicuous aspect of the female life cycle, namely motherhood, with its concomitant status of wife. The only complete women are mothers, women who are officially reassuring to the imagination, because they have been domesticated by marriage and toughened by maternity.

Although humankind continues to exist because there were first men, the greatest difficulty, as Genesis 2–3 shows, is not so much to assign them birth as to give them posterity. After the flood Noah's sons produce a new human race that instantly engages in the process of reproducing itself, as each man fathers 'sons and daughters' (Gen. 11). In the end, and in spite of several false starts, 'a man is [still] born to a woman' (Job 14.1), and not of the unknown. The story of man is thus marked by two separations, one from a paradisiacal state, the other from the mother's womb. The origins of Israelite history are marked by a similar duality. One records Abraham's separation from 'family', 'paternal clan' and 'homeland'; the other commemorates separation from Egypt, and with it the birth of covenantal identity. Matriarchs are conspicuously absent at moments of male bonding.[24] Their absence signifies the dependence of Israel on its fathers, and the dependence of women on fathers, husbands and sons, because the birth of males is the surest way of securing status.[25]

Genesis' recapturing of myths of origins assigns ample space to preludes to birth, or tales of 'nativity'.[26] In all cases the subject is female sterility (Gen. 16.1; 25.21;

22. 2 Kgs 6.24-33, with Lasine, 'Jehoram and the Cannibal Mothers', pp. 27-53. This is also, symbolically, what happens in Exod. 2 when Moses' mother deposits him in a basket, thus exposing him either to death or to a completion of the birth cycle itself.

23. On the prestige of motherhood in ancient Israel, see Karel van der Toorn, *From her Cradle to her Grave: The Role of Religion in the Life of the Israelite and the Babylonian Woman* (trans. Sara J. Denning-Bolle; The Biblical Seminar, 23; Sheffield: JSOT Press, 1994), pp. 77-92.

24. Exum, *Fragmented Women*, pp. 102-103.

25. Bird, 'Images of Women in the Old Testament', esp. pp. 51-55 and 61-71. Cf. Esther Fuchs, 'The Literary Characterization of Mothers and Sexual Politics in the Hebrew Bible', in Adela Yarbro Collins (ed.), *Feminist Perspectives on Biblical Scholarship* (Chico, CA: Scholars Press, 1985), pp. 117-36.

26. For a comparative view of biblical annunciation scenes, see Yair Zakovitch, *The Life of Samson (Judges 13–16): A Critical Literary Analysis* (Jerusalem: Magnes Press, 1982 [Hebrew]), pp. 26-39.

30.1), and the object of birth is male.[27] The stories intertwine matrimony with maternity.[28] Their chief protagonist is a divinity predisposed to intervene to ensure sexual reproduction, in order to safeguard the seemingly superfluous role of fathers in the process of procreation. Promises of fertility are invariably addressed to males (Gen. 16–17).[29] No reference is made to a union of love. Marriage is motivated by a desire to bear children, which further contributes to an indiscriminate switch between maids and mistresses, demeaning both women, as the tale of Sarah and Hagar shows.[30]

The sterile matriarch's counterpart is the fertile patriarch. Not by chance does Gen. 17.6-12 associate male reproduction with circumcision and covenant.[31] As a symbol of the covenant, circumcision creates a symbolic link between reproduction, genealogy and masculinity, separating sons from the maternal and its associated female impurity. Concomitantly, the designation of menstrual blood and the blood of parturition as impurities further undermines women's importance in procreation, and provides a rationale for their isolation (Lev. 12.2-4).

Communications across generations in Genesis appear to contradict rather than confirm the Fifth Word. The anticipated reward of the respect shown by an elder son (Esau) to father (Isaac) is thwarted by a 'rebellious' younger son (Jacob), whose 'rebelliousness' is encouraged, indeed orchestrated by his mother. Stolen primogenitures demonstrate how transitions necessary to win identity are placed under the problematic emblem of motherhood. By planting Rebecca at the center of the story, Genesis 27 makes maternity a bearer of legitimacy. By entrusting Isaac with the ultimate authority to bestow patrimony, the narrative sanctions paternal power, but skirts issues of legality. Jacob's obedience to his mother, and disregard of both law and father, depend on Rebecca's exploitation of her husband's blindness and appetites. She is the exception that confirms the conventions that dictate the common terrain which situates fathers in the center, and extends beyond them to the dramas of their children.

Narratives of maternity in Genesis are predicated on oracles given in advance to potential mothers and fathers. The terms of these predictions extend beyond the recipients to affect those whom s/he engenders. Isaac and Jacob are children of their fathers, but also fathers themselves, an interdependence emphasized by sharing a double kinship with both father and mother who are also closely related to each other. This is one reason why the stories in Genesis only reach their 'end' with

27.   On the monochromatic dimension of the narratives depicting mothers vs. the complexity of those dealing with their male counterpart, see Fuchs, 'The Literary Characterization of Mothers'.

28.   On Genesis family combinations, with an emphasis on maternal roles, see the suggestive analysis of Exum, *Fragmented Women*, pp. 94-114 (Chapter 4, 'The Mother's Place').

29.   Exum, *Fragmented Women*, pp. 94-95.

30.   Exum, *Fragmented Women*, p. 122.

31.   Exum, *Fragmented Women*, pp. 124-27, with Gerda Lerner, *The Creation of Patriarchy* (New York: Oxford University Press, 1986), pp. 191-93, and Howard Eilberg-Schwartz, *The Savage in Judaism: An Anthropology of Israelite Religion and Ancient Judaism* (Bloomington: Indiana University Press, 1990), pp. 141-76. On circumcision, see L. Hoffman, *Covenant of Blood, passim*.

another installment of the family's history, and in the retrospective understanding of the network of generational relations. This is also why there are striking similarities of dramatic structure and theme in the story of the first family, as well as in the ancestral narratives. All have a common point of reference, since they each treat events that are rooted in principles of universal creation and human procreation. 'Myth' and 'history' associate through integration into a familial space which revolves, ultimately, on symbols of motherhood.

4. *Moses and Maternity*

Cast in the mold of heroic myths, Exodus 2 explores implications of the Fifth Word by fragmenting maternity, and by distributing its components among several female bearers of identity.[32] From start to end, the story incorporates subversions of familial themes. There is no announcement, and not even a sterile wife.[33] No word of God, or of an angel, alerts the parents to the birth of a son destined to fulfill a special role in the annals of Israel. The birth itself is inscribed into a context of general oppression, marked by an underlying contest between the whim and will of an earthly potentate (Pharaoh) and Yahweh. To re-channel and control Hebrew reproductive energy, the Pharaoh recruits Egypt's natural geography. Disrespectful of parenthood, the monarch orders the Hebrews to throw their newly born, if male, into the river that, ironically, constitutes Egypt's most vital giver of livelihood.

Saving Moses involves not only parental disobedience to the law of the land, but also a challenge to parental authority. Moses' first savior, his mother, builds a basket and deposits both basket and baby in the water of the Nile, thus challenging the river to live up to its traditional role of sustenance. Moses' second savior, a daughter of the king of the land, defies the wish of her own father by rescuing a baby whom she instantly recognizes as a scion of the enslaved Hebrews. Exodus 2 accords the naming of the child to this Egyptian princess who, herself, remains nameless, as does her mighty father. Biblical annals often entrust the naming of the newly born to their mothers. Exodus 2 transfers this maternal right into the hands of a woman who is neither the natural mother nor a Hebrew. The name she chooses designates the circumstances of her discovery, in themselves, a 'rebirth'.

What makes the female biblical collusion of Exodus 2 remarkable and unique is the fact that the women, like the water of the Nile, incorporate the power of life-giving and of death. They take crucial initiatives in a deadly *agon* between the feminine and the masculine, made all the more remarkable by the disappearance of Moses' father from the records of his family right after the recording of his marriage. The language of generation, familiar from Genesis, reappears in Exodus 2, but all the roles are played by women. Because Moses is both born and made, the link forged at birth is permanently set asunder. In this tangle of ambiguities, the exposure of a son implies a denial of paternity. Yet, the story also suggests that the

32. What follows is based on my 'Moses the Persian?'
33. Robert Alter, 'How Convention Helps us Read: The Case of the Bible's Annunciation Type-Scene', *Prooftexts* 3 (1983), pp. 115-30.

mother could decide, independently of males (husband/father/older sons), whether to raise or expose the child. The consequence of a union between two ordinary Hebrews is, therefore, not a foregone conclusion. Procreation and multiplication is a command that cannot always be carried out, because the presence of couples does not suffice to ensure the continuation of the clan. Nor can the Fifth Commandment always be carried out, because the presence of a child does not guarantee either a 'family' or respect.

Because birth can be condensed into a meaningless moment, there is also a total impasse. Moses is not an Egyptian, but rather an intruder into the princely house whose daughter had adopted him in violation of all the rules of the kingdom. She endows him with name and power, that is, with an autonomy that runs counter to the state of his own people. In this story, there is no position with an unequivocal interpretation, and no way to account for legal positions. At the princess's hearth Moses is what a woman is at her husband's hearth—an external element introduced from the outside. At the same time, his very existence potentially undermines the status of both his mothers, the natural and the adoptive.

Moses never discovers his father. Nothing, in fact, is regular and straightforward in the matter of his birth or upbringing. Genesis's orthodoxy defines membership in terms of legitimacy and endogamic descent. In Exodus, Moses' nativity myth, although providing the son with legal and closely related parents, does little to resolve the question of his standing and his relations with either biological mother or father. The tension in the drama further lies in the distinction between birth from human beings, and (re)birth from water. The fecundity of the Nile and sexual reproduction have been confused with each other, because to restore Moses, product of both sex and river, to his original familial alliance, separation and covenant must be effected. In the passage between births, in Exodus 2, and 'rebirth' in Exodus 4, the parental couple becomes irrelevant.

5. *Deuteronomy's Disobedient Sons and Unruly Daughters*

Honor your father and your mother as the Lord God had commanded you so that you will live longer and so that you will prosper on the land that the Lord God is giving you. (Deut. 5.16)

Cursed be he who dishonors his father or his mother. (Deut. 27.16)

If a man has a rebellious and contentious son who does not listen to his father and mother and who, in spite of their remonstrance, still does not listen, then his father and his mother shall seize him and take him out to the elders of the town and to the gate of this place, and shall say to the elders: Here is our rebellious and contentious son who does not heed our voices and who consumes our goods. Let all the people of the town stone him to death so that the evil will be uprooted and so that all of Israel may hear and fear. (Deut. 21.18-21)

If any man takes a wife and goes in to her and then spurns her and charges her with shameful conduct and brings an evil name upon her saying; 'I took this woman and when I came near her I did not find in her the tokens of virginity'.

Then the father of the young woman and her mother shall take and bring out the tokens of her virginity to the elders of the city in the gate. And the father of the young woman shall say to the elders: 'I gave my daughter to this man, to wife, and he spurns her, and he has made shameful charges against her saying: 'I did not find in your daughter the tokens of virginity', and yet these are the tokens of my daughter's virginity'. And they shall spread the garment before the elders of the city and then the elders of that city shall take the man and whip him and they shall fine him a hundred shekels of silver and give them to the father of the young woman because he has brought an evil name on a virgin of Israel. And she shall be his wife, he may not put her away all his days. But if this thing is true, that the tokens of virginity were not found in the young woman, then they shall bring out the young woman to the door of her father's house and the men of her city shall stone her to death with stones because she has wrought folly in Israel by playing the harlot in her father's house. (Deut. 22.13-21 RSV)

In (re)casting the command to honor parents, the Deuteronomic version adds two significant phrases to the Exodus formulation. It insists on the divine origins of the command ('as the lord your God has commanded you'), thereby embedding it within the larger theophanic context, and it dangles the specter of not only longevity, but also of prosperity, as rewards for compliance.[34] Pedagogy and history mingle, reinforcing each other as parents emulate Yahweh, becoming teachers of piety and memory in their respective homes (Deut. 4.10; 11.19-21). Parenthood, then, acts as repository of the collective history which, in turn, accounts for the Commandment to honor parents.[35]

Reiterating Levitical prohibition on cursing parents, Deuteronomy, too, prescribes death to offenders (Deut. 27.16; Lev. 20.9). The penalty may reflect a viewpoint that deemed unwarranted 'every wrongdoing of sons against their parents which presupposed a rupture of the relationship of respect and deference'.[36] The Fifth Word itself does not propose penalties but rather blessings and rewards for correct conduct. Just how seriously did the law deem breaches of the Commandment may be measured in two instances which deal with two types of insubordinate 'children', a disobedient son who diminishes parental property (Deut. 21.18-21), and a wayward daughter who injures the standing of her parents in the community (22.13-21). Both cases delineate rebellious and deviant behavior, each dependent on gender perceptions, and each processing its protagonists as passive participants.[37]

---

34.   On the Deuteronomic character of these expressions, see Jose Loza, *Las palabras de Yahvé. Estudio del Decálogo* (México: Universidad Pontificia, 1989), pp. 123-25; Andre Lemaire, 'Le décalogue. Essai d'histoire de la rédaction', in Andre Caquot and Mari Delcor (eds.), *Mélanges bibliques et orientaux en l'honneur de M. Henri Cazelles* (Kevelaer: Butzon & Bercker, 1981), pp. 259-95 (284).

35.   On the historical circumstances, namely exile, which accounts for the Deuteronomic changes of the Exodus Commandment, see Briend, 'Honore', pp. 209-10, and Carrón, 'Honor', p. 39.

36.   Loza, *Las palabras*, p. 231.

37.   Joseph Fleishman, *Parent and Child in the Ancient Near East and the Bible* (Jerusalem: Magnes Press, 1999 [Hebrew]), Chapter 9, traces a basic comparison between the components of each pericope. On the similarities, see also Alexander Rofé, 'Family and Sex Laws in Deuteronomy

Deuteronomy 21.18-21 considers sons with gross appetites to possess eating habits which undermine the integrity of parental property. To restore harmony into households marred by gastronomic greed, the law calls on parents to transfer the matter from the domicile to the public and to accuse their offspring of rebellious-ness and insubordination, rooted, it seems, in incessant consumption of their goods.[38] Focusing on a young woman with concealed sexual appetites, Deut. 22.13-21 penetrates two domiciles, the woman's original and marital homes, which are disrupted by an alleged lack of parental control over a betrothed daughter.[39] The law allows husbands to accuse their wives of infidelity during betrothal, calling upon the women's parents to bear the double role of defenders and accusers. In each instance, namely that of the consuming son and of the unchaste daughter, the very exposure of the 'delinquent child' to public judgment suggests a willing forfeiture of parental authority.[40]

Procedures differ. There is no investigation in the case of the rebellious son because the 'crime' is self-evident, and the very accusation by the parents already constitutes its proof. An accusation of premarital sex, by contrast, is beyond deci-sive proof. Nor is the matter of female unchastity in Deuteronomy 22 settled through an investigation of the woman herself, or through a search for an elusive paramour. Instead, the parents are required to produce their daughter's 'tokens of virginity', because their word alone is insufficient to counterbalance the husband's accusa-tion.[41] The law envisages parents defending their daughter by resorting to counter-accusation which depicts the husband as harboring hatred towards an innocent wife.

To judge the parameters of trust violation between men (father/husbands), and between generations (parents/daughter), local elders must arbitrate between the two males who stand to be damaged not only by the alleged crime of the daughter/wife, but also by its very exposure. If the guilt of the gluttonous son seems a foregone conclusion, that of the wayward daughter must be established by intuition, and pre-sumably according to the social status of the accuser and defender. A disobedient son dies by stoning; a wayward daughter, if found guilty, meets the same fate, but at the very gate of her parental home (Deut. 22.21).

Who, then, is to blame for reproachable behavior of 'children'? Rabbinic inter-pretation of Deut. 21.18-21 excludes daughters from the orbit of dietary 'rebellious

---

and the Book of the Covenant', *Henoch* 9 (1987), 131-59 (143-44), especially on the semantic fields of 'wayward' (סרר) and 'licentious' (זנה).

38.   Bellefontaine, 'Deuteronomy 21:18-21', pp. 13-31, sees the two parts of the accusation as distinct, seeing the second as illustrative of the first and both as an exegesis of the Fifth Word; this latter is my view which I share with Gerhard von Rad, *Studies in Deuteronomy* (trans. David Stalker; London: SCM Press, 1961), p. 22, and *Deuteronomy: A Commentary* (trans. Dorothea Barton; Philadelphia: Westminster Press, 1966), p. 138.

39.   For a full discussion of this pericope, see Pressler, *View of Women*, pp. 21-43; see also above, Chapter 3 §3, and below, Chapters 6 (on 'murder' by language) 7.

40.   See Fishbane, *Interpretation*, p. 244, on the increased 'rationalization' of the judicial proc-ess in the book of Deuteronomy, including the introduction of a stratum of elders, and implying that the procedure of Deut. 21.18 relates to an early phase before family matters received 'national' legislation.

41.   Cf. my discussion of rabbinic investigative procedures in *Dinah's Daughters*, Chapter 4.

children' (*b. Sanh.* 69b-70a). The rabbis asserted that gluttony is a form of rebelliousness intimately linked with manhood. They further determined that neither a minor son (a boy who is not yet obliged by *mitzvot*), nor an adult man could be considered 'rebellious', but only an adolescent, the extent of whose liability is determined by the quantity of his genital hair. To magnify the enormity of rebelliousness, the rabbis relied on Prov. 31.1-9 (below) which regards filial insubordination as a rejection of the maternal womb itself (*b. Sanh.* 69b-70a). The verse assisted the rabbis in alleging that when the character of the father is flawless, the son's faults are inevitably inherited from the mother. In the maternal monologue concocted by the rabbis about a rebellious son, the mother is made to express a sense of betrayal because her investment in motherhood had been rendered futile by mothering a wayward child.

Lack of respect to parents constitutes, then, a rebellion against the womb. This is the organ that, implicitly, stands in the center of Deuteronomic inquiry into the behavior of a wayward daughter. Nor is it a coincidence that the case of male rebelliousness focuses on the belly, the closest equivalent to woman's womb. In both instances, the transgression becomes evident when the son gains weight, and if the woman falls pregnant. Such a focus also reflects the minutiae of gender stereotyping in a society which generates standards that project masculinity and femininity in terms of dogmatic assertions and specific modes of behavior. The Deuteronomic juxtaposition of the two cases as two sides of the same coin shows that males and females are subject to criteria of judgment that conscript 'parents' into an ideogram which divides society, in terms of the Fifth Word, into two hierarchies: commanding parents and obedient/deviant 'children'.

6. *Mothers and Super-Sons: The Story of Samson*

Inner-biblical exegesis captured icons of filial rebellion by appointing a mother a preacher of morality to her son:

> The words of Lemuel the king, the speech with which his mother chided him: What is it, my son, what is it, son of my womb, son of my vows? Do not let women capture your manhood and your strategies to vanquish kings. Kings ought not, Lemuel, kings ought not to drink wine. Nor should rulers desire drink. Lest they drink and forget the law and distort the right of the afflicted. Give a drink to him who is perishing, and wine to those whose soul is bitter. Let them drink and forget their poverty and their misery... (Prov. 31.1-9 RSV)

Proverbs' wayward son is a man who betrays the hopes that his mother had cherished while pregnant. He is a son who indulges in drink and in sex with foreign women. The proverbial stereotype fits well the figure of Samson who loved banquets and foreign women, in spite of maternal Nazarite vows and contrary to repeated parental and Pentateuchal strictures. The story is especially instructive. Indeed, in no other biblical narrative does the phrase, or cliché, 'father and mother' appear as often as it does in Judges 13–16. Yet, the scenes depicted are conspicuous in their demonstrable absence of filial respect. They show how Samson's rebellious body acts as a reflective mirror of the scope of generational conflicts that draw the limits of the Fifth Word.

Born in a domicile which hardly sets an example of spousal harmony and concord, the story of Samson, from its start, stretches along a fundamental, yet ultimately misleading opposition between the female body of mothers, wives and lovers on the one hand, and a male who becomes a symbol of virility on the other hand. Because Samson is a 'hero of manhood', he is identified with his body, and his invincible strength must be carefully nurtured from the moment of conception.[42] The centrality of Samson's mother, although a woman without a name, forecasts the significance of women in Samson's life.[43] In overcoming sterility, Manoah's wife engineers a break in the chain of Israelite subordination to non-Israelite powers. She is not just the mother of Samson but, through him, a symbol of an ideal motherhood that promises national delivery from the yoke of foreign domination.

In Judges 13 unusual encounters follow each other rapidly: a barren wife becomes an object of two annunciation scenes; an angel freely communicates with a mortal woman; and a distrustful husband (Manoah) proves resistant to divine messages. The would-be mother defies expectations—she neither responds to an angel who brings her tidings of future pregnancy, nor does she share with her husband the full angelic announcements.[44] A sense of mistrust and secrecy permeates these preliminary scenes. The words and actions of the would-be parents highlight dangers of unmonitored motherhood, rather than the happiness that this type of news is supposed to introduce.

Communications regarding the vital issue of procreation and legitimate birth are confined, in Judges 13, to the prospective mother and to an unidentified 'man of God'. While casting the mother as the more significant partner in the process, the tale's juxtaposition of women and angels also reveals a deep-seated male anxiety regarding the prospect of birth after years of childlessness. Samson's birth threatens to become a bone of parental contention rather than contentment. He is both the son of his parents, yet a product of an asexual process.

Such an ambiguous beginning ensures that Samson's path to a fulfillment of his destiny will be paved with transgressions, not the least a violation of the Fifth Commandment. In a preliminary encounter between the grown-up son and his parents, Samson informs 'his father and his mother' (Judg. 14.2) that he wishes to

42.   See Nicole Loraux, *The Experiences of Teresias: The Feminine and the Greek Man* (trans. Paula Wissing; Princeton, NJ: Princeton University Press, 1995), p. 116, for the expression (which she uses for Herakles). Zakovitch, *Samson*, p. 80, remarks on the dominant role of the mother in the nativity scenes of both Samson and Heracles.

43.   See, among many, J. Cheryl Exum, 'Samson's Women', in her *Fragmented Women*, pp. 61-93, and esp. pp. 63-68 ('Ideology and Reading: The Politics of Motherhood'). On Judg. 13–16 as power play, see Carol Smith, 'Samson and Delilah: A Parable of Power?', *JSOT* 76 (1997), pp. 45-57.

44.   Robert Alter, *The Art of Biblical Narrative* (New York: Basic Books, 1981), p. 101, on the variation in the repetition as 'setting the scene for a powerful but spiritually dubious savior of Israel; and cf. Alter's discussion of the tale of the birth of Samuel (p. 81), which he sees as another annunciation type-scene.

marry a Philistine woman and asks them to mediate matrimony on his behalf.[45] Appearing as a dutiful son, Samson's model of filial regard is shattered over the revelation of the bridal non-Yahwist identity. For Samson's parents the prospect is unacceptable. They ask in unison: 'is there none among the daughters of your own brothers, and none among all your people, that you need take a wife from among the idolatrous Philistines?' (14.3).[46] Samson's response addresses only his father: 'Her, you (masculine singular) must take for me, because she is the one I like most' (14.3). In the paradigm of manhood that Samson attains, he 'wins' his first battle by overcoming his parents, using as weapon a rhetoric of a free choice.

This parental-filial clash over matrimonial plans also reveals the limits of parental authority and of filial obedience. Biblical narratives endorse absolute parental control and legal pronouncements censure intermarriage (Exod. 34.15-16; Deut. 7.3-4). Samson's choice of a bride becomes a manifestation of filial disregard and an infraction of rules regarding marriage and the Fifth Commandment. Moreover, by marrying outside the covenantal community Samson runs the risk of fracturing the special relationship between Yahweh and Israel that entails, *inter alia*, the delivery of barren wives from the stain of sterility. This is why the redactor is careful to add that 'his father and mother did not know' that Yahweh had planned it all (Judg. 14.4).[47]

Seemingly complying with their persistent son, the parents accompany Samson to Timnah (Judg. 14.5).[48] They are apparently absent from Samson's heroic encounter with a lion, but are the main beneficiaries of his resourcefulness (14.9). Ironically, it is the 'rebellious child' who provides his parents with nourishment, thereby defying Deuteronomic definition of a sinning son (above). Samson's parents appear yet again as a stereotypical image of 'father and mother' in the course of a fateful 'fight' between Samson and his Philistine bride. The woman prods Samson to provide her with a solution to a riddle which had tantalized her Philistine co-patriots (14.16). He does not know that they had threatened to kill her and her father. She, paradoxically, uses precisely the same rhetoric which Samson had employed to win his argument with his own parents. She accuses Samson of 'hating' her, implicitly suggesting that he does not love her as he should; he responds by stating

---

45. Cf. Gen. 34.4, for a similar request and its disastrous results for the woman; see also Zakovitch, *Samson*, p. 96. On the passage as 'an extended polemic against intermarriage', see Shaye J.D. Cohen, 'Solomon and the Daughter of Pharaoh: Intermarriage, Conversion, and the Impurity of Women', *JANES* 16-17 (1984–85), pp. 23-37 (25, for quote).

46. Their objection has been regarded as perfunctory (Zakovitch, *Samson*, p. 97), namely a redactional touch catering to contemporary (redactional) audience, above Chapter 3 §2.

47. Cf. Gen. 24.50 where the proposed marriage (between Rebecca and Isaac) is a carefully calculated endogamic alliance.

48. The information, however, contradicts Judg. 14.6, which implies that the parents were not with Samson when he killed the lion. Zakovitch, *Samson*, pp. 86-88, 96-100, asserts that the parents had been absent from the 'original' plot but are late redactional additions. On Judg. 13–16 as a parable on the theme of obedience/disobedience of Israel *vis-à-vis* Yahweh, see Mark Greene, 'Enigma Variations: Apsects of the Samson Story Judges 13–16', *Vox Evangelica* 21 (1991), pp. 53-79.

that even his 'father and mother' had not been privy to his secret, implicitly suggesting that her demand transgresses wifely limits.

The brief dialogue juxtaposes spousal with parental 'love'. For Samson's bride the meaning of love is the sharing of secrets; for Samson it is the unquestioned acceptance of his own plans and council by both bride and parents. The comparison between the two types of relations places blood (parents) ahead of social conventions (wives). Yet, the encounter between Samson and his Philistine bride, rooted as it is in a violation of the Fifth Word, provides a model of filial devotion not, however, of an Israelite male 'child' but of a non-Israelite one, a female. She chooses, or rather is made to choose a parent (father) over her husband, and she pays for the choice with her life, bringing calamity on her entire household. Samson, who remains defiant, emerges unscathed, ready to fall in love again.

As it stands, the story of Samson begins with a woman, his mother, and ends with another, his lover Delilah, who, by cajoling the secret of his birth, becomes a surrogate mother.[49] Shaving him, Delilah engineers his death, just as his mother had ensured his destiny by leaving his hair to grow. Delilah unmans Samson for money while his mother secures his manhood through the purity of her body. The gestures of the two women reveal a discourse of parenthood in which the mother has an exclusive shaping role which excludes fathers, in spite of the text's tenacious inclusion of Manoah.

A conspicuous lack of reciprocity characterizes the relationships that the story delineates between couples, as well as between parents and 'children'. Even when Samson avenges the murder of his Philistine bride, the revenge is merely an excuse to indulge in his customary Philistine bashing. No relatives of the dead woman appear to express gratitude on her behalf, and Samson's own people are worried lest his 'feats' sour their relations with the Philistines. Love and hatred are two threads that run throughout the narrative alongside the themes of respect and disrespect. For Samson's Philistine bride and for Delilah love means the full disclosure of secrets. For Samson, wives and lovers provide temporary gratification and a peculiar source of identity. Never leading a national Israelite army, Samson derives his Israelite definition from his constant clashes with Philistines, females and males alike.

Deuteronomy 5 links the demand to show respect to one's parents with a promise of prosperity and longevity on the land that Yahweh had allocated to Israel. In Judges 13–16 this land is, however, under foreign domination, while the man destined to break this mold is, himself, a model of rebelliousness against familial and national values. Samson's failure to obey parental wishes regarding marriage results in a life that is spent among strangers and in a 'diasporic' existence. He also dies prematurely. His life and death provide a precise demonstration of the implied penalties of transgressing the Fifth Word, namely short life rather than longevity, and a subsistence at a nomadic level of living rather than agricultural affluence.

---

49. Zakovitch, *Samson, passim*. On Delilah as a Philistine Jael, see Susan Ackerman, 'What if Judges had been Written by a Philistine?', *BibInt* 8 (2000), pp. 33-41.

Only as a corpse does Samson return to reside, for good, among his own people and in the land of his parents.

Samson's story suggests that 'honoring' parents is tantamount to compliance with social rules or traditions as represented by older generations and incorporated in communal memory. The narrative paradox resides in the fact that Samson's disregarding of parental ideology is not only divinely preordained, but that it also paves the way to national redemption. But Samson remains a peculiar hero. He burns fields and fails to impregnate a single woman, in spite of his overabundant masculinity.

Perhaps, if asked, Manoah's wife would have elected to remain childless. The habitual dichotomy of sex vs. gender (= body vs. society, nature vs. culture) that permeates biblical presentations of women obscures complex issues of psychosexual identity and collective culture. She is not given a chance to negotiate between private wishes and public requirements which, in this case, are grafted in a rigid, yet subtle opposition. The narrative attaches variables of femininity and masculinity to anatomical females and males, but also confounds gender/sex assumptions. Samson's mother is anything but maternal; Samson himself is anything but a Nazarite-type savior. Both mother and son are, in fact, 'rebellious': she, because the identity of the child's father is never quite settled; he, because of systematically acting in defiance of Pentateuchal iconic images of Israelite 'heroes'.

Parents transmit name and legitimacy. In Judges 13, however, the biological father is a late comer, a 'foreigner' of sorts. He is also lame with words, showing singular ineptness when talking with angels and with his own child. His paternal status, so extolled in the Fifth Word, seems irrelevant in the micro-cosmos which his wife and son inhabit and within a context of national crisis. Samson's story unfolds a solution to Israel's nadir which associates 'redemption' not with the discharge of filial duties but with consistent violation of the Fifth Commandment. Salvation depends on deviant behavior, just as birth 'saves' a barren wife from social ruin.

In a way, Judges 13–16 is a tragi-comic variation on the theme of matrilineal filiation and on Decalogue's ideology. The story involves a systematic distortion of all the dominant (male) values of society. Between father and son there is a nameless mother who appears when the figure of the father is usually anticipated. Samson seeks the maternal embrace throughout, but in the wrong pair of arms. Something is suspect at the very heart of the representation of paternity. A mother links the chain of generations in which a son takes over from father to become the 'defender' of the 'fatherland' whose wealth stems from procreation and from adherence to rules that the protagonists continually transgress.

Chapter 6

THE MAPPING OF MURDER
(WORD SIX)

You see, the interesting thing is that you still could have killed me. There were no witnesses, and no judge would have convicted you, everyone would have rushed to surround you with sympathy, because we were the legendary friends, Castor and Pollux, together for twenty-four years through thick and thin, we were their reincarnation. If you had killed me, everyone would have reached out to you, everyone would have mourned with you, because *the world believes there could be no more tragic figure than someone who accidentally kills his friend. What man, what prosecutor, what lunatic would make the unbelievable accusation that you had done it deliberately?* There is absolutely no proof that you were harboring any deadly animosity toward me. The previous evening we had all dined together-my wife, my relations, our hunting comrades—as a friendly circle in the castle where you had been welcome, no matter what the day, for decades... You did not owe me any money, you lived in my house like a member of the family. Who could imagine you would do such a thing? No one. What cause would you have to murder me? Who could be inhuman enough to imagine that you, my friend-of-friends, would kill me, your friend-of-friends, when you could ask anything in life of me, receive anything you needed by way of psychological or material support, treat my house as yours, my fortune as yours to share, my family as your second family?

—Sándor Márai, *Embers*[1]

Nanna-sig son of Lu-Suen, Ku-Enlilla son of Ku-Nanna, the barber, and Enlil-ennam son of Adda-kalla, the orchard keeper, murdered Lu-Inanna son of Lugaluru, the (nishakku-)priest. After Lu-Inanna was dead, they told Nin-dada daughter of Lu-Ninurta, wife of Lu-Inanna, that her (husband had been murdered). She did not open her mouth. She kept it secret. Their case was brought to Isin before the king. The king ordered that the case be tried by the assembly of Nippur.

...

Addressing (the assembly) the (elders?) said: 'As men who have killed a man, they are not (fit to be) alive. Those three males and that woman should be killed in front of the (official) chair of Lu-Inanna...

[But others said]: Granted that Nin-dada daughter of Lu-Ninurta might have killed her husband, [seeing that she is only a woman,] what can she do that she should be killed?

1.   Sándor Márai, *Embers* (trans. Caroline Brown Janeway [from the German translation, *Die Glut as Embers*, of the Hungarian original, *A gyertyák csonkig égnek*] New York: Viking, 2001), pp. 146-47 (my emphasis).

In the assembly of Nippur they (the elders?) responded: A woman who does not treasure her husband might surely have intercourse with his enemy, and he would then murder her husband. Should he then let her know that her husband had been killed—why should she not then keep silent about him? [or: why should he not make her keep her mouth shut about him?] It is certainly she, who virtually murdered her husband. Her guilt exceeds that of one who (actually) kills a man.

The assembly…(condemned all four)…to execution.

—*ANET*, III, p. 542 (trans. J.J. Finkelstein[2])

1. *'Law' and Ethics*

What is 'murder'? Is it, as the quote from Márai's magnificent *Embers* intimates, a matter strictly between men?[3] And if so, what precisely happens when a woman 'murders', or remains silent about a murder, or is herself the victim of a 'murder'? In ancient Mesopotamia, as the trial of Nin-dada for murder shows, a woman need not wield a murderous weapon, or even be on the scene of the murder, to face a trial for murder and be found guilty. The recorded Mesopotamian proceedings further suggest that all five protagonists, namely the murdered husband, the silent or silenced wife, and the three murderers, had known each other prior to the fatal encounter. It is precisely this implied association that brought the wife to the gallows.

Nin-dada had not participated in the actual murder, nor did the prosecution have proof of her complicity in the murderous plot. But the unanimity that all the attendants expressed regarding her culpability is remarkable. It reflects the dependence of an exegesis of 'facts' on gender distinctions that organize women in the social hierarchy in terms of their relations with males. The Mesopotamian case demonstrates a filament of thought that opposes wifely responsibility with inactivity, and equates wifely silence with adultery and murder.[4] Nin-dada's incriminating silence, whether voluntary or forced, 'resounded' with male assumptions regarding her share in the crime. A murder, then, is not only a conclusion of a direct physical clash between males but also a result of a mindset, at least when it involves women.

While the Sixth Word categorically forbids 'murder', most translations render the prohibition as 'You shall not kill'. Whether in the context of the Decalogue the verb simply means 'to kill a man' (i.e. a human being) is, perhaps, not as clear-cut as has been generally assumed.[5] To support an interpretation that espouses a broad

2.   Slight modifications are based on Martha T. Roth, 'Gender and Law: A Case Study from Ancient Mesopotamia', in Matthews, Levinson and Frymer-Kensky (eds.), *Gender and Law*, pp. 173-84, translated text on pp. 176-67.

3.   In the story a murder never actually takes place. Rather it is analyzed to death by the intended victim. The real casualty in this proverbial triangle is the woman/wife/lover(?) who is driven to will herself to die.

4.   Cf. the so-called 'second tablet of Shurpu' in Walter Beyerlin, *Near Eastern Religious Texts Relating to the Old Testament* (Philadelphia: Westminster Press, 1978), p. 31, which associates adultery with murder.

5.   Andrew D.H. Mayes, *Deuteronomy* (NCBC; London: Oliphants, 1979), p. 170, for quote and the assumption. He is supported by Rodd, *Glimpses*, p. 98 n. 14. Phillips, *Ancient Israel's Criminal Law*, p. 83, suggests that the Decalogue deals with the space where the killing occurs (i.e. the covenant community) rather than with the nature of the crime.

and gender-impartial base of the Sixth Word, scholars have pointed out to verbal statistics that show how words formed with the root to 'kill' (הרג) and to 'cause one to die' (המית) occur with much greater frequency than 'murder' (רצח).[6] It further appears that, regardless of circumstances, words formed from the root 'murder' are used to describe both intentional killing (i.e. 'murder') and homicide (i.e. unintentional killing).[7] Numerical calculations, coupled with an apparent lack of clear-cut distinctions between one type of death and another, seem to indicate that biblical authors and redactors paid little attention to niceties of semantics. Yet, and unambiguously, the application of the term 'murder' to homicide in the Pentateuch and in the Dtr History is limited to 'legal' texts, with few but significant exceptions. In the rare narratives that use the term of the Sixth Word, the 'murder' cases are far from simple. Nor do they conform to any legally laid procedure. To render matters more complex, each of these stories features a woman in a prominent position, either as a casualty, namely the murdered entity (Judg. 19), or as the mind behind the murder, namely the 'murderer' (1 Kgs 21).

Curt to the point of obscurity, the Sixth Word draws no distinctions between different levels of accountability nor does it provide penalties.[8] The Covenant Code (Exod. 20.12-14) and the Holiness Code (Lev. 24.17, 21) propose capital punishment for killers, modified by a distinction (in the Covenant Code) between accidentally inflicted death vs. killing by design. For the former, there is an option of seeking refuge in one of the designated cities of asylum.[9] Complementary legal texts (Num. 35.9-34; Deut. 4.41-43; 19.1-13) briefly allude to issues such as intent, prior relations between murderer and murdered, and degrees of culpability; but, largely, they focus on the aftermath of untimely death and on how to shield an inadvertent killer from vengeance. Extending communal protection to unwitting and accidental murderers, these regulations emphasize an extraordinary aspect of the Sixth Word, namely that 'murder', at least as discussed in the legal portions of the Pentateuch, is the only transgression that can be committed unintentionally.[10]

---

6.   Stamm and Andrew, *The Ten Commandments*, pp. 98-99, count 42 of the latter, 165 for הרג and 201 for המית.

7.   See Deut. 22.26 (comparing rape with murder, see below); 1 Kgs 21.19 (murder and unlawful possession or theft, see below); Isa. 1.21 (juxtaposing fornication and murder); Hos. 4.2 (cursing, denying, murder, theft, adultery), 6.9 (murder and fornication); Jer. 7.9 (grouping theft, murder, adultery, false swearing and apostasy); Job 24.14 (murderer as a thief)—all these texts deal with what may be termed 'intentional killing' or 'murder'; for 'killing' as 'unintentional murder' see Deut. 4.41-44; 19.1-13; Num. 35; Josh. 20; 21 (all legal prescriptions, see below). In general, see Tate, 'Legal Traditions', p. 493.

8.   Rodd, *Glimpses*, p. 98.

9.   On the expansion of the subject of homicide (in the Covenant Code) to include bodily damage that may lead to death (Exod. 21.18-21), see Van Seters, 'Comparison of Babylonian Law Codes with the Covenant Code', p. 23. I doubt, however, whether the Covenant Code depends on Deuteronomy and the Holiness Code (as well as on Babylonian law codes), as Van Seters suggests.

10.   For scholarly debates regarding the development of the laws on homicide, see Phillips, *Ancient Israel's Criminal Law*, pp. 83-109; *idem*, 'Another Look at Murder', *JJS* 28 (1977), pp. 105-26; Henry McKeating, 'The Development of the Law on Homicide in Ancient Israel', *VT* 25 (1975), pp. 46-68; Haas, '"Die, She Shall Surely Die"', pp. 76-81, on categories of homicide

2. *The Meaning of Murder According to Numbers*

Dealing with simple and unadulterated death, yet unauthorized and unacceptable (by Yahweh's standards), the Sixth Word aspires, it seems, to castigate any kind of killing that contradicts communal interests and undermines the vision of a regulated society.[11] By implicitly forbidding specific types of killing it conjures sets of circumstances and configurations that may lead to violent and premature death.[12] In the Tetrateuch account of early Israelite history (Genesis–Numbers), from creation to the dawn of conquest, the precise conditions that result in a 'murder' are, therefore, a theoretical issue of some significance. Numbers 35.9-34, the only pericope in the Tetrateuch which repeatedly uses the term of the Sixth Word, provides incidences of potentially murderous encounters, as well as prescriptions regarding the fate of murderers:[13]

> And the Lord said to Moses: Say to the people of Israel: When you cross the Jordan into the land of Canaan then you shall select cities to be cities of refuge for you so that a murderer (רוֹצֵחַ) who hits (and kills) a person without intent may flee there. The cities shall be for you a refuge from the avenger, so that the murderer may not die until facing trial before the congregation... These six cities shall be set up as refuge for the people (sons) of Israel, and for the stranger (resident alien, גֵּר), the sojourner (תּוֹשָׁב) among them, so that anyone who kills unintentionally may flee there.
>
> If (one) hits (another) with an iron instrument and the other person dies, (the one whose hand had wielded the object) is a murderer; and the murderer must be put to death. Similarly, if (one hits another) with a stone...or with a wooden tool... (In such cases) the blood avenger may put the murderer to death; if he encounters him he may kill him.
>
> Whether one pushes (another) in hatred, or hurls (something) deliberately and he dies, or hits by hand in enmity and he dies, the one who struck the blow will be put to death since he is a murderer, and the blood avenger may put him to death upon encountering him.
>
> But if suddenly and without enmity one pushes another, or hurls at him whatever he happened to have in his hand unintentionally, or drops a deadly object of stone without noticing a person who subsequently dies, but he had not been his enemy nor sought to inflict harm on him, let the congregation judge between the one who hits and the blood avenger, according to these ordinances...

with and without blood-guilt. On the development and meaning of the term 'murder' (רָצַח), see Childs, *Exodus*, pp. 419-21. Cf. the issue of intent and lack of it with Lev. 4.2-12's attitude to inadvertent sin and its modes of expiation; see Douglas, *Leviticus as Literature*, pp. 124-28.

11. Philip J. Hyatt, *Exodus* (NCBC; Grand Rapids: Eerdmans, rev. edn, 1980 [1971]), p. 214.

12. As opposed to killing in war and to judicial execution, as well as, by some accounts, to the laying of animals; see Rodd, *Glimpses*, p. 98.

13. Num. 35.1 is also the only place where the term 'city of refuge' makes an appearance in Genesis–Numbers. Cf. Josh. 20.2, which may depend on Num. 35. I refrain from delving into chronological and provenance problems connected with each of the biblical references to cities of refuge since these are irrelevant to my argument, nor have I been convinced by the arguments so far advanced. For a survey of scholarly speculations, see Phillips, *Ancient Israel's Criminal Law*, pp. 99-109. See also Greenberg, 'Some Postulates of Biblical Law', on approaches to analysis of biblical laws on the same subject.

> If anyone kills a person and there are witnesses to the murder, that person shall
> be put to death, but not on the testimony of one witness. Nor will you take ransom
> for the life of a vicious murderer but he is to be put to death. Nor will you accept
> ransom for one who had fled to a city of refuge to facilitate a return home before
> the death of the high priest.
> You will not pollute the land where you are because the blood pollutes the earth.
> No expiation can be made for the blood that had been shed other than the blood of
> the person who had shed it. You shall not defile the earth where you live and where
> I dwell because I am the Lord who dwells among the sons of Israel.[14]

In the plainest sense of the word, Numbers 35 states that 'murder' is an act committed, intentionally or unintentionally, when a man confronts another, openly or
stealthily, and with a potentially deadly instrument in hand. Based on intent,
weapon and previous relations, the passage distinguishes between two types of
'murder', namely deliberate and unpremeditated. The right of a murderer to seek
asylum depends, then, on the calculated or the unforeseen result of a fatal clash.[15]
According to the Numbers 35 exegesis of murder, the spilling of blood breeds more
bloodshed, and the threat of interminable revenge carries with it seeds of communal
disruption. The regulations regarding asylum, with the limitations imposed on the
action-sphere of the blood avenger, respond to a basic tenet of male self-perception:

> Listen to my voice, lend your ears to my words: I had killed a man for wounding
> me and a child for striking me. If Cain is avenged sevenfold, Lamech will be
> avenged seventy-sevenfold. (Gen. 4.23-24)[16]

That blood has the power to speak beyond the grave is clearly reflected in
Yahweh's address to Cain after Abel's blood 'cried out from the ground' (Gen.
4.10).[17] Killing curses the land and the taking of life of one person by another must
be punished. But Cain expresses remorse and is spared. At the end of the discussion
of murder and refuge in Numbers 35, a coda (35.33-34) forges a direct link between
murder and motherland by deeming the willful shedding of human blood a pollution. The only atonement for this act of impurity is through the blood of the killer.[18]
No other form of settlement, such as monetary compensation, can atone for the
deliberate spilling of blood (35.31-32).

---

14.   Cf. Exod. 21.12-14, which prescribes death to whoever strikes a man and kills him, like the
Sixth Word, without distinction between murder and manslaughter, but which is followed by two
casuistic additions that define the latter as accidental killing, allowing the killer to seek altar asylum,
and murder as an act performed by one who lies in wait for his victim, attacks him in hot pursuit,
and killing deceitfully. Rodd, *Glimpses*, pp. 98-99.

15.   Rodd, *Glimpses*, p. 103. On the chronology of refuge locations, see Milgrom, *Numbers*,
Excursus 75, pp. 504-509, who traces the restructuring of the law of asylum from the establishment
of the altar asylum (Exod. 21.13-14) through the abolition of its asylum status under Solomon and
replacement by asylum cities, to the Deuteronomic adoption of the P system of asylum (for the D
system see below).

16.   Stanley Gevirtz, 'Lamech's Song to his Wives (Genesis 4.23-4)', in Richard S. Hess and
David T. Tsumura (eds.), *I Studied Inscriptions Before the Flood: Ancient Near Eastern, Literary
and Linguistic Approaches to Genesis 1–11* (Winona Lake, IN: Eisenbrauns, 1994), pp. 405-15.

17.   Gunkel, *Genesis*, p. 45, on the 'speaking blood' as a common fairytale motif.

18.   Cf. Ezek. 36.17-18 on polluting the land through bloodshed, idolatry and incest (adultery).

The Numbers 35 discussion of murder deals exclusively with direct and un-mediated encounters between two individuals. It further assumes the presence of the killer on the scene of the murder. The text does not address cases that involve plotting rather than executing a murder, nor does it concern itself with murders that result from sexual violence.[19] Such omissions are crucial. Their importance is well reflected in Deuteronomistic narratives which focus on precisely these aspects (1 Kgs 21; Judg. 19). Accounts of the early phases of Israelite history (Genesis–Numbers) provide, by contrast, an assessment of circumstances that contain the potential of murder but that are resolved through adultery (below).

Whether the Numbers pericope on asylum for murderers and its Deuteronomic parallels (below) encompass a vision of women as murderers seeking asylum, or as victims of willful killing that justifies revenge, is unclear.[20] On the basis of refer-ences (in Num. 35) to conditions, types of encounters, manners of inflicting death and weapons wielded (not to mention the consistent use of the masculine form of nouns and verbs), this lengthy exposition envisages primarily, if not exclusively, males as murderers and as murdered entities. That the blood avenger is a male member of the family of the dead is not in doubt.[21] Should one further surmise that the Sixth Word likewise deals with willful killing of males only? Does it therefore incorporate a value judgment regarding the life of a man by comparison with that of a woman?

It would be naïve, perhaps, to infer with certainty gender attitudes from 'legal' texts. Yet, in the Hebrew Bible women never kill other women. Genesis–Numbers, focusing on survival, on motherhood as means of forming and perpetuating the ancestral clan, and on midwives and daughters as preservers of males and of male identity (Exod. 1–2; Num. 36), has consequently little to say about modes of mur-der in general and of the killing of and by women in particular. Throughout the for-mative period of early Israel, as envisioned in the Tetrateuch, women are producers of life and not of death. On them depends the fate of the land, as a fragmentary Ugaritic text, which provides broad cultural context to biblical visions of women, strikingly illustrates:

> If [a woman gives birth…],
> The land […].
> If [a woman…] gives birth,
> He will have power over […].

19. Cf. the Egyptian catalogue of sins which includes: 'I have not killed/I have given no order to a killer' (*Book of the Dead* 125 [see *ANET*, I, p. 34; Beyerlin, *Near Eastern Religious Texts*, pp. 131-32]).

20. Phillips, *Ancient Israel's Criminal Law*, pp. 15-17, 110, argues that women had not been subject to Israel's criminal law prior to the Deuteronomic reforms.

21. On the identity of the blood avenger as a familial legal representative rather than as the one appointed to kill the killer, see Phillips, *Ancient Israel's Criminal Law*, pp. 102-104, who also points to the absence of evidence for the practice of blood feud, maintaining that the execution of a murderer was in the hands of a communal panel of judges and not in the hands of kin. The evidence remains ambiguous. Judg. 19–21 reflects a state in which all of Israel seeks revenge on all the direct kin of the 'murderers' (see below); in the case of Absalom and Amnon the 'killer' goes to exile but it is unclear whether this was done to avoid a blood avenger (see below).

If [a woman…] gives birth,
The land of the enemy [will be destroyed].
If [a woman…] gives birth,
There will be help […].
If [a woman…] gives birth,
The prosperity [of the king…, the king]
will have no [descendants]…[22]

Mediating between the past and the future, the maternal body symbolizes a vessel of temporal communications, a bridge to link men in war and in peace. Nothing is said of the potential death of the mother herself. Women do not die, they merely disappear out of narratives. Even in the books of Genesis and of Numbers, two texts brimming with women, death-scenes of women rarely intrude the tenor of male history.[23] The omission is singular, signaling a consistent elevation of the primary function of women, namely reproduction or the giving of birth, at the expense of their dying moments. Instead, narratives in Genesis and Numbers reflect on the potential of murder that women carry in their very bodies; they also ponder how the landscape allocated to femininity correlates or contravenes the horizons of murder that threaten male interaction.

3. *Metaphors of Murder: The Genesis Variation*

Repeated assurances to Abraham regarding multiplicity of seed (Gen. 12.2; 13.16; 15.5) appear as a delirium of a myth. Sarai is sterile; Abram is aging; and still nothing happens. Even the promised land fails to produce livelihood, a fact that induces two ancestral couples (Sarai–Abram; Rebecca–Isaac) to leave home in search of food. This is the background of a series of narratives known, in scholarly parlance, as the 'sister–wife' tales (Gen. 12, 20, 26). Succinctly recaptured, the first tale (Gen. 12.10-20) temporarily plants Sarah (still Sarai) and Abraham (still Abram) in Egypt. There the beautiful wife must pretend to be her husband's sister so as to prevent the husband's potential murder by lustful Egyptians. The wife then joins the royal harem; the husband is handsomely rewarded. Yahweh strikes the household of the local ruler with plague. Pharaoh hastily relinquishes the 'sister' back to the 'brother'. A happy end, at least for the husband.

The second 'brother–sister' episode plants the same couple, still searching for nourishment, in Philistine Gerar (Gen. 20.1-18). Once more the wife pretends to be the sister, fearful but resourceful the husband assiduously avoids being murdered, the local ruler collects the 'sister' into his harem, and observant Yahweh intervenes to stop the completion of the adulterous transaction. There follows a happy end with the couple amply rewarded for the enterprising charade. In the third 'brother–sister'

22. Olmo Lete, *Canaanite Religion*, pp. 358-59.
23. Only Rachel receives a fleeting reference when she dies, painfully and prematurely, in labor (Gen. 35). The killing of Cozbi the Midianite receives lengthier treatment (Num. 25). Her ruthless elimination constitutes a commentary on both intermarriage and on the role of the priests in the community.

tale (26.1-11), the son of the protagonist of the first two tales follows the family tradition by presenting his wife as his sister. The background is, again, Philistine Gerar, to which Rebecca and Isaac move after Yahweh prevents them from migrating to Egypt. The husband fears for his life on account of his wife's desirability. The ruse, this time, is discovered by the local ruler before the wife is appropriated. The couple is allowed to stay; the locals are warned off. Murder is averted, as is adultery.

All tales basically revolve around husbands who force a change of familial identity on their female partner for fear of being killed.[24] Two of these narratives accompany the transfer of silent (or silenced?) wife from her unsafe domestic environment to a gentile home.[25] The move ensures the safety of the 'husband–brother' in his own house, but exposes the 'wife–sister' to the mercy of other men.[26] Murder is prevented at the cost of actual or potential adultery. The prospective 'murderers' are all gentile, as are the would-be adulterers who must also learn a lesson through suffering.[27] Thus a plague visits the entire household of the Egyptian ruler who desired Sarah (Gen. 12), while at Gerar Yahweh imposes general sterility on all the female members of the palace (Gen. 20).

Why do the patriarchs fear for their lives in a territory where they seek livelihood and refuge from hunger? Perhaps the oddest explanation of the bizarre husbandly behavior, provided by the man himself, is Abraham's insistence on a lack of 'fear of God' (Gen. 20.11) at Gerar. The claim, in fact, is belied by the behavior of both

24. David J.A. Clines, 'The Ancestor in Danger: But Not the Same Danger', in *idem, What Does Eve Do to Help? And Other Readerly Questions to the Old Testament* (JSOTSup, 94; Sheffield: JSOT Press, 1990), pp. 67-84 (70), offers a salutary reminder, perhaps, of the complex issues at stake in each of the narratives. Irmtraud Fischer, *Die Erzeltern Israels: Feministisch-thelogische Studien zu Genesis 12–36* (Berlin: W. de Gruyter, 1994), *passim*, highlights the issue of pregnancy and progeny, as does Naomi Steinberg, *Kinship and Marriage in Genesis: A Household Economics Perspective* (Minneapolis: Fortress Press, 1993), *passim*. Fischer dates these narratives to the early monarchy since they show Yahweh intervening in favor of women rather than making promises to the primal ancestors; Fischer also maintains that the texts aspire to achieve a balance through shifting Yahweh's favor from matriarchs to patriarchs. For a different, folkloristic analysis, see Susan Niditch, 'The Three Wife–Sister Tales of Genesis', in *idem, Underdogs and Tricksters: A Prelude to Biblical Folklore* (San Francisco: Harper & Row, 1987), pp. 23-69, with an emphasis on difference and similarities. She reads all three as reflections of concerns regarding identity, exogamy and endogamy (p. 66). See also Ilona N. Rashkow, 'Intertextuality, Transference and the Reader in/of Genesis 12 and 20', in Danna N. Fewell (ed.), *Reading between Texts: Intertextuality and the Hebrew Bible* (Louisville, KY: Westminster/John Knox Press, 1992), pp. 57-73. On the question of one or thrice-told tale, see already David L. Petersen, 'A Thrice-Told Tale: Genre, Theme, and Motif in Genesis 12, 20, 26', *BibRes* 18 (1973), pp. 30-43.

25. Cf. the implantation of Esther in the palace in order, eventually, to avert a similar if more general danger, discussed in my *Dinah's Daughters*, Chapter 3.

26. As Exum remarks, 'it is not the woman's honor so much as the husband's property rights that are at stake' ('Who's Afraid of "the Endangered Ancestress"?', in *idem, Fragmented Women*, pp. 148-69 [quote on p. 151]).

27. Obviously ignoring the common wisdom which casts 'women from abroad' or 'strange women' as dangerous (*ANET*, III, p. 420; Beyerlin, *Near Eastern Religious Texts*, p. 48; Prov. 7.5-23).

the Egyptian monarch and the pious Abimelech of Gerar, who immediately comply with the divine order to release the Hebrew woman. Perhaps, then, Abraham's fear was rooted in the unpredictability of living as a stranger in a strange land. His apprehension of mortal danger, captured in the presumed 'primitiveness' of the local gentiles, poses a neat parallel to Exodus 1, where this state of mind (i.e. 'fear of God') characterizes actions that usher life rather than inflict death. The actors in Exodus are all women who live, generations after Abraham and Isaac, in the same Egypt that had given refuge to needy ancestors but that also produces a murderous monarch who aspires to curtail Israelite rate of procreation. The midwives ordered to execute all the Hebrew male babies, pious women and full of fear of God, defy the Pharaoh and save these infants. In each instance, piety, or its presumed absence, result in two drastically different patterns of behavior, one subversive of criminal authorities (Exod. 1), the other anxious to conform to the local male culture (Gen. 12). The bearers of piety in Exodus 1 are women; in Genesis 12, 20 and 26 the impious one are invariably gentile males although, ultimately, the rulers display greater piety than their fearful foreign subject.

Genesis 20, which appears to constitute the centerpiece of the brother–sister narrative triplet, weaves a web of curious but instructive contrasts. The story contains a death threat for potential adultery (20.3), balanced by the possibility of murder (20.11), both transgressions of basic Decalogue precepts and both modulating male relations. Then there is a matriarch blessed with promised procreation whose potential of life-giving is neatly juxtaposed with the sterility which strikes the womenfolk of her husband's host. The imagery captures two basic poles of female life span. In biblical perceptions of women and of family, wealth stems from the procreation of legitimate children. No greater disaster than barrenness can befall a woman. With a 'dead' womb, the wife stands to lose her status and, consequently, undermine the family's standing. Fecundity and sexual reproduction are inseparable. A third contrast in these tales balances penury with wealth. The protagonists, invariably a penniless couple, arrive in a land of plenty, only to leave from there richly endowed. An intimate link is forged in all these tales between maternity and money, as between murder and adultery. A hint, but merely a hint, of a systematic distortion of all dominant male values hangs over the plots.

Because the tricky situations in Genesis 12 and 20 are happily resolved, the issue of killing is obfuscated. Only the third 'sister–brother' tale (Gen. 26), featuring Rebecca and Isaac at Gerar, drives home the moral dimension not only of adultery but also of killing, by linking the two through a royal edict that threatens death to potential killers (of Isaac) and takers (of Rebecca) (26.11). A cynical observer might conclude that dying for the sake of one's wife is hardly an option that the venerable patriarchs wished to entertain. Underlying these three tales, however, is a perception of the inherent danger of femininity that can engender uncontrolled emotions by becoming an unwitting if not an unwilling arbiter of killing and of living.[28]

---

28. On the position of women in Genesis, see Ita Sheres, *Dinah's Rebellion: A Biblical Parable for Our Time* (New York: Crossroad, 1990), pp. 22-37.

Such indeed is the 'rationale' that dictated the harsh words which the Mesopotamian judges addressed to Nin-dada, whose husband had been murdered by three men (above). Based evidently on little more than the woman's silence, the 'prosecution' conjured a vision of adultery aggravated by murder. Seen otherwise, the Mesopotamian proceedings demonstrate the extraordinarily fragile legal position of wives. Whether present or absent from the scene of the murder, the wife was held responsible for the fate of her husband as though she had the ability to give life and to confer death.

The Mesopotamian case provides the kind of scenario which Abraham and Isaac had endeavored to dodge by passing off their wives as their sisters. Perhaps the ruse also shielded Rebecca and Sarah from accusations such as those which Nin-dada had to face after the death of her husband. But the Genesis tales stop short of linking actual adultery with virtual murder, although they hint at the destructive power that radiates from the desired body of a woman. It is difficult, in addition, to gauge the 'normativity' of this type of situation. Genesis 12, 20 and 26 delineate circumstances in which the ancestors are strangers in a strange land full, potentially, of gentile murderers and adulterers. The narratives further project major transgressions (i.e. murder and adultery) of basic Decalogue precepts in conjunction with improbable figures such as a barren matriarch and a mother whose bodies are designated as insurers of the most important covenant between Yahweh and the patriarchs.[29]

To guide readers back 'home' to Canaan and to 'normalcy', away from adultery and from gentiles but back to the basics of murder, Genesis 27 places maternal sentiments at the center of an exploration of familial feuds. Reverting to the pattern of Abel–Cain fraternal rivalry, the roots of the saga of Esau and Jacob are anchored already in their rivalry in the maternal womb and reinforced by the maternal predilection.[30] As the text succinctly states, 'Isaac loved Esau because he ate of his game; and Rebecca loved Jacob' (25.28). Love is a powerful emotion. In biblical texts, where emotions are rarely displayed, the rare references to 'love' born by women challenges the paternal principle that it often reinforces. Rebecca is placed in an equivocal position of a woman acting in place of man, a mother standing in for a father. She engineers a transfer of primogeniture privileges from her elder to her favorite younger son. She upsets Isaac's plan but carries out what had already been predestined (25.23). Depriving Esau of maternal protection, Rebecca recognizes what had been played out in her womb.

29. Perhaps, then, Exum is right in regarding the tales as male fantasy (*Fragmented Women*, Chapter 5, *passim*).

30. Although the motif of fraternal strife is hardly novel both in the Bible and in other ancient cultures, the prominent role of the mother seems exceptional. In only one other tale does the mother interfere in sibling's strife (Bath Sheba in 1 Kgs 2). In general, on 'brother language', see Michael Fishbane, *Text and Texture: Close Readings of Selected Biblical Texts* (New York: Schocken Books, 1979), p. 51, especially on the centrality of the fraternal element; cf. J.P. Fokkelman, *Narrative Art in Genesis: Specimens of Stylistic and Structural Analysis* (The Biblical Seminar, 12; Sheffield: JSOT Press, 2nd edn, 1991 [1st edn = Assen: Van Gorcum, 1975]), pp. 106-107, and Niditch, *Underdogs*, Chapters 3 and 4.

Problems arise when the dispossessed son plans murder in revenge. With healthy maternal instincts, recalling Abraham's lively sense of self preservation, Rebecca divines the murderous scheme (Gen. 27.41). She designs a clever and timely escape in an ingenious combination of need (to prevent murder) and desire (to see her son married to a woman of her choice and of her lineage). Potential murder leads to potential marriage via the words and acts of the mother. Esau goes his way, selecting an additional bride whose lineage is carefully calculated to defy paternal desires and directives (28.8-9).

Faced with loss of life, real or potential, male and female characters in Genesis behave according to gender patterns. Abraham and Isaac care for themselves. Rebecca, who, like other matriarchs, seems at first destined to sterile repetition, must find confirmation of the fact that the union with the masculine principle, embodied in a man and in the covenant, is characterized by fissures. Conceiving sons, she must either face their loss or make a choice. Appropriating Jacob, she reduces him to the status of his mother's son. Isaac is ready to conform to patterns of primogeniture. The parental couple seems a fiction, a way of masking the inevitable disjunction between paternal and maternal role. The dissociation crystallizes through potential sibling murder. A similar dilemma is unfolded by a 'wise woman' of Tekoah whose 'tale' of death and revenge likewise highlights a discourse of filiation ruptured by untimely demise (2 Sam. 14). Rebecca's worst fear focuses on the loss of both her sons, the one she had already disowned and the one who faces death (Gen. 27.45). The text reveals the repercussions of murder within the family and, specifically, the power of maternal bereavement.

Jacob's flight, precisely because it aborts the application of the law of homicide, highlights the limits of its applicability. The Sixth Word categorically proscribes murder; but when Yahweh does not act as an arbiter, human agents must apply a general law to specific cases, whether applicable or not. Because in biblical chronology the establishment of the cities of refuge is not an option that Genesis protagonists can entertain, Jacob must leave home.[31] The would-be murderer (Esau) stays. Here is a curious reversal of the 'original' sibling clash which depicts a murderer (Cain) doomed to perpetual exile. Maternal presence (Rebecca) or absence (Eve) activates different dynamics of familial relations. Instituting herself as her sons' arbiter of fate and as the mediator of the ancestral succession, Rebecca has to protect her choice, because the dilemma of a potential sibling murder is primarily a mother matter.

The issue is graphically delineated in the parable of 2 Sam. 14.5-17, where a mother already hit by the killing of one son by another must confront the demand of the family to execute the killer; the tragic possibility of childlessness and the prospect of the complete extinction of the paternal line.[32] In both cases mothers must find a way out of the predicament. While Rebecca designates a place of refuge for her beloved son (the house of her own brother), as well as a purpose for this

---

31.   Whether or not these tales are also the product of Deuteronomistic redaction is irrelevant here.

32.   See below, Chapter 6 §7.

involuntary 'exile' from home (securing an appropriate bride), the seemingly destitute widow in 2 Samuel 14 must appeal to the king. And although she is as 'wise'
as Rebecca, she cannot rely on her own wit nor on her relatives, but at least she can
and does speak in the name of divinely ordained principles which override familial
forms of justice (14.16).[33]

To judge by the Genesis tales, the most common form of killing at the dawn of
ancestral history was the murder, actual or potential, of one brother by another, or
by other brothers. The Sixth Word and its legal exegesis (Exod. 21.12-13; Num. 35)
do not contemplate such specificity nor the role of family members in the aftermath, with the exception of the so-called 'blood avenger'. The narratives fill the
gap. Considering an actual or potential sibling murder, the stories explore the context of murder and how a mother's love shapes the relations of sons. While there are
no corpses in either Genesis 12, 20 or 26 (the 'sister–wife' narratives) or in Genesis
27 (the Rebecca–Esau–Jacob narrative), murder remains a powerful metaphor that
motivates the actions of the protagonists. It also serves to delineate the position that
women *qua* wives and *qua* mothers occupy in familial settings. Sarah's and
Rebecca's passivity in the wife–sister stories is crucial in shielding their husbands.
Curiously, it is this very aspect of silence, thus implied collaboration, that seals the
fate of Nin-dada. Such wifely quiescence emerges in striking opposition to the
loquacity and actions of mothers when the fate of beloved sons hangs in balance.
Women, then, are inexorably embroiled in the dangers facing males, particularly
when a threat of death is hanging over husbands and sons, and with it the possibility of losing the all-important maternal status or entering the precarious position of
widows. They must survive through, for and because of men.

4. *Is the Killing of Women Justifiable? Murder as Metaphorical Rape*

If circumvention of murder of males by means of adultery or maternal connivance
appealed to the narrators of Genesis, scenes of female demise hardly intrude the
sequence of Israelite 'ancient' history. The single exception merits discussion but
the identity of the female victim obfuscates the legal and moral aspects of the case.
She is a Midianite who meets violent death at the hands of an Israelite priest in the
heart of the Israelite camp (Num. 25). Her story vividly illustrates the depth of patriarchal apprehensions (in Gen. 12, 20, 26) of dying an untimely death in a foreign
land. In her instance, however, the murder is carried out and the murderer is handsomely rewarded. The case of Cozbi also provides a useful if subversive example
of the application of the rules regarding murder.

As it stands, the story of Cozbi, unfolded in Numbers 25, appears to have neither
rhyme nor reason.[34] It ushers into public view, seemingly out of nowhere, a respect-

---

33. Cf. 2 Sam. 20.19, where the term ה נחלת is used by a woman who confronts Joab who had
intended to storm her city for giving asylum to a usurper, and who ends up by handing the head of
this usurper to Joab in order to save her city.

34. For much of what follows, see my 'The Rape of Cozbi', where I also deal with the structure of the chapter (two distinct and originally different tales juxtaposed to create a tissue of transgressions dependent on association with foreign women).

able mixed couple, each a member of a highly distinguished clan, only to kill them in the privacy of their own bedroom. Their murder apparently puts a stop to a general plague and thus saves Israel from complete extinction, just as Rebecca's initiatives ensure the continuance of the covenant. The killer, a self-appointed avenger of blood of men unrelated to him, becomes an arbiter of communal fate and a subject of divine praise rather than censure. The episode is juxtaposed with an equally curious record of sex and apostasy in which an untold number of Israelite males copulate *en masse* with Moabite women after sharing in the women's sacrifices to their god (Num. 25.1-5).

In the redacted version of this unfortunate couple's record, the male partner, a 'man of the sons of Israel' (איש ישראל, Num. 25.6, 8) identified as Zimri the Shimonite (25.14), approaches the tabernacle in the company of a 'Midianite woman' (25.6) identified as Cozbi, daughter of a Midianite nobleman (25.15). The narrative does not inform why they came there in the first place. According to the present sequence of Numbers 25, their appearance was singularly ill-timed. Moses and all the Israelites had been mourning the rash Israelite males whose indulgence in sex and apostasy had ushered a divinely ordained plague. Amid so much lamentation it would appear, at first, that the presence of yet another mixed couple was hardly likely to exacerbate the already gloomy picture. Yet, it does, and it leads to a deliberate chase and to the wielding of a deadly weapon with the clear intention of killing.

Phineas the priest, the identified killer of the couple, uses a lance to pierce Cozbi through the belly (Num. 25.8). No precise location is given in the case of Zimri's body. Nor is the selection of the female bodily part to be penetrated an accident. By choosing the locus of pregnancy, Phineas' action highlights the danger of an association between gentile women and Israelite men, simultaneously delegitimizing the connection. The choice of the womb as the organ of death also casts the murder as a metaphorical rape, carefully calculated to recall the 'rape' of Dinah (Gen. 34).[35] But the killing of a Shimonite (Zimri) by a Levite (Phineas) subverts the pattern of deadly fraternal collaboration. In a reversed re-enactment of Genesis 34, Phineas 'reclaims' the honor of Israel by killing not only the foreign partner of an Israelite, as do Dinah's brothers, but also the Israelite spouse.

The murder of Cozbi occurs at a moment when the great promise to the ancestors was at risk of unfulfillment. The plague had decimated numerous people. At the conclusion of Cozbi's tale, the Israelites are enjoined to avenge the Midianites because she was their 'daughter' and 'sister' (Num. 25.17-18). This time the plan of a general massacre which, in Gen. 34, Levi and Shimon carried out without

---

35. Num. 25 can, in this light, read as a deliberate counterpart of Judg. 19 in which rape precedes and leads to murder. On rapes as a political gesture, see Don C. Benjamin and Victor H. Matthews, *Social World of Ancient Israel 1250–587 BCE* (Peabody, MA: Hendrickson, 1993), pp. 180-86. On Dinah's 'rape', see my *Dinah's Daughters*, Chapter 1. Note, however, the textual problems of this pericope, with its deliberate play on קבה (Num. 25.7) and קיבה (Num. 25.8), the former a hapax designating, perhaps, the woman's quarter (Ludwig Koehler and Walter Baumgartner, *A Bilingual Dictionary of the Hebrew and Aramaic Old Testament* [Leiden: E.J. Brill, 1998]), the second referring to the stomach (cf. Deut. 18.3).

paternal sanction, receives the stamp of divine authority. Cozbi's death is, para-doxically, to be avenged by more killing but not of her murderer, rather of her own people.[36] The plan of punishment further leads to more pairing of Israelite males with non-Israelite females, this time in order to save Israelites from extinction (Num. 31).

The episodes commemorated in Numbers 25 begin with a public display of pas-sion and idolatry and continue with a violation of privacy as Phineas invades Cozbi and Zimri's intimate space. Yet, the legal grounds for the murder are problematic. Other than castigating intermarriage in general (Exod. 34; Deut. 7), the Pentateuch fails to provide ordinances in case intermarriage does take place; nor are there 'laws' that condone the ruthless elimination of a mixed couple or that legitimize their relationship. To resolve textual tensions between what is stated and what may be implied, Cozbi must die.

Ultimately, narratives of this type problematize murder by casting a gentile woman as a legitimate victim of a priestly 'sacrifice'. Because the 'history' of Genesis–Numbers is basically about survival, the life and death of the female spe-cies is inserted within a narratological genealogy that leads from a universal 'crea-tion' to 'national recreation'. Read within a larger context of killing, from Cain's murder of Abel (Gen. 4) to the allocation of cities of refuge to unintentional mur-derers (Num. 35), the narratives that ponder the role of women in preventing murder or as victims illuminate the complexity of the underlying ideology of the Sixth Word. With its endorsement of the deliberate killing of a gentile woman allied with a noble Israelite, Numbers 25 highlights a crucial exception to the rules of intentional murder. The murder of a woman, especially a foreign one, is easily excused by elevating her elimination into a level of 'national' salvation. Distilling the religious experience of the community and its relationship with its God, the narratives that deal with hypothetical murders of men and the actual murder of a woman probe gender distinctions. Ambiguity lingers. In Genesis adultery and murder remain intimations of sin. What happens when they do happen? In Numbers 25 a gentile woman is killed and her murderer, as well as his descendants, are glorified. What if a gentile woman is a killer?

5. *A Deuteronomic Anatomy of Murder*

In the Exodus account of the Decalogue, detailed preparations for theophany alert participants and readers to the great moment of law-giving. In the Deuteronomic recapturing of these same events (Deut. 5), the redactor(s) elected to preface the same charter with a list of asylum cities for unintentional murderers (4.41-43).[37]

36. Susan Niditch, 'War, Women and Defilement in Numbers 31', *Semeia* 61 (1993), pp. 39-57. Cf. Mieke Bal, 'Scared to Death: Metaphor, Theory and the Adventure of Scholarship', in David Jasper and Mark Ledbetter (eds.), *In Good Company: Essays in Honor of Robert Detweiler* (Atlanta: Scholars Press, 1994), on the studious avoidance of referring to rape.

37. Brueggemann, *Deuteronomy*, p. 59, suggests that this otherwise perplexing addendum intended to protect people from neighborly violence and with breaking a cycle of violence (p. 197, on Deut. 19.1-13).

The information appears, at first, misplaced. It suggests, however, that redactional strategies viewed procedures relating to the matter of murder as prime regulators of manhood. Yet, the very essence of murder subverts one of Yahweh's prime promises to Israel: longevity (4.40). Intimately linked with this ideology of law-keeping and longevity, already expressed in the Commandment of the Sabbath, are safeguards which ensure life for an unintentional killer.[38]

Both Deut. 19.1-13 and Josh. 20.1-9, two complementary pericopes that deal with the aftermath of a killing, set in place a structure to regulate relations between the avenger of blood and the killer, as well as between the killer and the community of the asylum city.[39] Deuteronomy 19.5 invokes a bucolic, all-male setting turned sour as a man wielding an axe to cut trees hits, accidentally, another man. Premature death results. The action itself seems both innocuous and routine. 'Realistic' as this lively illustration of a casuistic law may appear, not a single narrative of killing lends 'concrete' imagery to this type of unintentional killing among men. While in Deuteronomy 19 the asylum city acts as a barrier between a hot-headed avenger of blood and an unintentional killer, in Joshua 20 the same asylum space becomes a scene of judgment. The Joshua pericope provides a precise procedure to mediate between asylum seekers who plead their case, and the elders of the cities of refuge who must establish whether the person is indeed innocent of a willful murder. Judged sinless, the elders then proceed to protect the man from the avenger of blood until the killer can return home.

Like Num. 35.25, but unlike Deuteronomy 19, Josh. 20.6 allocates a specific period for the sojourn of a killer in a city of asylum (the lifetime of the great priest), emphasizing the temporality of the shelter. Only Deut. 19.11-12, however, deals with the fate of a man deemed guilty of an attempt to abuse the laws of asylum. Its dictum is theologically rather than legally driven, demonstrating concern over the shedding of 'innocent blood' in general, but without an emphasis on a concomitant pollution of the land.[40] Like Numbers 35, Deuteronomy 19 echoes the basic ideology of blood-for-blood as set out in Gen. 9.5-6:

---

38. Note also the curious juxtaposition of the ritual of the 'slain heifer' (Deut. 21.1-9) meant to atone for an unsolved and irresolvable murder with the rules relating to the treatment of a 'beautiful captive' (21.10-14).

39. Robert R. Wilson, 'Enforcing the Covenant: The Mechanisms of Judicial Authority in Early Israel', in Herbert B. Huffmon, F.A. Spina and A.R.W. Green (eds.), *The Quest for the Kingdom of God: Studies in Honor of George E. Mendenhall* (Winona Lake, IN: Eisenbrauns, 1983), pp. 59-75; and *idem*, 'Israel's Judicial System in the Pre-Exilic Period', *JQR* 74 (1983), pp. 229-48; cf. Herbert Niehr, 'Grundzüge der Forschung zur Gerichtsorganisation Israels', *BZ* 31 (1987), pp. 206-27.

40. Pressler, *View*, p. 199. Cf. Stulman, 'Sex and Familial Crimes', pp. 53-54, on Deut. 19.1-13 as law formulated to protect unintentional killers and not primarily to appoint the state as an avenger of the offense. He also argues that the Deuteronomic text serves as an intermediate stage between ancient laws that did not differentiate intention and the priestly transformation of homicide into a sacral crime by monitoring the blood avenger. This, however, is also indicated in Num. 35. The dates of the two pericopes on murder are unclear, but Deut. 19, with its reference to the three cities and an additional three, may have antedated Num. 35 which knows of six total.

For your lifeblood I will surely require a reckoning. Of every beast I will require it and of man. Of every man's brother I will require the life of a man. Whoever sheds the blood of man, by man shall his blood be shed. For God made man (אדם) in his own image. (RSV)

God emerges as the blood avenger *par excellence*. What, then, of the law of mortal avengers?[41] To judge by the harsh Genesis words just quoted, divine involvement is limited to the unjust killing of males. Neither the Sixth Word, nor its legal amplifications, in either Numbers 35 or Deuteronomy 19, suggest that God is similarly active in the case of an untimely and violent death of a woman. Whether or not a woman may join the crowds of asylum seekers, if she happens to kill intentionally or unintentionally, is also not entertained. The possibility of designating a woman as a blood avenger can be easily ruled out. Yet, the rules do not deny that the spilt blood of a woman calls for a suitable revenge.

Generalizing the specific circumstances that Deuteronomy 19 depicts, Joshua 20 suggests that the 'history' of each case is a prime factor in determining whether death had been premeditated or accidental. This is why each asylum seeker must account for his presence at the gate of the asylum city, and this is why the elders play such an instrumental role in the aftermath of the killing. Criminal law, in either Numbers 35 or Deuteronomy 19, fails to delve into the 'historical' context of a murder (vs. killing). Why would one hate another to the extent of contemplating and executing a murder? This is precisely what narratives do as they probe the past in order to trace specific actions and behaviors that lead to crime. Even then, however, the question of discerning intent from accident remains problematic, because a person suspected of an intentional murder is not subjected to an ordeal, unlike a woman suspected of adultery (Num. 5).[42] Intention must, therefore, be determined on the basis of prior intercourse between the two parties, the would-be murderer and the would-be victim. This is why the elders of each city of asylum must serve as a board of inquiry, as well as jury and judges.

Perhaps the most remarkable contribution of Deuteronomy to the legal anatomy of 'murder' is its deliberate intrusion into a domicile, rather than into an open and all-male space, and into marital relations, rather than an all-male network. Deuteronomy 22.13-21, known as 'the case of the slandered bride', nicely illustrates both the application of legal procedures to instances that can lead to judicial execution, and what Roland Barth so aptly calls 'murder by language'.[43] Its weapon is the

41. Bernard S. Jackson, 'Reflections on Biblical Criminal Law', *JJS* 18 (1973), pp. 8-38, regards God as the one who inflicts the punishment in Gen. 9 (pp. 24-25).

42. Rodd, *Glimpses*, p. 106.

43. See Roland Barthes, *The Pleasure of the Text* (trans. Richard Miller; New York: Hill & Wang, 1975), who regards the term as synonymous with gossip. See also below, Chapter 7. Cf. Victor H. Matthews, 'Honor and Shame in Gender-Related Legal Situations in the Hebrew Bible' in Matthews, Levinson and Frymer-Kensky (eds.), *Gender and Law*, pp. 97-112 (108-12), who views these as cases of malicious speech designed to evoke a reaction of public condemnation in order to degrade the object of the slander, and, in the same volume, Tikva Frymer-Kensky, 'Virginity in the Bible', pp. 79-96 (and esp. pp. 93-95), on the value of virginity. On this pericope see also Chapters 3 §3 and 7 §5.

tongue. The object of assault and accusation is the female hymen and, ultimately, the life or death of the wife. The pericope envisions the following: a man marries a woman; a man repudiates a woman; a man charges a woman with infidelity prior to the marriage.[44] Matters move from the marital bed back to the wife's parental home. The father (and mother) set out to protect family's reputation. A fight ensues over the chronology of daughter's sexual history. An offended father and seemingly injured husband face each other in public. The integrity of the female hymen becomes a subject of slander in a potentially deadly male interaction.

For the Deuteronomist, the absolute principle of undivided allegiance privileges the husband. The issue of the wholesome female body is the focal point at which two coordinates of space and time converge. Its symbolic value refers back to the critical problems of adultery, genealogy and, in a finite form, to the very relations between Yahweh and Israel. If found guilty of a fractured hymen, the communal killing of the woman at the gate of her father's home determines the most important boundary of all, that between 'before' and 'after'. Death of this type signals both an ending (of 'adultery' and of life) and a return (of the problem itself). It is precisely the recurrent nature of this situation that makes the Deuteronomic 'murder by language' a generic model.

Verbal aggression, as the one embedded in the battle over the basic tenets of idealized womanhood, illustrates the agonistic culture that marks the ideology of manhood. The battlefield is the body of the daughter/wife. A relatively peaceful resolution can find the husband guilty of unfounded accusation. A deadly resolution can find the woman guilty. If this happens, she faces execution by communal stoning. No room is allowed for doubt or for refuge. The legal sphere constructed in Deuteronomy accommodates men motivated to murdering wives by language, and undeterred by publicity. The rules extrapolate constraints of female conformity and hint at domestic spaces populated by female fears.[45]

There is no narrative of murder by slander; but the very existence of the law, and its authorization of public execution, shows how public opinions determine the moral worthiness of males by that of their wives and daughters. A shade of suspicion on the moral and bodily integrity of the female body is sufficient to induce the loss of the family's good name in the community. What Deut. 22.13-21 also suggests is that a man who cannot guard his daughter's modesty after betrothing her spreads the damage from one household to another and from one man (father) to another (husband), thus undermining both manhood and neighborhood. Blame and shame go hand in hand. The image of the cuckolded husband has haunted pages of European literature. But in Deuteronomy it does not generate laughter. Rather, suspicions of wifely pre-marital sex engender a smear campaign, marital rupture, male rivalry (rather than unity) and possible death for the woman. In this logic of

---

44. The precise meaning of עלילת דברים is unclear. For discussion see Pressler, *View*, p. 23.

45. Cf. the Roman ideology of manhood, discussed in David Wray, *Catullus and the Poetics of Roman Manhood* (Cambridge: Cambridge University Press, 2001), *passim*, and Maud W. Gleason, *Making Men: Sophists and Self-Representation in Ancient Rome* (Princeton, NJ: Princeton University Press, 1995), *passim*.

manhood, female sexual excess is a symptom of general moral and ethical weakness and of male impotence.[46] Only death can put a stop to it.

6. *Killing for Lust? The Female Body as Motivation of Murder*

In the book of Genesis, sister–wife tales (Gen. 12, 20, 26) that feature husbandly ruses in partnership with wifely compliance hint at potential double transgression of two Commandments, the Sixth and the Seventh. This implied association between adultery and murder, always potent, becomes a 'reality' in the well-known story of David and Bath Sheba (2 Sam. 11), which begins with adultery and continues with murder, two criminal preludes to a succession sequence marked by sex and violence.[47] Casting men in the role of messengers of death and of executioners, these Dtr narratives advance an encoded message that subtly shifts the blame from the shoulders of men to those of women.[48]

A one-night-stand involving a beautiful married woman and a lusty (married) king culminates in the death of the cuckold husband and the reunion of the sexual partners.[49] From the start of the Dtr presentation, the tale bathes in oddities and implied criticism. The narrator presents Bath Sheba bathing on a roof, but passes no comment on this matronly occupation with hygiene.[50] She spends a night with a man other than her husband. Whether she was a willing or unwilling participant, the text does not disclose. Female emotions are left outside the scope of the narrated events. By minimizing the encounter between Bath Sheba and David to a process devoid of sentiment besides pure lust, the text testifies to possible collusion while, simultaneously, stressing the initiative of the king.

---

46. Cf. Ben Sira 26, fulminating on 'bad' and 'good' women and on wives, with Warren C. Trenchard, *Ben Sira's View of Women: A Literary Analysis* (Chico, CA: Scholars Press, 1982); see also Claudia V. Camp, 'Understanding a Patriarchy: Women in Second-Century Jerusalem through the Eyes of Ben Sira', in Amy-Jill Levine (ed.), *'Women like This': New Perspectives on Jewish Women in the Greco-Roman World* (Atlanta: Scholars Press, 1991), pp. 1-39.

47. J.-P. Fokkelman, *Narrative Art and Poetry in the Books of Samuel: A Full Interpretation Based on Stylistic and Structural Analysis* (Studia Semitica Neerlandica, 20, 23, 27, 31; 4 vols.; Assen: Van Gorcum, 1981–93), I, p. 99 and *passim*; Regina M. Schwartz, 'Adultery in the House of David: The Metanarrative of Biblical Scholarship and the Narratives of the Bible', *Semeia* 54 (1991), pp. 35-55, focuses on the twin themes of sexuality and politics, and on adultery and rape as ruptures of social norms relating to the exchange of women. See below, Chapter 7 §6.

48. Exum, *Fragmented Women*, p. 193.

49. In addition to the bibliography cited below, Chapter 7, see Moshe Garsiel, 'The Story of David and Bath Sheba: A Different Approach', *CBQ* 55 (1993), pp. 244-62; George G. Nicol, 'David, Abigail and Bathsheba, Nabal and Uriah: Transformations within a Triangle', *SJOT* 12 (1998), pp. 130-45; and Thomas Naumann, 'David als exemplarischer Konig: Der Fall Urijas (2 Sam. 11) vor dem Hintergrund altorientalischer Erzahltradition', in Albert de Pury and Thomas Römer (eds.), *Die Sogenannte Thronfolgegeschichte Davids* (Freiburg: Universitätsverlag, 2000), pp. 136-67.

50. David M. Gunn, 'Bathsheba Goes Bathing in Hollywood: Words, Images and Social Locations', *Semeia* 74 (1996), pp. 75-101.

By one reading, Bath Sheba seems the direct opposite of the icon of wifely chastity as embodied, for example, in the Roman Lucretia.[51] There is no vision of a matron surrounded by maids, nor of one engaged in weaving. Unlike Lucretia, Bath Sheba does not entertain an honored male guest at her husband's home and in his absence, nor does Uriah's wife have to confront a guest-turned-intruder who threatens rape or public shaming. The biblical narrative does not provide a character judgment of Bath Sheba. It merely states that her resultant pregnancy prompted the 'lover' to recall the husband from the battlefield in what appears to be a vain attempt to correct ascription of paternity. Problems arise when the third member of the proverbial triangle refuses to play by the rules of the king. He stays put at the gate of the palace which had witnessed the passage of his wife from domestic to royal bedchamber. Failing blandishments, the 'lover' sends the husband to certain death in the same war from which he had previously recalled him. The husband reassumes soldier's garb. He dies in a siege of a city. Wifely mourning follows. Bath Sheba joins the harem. A son is born.

Such is the elegant if gory solution to the problem of pregnancy resulting from adultery. A history of murder is, nearly, fully disclosed. The story operates along gender life-cycle which are both distinct and overlapping. A female life-cycle highlights the movements of Bath Sheba as she goes through distinct stages, a wife, a mistress, a widow and a wife again. Yet, she is never seen in the seclusion of her own home. Another, a male life-cycle, accompanies Uriah from the battlefield to the gate of the peaceful palace and back to the walls of a beleaguered enemy's city. A third male life-cycle David encroaching on the domain of other men as he appropriates their wives and abuses his royal authority to get rid of the husbands. Sex and death are not far apart.

Legally speaking, there is no murder, as such, in the sense of Deuteronomic legal purview. David confronts Uriah with words and not with weapons. The identity of the Ammonite who killed Uriah is neither made known nor is it material. But the intent to kill is unmistakable, substantiated in writing and in the king's own hand. Because the 'killer' is a king and because murder as prescribed in either Deuteronomy 19 or Numbers 35 had not occurred, Uriah's death cannot be resolved through ordinary legal procedures. Like Abel's death, the issue calls for divine arbitration. The scenario of murder is further complicated by the ethnic identity of the murdered. Uriah is a gentile, a Hittite. Yet, his self-appointed avenger of blood is none other than Yahweh, through Nathan the prophet. Strikingly different is the case of Cozbi, another gentile who elects of her own accord to join the Israelites, whose murderer, Phineas the priest, is extolled by Yahweh (Num. 25). Should we infer, then, that the blood of a gentile woman married to an Israelite man is of lesser value than that of a gentile man allied with an Israelite woman?

Ambiguity lingers. *Cui bono*? Who stood to gain from Uriah's premature death? For Bath Sheba the demise of Uriah paves the way to become a wife of a king; for David, Uriah's removal engineers the permanent annexation of a desirable woman

---

51. Livy, *The Early History of Rome* 1.57-59, with my comments in *Dinah's Daughters*.

with proven reproduction capability. Love, which remains curiously invisible and inaudible throughout, may have also played a role. By prophetic reckoning, however, the affair raises serious issues that touch on morality and law. The king already has other wives in the harem; Uriah has only one. The king has children; Uriah has none. As Bath Sheba is transported from home to palace, the potential inherent in her body maps a territory of a murder motivated by greed and lust alone. To unravel the muddied threads of a murderous adultery Yahweh sends a prophet. As operators of intelligibility, both prophet and God must harmonize 'law' and 'reality' in order to ensure justice where there is no recourse to law.

In the prophetic recasting of the events, Nathan cleverly changes the identity of the protagonists in order to highlight the repercussions of unbridled greed and to make the king his own judge and the blood avenger. The prophet turns Bath Sheba into a dumb animal which is slaughtered by a greedy rich protagonist. Who, then, is the real victim of the 'murder'? The animal which is butchered to death to cater to an already satiated palate, or its owner who is left destitute? The wife who becomes a widow, and hence potentially a marginal member of society, or the husband who faces a tough choice between conceding paternity not of his seed or facing near-certain death in war? Narrative and prophetic parable highlight a male dilemma but also convey the vulnerability of women whose husbands are absent, and of 'daughters' whose 'fathers' are without means.

The prophetic discourse of 2 Samuel 12 does not provide a readily available punishment suitable to the crime. The 'law' of murder does not deal with murder induced by the pen, especially when the victim dies in the course of fighting Israel's enemy, and when the 'murderer' is Yahweh's chosen king. Nathan must devise a specific penalty for David. For Bath Sheba Yahweh reserves a punishment of double bereavement, generated by the untimely deaths of her first husband and of her firstborn. Even here, the text does not allow mothers to vent their emotions. As the child lies sick it is the father, not the mother, who is seen in anguish and remorse (2 Sam. 12.15-23). But the child dies. The king 'consoles' the mother by reproducing another child. A happy end ensues. The adulterer, although doomed by prophecy to witness 'war' in his own family, nevertheless survives to a grand old age and to see this child becoming a king. Bath Sheba is destined to become the queen mother. Does murder, then, pay?

Juxtaposed with the tale of Cozbi, the story of Bath Sheba and David generates contradictory propositions. The shedding of human blood, any human blood, Israelite or gentile, if induced by evil intention, pollutes Yahweh's ideology of justice. The killing of women, if gentile, has the ability to exonerate the whole of Israel. The killer of Cozbi gains Yahweh's lasting favor, extended from himself to his progeny. The killer of Uriah becomes the object of prophetic wrath and of divinely inspired penalties. Cozbi brings calamity. Bath Sheba's beauty brings death to her husband. The murder of Cozbi effectively puts a stop to a process of procreation that threatens covenantal concepts of the right lineage; the killing of Uriah secures David's throne.

Cozbi, although named, remains faceless. Israelite women whose body provokes violent reactions are invariably endowed with beauty. Thus Bath Sheba and thus

Sarah and Rebecca.[52] To show that female beauty is not only a dubious asset but downright dangerous, beautiful women who are married to Israelite males are made to experience humiliation and trauma prior to becoming 'full' members of the community by discharging maternity. The birth of Solomon is inscribed in tragedy. That of Isaac comes only after Sarah must witness the successful copulation of her own maid with her husband. Both cases call for the active intervention of Yahweh, who must alter a fragile domestic balance as well as the state of the womb. Delivery and dying are paired in a close and deliberate sequence.

True to prediction, the birth of Solomon and the capture of the Ammonite capital by David's army, both events that signal David's singular success in the fields of love and war, usher a second cycle of sex and violence. Repetition is the essence of the narrative.[53] Thus the thrice-told brother–sister tales of Genesis, and thus the stories of the princess Tamar and the wise woman of Tekoah, each further elucidating the scope and repercussions of transgressing the Sixth Word.

7. *Metaphors of Murder: The Rape of Tamar*

Seemingly scripted according to Deuteronomic precepts, the tale of Tamar, David's daughter, and her half-brother Amnon (2 Sam. 13), features a (metaphorical) murder, a blood avenger and a bloody revenge.[54] The motive is pure greed. The catalyst is the beautiful body of a woman. The murder weapon is male desire. The result is not the elimination of husband by lover but of one brother by another. The real victim is the compromised virgin. The outline is familiar: enamored of Tamar and pretending illness, Amnon asks David to send her to nurse him. In his room he rapes her against her expressed will. With equally blinding passion he sends her away, refusing to marry her (2 Sam. 13).[55] Tamar turns to a pubic demonstration of grief in a vain search of a remedy to an affliction which the law fails to address or redress.

---

52. Frymer-Kensky, *In the Wake of the Goddesses*, p. 206, argues that the Bible does not consider female beauty a power stratagem of women but rather a subversive asset that makes them objects of attention and 'victims of the superior male'. Perhaps Abraham's stratagem would not have worked without Sarah's collusion, and Bath Sheba's silence can be read as an indictment.

53. On David's own rise to power along a path punctuated by rape and murder, see Kenneth A. Stone, *Sex, Honor and Power in the Deuteronomistic History: A Narratological and Anthropological Analysis* (JSOTSup, 234; Sheffield: Sheffield Academic Press, 1996), pp. 85-95. On 2 Sam. 12 in the context of the so-called 'court history', see Stuart Lasine, 'Melodrama as Parable: The Story of the Poor Man's Ewe-Lamb and the Unmasking of David's Topsy-Turvy Emotions', *HAR* 8 (1984), pp. 101-24.

54. Mark Gray, 'Amnon: A Chip Off the Old Block? Rhetorical Strategy in 2 Samuel 13.7-15: The Rape of Tamar and the Humiliation of the Poor', *JSOT* 77 (1998), pp. 39-54. On parallels with Gen. 39 (Amnon as Potiphar's wife), see Zakovitch, 'Through the Looking Glass', p. 145.

55. See the important comments of E. Levine 'On Exodus 21,10', p. 145, on the meaning of the much-discussed verb ענה, which does not signify rape in legal or narrative diction but rather an act of opening, namely a crucial step in a sequence that entails grabbing or overpowering, laying and opening.

Just as the earth cannot revive the murdered dead, there is no reconstitution of a fractured hymen.[56] Tamar's blood brother, Absalom, aggravates her plight by imposing isolation and silence. Tamar is consigned to oblivion but the memory of the affront lingers.[57] She has recourse neither to law nor to paternal protection or reprisal because fathers never side with daughters against sons. Like Jacob's bafflement when confronted with Dinah's 'rape', David remains reticent. Yet, by law and by custom, a rape calls for revenge, precisely like murder. Tamar must entrust her vindication to an avenger of rape. The natural choice, Absalom, deems her initiative of advertising the disaster a singularly inappropriate means of settling scores. Rape becomes a matter of manhood, to be pursued by men and according to criteria of masculinity. Tamar's excision breeds ambiguity. It reinforces the disastrous consequences of a rape within the family but it also highlights the expendability of women from subsequent proceedings. Males can settle their disagreements in a dozen ways and reach satisfactory conclusion. Females who either intervene actively in brawls among men (Deut. 25.11-12) or cause a deadly male clash must bear the serious consequences of 'intrusion'.

Absalom contrives the killing of Amnon. His avenging of Tamar's rape goes beyond the scope of the crime. Deuteronomy 22.28-29 (cf. Exod. 22.15-16) prescribes negotiations, rather than retaliation in the case of a rape of an unbetrothed woman.[58] This is indeed what Tamar had proposed to Amnon (2 Sam. 13.12-13). His refusal is not anticipated by the rules and consequently no procedure exists to deal with reluctant rapists. The laws relating to seduction envision a father who does not want to condone the alliance of his daughter with her rapist. But Deut. 22.25, 27, which relate to rape of a betrothed woman 'in the field' where resistance would be futile, call for the execution of the rapist. In remarkably strong language, the law insists that 'this case (i.e. rape of a betrothed woman in the field) is like that of a man attacking and *murdering* (רצחו נפש) his neighbor' (Deut. 22.26 RSV, my emphasis).

In Deuteronomistic ideology, then, a rape of an affianced woman by a man to whom she is not engaged is tantamount to murder. This choice of terminology, strikingly echoing the Sixth Word, seems hardly a coincidence. It is this perception of rape as murder that enables Absalom to advance his own interpretation of Tamar's rape in terms of a (metaphorical) murder. Amnon then must die. The murder is planned and the murdered man is caught in an 'ambush' at a moment of drunken weakness. Legally speaking, this is a murder in the full and exact sense of both Numbers 35 and Deuteronomy 19. Yet, the murderer, like David in Uriah's case, had not wielded a deadly instrument himself but entrusted the execution to others.

56. This is why an elaborate purification ritual is required when a corpse, clearly slain, is discovered 'in the soil' (Deut. 21). The dead is mute; the soil cannot resuscitate humans.

57. Fokkelien van Dijk-Hemmes, 'Tamar and the Limits of Patriarchy: Between Rape and Seduction (2 Samuel 13 and Genesis 38)', in Bal (ed.), *Anti-Covenant*, pp. 135-56 (137). Cf. 2 Sam. 20.3, which condemns David's concubines to a 'lifelong widowhood' because of his deliberate abstinence from sex with them.

58. See Pressler, *View of Women*, pp. 35-41.

No reference is made to any of the appointed cities of refuge. Had they existed, none would do because Absalom does not fit the categories of inadvertent killer. He leaves Jerusalem to seek asylum in a non-Israelite territory (Geshur) (2 Sam. 13.37). His departure marks the apex of a development that causes the royal palace to lose, in a remarkably rapid succession, no less than two princes and one princess. Amnon is dead, there is no healing of Tamar's lost virginity, but reconciliation with Absalom can still be effected. It is achieved, somewhat surprisingly, through a wholly unrelated 'wise woman' who, coached by Joab, concocts a story dominated by the theme of sibling murder and its familial repercussions. Instead of presenting a predictable parable of rape and revenge, the 'wise woman' of Tekoah introduces a 'contemporary' version of the Cain–Abel/Esau–Jacob tales.

As the Tekoan woman unfolds her 'story', recent events are recast. A brother still kills a brother, as Absalom had killed Amnon, but the killing is done without stated motivation and by accident (2 Sam. 14). There is no grieving or silent father but rather a grieving and loquacious 'mother'. Neither lust nor rape accounts for the sibling murderous encounter in Tekoah. The woman's family, however, interprets the death as murder and demands the blood of the killer, just as the law prescribes. The mother appeals to the king.

The Tekoan narrative, presented as pure invention, focuses on a real dilemma which juxtaposes 'law' and morality with maternity. Her exposé highlights an absurdity inherent in the consistency with which narratives elevate maternity as women's chief desire and attribute. What can a woman do when the 'law' becomes a weapon of depriving mothers of this very same asset by subjecting their sons to a male communal justice that espouses retaliation of killing with killing?

Law of land vs. law of mothers? Continuous membership in the covenant community depends on procreation. The law of 'murder' calls for revenge. The woman's discourse drives home the illogical extension of the rules of blood-avenging based on, perhaps, an erroneous interpretation of both facts and rules. Her text conveys parental plight in such circumstances through maternal rather than paternal imagery. It suggests sympathy with the problems that women face when faced with the inexorable demands of reproduction and of nurturing infants to healthy adolescent. Thus the Tekoan woman is a widow, unlike David. And thus, in the case of the great woman of Shunem, the husband becomes immaterial, although aging and unlikely to produce a replacement for his dead son (2 Kgs 4).

Such stories highlight a yawning gap between legal theories and 'realities'. Deuteronomistic narratives of rape provide their own exegesis of the rules, as well as a commentary on similar tales. The narrative of Tamar, Amnon and Absalom provides a significant variation of Genesis 34. There is an 'ancestral' law which empowers brothers to avenge in blood the 'murder' of a sister. But there are also rules that deal with murders as such. Only the king can mediate between two such dissenting courses of action. In her plea the 'widow' asks David to override familial jurisdiction. She thus admits her own inability to act as an arbiter in a matter that so closely concerns her welfare and the survival of her family. Tamar's vocal appeal to immediate remedy remains unanswered. When the widow secures royal help, she states that 'the word of my lord the king is like the angel of God to discern good and evil' (2 Sam. 17 RSV). The words must have sounded ripe with irony.

To drive home the problematic aspects of actual and metaphorical murders, the women in 2 Samuel 13–14 change role—instead of a raped sister the Tekoan parable casts a widowed mother as the protagonist. It indicates that childless widows are marginalized into a limbo of social non-existence just as Tamar's neutralization effectively removes her from society as well as from the list of potential successors to the throne. Between the silenced Tamar (2 Sam. 13.20) and the loquacious (if not blabbering) woman of Tekoa, the matter of murder raises questions about the meaning of killing and the application of law to specific cases (or vice versa). Both Numbers 35 and Deuteronomy 19 attempt to put a stop to cycles of revenge prompted by murder. The parable of the widow's sons provides a striking illustration of the general repercussions of familial revenge. But in her story the murderer appears without guile, hardly relevant to an Amnon or an Absalom.

How 'wise', then, is the 'wise woman'?[59] The case that she unfolds seems to relate directly to the ideology of Deuteronomy 19 that allows unintentional murderers to seek asylum. But there are no cities of refuge in the tale, although Absalom seeks refuge as though entitled to asylum. The picture presented by the wise woman muddles the laws. It contains a family that seeks revenge where no revenge ought to be sought; it makes no reference to laws dealing with murder; and it appeals for justice to a king who had authorized murder and rape. Yet, unlike the 'wise' counselor of Amnon who had proposed feigning malady in order to entice Tamar to his abode (2 Sam. 13.3), female wisdom appears an instrument of harmony rather than of rape and discord.

At the heart of the thrice-repeated theme of 'murder' of 2 Samuel 13–14 (that of Tamar, of Amnon, and of the woman's son) lies an inner-biblical interpretation which extends the meaning of the Sixth Word to a deadly confrontation between the sexes through rape. Like a 'straightforward' murder between males, metaphorical murder of woman's virginity leads to bloodshed. Following the vicissitudes of the royal family, the narratives chart the disruptive patterns of relationships among its members as they revolve around murder. Taken in conjunction, the stories incorporated in 2 Samuel 11–14 provide an anatomy of provocation and of murder as these revolve around women's sexuality. Seen otherwise, the stories outline the incalculable and often murderous repercussions of the exposure, willing or unwilling, of the female's body to male lustful gaze. Stressing domestic policies, the narratives of Bath Sheba, Tamar and the Tekoan woman compliment and supplement the gaps in the legal material dealing with murder. They highlight the shortcomings of legal systems that aspire to protect the interests of males often at the expense of women.

59. See Brenner, *The Israelite Woman*, pp. 33-45, on wise women in general, and especially pp. 34-35, on the 'wise' woman as a manipulator; Claudia V. Camp, 'The Wise Women of 2 Samuel: A Role Model for Early Israel', *CBQ* 43 (1981), pp. 14-29; Patricia K. Willey, 'The Importunate Woman of Tekoa and How She Got her Way', in Fewell (ed.), *Reading between Texts*, pp. 115-31, especially on the layers of irony in the tale and on the parable as a parody of Nathan's presentation. See also Larry L. Lyke, *King David with the Wise Woman of Tekoa: The Resonance of Tradition in Parabolic Narrative* (JSOTSup, 255; Sheffield: Sheffield Academic Press, 1997), *passim*.

8. *The Killing Female of the Species*

No history of murder, or of monarchy for that matter, can be complete without the figure of Queen Jezebel. Wife of Ahab of Israel, Jezebel is neither an Israelite nor, at that point, a mother.[60] A foreign princess, like Cozbi, she breaks the biblical boundaries of gender, religion and law.[61] Few narratives in the Dtr History convey the problematization of premeditation as does the 'murder' of Naboth 'by' Jezebel and Ahab (1 Kgs 21).[62] Fewer still penetrate the mindset of a murder so acutely and minutely as this story does.

The account presents an intricate tableau which begins with an encounter between two males over property, and continues with the unexpected intervention of the wife of one of these men in an attempt to 'save' her husband. Superficially, then, the trio of 1 Kings 21 resembles the situation suggested in Deut. 25.11-12, in which a wife of one intervenes in a brawl involving her husband and another man, by pulling ('mutilating'?) the opponent's genitals. Deemed willful and unwarranted, the Deuteronomic law calls for the punishment of the extravagantly interfering wife by decreeing the amputation of her 'offending' hand.[63] But in 1 Kings 21 one man actually dies. The other male party and his wife, in this instance a king and a queen, are accused of murder in what amounts to an odd extension of *lex talionis*. In fact, neither husband nor wife had been present at the scene of the murder. The 'murdered' man had been executed by his own congregation and according to an acceptable judicial process.

The scenario in 1 Kings 21 is peculiar. At its heart is not a Deuteronomic 25 triangle of two contesting males and one interfering woman, but a wife, husband and Yahweh's prophet (Jezebel, Ahab, Elijah), cast, respectively, as a couple of 'killers' and one blood avenger.[64] Jezebel's relationship with these two men is diametrically opposed. She is a concerned wife and an implacable enemy at one and the same time.[65] The rivalry between Jezebel and Elijah is not only deadly. It threatens to become interminable, thus reflecting, oddly enough, the concerns of

60. The text pointedly ignores her motherhood, although she is certainly Ahazia's mother (1 Kgs 22.53 refers to Ahazia's following his 'mother's way' with regards to idolatry), and probably also Athalia's mother. Whether or not she is also Jehoram's mother is less clear (2 Kgs 3.2). The texts are problematic at this point: there is a contradiction between 2 Kgs 1.17 and 3.1, and a doublet in 1 Kgs 22.52-54 and 2 Kgs 3.1-3.

61. On the hostility of the Dtr theologians to Jezebel and her religious affiliation, see Phyllis Trible, 'Exegesis for Storytellers and Other Strangers', *JBL* 114 (1995), pp. 3-19 (4) and *passim*.

62. What follows is partly based on my 'From Jezebel to Esther'.

63. Although loss of virility, a potential consequence of Deut. 25.11-12, may have been tantamount to 'death' as well; see Miriam Y. Shrager, 'A Unique Biblical Law', *Dor le Dor* 15 (1987), pp. 190-94.

64. On the violent relations between Jezebel and Elijah, see Phyllis Trible, 'The Odd Couple: Elijah and Jezebel', in Christina Buchmann and Celina Spiegel (eds.), *Out of the Garden: Women Writes on the Bible* (New York: Fawcett Columbine, 1994), pp. 166-79.

65. No sooner is she installed in the palace Jezebel embarks on a wholesale elimination of Yahweh's prophets (1 Kgs 18.4). The zealousness with which she carried out this task may be ascribed to her position as a priestess of the Baal (Brenner, *The Israelite Woman*, pp. 24-25).

Numbers 35, Deuteronomy 4 and 19 regarding the endless cycle of disorder that murder generates.

When Ahab covets Naboth's vineyard, Jezebel sets the stage for a trial which involves, as the text insists, false witnessing. But for those not in the knowing, the execution of Naboth in Jezreel appears to have been conducted according to a correct legal protocol. It may be, therefore, asked why does Elijah accuse Ahab and Jezebel of murder (1 Kgs 21.19) rather than, say, of killing or of master-minding a murderous plot. Here the answer must be that there was no penalty by law for plotting a murder, or for a murderous intention, as Nathan's castigation of David's 'killing' of Uriah plainly shows. The Tenth Commandment prohibits the coveting of other men's property. It does not assign a penalty and does not directly contemplate murder as a result of covetousness. This is, in fact, what the narrative of Jezebel does when it presents a covetous king and a murderous wife.

The tale of Naboth's execution highlights the essence of murder not as an act of killing *per se* but as a carefully calculated plot in which innocence battles guilt in vain; and writing, speaking and gossip prove as deadly as the wielding of a blunt instrument. There is no resolution in this case, either by allowing the 'murderer' to seek refuge or by bringing him/her to judgment. According to Num. 35.6-21 and Deut. 19.11-13, a man who kills another deviously, and through deceit, is not entitled to the privilege of asylum. In the royal setting of the affair of Naboth's vineyard, kings and queens are evidently not subject to such judicial processes. Nor is there a relative to act as a blood avenger, other than Yahweh and Yahweh's prophet.

Killing, then, like fighting, is an action that entails direct confrontation between attacker and attacked. Causing someone to die is a different matter. Behind the word distinction lays two distinct discourses, one that places the idea of execution at the center, even at the expense of a description of the means employed; and another that focuses on the social practice of death through what is left unsaid.[66] Naboth represents a culture that resists alienation. Ahab and Jezebel are products of a culture in which kings consolidate landed properties, and questions of ownership are determined not by individuals but by royal will. At the heart of the confrontation between the royal couple and their subject is, therefore, an issue of arbitration. Who has the authority to determine land affiliation? Kings whose throne had been sanctified by Yahweh, or private citizens who abide by a law that may no longer carry relevance? 1 Kings 21 sides, through Yahweh and Elijah, with the latter. It further suggests that while Ahab might have abandoned his desire for the neighbor's vineyard, the intervention of Jezebel, a foreign women and a queen, undermined this potential resolution.

One striking feature of the grand narrative that covers the reign of Ahab and Jezebel is its appropriation of the terminology of the Sixth Commandment. Variations of the root 'murder' (רצח) appear twice (1 Kgs 21.19; 2 Kgs 6.32), and on each occasion the term seems singularly out of place. In the encounter between

---

66. Cf. the Athenian discourse of death by design, discussed in Loraux, *The Experiences of Teresias*, p. 101.

Elijah and Ahab over the royal appropriation of private property, Naboth's death is described as a 'murder' (1 Kgs 21.19). But Elijah, and perhaps Ahab, know that this is no 'murder' in the plain legal sense of the word. Kings or queens need not resort to bloodying their hands. The punishment to which Ahab and Jezebel are subjected as a result of Naboth's death makes, therefore, little sense. In the annals of the Israelite monarchy a similarly motivated murder, notably that of Uriah by David (2 Sam. 11, above), is cast as an act of impiety against God.[67] And although the prophet Nathan pronounces a twofold punishment, neither David himself nor his dynasty are destined to immediate extinction as Ahab's is. Furthermore, Ahab meets his death through a ruse (1 Kgs 22.29-38), precisely the same type of stratagem that his wife had employed to secure his happiness.

What the redactional recording of the Jezreel proceedings leaves in no doubt is its 'reading' of the entire affair as blasphemy. In this interpretative fashion the tale is launched with Naboth's (futile) appeal to Yahweh, continues with Ahab's (fruitfully) relinquishing resolution to the queen, and ends with a fatal accusation of blasphemy. In the process, Jezebel, already cast as the persecutor of Yahweh's prophets, is characterized as a prosecutor of Yahweh's innocent worshipper.[68] The transformation of a private grievance (between Naboth and Ahab), through Jezebel, into a public charge is the dominant motivation of the false swearing and of murder.

In royal annals when kings commit crimes they are reprimanded by prophets, retract, and are duly punished by Yahweh. But when the motivating agent of the 'crime' is a woman, a foreigner and a queen, the story gains a twist. The king appears to lose his will and to recede into inactivity. The queen adopts royal tactics and commands the scene. Like David, Jezebel entrusts visibility to trusted brokers. Unlike David, she is never confronted directly either by Yahweh or by a prophet. Such a privileged mode of communication is solely the right of impious kings.

To justify in full the elimination of a legitimate monarch (Ahab) and of his legitimate queen, the Dtr narrative(s) compound(s) Jezebel's guilt with other charges, namely sorcery and prostitution (2 Kgs 9.22b), that appear to have little relevance to her role in the Naboth's affair. The allegation is puzzling. The queen could have hardly been either a whore or a witch, at least in the crude sense of these terms. But they fit a discourse which aims at tracing royal violations of the covenant through transgressions of the Decalogue precepts, namely of impiety and of apostasy. By pitting traditional covenantal ideology of property possession against royal rights

---

67. See Marsha White, 'Naboth's Vineyard and Jehu's Coup: The Legitimation of a Dynastic Extermination', *VT* 44 (1994), pp. 68-69, on parallels between the two tales and the casting of see 1 Kings in the mold of the David–Bath Sheba–Uriah tale.

68. Hence the seemingly irrelevant appeal of Naboth to Yahweh in the initial encounter between him and Ahab because no law prohibited the alienation of ancestral property. However, as Terence E. Fretheim, *First and Second Kings* (Westminster Bible Companion; Louisville, KY: Westminster/John Knox Press, 1st edn, 1999), p. 118, emphasizes, priestly law (Lev. 25.23) insists that all the land belonged to Yahweh and, by implication, cannot be sold for any reason or in perpetuity.

of appropriation, the narrative of Naboth's vineyard traces the complex web of emotions, actions and reactions that result in murder.

What makes the tale of Jezebel, Ahab and Naboth particularly useful for the promotion of the morality advocated in the Decalogue is its association with other Commandments and other legal texts. Deuteronomy 5.17-21 lists murder, adultery, theft, false testimony and covetousness as major moral transgressions. The order of the Naboth affair (with the exception of adultery) is precisely the opposite: it begins with covetousness, proceeds with false testimony and murder, and ends in theft. A similarly deliberate inversion, highlighting the inseparable nature of all these crimes, appears also at the conclusion of the Deuteronomy 19 pericope on asylum (19.2-13). Deuteronomy 19.14-21 deals with unlawful removal of landmarks in order to acquire property and with false testimony, ostensibly issues which do not belong together.[69] Yet, the juxtaposition of insidious murder, illegal acquisition of neighborly property and lying in a court of law (the sum total of Deut. 19), makes perfect sense in light of the Naboth affair. It is clear that the redactor had envisaged all three crimes as a possibly inseparable chain, exactly as 1 Kings 21 shows.

By juxtaposing several transgressions, the story of Jezebel and Naboth illustrates the scope and various configurations of murder. In this reading, murder cannot and does not stand as an independent category. Its perpetration depends on a chain of events that encompasses unacceptable modes of human morality. A similarly chilly message is reflected in the narrative's intimations of sins of writing and of speaking.[70] 1 Kings 21 traces the winding path that leads from a verbal quarrel between men to an execution motivated by false witnesses and orchestrated by a woman. Its imageries mirror the legal proceedings of Deut. 22.13-21 that deal with accusations of sexual immorality. There, too, a false accusation, anchored in desiring gain through attributing guilt, has the potential of inducing a judicial 'murder'. Yet, Deuteronomy 22 makes hatred a prime motivation; 1 Kings 21 implies spousal love as the moving spirit. Both emotions become potentially destructive if aired in public, either by the tongue or through the pen.

9. *Postscript: The Female Body as a Deadly Weapon*

By way of conclusion I would like to discuss, briefly, two episodes that have engaged many feminist critics, namely Jael's killing of Sisera (Judg. 4–5) and the rape (and murder) of a woman of Bethlehem (Judg. 19–21).[71] Each narrative presents a different view of killing by attempting to harmonize 'law' and 'reality' as

---

69. These are also issues which have taxed modern ingenuity, as diagrammed in Campbell and O'Brien, *Unfolding*, p. 73.

70. See above, Chapter 3 §3 and 6 §5.

71. See Mieke Bal, *Murder and Difference. Gender, Genre and Scholarship on Sisera's Death* (trans. Matthew Gumpert; Bloomington: Indiana University Press, 1988), for a detailed study of Judg. 4–5, and above Chapter 3 §5. There is no lack of female killers in the book of Judges, including women who kill in war, such as the woman of Thebez (Judg. 9.50-57) and Deborah, and women who deal death, like Delilah; see Mieke Bal, *Lethal Love: Feminist Literary Readings of Biblical Love Stories* (Indiana: Indiana University Press, 1987).

they converge on women, both in and outside the domicile. The story of Jael (Judg. 4–5) focuses on a single encounter between a Kenite(?) woman and a Canaanite general. It forms the conclusion to a war of liberation between the Israelites, led by Deborah and Barak, and the Canaanites, led by Sisera.

When Sisera, after an unexpected Canaanite defeat, reaches Jael's tent, he believes that he has reached an 'asylum', a safe haven which provides protection and sustenance. When, satiated, he relapses into sleep, she kills him with a peg, an impromptu instrument of death taken from the very structure that has sheltered them both. In Deborah's victory paean (Judg. 5) the killing becomes a singular achievement, just like the killing of Cozbi by Phineas (Num. 25). Yet, by a different and less complimentary reading, Jael was in breach of hospitality. Her motions, directly imitative of male patterns of behavior, highlight both the general obligatory nature of hospitality, as well as the exclusion of women from this specific mode of male host–guest communication. At one level, then, Sisera simply failed to interpret Jael's rhetoric correctly—while inviting him to her domain she did not have, nor intended to abide by the rules set by males. At another level, Jael emerges as a traitor to the friendship between Canaanites and Kenites, a bond forged by males and only implicitly extending to their womenfolk.

Jael lures Sisera to safety because he sees that she is alone, and hence believes her to be weak and defenseless.[72] His estimate, based on stereotypical male perceptions of innate female feebleness, is proven deadly wrong. Judges 4 and 5, a discourse dominated by the female voice, exposes situations in which women act like men and win praise like men for exceptional feats, from other women.[73] Because the presentations in both Judges 4 and Judges 5 are unusual in biblical records, none of the protagonists behaves in a predictable or legally prescribed manner. The story suggests that women can kill just like men, namely by wielding deadly weapons, stealthily and intentionally. But the tales stop short of providing a match of might, pitting a woman against a man in a direct physical confrontation, because the Hebrew Bible knows of only a few specific ways in which males and females interact in an unmediated manner (Josh. 2; Judg. 1; 1 Sam. 1; 25). The killing of males by females is not one of these.

If read in the light of the Sixth Word, Jael's killing of an enemy in war hardly relates to the moral message of the Commandment. But she had not been an enemy of Sisera, nor had her clan participated in the war. Neither was she an Israelite(?), nor a representative of people who had been oppressed by the Canaanites.[74] Was

72.   Judg. 4 also betrays uneasiness about women warriors, a trait absent from Debora's poem; see Gale A. Yee, 'By the Hand of a Woman: The Metaphor of the Woman Warrior in Judges 4', *Semeia* 61 (1993), pp. 99-132; Ellen J. van Wolde, 'Ya'el in Judges 4', *ZAW* 107 (1995), pp. 240-46; Susan Ackerman, *Warrior, Dancer, Seductress, Queen: Women in Judges and in Biblical Israel* (New York: Doubleday, 1998).

73.   For a discussion of the complex relationship between the two texts, see Heinz-Dieter Neef, 'Deboraerzahlung und Deboralied: Beobachtungen zum Verhaltnis von Jdc. IV und V', *VT* 44 (1994), pp. 47-59. On the 'meeting' of Jael and Sisera, see Yairah Amit, 'Judges 4: Its Contents and Form', *JSOT* 39 (1987), pp. 89-111.

74.   Nehama Aschkenasy, *Women at the Window: Biblical Tales of Oppression and Escape* (Detroit: Wayne State University Press, 1998), pp. 29-30, also links the tale of Jael with the

the death of Sisera, then, a 'first degree' murder or rather a killing in war where death is a routine? That Jael intended to kill Sisera from the moment she glimpsed his presence on her territory seems plausible, but Judg. 4.21 presents an odd order of events. First, she seizes a peg and a hammer, then she approaches Sisera quietly, lastly she crushes his temple with the peg. Only then the text divulges that Sisera had fallen asleep, and then he dies. It is interesting to note that Deborah's praise poem recasts the killing as an encounter between the doubly armed Jael (with milk and peg) and the mighty Sisera (once fortified with chariots and probably still carrying weapons), as though the two faced each other squarely and directly (Judg. 5.25-26).[75]

The killing of Sisera takes place in a context of war, just as the murder of Cozbi is embedded in a deadly plague. The two killers, a gentile woman and an Israelite priest, emerge as heroes who save the people from a national disaster and from oppression.[76] But under 'ordinary' circumstances of neither plague nor war, the violation of the rules of hospitality, and of man's exclusive right to his own living body and to the living body of his sexual mate, are perceived as a grievous threat to a fragile social order. To illustrate the repercussions of the fragmentation of basic ideologies of manhood, the book of Judges, although a recital of Israel's efforts to fight off foreign oppression, ends with a civil war.

Judges' closing chapters (19–21) question the meaning of murder as they probe the repercussions of an assault on ostensibly insignificant individuals within a context of hospitality. The narrative begins with a breach of domesticity of a nameless couple (he a 'Levite', she a 'concubine' from Bethlehem), continues with the couple's ostensible reconciliation and journey home, their vain search for hospitality in Benjaminite Gibeah, the rape of the female guest by a group of local men, her subsequent death, and the husband's call for revenge.[77] Yet, who, exactly, was

---

proverbial stereotype of the 'strange woman' of Prov. 7.6-27, which inspires males with dread, as well as with the unusual figure Deborah, a she-prophet who sits under a tree, away from home and from domestic constraints.

75. The poem is generally held to be much earlier than its prose counterpart. For the purpose of the present analysis the differences, especially regarding the reconstruction of intent and action, are crucial but not the date of each.

76. All feminist commentators have dwelt on the sexual connotations of the scene between Jael and Sisera. See, among others, Susan Niditch, 'Eroticism and Death in the Tale of Jael', in Day (ed.), *Gender and Difference in Ancient Israel*, pp. 43-57. This is, of course, an important aspect of the irony of the situation in which the wife of the host takes the limits of hospitality to its illogical conclusion.

77. For full analysis, see H.-W. Jüngling, *Richter 19: ein Plädoyer für das Königtum* (Rome: Biblical Institute Press, 1981), and Trible, *Texts of Terror*. See also Kaola Jones-Warsaw, 'Toward a Womanist Hermeneutic: A Reading of Judges 19–21', in Athalya Brenner (ed.), *A Feminist Companion to Judges* (The Feminist Companion to the Bible, 5, 2nd Series; Sheffield: Sheffield Academic Press, 1993), pp. 172-86, as well as Peggy Kamuf, 'Author of a Crime', and Mieke Bal, 'A Body of Writing: Judges 19', pp. 187-207 and pp. 208-30 respectively in the same volume. See too the other contributions to Brenner (ed.), *A Feminist Companion to Judges*. Critics have been puzzled by the choice of verb in Judg. 19.2, which implies that the woman 'went whoring'. Most resort to the reading of the LXX that makes her 'angry'. See also, Susan Niditch, 'The 'Sodomite' Theme in Judges 19–20: Family, Community and Disintegration', *CBQ* 44 (1982), pp. 365-76; and

responsible for the death of the woman? The unnamed rapists who repeatedly violated her body, or the Levite who carved it into twelve fragments when she failed to respond to his command to get up and get ready? The text never specifies the moment of her death, nor, for that matter, does it list the Benjaminite rapists among those who later perish in the civil war.

The archaeology of murder in Judges 19 is multilayered. Ostensibly, the main crime of the Benjaminite men is the rape of another man's woman. Their intent, however, had been to rape the man. Judged according to intention, the Benjaminites are guilty of first-degree murder. Judged according to the actual deed, the precise crime is problematic. As rapists of a betrothed woman, the Benjaminites deserve death, at least according to Deut. 22.25, although the precise location of her gang rape is not given. But the woman had been raped with the tacit approval of her husband, a fact that may appear to exonerate the rapists of the crime. The text advertises the Levite as the 'man (or husband) of the murdered woman' (איש האשה הנרצחה, Judg. 20.4), an unusual description which uses the terminology of the Sixth Word, and is all the more striking by its very rarity. Yet, murdering had not been the intent of the violence that the Benjaminites had inflicted on the woman.

By resorting to the Sixth Word to qualify the Benjaminite crime, the redactor of the story highlights a cycle of violence that begins with a verbal interchange between men over tenets of hospitality and ends in rape and murder. Both transactions underlie a metaphorical murder of hospitality. In the Levite's rendering of the events of the fateful night at Gibeah, the woman's body becomes a border zone exemplifying the double nature of the Benjaminites' transgression. They had violated the basic principles of hospitality by demanding that a host relinquish his guest to an uncertain fate, and they appropriated and abused the symbol of manhood and ordered society, namely man's privileged access to the body of his wife.

In his public recapturing of the trauma, the Levite informs the Israelite audience that the Benjaminites had intended to kill him and that they raped his concubine in a manner that resulted in death (Judg. 20.5). In his eyes, the real victim of the crime is himself and not the dead woman. He interprets his carving of her body as a symbol encapsulating the enormity of the Benjaminite 'abomination and wantonness' (זימה ונבלה, 20.6 RSV). His listeners accept his version. For them, the injuries inflicted on man's pride and property are serious enough to warrant a wholesale war against all the Benjaminites who display an astonishing solidarity by refusing to hand over the villains of Gibeah. Nevertheless, the scale of the planned vengeance appears well beyond the proportion of the crimes that the men of Gibeah had committed.

Nor is the civil war, for that matter, a foregone conclusion in spite of the ratio of power. The Israelites lose the first two rounds. They gain victory only after consulting Phineas the priest, seemingly the same Phineas of Numbers 25 who appears

Stuart Lasine, 'Guest and Host in Judges 19: Lot's Hospitality in an Inverted World', *JSOT* 29 (1984), pp. 37-59. On the rape as fiction invented in the Saul–David polemics, see Simcha S. Brooks, 'Was There a Concubine at Gibeah?', *Bulletin of the Anglo-Israel Archaeological Society* 15 (1996–97), pp. 31-40.

miraculously active. This astonishing choice of a priestly mediator with its sublime indifference to even literary chronology suggests that the redactor wanted to forge direct and evocative links between Israel's 'ancient' wilderness history, with its bloody vindication of sexual apostasy in Numbers 25, and its 'contemporary' vicissitudes. In both instances, unlawful sex erupts in a general catastrophe (plague in Num. 25, civil war and numerous casualties in Judg. 20). And in both, only a priest, Phineas to be exact, can save the situation.

Parallels abound. The murder of Cozbi the Midianite ushers a war with Midian which brings numerous Midianite virgins to the Israelite camp as brides of Israelite males (Num. 31.16-18). The murder of the woman of Bethlehem (= the Levite's 'concubine') results in a wholesale abduction of Gileadite and Shilonite virgins as brides of Benjaminite males (Judg. 21.11-12, 21-23). A 'happy' end indeed, at least for the surviving Israelites and Benjaminites. Both narratives also touch on issues of purity and pollution. Judges 20.13 qualifies the Benjaminite crimes as 'evil' to be eradicated, suggesting that the criminals pollute a 'buffer zone' and create an intolerable anomaly in the social and moral order. The perception is similar to the operational logic which had dictated the massacre of all the Midianites in Numbers 31, and of all the Shechemites in Genesis 34, retaliation. The woman of Bethlehem, like Cozbi, and unlike Dinah, was not a virgin. Both women were allied with a man and identified in terms of provenance and paternity on the one hand, and of domicile and 'marriage' on the other hand.

Judges 19–21 articulates dogmas regarding murder and marriage through an uncanny juxtaposition of physical-sexual violence that leads either to death and to marriage. The threat of death to the Levite leads to a murderous rape; the rape of the woman of Bethlehem ushers her demise; the civil war between Israel and Benjamin leads to enforced celibacy (in itself a form of death), but the siege of Yabesh-Gilead produces virgins for these Benjaminite 'celibates'; and the festival at Shiloh provides more virgin-wives. The prospect of life is balanced against the ubiquity of death through the acquisition of eligible female partners on the one hand, and the demise of potential child-bearers on the other hand.

In the double articulation of this singular past, the memory of the woman of Bethlehem had been effaced to give way to the living virgins of Shiloh. The souvenirs of the deadly night had to be erased through a civil war. In the redactional reconstitution of the 'original', the murderous rape becomes a catalyst of the appropriate relations between males. This is one reason why the precise identity of the protagonists, with the exception of Phineas, is not articulated.[78] It made no

---

78. Anonymity and specificity of names in biblical narratives is a problem. Adele Reinhartz, *Why Ask my Name? Anonymity and Identity in Biblical Narratives* (New York: Oxford University Press, 1998), claims that names carry meaning inherently, give unity to a single character who appears in several contexts, offer a simple way of referring to a specific person, and distinguish people from one another. See also the comments and criticism of G. Posner, 'Anonymity in Genesis: The Pattern of a Literary Technique', *Nahalah* 2 (2000), pp. 103-29. On anonymity in Judges as a metaphor for the dictum 'everyone doing what is right in his eyes', see Don M. Hudson, 'Living in a Land of Epithets: Anonymity in Judges 19–21', *JSOT* 62 (1994), pp. 49-66.

difference. What mattered was the woman's marital status and the manner in which her violated body came to represent the repercussions of the Benjaminites' covetousness of what was not rightfully theirs.

In the complex web of relationships that binds humans to God, human sexuality embodies unruly filaments and, hence, loci of transgressions that entail an irreversible fate. This discourse of murder, in both the 'histories' of Genesis–Numbers and of Joshua–2 Kings, is punctuated by harsh and unpredictable images that involve the killing of and by woman. Whether coined as victims or culprits, as 'sisters' averting the murder of 'brothers/husbands', as mothers preventing domestic violence, as murdered or murderous gentile wives, as daughters of Israelite aristocrats, or as Israelite wives of gentile mercenaries and of Levites—the tales surveyed here confirm, yet also confuse, stereotypical feminine attributes. For the women are activated, motivated or victimized by threat of murder, and the cumulative impact of their presence is a measure of the extent of the transgression committed.

In a way, then, the murders not committed in Genesis are perpetrated in the Dtr History, with Numbers 25 serving as a prelude of sorts. The narratives endow the prohibition of the Sixth Word, and the prescriptions of Numbers 35 and Deuteronomy 19, with 'concrete' meaning. They also problematize the attendant issues of murder precisely by focusing on the female body as a buffer zone: Is the blood of women as valuable as that of men? Is 'murder', as defined by 'law' and ethics, the exclusive killing of males by males? Deuteronomy 22.26 equates rape with murder, and the raped Dinah, Tamar and the woman of Bethlehem are suitably avenged through the killing of the culprits. But these are vindications of male honor. Women are left to languish or to die. There is no accounting for sanctified and for unsanctified death when it comes to women. The vocabulary of 'murder' of and by women coexists with that of sexuality and marriage.

Within the structures of power outlined in the Hebrew Bible, the extension of the meaning of murder through narratives also hints at subversion of 'normativity'. Because the Bible puts such a premium on men's lives, the marginality of women, in general, also reflects the fragility of the morphology of the body as a basis of gender and legal distinctions.[79] In the biblical cosmos, as directed by Yahweh, the energy that guides human affairs is often channeled through the feminine other. She serves as God's instrument when she is acted upon, and even when she acts or seems to act on her own terrain and for her own reasons.

When women control the plot and the activity of plotting, they manipulate male duplicities and illusions. In spite of their exclusion from the central arena of masculine public life, women have special access to powers in and beyond men's control, thus unsettling typical male assumptions. The same exclusion which relegates women to an interior space of their own, also equips them for deviousness and

79.   I am echoing here Butler, *Gender Trouble*, and various points raised by contributors in Caroline Walker Bynum, *Fragmentation and Redemption: Essays on Gender and the Human Body in Medieval Religion* (New York: Zone Books, 1991), *passim*, as well as Jane Gallop, *Thinking Through the Body* (New York: Columbia University Press, 1988).

gives them a talent, or rather a reputation, for weaving wiles. Women know when men are ignorant (Jezebel–Ahab; Rebecca–Isaac); they read where men misread (Jael–Sisera); and they communicate, verbally and physically, in ways that reflect the beliefs of men about their nature. Narratives involving the killing of and by women invite audiences to engage in fits of interpretation precisely because the invariably disastrous nature of the outcome illuminates how feminine configurations shape a mythic quest for manhood.

Chapter 7

Conjugality and Covenant
(Word Seven)

You shall not commit adultery. (Exod. 20.14; Deut. 5.18)

Rabbi Samuel ben Unya said in the name of Rab: [Prior to her marriage] a woman is like a shapeless lump (*golem*) who concludes a covenant only with him who transforms her into a [useful] vessel, as it is written: *For your maker is your husband (or: the one who deflowers you is the one who creates you), the Lord of Hosts is his name* (Isa. 54.5). (*b. Sanh.* 22b [Soncino—modified])

1. *Prelude: Whose Adultery is it Anyway?*

Accused of committing adultery with her step-son (Asqudun) in the absence of her husband, and dreading a river ordeal, the wife of Sin-iddinam defended herself at court by describing how she had been accosted by the young man at home.[1] According to her testimony Asqudun said to her: 'I want to wed you'. He further kissed her lips, touched her genitals, but 'his penis did not penetrate [her] sex'. Her reply to his sexual assault was: 'It is not possible that I should sin against Sin-iddinam!' She concluded her public assertion of innocence with the statement that 'in the house where I was I did not do that which I should not do to my lord'.

To what extent the defendant's past of prostitution, which included both father and son as clients, had been taken into account as evidence of moral standing is unclear. Nor is it clear whether Asqudun had tried the path of seduction more than once. What the woman's words reflect, however, is the perennial problem of adultery not outside the domicile but within the family and at home. Had the wife of Sin-iddinam consented to the proposed adultery and fallen pregnant, the issue of paternity would have posed insoluble problems. The case also highlights the vulnerability of women whose husbands happen to be away and whose isolation (and in this case the assumption of availability based on a certain past) is exploited by male relatives.[2]

---

1. For the text, see Kuhrt, *Ancient Near East*, I, p. 106, translating Dominique Charpin *et al.*, *Archives épistolaires de Mari* I/2 (Archives royales de Mari, 26; Paris: Editions Recherches sur les Civilisations, 1988), no. 488.

2. For an analysis of Neo-Babylonian adultery clauses in marriage contracts, see Roth, '"She Will Die by the Iron Dagger"', pp. 186-206. Cf. the penalty of public shaming and divorce, rather than death, meted out to wife discovered *in flagrante*, discussed in Greengus, 'A Textbook Case of

This much for Mesopotamian reality. In a proverbial biblical tale of intended 'adultery' (Gen. 39), the seducer, a gentile woman, is the wife of a distinguished member of the Egyptian Pharaonic administration; the object of seduction, a Hebrew male, is a good looking slave in her household. Despite distances of space and time(?), the tale of the wife of Potiphar and of Joseph presents striking similarities with the Mari document.[3] Both scenes of seduction take place at home and in the absence of a husbandly figure of authority. The dialogue between the two protagonists seems scripted on the basis of legalities. Like Asqudun, Potiphar's wife accosts Joseph with the words: 'sleep with me' (Gen. 39.7). And like the wife of Sin-iddinan, the desired partner refuses on the ground that

> With me (here) my master has had no concern regarding what is in the house. Everything that he has he had entrusted into my hands. No one is more elevated than myself in this house, nor has he held back anything from me but you, because you are his wife. How, then, can I commit so great an evil and sin against God? (Gen. 39.8-9)

Adultery emerges, at least in Mesopotamia and biblical Egypt, not so much as a mode of sexual behavior as an act of betraying trust among males.

Genesis 39 and the Mari trial reveal the seduced as a person in the power of the seducer. Because of her past, and especially her previous relations with Asqudun, the wife of Sin-iddinam appeared a natural object of conquest to her unscrupulous step-son. Because of his servile position, the wife of Potiphar regarded Joseph as a man susceptible to an illicit sexual liaison. The two seducers exploit the temporary removal of paternal/husbandly authority to advance their plans, and both are apparently unmoved by the virtuous words of their intended victims.

In the textual retelling, following the failed seduction and the husband's return, Potiphar's wife shifts the essence of the 'crime' that, in fact, had not taken place, from adultery to rape. This is precisely the stance that the wife of Sin-iddinan had taken in her trial for adultery. Here, in principle, the aggressor is invariably male. The female narrative of what transpired, in both Mari and in Egypt, further reflects the fragility of the woman's position in her own home, despite her status, and her vulnerability to possible accusations of having sex with slaves or with relatives of her husband. Underlying both accounts of adultery/rape is, perhaps, a latent power struggle between a younger, ambitious member of the household (son/slave) and a

---

Adultery', but the reading may be controversial. None of these cases deals with liaisons between free married women and bonded men. The implication is that such liaisons were considered a private offense and were dealt with in private.

3.   On the structure of the Joseph narrative, see Donald B. Redford, *A Study of the Biblical Story of Joseph, Genesis 37–50* (VTSup, 20; Leiden: E.J. Brill, 1970); George W. Coats, *From Canaan to Egypt: Structural and Theological Context for the Joseph Story* (Catholic Biblical Quarterly Monograph Series, 4; Washington: Catholic Biblical Association, 1976); Walter Brueggemann, *Genesis* (Interpretation; Atlanta: John Knox Press, 1982), pp. 288-380, with a visual summary on p. 297; and James L. Kugel, *In Potiphar's House: The Interpretive Life of Biblical Texts* (Cambridge, MA, Harvard University Press, 2nd edn, 1994 [1st edn = San Francisco: Harper & Row, 1990]).

woman who feels threatened by the implied favor of the husband and by the physical proximity of the favored male.[4]

Nowhere in the Pentateuch are there, in fact, legal provisions regarding sexual liaisons between free women and bonded men.[5] The omission is both understandable and astonishing. Understandable, because this kind of 'adultery' was a matter to be dealt with in private. Astonishing, because this type of relationship, at least between free males and bonded females, both Hebrew and gentile, features prominently in the Pentateuch.[6] Deuteronomy 22.13-29 is quite eloquent in its visualization of situations that betray actual or potential adultery, but refrains from referring to the identity or status of the adulterer. It may be asked, then, whether Genesis 39 deals with adultery, as defined in Pentateuchal law (below) and prohibited by the Seventh Word. What relationships are there between legal theories and narrative 'realities' when it comes to undesirable sexual intimacy between men and women? The episode that pits Hebrew (male) virtue with gentile (female) vice in Genesis 39 also raises crucial questions about the identity of the addressees of the Seventh Word, and about the nature of the 'crime'. Above all, what is the meaning of adultery for a covenant community that defines its relationship with God in terms of marriage?[7]

2. Adultery: The View of Leviticus

The Seventh Word provides neither a definition of the offence of 'adultery' nor a punishment, and not even a hint of circumstances, extenuating or otherwise.[8] Like other Commandments, it, too, assumes the familiarity of its audience with its ideology and meaning. Slightly more elaborate, Lev. 20.10 defines the 'actor' and the one acted upon, advocating death for both:

> If a man commits adultery with the wife of another man, the man who commits the adultery with his neighbor's wife will be put to death, both the adulterer and the adulteress. (Lev. 20.10)

What is curious about this Levitical condemnation of adultery is its use of the terminology of the Seventh Word as well as the harsh penalty meted to both

4.   Alice Bach, 'Breaking Free of the Biblical Frame-Up: Uncovering the Woman in Genesis 39', in Athalya Brenner (ed.), *A Feminist Companion to Genesis* (The Feminist Companion to the Bible, 2; Sheffield: Sheffield Academic Press, 1993), pp. 318-42 (320-32) (on Joseph's aspiration to power).

5.   Unlike multiple references to mixed marriages between free female Israelites and free gentile males. See my *Dinah's Daughters*, Chapter 1.

6.   Deut. 21.10-14 (rules regarding beautiful gentile captive), with Pressler, *View of Women*, pp. 8-15. Exod. 21.7-11 (on bonded Hebrew women), with E. Levine, 'On Exodus 21,10'. Phillips, *Ancient Israel's Criminal Law*, p. 121, suggests, 'neither the Book of the Covenant nor Deuteronomy were interested in sex *per se*' but only in guaranteed paternity.

7.   See, recently, Peggy L. Day, 'Adulterous Jerusalem's Imagined Demise: Death of a Metaphor in Ezekiel XVI', *VT* 50 (2000), pp. 285-309, and below.

8.   Rodd, *Glimpses*, p. 28. For an example exonerating a woman who claims that she had committed adultery under pressure, see *Middle Assyrian Laws* A 23 (the most recent edition is Claudio Saporetti, *The Middle Assyrian Laws* [Malibu: Undena Publications, 1984]).

adulterers. It further implies that the community, acting as a single body, has the power to execute the offending parties. Communal interest in such sins of sexuality is further in evidence through the insertion of this ban into a list of other sexual offenses, including sex between a man and a host of female relatives by blood and by marriage (Lev. 20.11-21).[9]

Adultery, then, or sex with the wife of another man, is an offense that must be regulated to ensure the sound foundations of the society envisioned in Leviticus. This social order calls also for clear distinctions between the Israelites and their gentile environment (Lev. 20.23), suggesting that the body of a woman belonging to another man, if invaded by another, engenders a communal pollution—as do gentiles, if mixed (in marriage/sex) with Israelites. Compliance with these 'laws' guarantees, then, not only familial and communal harmony but also an intimate and unbroken bond between land and men (20.22).

No narratives in Genesis–Numbers bear out the death penalty which Lev. 20.10 prescribes for adultery. The only narrative in which an 'adulteress' is nearly burnt alive (Gen. 38) suggests that sex between a man and his own daughter-in-law is, under certain circumstances, not a crime, in spite of Lev. 20.12. Stated otherwise, although Genesis 38 issues a threat of execution for adultery, or rather for a perceived adulteress, the verdict is not implemented.[10] Such discrepancies between 'law' and 'actuality' seem to indicate that the laws aspired primarily to define an ideal community rather than to prescribe specific penalties for specific 'crimes'. Regulations and threats were meant to deter rather than to deal with actual adultery.[11]

With its sole emphasis on male initiators of adultery, Lev. 20.10 appears to reinforce the common scholarly opinion regarding the exclusive male identity of the recipients of such strictures, including the Seventh Word itself. The double death penalty for both actor and acted upon parties seems, at first, an afterthought. Logic suggests that the law had initially set out to curb male overtures *vis-à-vis* wives of other males. At a later stage it was deemed 'prudent' to condemn both participants to death, regardless of consent or coercion. This 'extension' of the original indicates an awareness of women's potential not only to be acted upon but also to act as men do. The story of Genesis 39, albeit deliberately casting a foreign woman as a promoter of 'adultery', provides a striking illustration of this shift of the geography

9. Phillips, *Ancient Israel's Criminal Law*, pp. 121-29, provides a minute analysis of this 'coda' (Lev. 20), which he regards as a heavily edited priestly post-exilic extension of Deuteronomical regulations (below) which forms 'the first stage of the reinterpretation of the crime of adultery to include all unnatural sexual unions' (p. 125) that are punishable with excommunication. Phillips does not discuss, however, the precise circumstances under which the act of adultery is revealed (or concealed) (see below). See B.A. Levine, *Leviticus*, p. 255, for a diagram of prohibited relations.

10. Rodd, *Glimpses*, p. 25, with Henry McKeating, 'Sanctions against Adultery in Ancient Israelite Society, with Some Reflections on Methodology in the Study of Old Testament Ethics', *JSOT* 11 (1979), pp. 57-72.

11. Or, in Ska's words 'to convince and educate' rather than to repress crimes and settle conflicts, J.L. Ska, 'Biblical Law and the Origins of Democracy' (unpublished paper delivered at AAR 2001, text accessible on <www.biblicallaw.org>), p. 8.

of sex and gender. What the law omits are situations in which husbands initiate adultery between their wives and other men, precisely the circumstances delineated in Genesis 12, 20 and 26. Nor does Lev. 20.10 disclose how exposed adulterers were to be executed or who were the agents that had a hand in revealing the very existence of adultery. In Tamar's case (Gen. 38), someone in her neighborhood 'discovered' and reported the 'crime' to her father-in-law who, although quick to condemn her to death, also happened to be the unwitting partner of her 'adultery'.

A mere shade of suspicion of illicit sex, even without proven pregnancy, was sufficient to subject a wife to an ordeal initiated by her own husband (Num. 5). Ironically, the anthropology of adultery, by law at least, embraced attackers and attacked in a battlefield over manhood in which the body of a married woman was both penetrated and protected, at a cost to herself. Not surprisingly, underlying the regulations regarding adultery is a fear of misplaced paternity. Suspicions could have been nurtured by neighborly gossip, an insidious factor regulating communal customs.

In Lev. 18.20, adultery was indeed perceived as an expression of unneighborly behavior, bearing far reaching consequences for the basic purity of the entire covenant community:

> You shall not lie carnally with a wife of your neighbor and defile yourself with her.

Because of linguistic difficulties, it has been suggested that the prohibition incorporated in this text does not relate to adultery at all but, rather, to a sort of gentlemanly agreement that empowers a male friend to fertilize the wife of a neighbor.[12] This seems farfetched. While a sexual liaison between a 'neighbor' and a wife of another man, authorized or unauthorized, is castigated in Lev. 18.20 in terms of purity and pollution (as do other precepts in the Holiness Code), the basic problem of the violation of a woman's body that is specifically associated with a specific male remains unaltered. Here, as in Genesis 39, sexual contacts outside the legitimate marriage bed are deemed a moral issue and subject to self-restraint.[13]

Both Lev. 18.20 and 20.10 put a premium on the relations between the males most closely concerned with adultery, namely the husband and the lover. The adulteress appears as an afterthought. Repeated use of the terms 'fellow' and 'neighbor' (עמית and רע) in these biblical regulations adumbrates adultery as a transgression of communal boundaries and of the sanctified realm of neighborly property. The rules indicate that the loyalty of both wife and 'neighbor' to the husband is much more important than that of the husband to his wife.[14] The imbalance seems motivated by sheer fear that gaining access to one's wife could result in divulging the

---

12. Raymond Westbrook, 'Adultery in Ancient Near Eastern Laws', *RB* 97 (1990), pp. 542-80 (568 for Lev 18.20).

13. See also below, Chapter 9.

14. Which is why all commentators agree on the restricted sphere of the law of adultery to sexual intercourse with a married woman whose responsibility was to ensure the continuance of the husband's name through correct paternity; see Phillips, *Ancient Israel's Criminal Law*, p. 117.

secrets of the home to the entire neighborhood. A tyranny of gossip becomes a powerful social tool in shaping gender relations and the ideology of gender behavior.[15]

There is no penalty, in Lev. 18.20, for 'lying carnally' with the wife of one's 'neighbor'. Perhaps the omission betrays a certain recognition of the limits of the law when a crime committed could be concealed with grave results (particularly with regards to paternity), as well as presented or rather misrepresented by partners who were not caught in the act. Leviticus 18.20, like 20.10, is embedded in restrictions on other types of sexual contacts, primarily between relatives by kin and by marriage (18.6-19; 20.11-12), such as sex between father and daughter-in-law.[16] The grouping of all matters relating to forbidden sex in both pericopes suggests that all these types of illicit sex may have fallen under the criminal category of adultery. If this is the case, the association of 'adultery' with 'incest' extends categories of potential adulterers to practically all male relatives besides the husband himself.[17]

3. *Adultery According to Genesis*

Two tales of adultery take place in Egypt, one (Gen. 39, above) features a gentile woman and a Hebrew male, the other (Gen. 12) a Hebrew woman and a gentile male. In spite of this neat symmetry and the commonality of geography, the stories provide widely differing lessons. Genesis 39 insists on the personal purity of its (male) 'hero' by removing the husband from the scene of seduction; Genesis 12 presents the husband, rather than the male 'lover', as a man ready to compromise the virtue of the female protagonist. While both stories show affinity with the legal ideology of the Levitical strictures regarding adultery and with the Seventh Word, each highlights different gender attitudes.

The tripartite saga of Joseph in Egypt (Gen. 37–50: separation and slavery, seduction and incarceration, salvation and success) traces the rise of Joseph from rags to riches through the favor of mighty Egyptians, including Potiphar and the Pharaoh himself. To effect these 'miraculous' transitions, the narrative introduces a woman into a story which is otherwise remarkable for the absence of the feminine.[18] She is Potiphar's wife, a woman of action whose lack of name seems to suggest that all

---

15. Lev. 19.16 prohibits slandering or vicious gossiping (רכיל), comparing slander to blood. Cf. Gilmore, *Aggression and Community*, p. 53 (esp. the proverb 'la lengua no tiene dientes, y mas que ellos muerde', 'the tongue has no teeth but it bites deeper').

16. See Phillips, *Ancient Israel's Criminal Law*, pp. 123-25, especially on Leviticus' reinterpretation of the crime of adultery to include all unnatural sexual unions. On difficulties relating to the provenance and dating of the sexual legislation of Lev. 20, see David Daube, *Studies in Biblical Law* (Cambridge: Cambridge University Press, 1947; repr. New York: Ktav, 1969), pp. 78-88. See also Athalya Brenner, 'On Incest', in *idem* (ed.), *A Feminist Companion to Exodus–Deuteronomy*, pp. 113-38, for legalities, theories and narratives about incestuous relations; and Madeline G. McClenney-Sadler, 'Women in Incest Regulations', in Myers *et al.* (eds.), *Women in Scripture*, pp. 206-208.

17. See Phillips, *Ancient Israel Criminal Law*, pp. 121-29, on priestly legislation.

18. Even Joseph's marriage is tersely recorded (Gen. 41.45).

gentile women share her characteristics. In Genesis 39 she becomes a dangerous seductress and a violator of multiple boundaries, in other words the precise antithesis of the virtuous, obedient and trustworthy Joseph.[19]

The Genesis reworking of the common ancient folk-theme of married seductresses and innocent young men makes the Egyptian woman strong and resourceful. To exonerate herself from the kind of accusation that the wife of Sin-iddinam had to face, Potiphar's enterprising wife clings tenaciously to the only piece of 'evidence' which 'proves' her innocence and Joseph's guilt, namely the presence of Joseph's garment in her own room where, clearly, it should not have been. Potiphar apparently believed his wife. He did not question Joseph, perhaps because the evidence was overwhelmingly against him.

In view of the incalculable repercussions of an accusation of 'adultery' with a slave, the woman's behavior is predictable. At stake was her own survival. Because of a crucial disparity of status and rank between the two protagonists in Genesis 39, the mere suggestion—not to say the reality—of sex with a slave implied a grievous transgression and, above all, shaming the husband.[20] The severity of this particular type of 'adultery' is reflected in Joseph's words about trust, and in the woman's second version of what had transpired which refers not to Joseph's maleness (as does the first presentation of the 'crime') but to his servile status (Gen. 39.17-18).

Although male resistance to temptation is a common stock of such tales, Joseph's allegation that adultery is abhorrent to God introduces an element of religiosity into the tale.[21] He incorporates Yahweh in the proverbial triangle by projecting God as an injured party besides the husband.[22] This extension of actors helps to account for the penalty that Joseph sustains and for which there is no correspondence in Levitical (or Deuteronomic) prescriptions. In Genesis 39 adultery, then, is a domestic crime to be judged by the husband, a god in his own household. Whether this form of judgment is only applicable to cases in which one party is a slave remains unclear.

Two (male) perceptions of the events are incorporated in the redacted version of Genesis 39. One, Joseph's, casts 'adultery' as a transgression of divine commands and an offense against the master, hence a moral and social sin. The second, the

19.   Jack Levison, 'An-Other Woman: Joseph and Potiphar's Wife—Staging the Body Politic', *JQR* 87 (1997), pp. 269-301.

20.   The ideology of female marital chastity and the public standing of married males is nicely articulated in an Egyptian marriage contract from Alexandria (92 BCE): 'It shall not be lawful for Apollonia to spend night or day away from the house of Philiscus (the husband) without his knowledge, or to have intercourse with another man or to ruin the common household or to bring shame upon Philiscus in whatever causes a husband shame') (in Mary L. Lefkowitz and Maureen B. Fant, *Women's Life in Greece and Rome* [Baltimore: The Johns Hopkins University Press, 1982], p. 59, quoting Bernard Grenfell *et al.* [eds.], *The Tebtunis Papyri* [4 vols.; London: Oxford University Press, 1902–]).

21.   Nor should one discount the issue of intermarriage in general and of sex across national lines in particular. Cf. Gen. 34, with my *Dinah's Daughters*.

22.   Supporting Paul, *Studies*, pp. 30-31: 'only in Israel does a legal collection embody the basis for the covenantal agreement between a deity and his elect'.

storyteller's, casts the confrontation between Potiphar's wife and Joseph as a straightforward case of adultery, with an adulteress indifferent to shame and to husbandly honor.[23] 'Actor' and narrator, both males, share a vision of God 'as the source of the ethics which Joseph feels bound to obey'.[24] Because the two invisible protagonists in the plot, God and Potiphar, remain powerful motivators, the woman's point of view is left outside the scope of the redacted narrative.[25] Based on post-biblical expansions, Bach suggests that the story of Joseph and the Egyptian lady could have come to a happy rather than a sore end (for Joseph alone?) had love (*eros*), rather than sin, been allowed to enter the plot.[26] Her proposal highlights a singular omission of the Hebrew Bible: with the exception of the Song of Songs, the text rarely addresses sensual love between a man and a woman. Perhaps, then, love is absent from Genesis 39 not by design but because it had been banished by lust.

Post-biblical expansions of the history of Joseph in Egypt, like Joseph's implied reading, draw a sharp contrast between male spheres of honor–shame and the female spheres of dishonor–disgrace in order to create a new model of Jewish masculinity with sexual chastity as a prime heroic attribute.[27] Such basic dichotomy highlights a later shift (in Judaism) of emphasis from 'adultery' in its basic biblical senses of an illicit sexual encounter) to adultery as an unlawful manipulation of the male body. Calculations of morality and ideology minimize the role of women to that of devil's advocate, testers of manly moral prowess.[28]

Egypt proves a fertile ground for potential adultery, enabling narrators to explore aspects that 'laws' fail to envisage.[29] In Genesis 12 the question of adultery acquires poignancy when the husband, a refugee in a seemingly hostile yet welcoming land, promotes rather than protects (or judges) wifely virtue.[30] Genesis 12.10-20, as well

---

23. Rodd, *Glimpses*, p. 33.

24. Rodd, *Glimpses*.

25. Bach, 'Breaking Free', p. 320.

26. Was Potiphar, then, indeed a eunuch? See R. Peter-Contesse, 'Was Potiphar a Eunuch?', *The Bible Translator* 47 (1996), pp. 142-46.

27. *Testament of Joseph*, with Bach, 'Breaking Free', p. 321. Cf. *Joseph and Aseneth*, with Ross S. Kraemer, *When Joseph Met Aseneth: A Late Antique Tale of the Biblical Patriarch and his Egyptian Wife* (New York: Oxford University Press, 1998), for a recent discussion of the many problems linked with this work. See also Boyarin, *Unheroic Conduct*.

28. It is not clear when a woman became liable to the law of adultery. Phillips, *Ancient Israel's Criminal Law*, claims that not before the Deuteronomic period (and by implication a Deuteronomistic editing of Genesis–Numbers), but Pressler, *View of Women*, pp. 33-34, disagrees, probably with reason.

29. I refrain from discussing the chronological relationship between Genesis and the rest of the Pentateuch, a thorny and controversial subject. See, above, Chapter 1, for current scholarly opinions. It would be difficult to sustain, as Calum M. Carmichael (*Women, Law and the Genesis Traditions* [Edinburgh: Edinburgh University Press, 1979]) does, the theory that the entire book of Genesis is woven around the Decalogue.

30. In addition to the bibliography in Chapter 6 (above), see Mark E. Biddle, 'The "Endangered Ancestress"' and the Blessing for the Nations', *JBL* 109 (1990), pp. 599-611; and Seth D. Kunin, *The Logic of Incest: A Structuralist Analysis of Hebrew Mythology* (JSOTSup, 185; Sheffield: Sheffield Academic Press, 1995), pp. 65-69 (Gen. 12), pp. 83-85 (Gen. 20), pp. 107-109

as its 'companions' (20.1-7; 26.6-11), cast the husband as a protagonist whose presence, not to say downright encouragement, rather than absence, motivates adultery.[31] In all three tales the husband is the guardian and arbiter of marital chastity, with power to trade his wife's bodily integrity. This husbandly hegemony contrasts sharply with the husband's own impotence *vis-à-vis* other men in Egypt (or in Gerar). It further makes the woman a doubly subjected object, to her husband as well as to the whims of local potentates.[32]

Sarah is a beautiful woman, but her beauty is seen as a double weapon: potentially a mortal risk for the husband (if murdered), but also a likely source of profit (through adultery). Circumstances, and especially the double alienation of the male (from promised land and from own wife), clothe Abraham's ruse with a nearly exemplary function.[33] Yet, self-centered insistence on self-preservation also inserts Abraham into the ranks of men ready to discard daughters and wives in times of peril.[34] This is why his rhetoric in Genesis 12 and 20 extols affinities between what men see and the desires such visions engender. In his 'reading' of the situation, adultery is an inevitable result of the misdirected male gaze.

The proposed adultery in Egypt takes Sarah's consent for granted. In return for trading her Abraham acquires wealth, slaves and maidservants.[35] Hagar inclusive? Because adultery must be punished, the Egyptian monarch who annexed Sarah to

(Gen. 26). Desmond T. Alexander, 'Are the Wife/Sister Incidents of Genesis Literary Compositional Variants?', *VT* 42 (1992), pp. 145-53, claims that there is no way to settle questions of archetype, namely whether we have a triplet or three separate stories.

31.   As Rodd, *Glimpses*, p. 32 n. 4, remarks, whether these three pericopes are variants of a stock theme or not is not important for investigating the ideology of adultery; the former possibility 'gives them increased significance'. In addition to the bibliography given in Chapter 6 see: Ephraim A. Speiser, 'The Wife–Sister Motif in the Patriarchal Narratives', in Alexander Altmann (ed.), *Studies and Texts*. I. *Biblical and Other Studies* (Cambridge, MA: Harvard University Press, 1963), pp. 15-28 (repr. in J.J. Finkelstein and Moshe Greenberg [eds.], *Oriental and Biblical Studies: Collected Writings of Ephraim A. Speiser* [Philadelphia: University of Pennsylvania Press, 1969], pp. 62-82); Robert Polzin, 'The Ancestress of Israel in Danger', *Semeia* 3 (1975), pp. 81-89. There is also no agreement regarding the relative dates of these three episodes. Rudolf Kilian, *Die vorpriesterlichen Abrahams-Überlieferungen: literarkritisch und traditionsgeschichtlich untersucht* (Bonn: Hanstein, 1966), p. 214, regards Gen. 26 as the oldest of the three; the reverse is surmised by Klaus Koch, *The Growth of Biblical Tradition: The Form-Critical Method* (trans. S.M. Cupitt; New York: Charles Scribner's Sons, 1969), p. 125.

32.   Kunin, *Incest*, pp. 66-67, also emphasizes the series of oppositions that the stories generate between insiders (sisters) and outsides (wives), reading them as allegories tracing the 'domestication' of wives through metaphors of sister–brother relations. He sees in all three precursors of the Exodus, a process that makes Israel a suitable wife for God.

33.   Fokkelien van Dijk-Hemmes, 'Sarai's Exile: A Gender-Motivated Reading of Genesis 12.10–13.2', in Brenner (ed.), *A Feminist Companion to Genesis*, pp. 222-34 (229).

34.   Van Dijk-Hemmes, 'Sarai's Exile', p. 230 with the obvious comparisons with Lot (Gen. 19.8); and the unnamed Levite (Judg. 19.25).

35.   As Cady Stanton remarks: 'It is a little curious that the man who thus gained wealth at the price of his wife's dishonor should have been held up as a model of all the patriarchal virtues' (Elizabeth Cady Stanton, *The Woman's Bible* [New York: European Publishing Company, 1895; latest reprint 1993], p. 44).

his harem is stricken by God not with death, as the Holiness Code prescribes, but with plagues. At Gerar, where the verbal exchange between Abraham and Abimelech the ruler (Gen. 20.11-13) suggests that adultery is a transaction handled by men for the benefit of men, the husbandly eloquence effects a reconciliation between husband and 'adulterer' because Abraham, although a needy stranger in a strange land, has the power to undo divinely inflicted penalties.[36] The 'battle' over female fertility and sterility is, predictably, won by Abraham whose 'victory' anticipates Sarah's own 'triumph', namely the birth of Isaac (21.1).[37]

Yet, one point in Genesis 20 tales remains unsolved. Abimelech maintains that Abraham had violated the law of the kingdom by his promotion of wifely adultery (20.9-10). Shifting the burden of guilt from husband to wife, the narrator, by contrast, concludes that 'on account of Sarah, wife of Abraham' (20.18; cf. 12.17) God had to demonstrate divine might. Whose fault, then, is it? Who is guilty of doing 'things that are not (or, ought not to be) done' (20.9).[38] Conflicting messages emerge. The Egyptian tale of Genesis 12 seemingly proposes that adultery between a Hebrew female and a gentile male is not sinful, under certain circumstances, although the tale underscores Yahweh's faithfulness *vis-à-vis* patriarchal behavior.[39] Paradoxically, the story also supports the Levitical stand which regards adulterers as criminals, regardless of motivation and particulars. And it exposes the tricky question of intent. According to the Pharaoh, he had acted not reprehensibly but rather unintentionally because of false pretenses of another man. An unwitting adulterer, the Pharaoh nevertheless has to sustain a punishment, as though abiding by the adultery rules of Leviticus. The narrator does not even state whether the plagues had been withdrawn after the king relinquishes Sarah back to her husband.

With each of the 'sister–brother' tales the moral tone becomes more strident. Gentile protagonists must learn a lesson through severe penalties because the basic narrative requires an ongoing demonstration of Yahweh's presence and power. In

---

36. Cf. Abimelech's behavior with the oath made by a suspected perpetrator to the husband in Assyrian law, discussed in Moshe Weinfeld, 'Sarah in the House of Abimelech (Gen. 20) in the Light of Assyrian Law and the Genesis Apocryphon', *Tarbiz* 52 (1982), pp. 639-42 (Hebrew) (reprinted in A. Delcor [ed.], *Melanges Bibliques et Orientaux en l'Honneur de Mathias Delcor* [Kevelaer: Butzon & Bercker, 1985], pp. 431-36).

37. And well after her own Egyptian maid provided Abraham with an heir (Gen. 16.4). On intriguing parallels between Gen. 12 and 16, see Exum, 'Who's Afraid of "The Endangered Ancestress"?', p. 150. On Hagar, see Savina J. Teubal, *Hagar the Egyptian: The Lost Traditions of the Matriarchs* (San Francisco: Harper & Row, 1990), and *idem*, 'Sarah and Hagar: Matriarchs and Visionaries', in Brenner (ed.), *A Feminist Companion to Genesis*, pp. 235-50. On the significance of the motif of bareness, as a link with the Abraham cycle and other Genesis narratives, as well as the reason for removing Sarah from the household, see Steinberg, *Kinship and Marriage*, pp. 52-55 (54).

38. The expression further refers to 'serious violations of custom that threaten the fabric of society'; see Kyle P. McCarter, *II Samuel*, p. 322 (AB, 9; New York: Doubleday, 1984), who compares Tamar's appeal to Amnon with Abimelech confronting Abraham in Gen. 20.9-10.

39. John H. Otwell, *And Sarah Laughed: The Status of Women in the Old Testament* (Philadelphia: Westminster Press, 1977), p. 79.

spite of the happy end for the Hebrew protagonists, the problematization of the plots remains unsolved. Because Yahwist sexual morality is hardly unique, the discussion of adultery in both biblical 'law' and lore is riddled with difficulties. Nor can narratological/redactional efforts to recast the ideology of adultery in specific Yahwist terms conceal the fact that in practically all ancient societies adultery was seen as a social sin and as a violation of both custom and law.[40]

This is why the third wife–sister tale (Gen. 26.7-11) fails to envisage even a separation between wife (Rebecca) and husband (Isaac). Nevertheless, sheer husbandly pretense still stimulates action. The wife is not appropriated because the king happens to be an observant man. The male gaze, a prime promoter of adultery in Genesis 12 and 20, galvanizes (in Gen. 26) the beholder into speech rather than action. Abimelech, already tried by Abraham's ruse, remains unimpressed by Isaac's 'logical' fear of death, just as Potiphar's wife shrugged off Joseph's pious argument (above). At Gerar, adultery under any circumstances 'would have brought guilt upon us' (26.10 RSV). This is Abimelech's argument. The law of his realm and divine precepts are unanimous in condemning adulterous intent. But Abimelech cleverly shifts the burden of guilt from the adulterer back to the husband while the decisive and deciding voice of Yahweh remains absent.

Ultimately, by silencing Isaac, the narrative also exonerates him. He is, after all, the sole bearer of the promise to Abraham.[41] Nor is the king punished. Rebecca at Gerar, unlike Sarah, is already a mother.[42] Maternity and barrenness form two invisible threads that link the three tales by suggesting that the most serious potential danger inherent in (concealed) adultery is the contamination of paternity and of genealogy.[43] Underlying these seemingly repeated narratives is a latent conflict between customary perceptions of adultery as a social sin that entails a general degradation of the society where it is practiced, and Yahwist theology that requires divine monitoring of all human actions, intentions and motivations, especially those

40.   Phillips, *Ancient Israel's Criminal Law*, p. 117, asserts that ancient Israel, because it considered adultery as a crime that threatened the covenant relationship (i.e. sacral offence), consequently demanded state and not private action or rather reaction while ancient Near Eastern societies (where adultery was a secular offence) allowed the husband to determine the fate of his wife and, by extension, of her lover, as though adultery was not a serious moral offence that undermined the basic morality of society. The case of the wife of Sin-iddinan (above) shows the state actively involved in a case of adultery through the imposition of an ordeal (cf. Num. 5). In Neo-Babylonia the ideology of wifely chastity and loyalty was so important as to create, in some cases, a specific adultery clause in marriage contracts, Roth, ' "She Will Die by the Iron Dagger" '. See also J.J. Finkelstein, 'Sex Offenses in Sumerian Laws', *Journal of the American Oriental Society* 86 (1966), pp. 355-72. On ancient Israelite attitudes, see Rofé, 'Family and Sex Laws', pp. 131-60. Practically every discussion of marriage and family also includes remarks on the issue of adultery.

41.   John Van Seters, *Abraham in History and Tradition* (New Haven: Yale University Press, 1975), pp. 179-83, on Isaac's cycle as an artificial tradition imitating Abraham's cycle.

42.   As Steinberg, *Kinship and Marriage*, p. 93, emphasizes.

43.   Steinberg, *Kinship and Marriage*; Karel van der Toorn, *From her Cradle to her Grave: The Role of Religion in the Life of the Israelite and the Babylonian Woman* (trans. Sara J. Denning-Bolle; The Biblical Seminar, 23; Sheffield: JSOT Press, 1994), p. 79.

surveyed in the Decalogue. This is why Genesis 12 implies that adultery had taken place while Genesis 20 deliberately sets out to prevent it and Genesis 26 discusses it as a remote possibility. And this is why the Tenth Commandment, ostensibly redundant, deals not with action but with intention as a crucial preliminary of sin.

Genesis 12 and 20 provide for a consideration of extenuating circumstances that lead to adultery through fear of murder. What they fail to consider is an 'adultery' committed not in order to recover the fortunes of a husband but, as Genesis 38 does, to avoid the plight of widowhood.[44] To bring Levitical strictures on unlawful sex closer to the Seventh Word, Genesis 38 features Tamar as a woman who actively solicits 'adultery' with her own father-in-law who had failed to provide her with a third husband.[45] Crossing the boundaries of sex and of 'incest', she selects Judah as a sexual partner. The choice is never fully accounted for, but it provides a perfect fit to the Genesis plots that feature illicit sexual liaisons in schemes of survival.

Genesis 38 casts Judah as a man who breaks with custom. But because the issue of involuntary widowhood is basically a familial matter Tamar has no recourse to 'law'. Rather, she must handle her dealings with Judah according to an invisible legal protocol which presents a deliberate subversion of Deut. 22.13-21. The battle over the sexual integrity of the widow, in Genesis 38, is pitched between the woman herself and her father-in-law, and not between two male relatives as Deut. 22.13-21 envisages. The guardian of female chastity is no longer a blood relative but a relation by marriage. The execution of his verdict becomes a communal activity which the 'judge' does not even witness.

When Tamar is 'caught', there is neither trial nor ordeal. No one looks for a putative father.[46] The neighborhood assumes that Tamar had become a regular prostitute and that her pregnancy constitutes a crime against her husband's family rather than against her own paternal home. Hovering between tragedy and farce,

44. The position of Gen. 38 in the overall narrative has been regarded as an anomaly; see Brueggemann, *Genesis*, pp. 307-308. But the links with the other adultery tales and especially with Gen. 39 account well for this seemingly unaccountable tale. On the legal status of widows, see Jan A. Wagenaar, '"Give in the Hand of Your Maidservant the Property..."': Some Remarks to the Second Ostracon from the Collection of Moussaieff', *Zeitschrift für altorientalische und biblische Rechtsgeschichte* 5 (1999), pp. 15-27.

45. It is out of place here to argue about the problematic aspects of the placing of this tale in the Genesis sequence. Ephraim A. Speiser, *Genesis* (AB, 1; New York: Doubleday, 1964), argues that Gen. 38 is a late and arbitrary insertion; but see the criticism of Bal, *Lethal Love*, pp. 89-91, who points out that unity is not textual but a readerly feature and a process, and who espouses a thematic unity between Gen. 38 and 39 based on 'tricky love' (p. 91). I would rather call it 'adultery', real and imaginary.

46. David M. Gunn and Danna N. Fewell, *Narrative in the Hebrew Bible* (Oxford: Clarendon Press, 1993), p. 42, correctly emphasize the community double-standard when it comes to judging the behavior of widows and of widowers, as in fact does Tamar herself. On the episode as a narrative sample of *lex talionis*, see Carmichael, *Women, Law*, pp. 119-20. On Tamar's alleged activity as a קדשה, see Mayer Gruber, 'Hebrew Qedesah and her Canaanite and Akkadian Cognates', *UF* 18 (1986), pp. 133-48.

Tamar's tale comes to a quasi-happy end. She presents tokens of her innocence to a 'judge' who used to own them and who is also the father of her unborn children. Judah reluctantly acknowledges the correctness of her actions, stopping short of admitting paternity.[47] Nor is he willing to marry her.

What, exactly, is Tamar's crime? Her behavior is described as 'prostitution'.[48] The penalty which the story issues for such an unwonted display of matronly lust is execution by fire. Leviticus 21.9 inflicts a similar one on a whoring daughter of a priest. Neither Judah nor, perhaps, Tamar's own father, were priests. Flames are also the penalty recommended for a man who engages in sex with his wife's mother (20.14). There are no provisions for widows who engage in sex outside widowhood. In legal retrospect, Tamar has become a prisoner and a victim of the law of levirate marriage.[49] The only way to free herself from the impasse imposed on her by Judah's reluctance to marry his son to her is to teach Judah a legal lesson through an elaborate deception. Poetic justice accredits Tamar with two sons as though to compensate for the two husbands she had lost.[50] Judah is deemed a promoter of 'adultery'.[51] And although ancient Jewish paraphrasing and exegesis of Tamar's tale recast him as the 'hero' of the affair, Genesis 38 seems to place the relative burden of guilt on Judah, while paying a tribute of piety to Tamar.[52]

In moral terms Tamar is superior to Judah, as she is to Potiphar's wife for whom she is clearly positioned as a counterweight. The latter behaves like a prostitute; Tamar acts like one, or rather as a woman free to make sexual choices.[53] Both Genesis 38 and 39 reflect norms that place an inordinate emphasis on the behavior of married or betrothed women and on female sexual chastity. Yet, they also appear

47. Judah's admission of Tamar's 'righteousness' (Gen. 38.26) is difficult to interpret. It may denote his resentment and even a sense of inferiority, as Gunn and Fewell, *Narrative*, p. 43, maintain. More likely it alludes to the inherent justice of her cause. E. Levine, 'On Exodus 21,10', p. 152, upholding the 'judicial historicity' of the tale, maintains with good reason that Judah's words constitute an admission of being *in delicto*. By forcing her to subsist without sexual relations he had imposed on her a pact without a reciprocal obligation. This unilateral 'agreement' made him guilty while rendering her *ipso facto* free of any marital constraints.

48. Gen. 38.24. The verb זנה is used almost exclusively with feminine subjects, while נאף ('adultery') can occur with either feminine or masculine objects; see Donald L. Slager, 'The Figurative Use of Terms for "Adultery" and "Prostitution" in the Old Testament', *The Bible Translator* 51 (2000), pp. 431-38 (433). See also the response to feminist critics of the negative sexual imagery conjured by these terms when relating to women in R. Abma, *Bonds of Love: Methodic Studies of Prophetic Texts with Marriage Imagery: Isaiah 50.1-3 and 54.1-10, Hosea 1–3, Jeremiah 2–3* (Assen: Van Gorcum, 1999), pp. 28-29, who views them as open ended.

49. Susan Niditch, 'The Wronged Woman Righted: An Analysis of Genesis 38', *HTR* 72 (1979), pp. 143-49.

50. Niditch, 'The Wronged Woman Righted'.

51. Etan Levine, 'On Intra-Familial Institutions of the Bible', *Bib* 57 (1976), pp. 54-59.

52. *Genesis Rabbah* 85.8. The exception is Pseudo-Philo, *Liber antiquitatum biblicarum*, which makes Tamar a mother in Israel and a fiery exponent of anti-intermarriage attitudes. For the latter see Pieter W. van der Horst, 'Tamar in Pseudo-Philo's Biblical History', in Brenner (ed.), *A Feminist Companion to Genesis*, pp. 300-304.

53. Bird, 'The Harlot as Heroine', pp. 119-39.

to contradict the moral verdict of Lev. 20.10, and possibly of the Seventh Word, which place initiation and guilt primarily on the shoulders of male adulterers. Perhaps the most intriguing aspect of all the Genesis tales of fornication and adultery is the fate of the woman involved. None is punished as Lev. 20.10 decrees, not even the enterprising wife of Potiphar, as far as the text divulges. The opposite is the case, with Sarah and Tamar 'awarded' pregnancies and sons.

By its very definition adultery is a by-product of marriage, and marriage was a carefully calculated step in biblical antiquity, as the stories of the marital arrangements regarding Rebecca and Rachel so clearly illustrate. Already in Old Babylonia marriage ceremonies and wedding rites were extremely elaborate, involving a substantial part of the community.[54] There, in addition to the formal transfer of various property items from one family to another, weddings entailed offerings in temples as well as feasts and living arrangements that touched on the lives and structures of the households of both bride and bridegroom. It is this mystique of marriage, this idealization of a series of commercial transactions that comprised belongings and bodies that explains, in part, the publicity attendant on detecting wifely adultery.[55]

Genesis tales of 'adultery' demonstrate how, in their bodies, women incorporate both the potential of order and of disorder. And because they hold the key to an orderly transmission of genealogy, as well as to a chaotic disruption of lineage, the discourse of the feminine explores facets of adultery which the law omits.[56] In Genesis 12 and 20 circumstances require divine intervention because at the heart of extra-marital or extra-social sex is the problem of secrecy with its wide-reaching ramifications of muddling of husbandly seed. This is why Lev. 18.20 forbids the 'giving of a male seed' to the wife of another man and regards violations as pollution. And this is why, although Genesis narratives and Levitical regulations place the brunt of committing (but not conceiving) 'adultery' on male perpetrators (Gen. 39 being the exception), the only legal procedure, or ordeal, that the Hebrew Bible articulates in order to detect adultery focuses on exposing suspected adulteresses (Num. 5).[57]

54. Greengus, 'Old Babylonian Marriage Ceremonies and Rites', *Journal of Cuneiform Studies* 20 (1966), pp. 55-72.

55. The terminology of marriage has been widely applied to describe the covenant between Yahweh and Israel, casting adultery as idolatry. Among numerous scholarly analyses, see Muffs, *Love and Joy*; Sakenfeld, 'Love', in *ABD*, VI, pp. 375-81; Gerlinde Baumann, 'Connected by Marriage, Adultery and Violence: The Prophetic Marriage Metaphor in the Book of Twelve and in the Major Prophets', *SBLSP* 38 (1999), pp. 552-69; and Day, 'Adulterous Jerusalem'.

56. Cf. Exum's analysis of Gen. 12, 20 and 26 as expressions of fear of women's sexuality and sexual knowledge, in her *Fragmented Women*, pp. 148-69.

57. On the rarity, or rather absence of river ordeals from ancient Israel in spite of their widespread use in cases involving fornication (*Laws of Ur-Nammu* 11), sorcery (*Code of Hammurabi* 2), and adultery (*Code of Hammurabi* 132; *Middle Assyrian Code* 17, 22, 24), in other words, female crimes, see Rodd, *Glimpses*, p. 31 n. 11. It is therefore striking that the only souvenir of such ordeals involves adultery. See also Eryl W. Davies, *Numbers* (NCBC; Grand Rapids: Eerdmans, 1995), p. 51, for a list of ordeal types in the ancient Near East.

4. *Revealing the Concealed: The Ordeal of the* Soṭah

A perennial preoccupation with adultery in ancient Near Eastern texts and images appears associated with perceptions of the bodies of women as seats of uncontrolled eroticism. Elamite and Syrian statuettes of naked women, called 'seductresses' by moderns, display generously proportioned genitals and breasts as a reminder of female exclusive attributes.[58] Conveying a message of corporeal communication, these blatant images of female sexuality project a constellation that pits femininity with male desire, making women the embodiment of purity and lust, victim and destroyer, bearers of beauty and of violence, and of the familiar and the unknown.

So ubiquitous is the presence of this multi-leveled blessing-threat that the only ordeal that the Hebrew Bible records revolves on a blatant attempt to control and subvert the very feminine. Numbers 5.11-31 preserves a lengthy 'constitution' that outlines the public exposure of a woman whom her husband suspects of betrayal. The issue at stake is adultery in its basic sense of extra-marital relations of a married woman with a man who is not her husband (although the term 'adultery' as it appears in the Seventh Word and in Lev. 20.10 is not used in Num. 5).

Briefly recaptured, the text stipulates that if a man suddenly suspects his wife of adultery but has no proof of it he can launch a legal procedure of detection that includes a 'sacrifice of jealousy' (Num. 5.15) and an elaborate ceremony orchestrated and conducted at the temple by a priest.[59] The suspected adulteress (סוטה) is brought before Yahweh (twice?, 5.16, 18), has to take an oath (twice?, 5.19, 21) and to drink the so-called 'bitter water' (twice?, 5.24, 26-27).[60] This liquid concoction is meant to bear out or to refute the woman's allegation of innocence. No alleged lover is interrogated. The ordeal further serves to exonerate suspicious

---

58.   Zainab Bahrani, *Women of Babylon: Gender and Presentation in Mesopotamia* (London: Routledge, 2001), pp. 83-84, for the appellation and the images (pl. 16 and 17 on p. 84, and pl. 36 on p. 156). These nude figures have often been associated with the goddess Ishtar and with her fertility aspects, an interpretation that Bahrani contests. Cf. Urs Winter, *Frau und Göttin: Exegetische und ikonographische Studien zum weiblichen Gottesbild im Alten Israel und in desssen Umwelt* (Freiburg: Universitatsverlag, 1983), and the objections raised by Edward Lipiński, 'The Syro-Palestinian Iconography of Woman and Goddess (review article)', *Zhumal prikladnoaai khimi* 36 (1986), pp. 87-96.

59.   On the passage see above Chapter 3 §1, and my *Dinah's Daughters*, Chapter 4.

60.   On the difficulties regarding the precise structure of the account, see Rodd, *Glimpses*, p. 31, who thinks that the account combines two rites of the same ordeal rather than two separate forms of the ordeal. Michael Fishbane, 'Accusations of Adultery: A Study of Law and Scribal Practice in Numbers 11–31', *HUCA* 45 (1974), pp. 25-45, likewise respects the integrity of the text, as does Herbert C. Brichto, 'The Case of the Sota and a Reconsideration of Biblical "Law"', *HUCA* 46 (1975), pp. 55-70, who also regards the pericope as an instance 'of remedial legislation regarding wives' (p. 67) aiming at protecting the woman as wife in a disadvantaged position which society had carved out for her (p. 67). On two distinct sources for the same text, see B. Stade, 'Beitrage zur Pentateuchkritik (3: "Die Eiferophferthora")', *ZAW* 15 (1898), pp. 166-75; G.B. Gray, *Numbers*; and Baruch A. Levine, *In the Presence of the Lord: A Study of Cult and Some Cultic Terms in Ancient Israel* (Leiden: E.J. Brill, 1974).

husbands of complicity (presumably in swearing to what transpires as false testimony). Underlying the ritual is a reliance on the 'religious protection of the matrimonial bond' that on occasion can be made explicit if not public, and on the power of an oath to demonstrate the 'truth'.[61]

Had adultery been suspected because the woman had fallen pregnant, as happened in Tamar's case?[62] The text does not ponder the possibility but merely projects a 'spirit of jealousy' as legal grounds of accusation. In case the charge proved groundless the husband was not punished, just like Judah who reneged a vow. Nor is there a complementary ritual to uncover concealed male adulterers. Revealing the *soṭah*'s potency to challenge gender definitions and authority in patriarchal society', the 'law' questions the ways in which a collectivity bases its exemplary status.[63] It suggests, however, that in societies, like the one encoded in Genesis–Numbers in which the position of women was largely determined by their status as wives and mothers, adherence to the rules of wifedom and motherhood was *ipso facto* crucial.[64]

In the settings of the *soṭah* ordeal the woman must condemn herself by her own words and through her own body. Her concealed activities can lead to her social 'suicide' because, if guilty, she becomes a pariah in her community. Even the attribution of guilt becomes a stain of shame. Hence, there is no need for an execution, pace Lev. 20.10, since the woman becomes her own executioner. The consequences for a guilty wife, if she is pregnant, entail miscarriage (as implied by some translations).[65] If not pregnant at the time but still guilty, she is assured of sterility (Num. 5.21, 27). There is no escape, as the midrashic tale quoted at the start of Chapter 3 so poignantly illustrates, even when the woman believes that she has fooled God.[66]

---

61.   Van der Toorn, *From her Cradle to her Grave*, p. 62, who also regards the trial by ordeal as a dramatized form of the oath in which the river functions as a lie detector and executor of the eventual punishment.

62.   Fishbane, 'Accusations', presents the ritual as a *de iure* conviction process of a *de facto* crime. Jacob Milgrom, 'A Husband's Pride, A Mob's Prejudice: The Public Ordeal Undergone by a Suspected Adulteress in Numbers 5', *BR* 12 (1996), p. 21 believes that the ordeal was meant to protect rather than to humiliate the wife.

63.   See Bonna Devora Haberman, 'The Suspected Adulteress: A Study of Textual Embodiment', *Prooftexts* 20 (2000), pp. 12-42, for a recent analysis. She sees the ritual as intending to 'diffuse male jealousy that transfers the woman from the domain of her wanton jealous spouse and potentially vengeful male courts towards the protection of the inner sanctum' (p. 16). The public humiliation that she suffers is, in this case, 'a ritual catharsis' (p. 16). Haberman also insists that the water of instruction is '*not* simply a lie detector, a mechanism to solve legal ambiguity' because it does humiliate the woman publicly (p. 18, emphasis added).

64.   Where such issues had no bearing on the status of women, as in archaic Sparta, the famed legislator Lycurgus could gently point out to an inquiring foreigner that there simply was no need to penalize adultery in a society, such as Sparta, where adultery has no place in defining social virtues and norms. Plutarch, *Lycurgus* 15.17-18.

65.   NEB translates: 'by bringing upon you miscarriage and untimely birth'. For William McKane, 'Poison, Trial by Ordeal and the Cup of Wrath', *VT* 30 (1980), pp. 474-92 (474), the main aim of the ordeal is to resolve cases of doubtful paternity. Haberman, 'Suspected Aldulteress', p. 19, disagrees.

66.   See above, Chapter 3.

Jealousy, impurity and sacrifice appear regularly in Num. 5.11-31. The husband who may have suspected an innocent wife must make a specific type of sacrifice, a commemorative one of either innocence or guilt. The notion of purity and impurity is heavily imprinted with water, either holy water from the tabernacle itself or the water that acts as an invisible witness of the action that the ordeal attempts to expose. In the absence of precise medical terminology it is impossible to gauge the nature of the condemning water. They constitute a fluid bond between the couple, between the woman and the wife, and between the sacred and the profane. She is a sacrificial victim, entangled in a 'snare and caught in a mortal and moral trap'.[67] Her survival depends on guile and not on open confrontation, once more as the midrashic excerpt indicates. The anomalous double 'weapon' of guilt-exposure highlights the anomalous nature of her alleged ignominious betrayal.

In a universe of women where the womb provided their most visible and crucial link with society, the 'bitter water' becomes the test of values of domesticity.[68] And since this universe, as elsewhere in antiquity, is contrasted with the masculine realm, exposing the belly is a manner of death unto itself and one specifically feminine.[69] The suspected adulteress does not shed blood and the medical results of the drinking of the concoction are unclear. But they appear visible enough in the eyes of a critical environment and ensure a lasting stain on her reputation in case of guilt.

Virility and femininity underlie the progression of the ordeal from its innocuous start to its potentially bitter or 'happy' end. The fate of the unknown lover remains outside the scope of the narrative in spite of 'laws' that demanded his execution (Lev. 20.10). What mattered was the preservation of a dichotomy, artificial and ideological, of the legitimate product of women's bodies. Like the Genesis tales that idealize silent and compliant wives, the image of the suspected adulteress coagulates male fears about the unknown and about activities of members of their household which they cannot control. And, like Lev. 18.20, which casts adultery as defilement, Num. 5.11-31 expounds the results of such a form of defilement and how an ordeal may turn impurity to purity.

What the text fails to encapsulate are women's fears of injustice in case the innocent is found guilty, of barrenness as a result of the ordeal, and of giving birth to a child that may not resemble the husband. This is exactly what an unknown woman expressed in a prayer to the goddess Ishtar whom she asked to ensure the kind of justice that men enjoy but that is often denied to women:

> You are the judge, procure me justice!
> You bring order, inform me of a ruling!...

---

67. See Loraux, *Teresias*, p. 109 for the expression (in a wholly different context).

68. This is one reason why it is so difficult to date such portions. Rodd, *Glimpses*, p. 31, believes that Num. 5.11-31, because of its emphasis on defilement and the central role of the priest, may be post-exilic. He also regards the inclusion of this ordeal as a souvenir of a clash between the formulators of the Israelite law codes and 'custom' or the mode of arbitration favored by ordinary Israelites.

69. Cf. 2 Sam. 11.17, 21, on the death of Abimelech (and Uriah?) at the hand of women during a siege.

May my transgression be forgiven and my guilt remitted…
Give me a name and a descendant!
May my womb be fruitful![70]

Viewing the body of a suspected adulteress as 'a textual territory', the ordeal of the *soṭah* delineates a frontier zone that surrounds the issue of adultery in ancient Israel of Genesis–Numbers.[71] It further illustrates the apparent impartiality of the 'laws' governing adultery, if detected *in flagrante*, and the one-sided 'reality' that espoused full husbandly control of the bodies of women. Yet, Num. 5.11-31 stands alone as a process of potential incrimination of a married woman not caught *in flagrante*. Its uniqueness must send a cautionary note when considering the vast and nebulous terrain of narratives of adultery in the Hebrew Bible.

5. *Adultery: The View of Deuteronomy*

Deuteronomy 22.22, like Lev. 20.10, defines adultery as a state in which 'a man has sexual intercourse with a married woman':

> If a man is caught lying with the wife of another man, both of them shall die, the man who lay with the woman as well as the woman. Thus you shall purge out the evil from Israel.[72]

The pronouncement appears to combine the ideology of Lev. 18.20, which regards the carnal knowledge of one's neighbor's wife as defilement, with the 'practicality' of Lev. 20.10, which prescribes death to a man who commits adultery with a wife of his neighbor as well as to his female partner.[73] Deuteronomy 22.22 does not even 'hint that the man (i.e. adulterer) has committed a wrong against his own wife, were he married'.[74] When a man commits adultery, then, he violates the marriage of another, while a wife violates 'only' her own marriage.[75] The object of the adultery is a woman who 'has known a husband', a rare expression which appears only once more in the Hebrew Bible, in Gen. 20.3, where the phrase is put in the mouth of Yahweh who warns Abimelech of Gerar of(f) sleeping with Sarah.[76]

---

70. Van der Toorn, *From her Cradle to her Grave*, p. 80, quoting Werner R. Mayer, *Untersuchungen zur Formensprache der babylonischen 'Gebetsbeschwörungen'* (Rome: Biblical Institute Press, 1976), p. 458.

71. Haberman, 'Suspected Adulteress', p. 12, for the quote.

72. Campbell and O'Brien, *Unfolding*, for the verse; Rodd, *Glimpses*, p. 28, for the quote. I refrain deliberately from entering the seemingly perennial debate about provenance, date and redaction of the text. Campbell and O'Brien (p. 76) offer a summarizing table of three scholarly views.

73. The vexed question of the chronological relations between the Levitical and Deuteronomic passages in the final redacted text is irrelevant to my discussion. For one hypothesis that regards the latter as the earlier, see Phillips, *Ancient Israel's Criminal Law*.

74. Rodd, *Glimpses*, p. 28.

75. Tate, 'Legal Traditions', p. 494.

76. Pressler, *View of Women*, p. 31, a resemblance which probably points to a Deuteronomistic redaction. Pressler further groups under 'adultery' all the regulations of Deut. 22.13-29 (i.e. 'rape', seduction, and the fractured virginity or the slandered bride).

Unlike Lev. 20.10, Deut. 22.22 seems to provide for specific circumstances of 'discovery' *in flagrante* as the only type of evidence that can be procured to prove the offense. But Deuteronomy does not supply rulings for a suspicious husband, an omission which implies the continuous validity of the ordeal of the bitter water.[77] How a couple caught in the act is to be executed is not specified. Perhaps they were to die by stoning, a mode of communal punishment that prevented the executioners from touching the guilty, thus ensuring the avoidance of pollution.[78] This was the penalty allotted to a betrothed virgin and to her rapist if the rape (seduction?) had taken place in town (Deut. 22.23-24). In both cases the consent of the woman seems to be taken for granted.[79]

Scholarly interpretations of Deut. 22.22 have accounted for the harshness of its penalties on various grounds, ranging from viewing the wife as her husband's property (hence the call for her death as well as for that of the male initiator), through assuming adultery to be a component of the purity system (hence the concern to the purge evil), to seeing adultery as a disruption of the patriarchal system and particularly of paternity (a latent common assumption).[80] Neither the first nor the last issue directly engage biblical narratives of adultery in the Dtr History (Joshua–2 Kings). Nor does fear of paternal contamination or of sexual laxity features explicitly in the ancestral wife–sisters stories that place legally wedded wives in bedrooms of men other than their husbands (Gen. 12, 20, 26, above).

It is instructive to turn, for a moment, to Wisdom literature in order to glean 'folk' perceptions of adultery. Proverbs 6.32-33 depicts an adulterer as 'a heartless man', a male body housing a corrupt soul whose 'shame will never be erased' (6.32-33), and who faces the risk of relentless vengeance on the day of payment (6.34). A graphic description of an adulterer (Job 24.14-15) pictures a man with adulterous intentions as a creature of twilight, a breaker of boundaries and a rebel against light. He is a man who must carefully watch for darkness lest he is observed. He also has to conceal his face, to dig through houses at night, and to shut himself up during the day.

This mode of anti-social behavior is stereotypical of societies in which a sharp distinction is drawn between the legal bodies of married women and the bodies of women to whom all men have legal access, namely prostitutes. What, then, makes a man an adulterer? Desire, it seems, as well as the allure and availability of would-be adulteresses. Proverbs 6.10-22 exposes the vulnerability of young men to

77. Cancelled, according to *m. Soṭ.* 9.9 only in the late first century CE; see Hauptman, *Rereading the Rabbis: A Woman's Voice* (Boulder, CO: Westview Press, 1998), pp. 26-27.

78. Rodd, *Glimpses*, p. 29, further sees in this type of death a support for the view that adultery was tantamount, above all, to impurity.

79. Nor is it clear whether the 'legislation' represents an attempt to wrest familial jurisdiction from the hands of the husband and a belief in the equal culpability of the two partners to the adultery. Pressler, *View of Women*, pp. 33-35, dismisses both David Daube, 'Biblical Landmarks in the Struggle for Women's Rights', *Juridical Review* 23 (1978), pp. 177-97 (177-80), and Phillips, *Ancient Israel's Criminal Law*, pp. 110-12, and insists that the identity of the prosecutors remains unclear while the executioners are a collective male communal body.

80. Mayes, *Deuteronomy*, pp. 170, 311.

seduction by women whose husbands are away from home, a familiar motif given a lively illustration in Genesis 39. Genesis 38 does not castigate the venerable Judah for venting his sexual energy in an intercourse with a 'prostitute'. Prostitution was useful in averting adultery. It provided an easy and legal outlet for lusts that might otherwise become misdirected and undermine the fabric of social stability.[81]

These are the premises that contributed to the imagining of adulterers as liminal beings whose participation in society is dictated by their lustful needs, and by the safeguards that society imposes on sexual behavior. But if we take the laws at face value, illegal amorous activities carried considerable risks that rendered adulterers near-professional. Job and Proverbs imply that seekers of other men's wives terrorize society precisely because, unlike other types of excessive behavior, it was difficult to identify an adulterer unless caught in the act. Since an adulterer had to keep his vice secret, this necessity put greater pressure on men who were anxiously watching other men for telltale signs of an action that remains by its very nature a secret.

Deuteronomy 22.13-29 delves into the 'discovery' of adultery by delineating various possibilities.[82] One case (22.13-21) features a suspicious husband who accuses his wife of pre-marital sex with another.[83] Because the husband evidently cannot subject the wife to the ordeal prescribed in Numbers 5 (or does not know of it) he has to state in public his suspicion regarding the state of her hymen upon the wedding night.[84] The affair involves not only the community's elders but also the parents of the bride, who are naturally eager to exonerate themselves of transferring tarnished 'goods'.[85] The woman disappears from the scene. Instead, 'tokens of her virginity' (Num. 22.15, 17 = first night sheet?) become a crucial piece of evidence in an elusive procedure in which the word of the father is pitted against that of the husband, as the 'tokens' are carefully examined for 'proof' of either chastity or infidelity.[86]

Legally speaking, an accusation of pre-marital sex implies an unacceptable mode of female behavior under paternal authority (Deut. 22.21b: 'prostituting her father's house'). At stake, too, is the issue of property as an extension of wifely integrity, as

---

81. Cf. James Davidson, *Courtesans and Fishcakes: The Consuming Passions of Classical Athens* (New York: HarperCollins, 1999), p. 84.

82. For discussion of this pericope, Pressler, *View of Women*, pp. 21-43.

83. See above, Chapters 3 §3 and 6 §5.

84. The precise meaning of the term בתולים (Deut. 22.14, 15, 17, 20) has been much contested. For summary of scholarly views, Pressler, *View of Women*, pp. 25-28, opting for a straightforward fractured hymen rather than pregnancy at time of wedding. Rofé, 'Family Law', pp. 135-56, regards Deut. 22.13-21 as a composite text, distinguishing between vv. 13-19 on the one hand and vv. 20-21 on the other. Stulman, 'Sex', p. 58, calls attention to the unilateral action of the husband and to the woman's recourse to court.

85. This is one case in which the family is represented by 'father and mother'. Cf. the case of the disobedient son (Deut. 21.18-21) and the Fifth Word (honor your father and your mother), above Chapter 5.

86. Gordon J. Wenham, 'Betulah: A Girl of Marriageable Age', *VT* 22 (1972), pp. 326-48, draws attention to the coincidence of term (of pregnancy) and the timing of the marriage and the accusation, believing that the woman had been pregnant at the wedding.

well as a code of conduct between males.[87] If the elders believe the father, the husband is heavily fined and must stay married to the woman till the end of her life, forfeiting a basic husbandly right to divorce one's wife. The gravity of this penalty is reflected in the dictum that husbands' unjustifiable slander tarnishes not only the wife's reputation but also that of all the virgins in Israel (Deut. 22.19). If the elders believe the husband, the woman is to be stoned to death, like a blasphemer (Lev. 24.23). The execution takes place at the entrance to her father's house, a grim lesson for all women who would 'prostitute' not only their body but also, and most crucially, the reputation of their fathers as honest dealers in their daughters' virginity and marriageability.[88] The disparity in sentencing is obvious. The woman must pay with her life for a crime committed with her body; the man, if his allegation proves groundless, must pay with money (and with infamy?) for sins of speaking, namely slandering the reputation of an innocent family. But he lives, in either case, while the woman's sin, if she is found guilty, must be eradicated through the obliteration of her body.[89]

Why would a husband even consider this mode of slander rather than, say, initiating a divorce? Numbers 5.14 stipulates a mysterious 'spirit of jealousy' as the moving force behind the sudden accusation for adultery. Deuteronomy 22.13 suggests that 'hatred' breeds slander, but the term used also denotes a legal cause for a divorce.[90] The two instances of suspicion may not be far apart since, in both Deuteronomy 22 and Numbers 5, the issue hinges not on the ability of the husband to provide proof of wifely infidelity (either before or after the marriage), but on a judicial process or ordeal that aims to uncover the concealed and to enable the husband to get rid of his wife without losing her dowry. Both result in a tarnishing of the reputation of the woman and of her family, if she is found guilty. And both may have also been intended to protect wives hated by their husbands by providing a public opportunity for vindication.[91]

87.   Which also accounts for Deut. 24.1, which allows divorce, presumably with recovery of dowry by the spurned wife, upon the will or whim of the husband.

88.   The penalty also suggests a link with the Fifth Word that calls for respect to parents (and by implication for their public image and standing in the community) and with the Word that deals with false witnesses, as well as, possibly, with Deut. 19.16-19; see Pressler, *View of Women*, p. 24 (for the latter). Note the presence of the mother of the bride in the public examination of the gown (Deut. 22.15).

89.   Cf. Deut. 22.28-29, which prescribes a similar punishment for raping an unbetrothed woman vs. Exod. 22.15-16, which leaves the father room for refusing to marry his daughter to her seducer. Tikva Frymer-Kensky, 'Law and Philosophy: The Case of Sex in the Bible', *Semeia* 45 (1989), pp. 89-102 (93), believes that death was merely a verbal threat intended to emphasize expectations of the virginal body of brides. Cf. similar expectations in Neo-Babylonian marriage contracts; see Roth, ' "She Will Die by the Iron Dagger" ', *passim*.

90.   If indeed it means a divorce, the whole process must hinge on the husband's desire to get rid of his wife but to keep the property she had brought into the marriage. Otherwise the procedure makes little sense since divorce was apparently easy enough for a man without imputing sullied virginity at marriage to his divorcee. On divorce, see Reuven Yaron, 'On Divorce in Old Testament Times', *Revue internationale des droits de l'antiquite* 3 (1957), pp. 117-28.

91.   As Stulman, 'Sex', p. 57, and Calum Carmichael, *The Laws of Deuteronomy* (Ithaca, NY: Cornell University Press, 1974), p. 168, maintain.

Deuteronomic concerns to explore specific situations of adultery, actual or potential, extend to cases that intertwine the fate of men with that of 'betrothed' women through an exploration of the geographical context of 'rape' and 'seduction' (Deut. 22.23-29). Seeking to link location and penalty, the regulations determine the degree of female collusion according to the topography of the crime. If seduction takes place within the earshot of people, the case becomes 'adultery' because the woman should have called for help. Both 'partners' are to be stoned at the city gate, like a woman with pre-marital fractured virginity. Had the sexual encounter taken place 'in the field', far from the watchful and potentially protecting eyes of family and community, it is deemed a rape. The man is to die but the method of execution is not specified. The fate of the compromised, betrothed woman is likewise omitted. Whether these Deuteronomic precepts also reflect a reform that diminished husbandly and paternal authority, as has been claimed, is equally unclear.[92]

Paradoxically, then, the will of a woman features as a component in a process that involves illicit sex.[93] She is the one who holds the key to her family's morality through the protection or exposure of her hymen. Yet, the female Israelite has barely an existence. At most, she is a betrothed or married woman, belonging to an Israelite citizen and reliant on the community. Prior to marriage, her main attribute is virginity. Betrothed, her engagement places her in a liminal position that has the potential of upsetting the delicate balance between father and (future) husband. Hence, the legal strategy of placing the burden of guilt for adultery on the woman herself is irony itself. While the law stakes a claim to entrench women in a specific familial context, the very presence of women invests a space with erotic connotations which, in turn, require monitoring.

If the Deuteronomic law code, of which Deut. 22.22 forms but one item, aspired to 'give guidance and direction to Israel throughout the course of its history', it may be asked: How did the Dtr History follow such guidelines?[94] Here, a curious omission emerges. There is no story that shows a man slandering his bride (22.13-21), and none to reveal rapes of a betrothed woman either in town or in the countryside (22.23-29).[95] Both may have been subjects of Deuteronomic preaching of sexual

---

92. *Pace* Stulman, 'Sex', pp. 57-58, with reference. Already in Lev. 20.10 the community becomes the proposed executioner; and state institutions hold a central place in resolving the issue of suspected adultery in Num. 5.

93. Whether or not this also denote a Deuteronomic innovation regarding the liability of women to the law of adultery, as Phillips, *Ancient Israel's Criminal Law*, *passim*, suggests, is another question. Pressler, *View of Women*, pp. 33-35, objects to this view, claiming that the severity reflects the gravity of the offence.

94. Campbell and O'Brien, *Unfolding*, p. 39, for the quote.

95. Deut. 22.21 which demands the execution of a woman who had sexual relations prior to her marriage since she 'had committed an abomination, to prostitute (at?) the house of her father' (vs. Pressler, *View of Women*, p. 30, who reads 'to engage in illicit sexual relations while under the authority of her father') recalls the problematic phrase in Judg. 19.2 that depicts the Levite's concubine as returning to her father's home after 'prostituting'. The abbreviated, not to say truncated narrative may conceal a dispute between the father and the 'husband' over the state of the woman's virginity upon her 'marriage'. See above, Chapter 6.

morality rather than the codification of a law-giver.[96] Only the subject of adultery detected *in flagrante*, in its plainest sense as a crime against the husband of the woman concerned and against Yahweh, is fully pursued in a complex story of lust, illicit sex, murder and revenge (2 Sam. 11–14). Even then, the adulterer is no ordinary member of the covenant community, the husband is not an Israelite, and the couple is certainly not executed, as Deut. 22.22 prescribes. This is, of course, the story of Bath Sheba and David, already discussed in the 'Mapping of Murder'. It will now be dissected under the microscope of the marriage bed.

6. *Does Sinning Pay? The Morality of Adultery in 2 Samuel 11*

In the Dtr History the tale of David and Bath Sheba (2 Sam. 11) provides a moralistic sermon of sorts on the subject of adultery and on its far-reaching ramifications.[97] As king confronts a wrathful prophet, the latter's metaphoric retelling of the affair becomes not a story of plain adultery but a sordid tale of pitiless oppression of one poor man by one rich man. For all appearances, this narrative has little to do with either adultery or murder. In prophetic perceptions, however, the adultery is, implicitly, a power contest between men. Decoding the parable for the benefit of his bemused royal listener, Nathan charges David with killing and with appropriating the dead man's wife (12.9), both actions, by prophetic parlance, betray conspicuous lack of gratitude to Yahweh (12.7-9). David expresses remorse and the prophet relents.[98]

Neither David nor Bath Sheba are punished with death, the penalty that both Lev. 20.10 and Deut. 22.22 assign to a man and a woman who are caught in adultery. Nor does the husband get a chance to subject his wife to the ordeal of the *soṭah*. The story does not even hint at such a possibility, nor does the prophet appear concerned with adultery as such. Since Deut. 22.22 stipulates death only in cases of adultery discovered *in flagrante*, the affair of David and Bath Sheba, although hardly a secret, falls outside the orbit of these regulations. The punishment, nevertheless, must suit the extent and intent of the crime. Yet, instead of meting death to the partners in the adultery, their firstborn son, the very result of the sexual act of betrayal, dies at birth. To 'console' Bath Sheba David sleeps with her

---

96. The distinction is introduced by Rofé, 'Family and Sex Laws'.

97. In general, see Randall C. Bailey, *David in Love and in War: The Pursuit of Power in 2 Samuel 1–12* (JSOTSup, 75; Sheffield: JSOT Press, 1990); Adele Berlin, *Poetics and Interpretation of Biblical Narratives* (Bible and Literature, 9; Sheffield: Almond Press, 1983 [repr. Winona Lake, IN: Eisenbrauns, 1994]); David M. Gunn, *The Story of King David: Genre and Interpretation* (JSOTSup, 6; Sheffield: JSOT, 1978); Sternberg, *The Poetics of Biblical Narrative*; John J. Kessler, 'Sexuality and Politics: The Motif of the Displaced Husband in the Books of Samuel', *CBQ* 62 (2000), pp. 409-23.

98. David's sentiments are beautifully captured in Ps. 51. See Barbara E. Rosenblit, 'David, Bat Sheva, and the Fifty First Psalm', *Cross Current* 45 (1995), pp. 326-40. Mayes, *Deuteronomy*, p. 78, suggests that the introduction of the possibility of repentance and forgiveness diffuses the tension between two ideologies, the one postulating that violation of the covenant entails punishment and destruction, the other casting Israel as Yahweh's people, independent of any covenant.

(2 Sam. 12.24) and she conceives. The birth of a son in legitimate wedlock appears to erase the memory of Uriah and of the adultery.

'From the beginning, the tale implies an existential divide between the male and the female sphere', between war and home, and between the conquest of cities and the conquest of women.[99] And it is especially striking because the one who dies is the husband, contrary to law and to morality. The narrator accompanies Bath Sheba from the rooftops of Jerusalem to the interior of the royal palace, and from her bathing body to her mourning cloths, in a quest for the full magnitude of the crime of adultery. According to the prophetic censure of David's adulterous activities, his main sin was not merely the violation of Bath Sheba and Uriah's marital space, but also a breach of basic familial conventions (namely patrilineality, patriarchy, patrilocality). The removal of the 'lamb-daughter' from the family further raised a much larger issue: Is David eligible to rule as Yahweh's chosen king over Yahweh's chosen people?

Neither Nathan nor Yahweh can forget or forgive that David's desire for Bath Sheba and her pregnancy caused the death of an innocent man at the hands of Israel's enemies.[100] The narrative thus elevates an affair that begins as a private passion between two individuals to the level of a national event that tarnishes not only Yahwist moral precepts but also the orderly conduct of wars between Israel and its neighbors. Such wars cannot become the scene of settling private scores, least of all between an adulterous king and a powerless husband of a desired woman.[101]

Penetrating, briefly, the domain of wives and mothers, 2 Samuel 11 peruses the course of adultery from the betrayal of the very ideology of marriage to the 'murder' of a man who is twice victimized, once as a husband and once as a subject. Few other narratives account so fully for the repercussions of the Seventh Word.[102] No other story dwells on the chain of transgressions that a single violation of the Seventh Word engineers. This is why David's punishment has to be exemplary even if hardly applicable to other Israelites. Bath Sheba's loss (and recovery) of maternity is equally symbolic. It seems directly related to the ordeal of the *soṭah* that aspires to reward chaste wives with pregnancy and adulterous wives with sterility (Num. 5.27-28).

In one way, all the tales of real or potential adultery in the Hebrew Bible have a common denominator: the inclusion of a gentile as a member of the inevitable

---

99. Aschkenasy, *Woman at the Window*, p. 108, although I do not entirely subscribe to her notion that 'the tale's true tyrant is not the king but the cycle of the woman's body' (p. 109).

100. 2 Sam. 12.14, a difficult phrase, 'you have utterly scorned or maligned the enemies of God', is translated in the RSV as 'you have utterly scored the Lord'.

101. Cf. Jer. 29.23, railing against false prophets who both lie and commit adultery, as though the two types of behavior are two sides of the same coin; and Mal. 3.5, for whom the days of national redemption are closely linked with a moral reform that brings to task adulterers, as well as magicians, men who swear falsely and the oppressors of widows, orphans and aliens.

102. As well as for the links between the Seventh Word and other Commandments through a chain of violations that include theft, murder and false witness; see Schwartz, 'Adultery in the House of David', p. 50. Schwartz also sees in the affair a reflection of the Decalogue's call for the exclusive love of Yahweh which translates into exclusive love of one's own wife (p. 50).

triangle.[103] Neither Decalogue(s) nor the 'legal' pronouncements of either the Holiness Code or Deuteronomy deal directly with gentile partners. Regulations regarding adultery, as other rules regarding sex, were basically intended to define the precise situation and status of the woman with whom one could 'copulate in safety'.[104] The universality of the moral code that endorses the limitation of the female sexual horizons in matrimony suggests that adultery is regarded as a universal crime against all males. Yet, none of the stories (with the exception of Gen. 39) puts the blame only on the women involved, directly and squarely. Equally curious is the presentation of the 'adulteresses' in these stories. While the 'legal' regulations forbear (with one exception) to explore the issue of consent or coercion, Genesis tales point to adultery under duress, a situation that renders adulteresses automatically innocent (Sarah) or eventually exonerated (Tamar). The 'adulterer', if gentile, remains liable to penalty regardless of culpability; if, however, the 'adulterer' is Israelite, he is excused.

Views of adultery in the Hebrew Bible relate to a drive to overcome human lusts which hinder full participation of males in Yahwistic rituals and in the covenant. Such are the limits which underlie both man's unlimited legal ability to control the body of his wife, and male fears of woman's emotional and uncontrollable nature. Scholarly analyses of the politics of gender, space and reputation have emphasized the normative application of honor and shame to the public and private dichotomy of sexuality.[105] Female honor involves sexual purity and the behavior requisite to maintain it in the eyes of a watchful community, while men's honor is defined largely through their control of female chastity.[106]

That the issue of adultery is intimately bound with that of lineage and with the 'politics of reputation' has been emphasized countless times. Because of the belief that divergent female behavior has the potential of ruining a lineage, a paradox of empowerment emerges. Female moral standards had to be controlled because men had an ever-present suspicion of them. In private and in public society sought to ensure a watchful eye over women, and particularly over wives, in order to ward off the roving eyes of other men. In the microcosm of the *soṭah* ordeal, the exposure of a suspected adulteress reverses the normative process by which a woman is, ideally, increasingly concealed from the public eye. It begins with revealing her hair and concludes, if she is guilty, with exposing her belly (womb) and her thighs (that opened to receive the seed of a man other than her husband). This is one biblical image of adultery. But the Hebrew Bible presents two irreconcilable images of adultery: one committed by a king and hence hardly a normative profile of an adulterer,

---

103. Tamar's precise identity is not specified.

104. Davidson, *Courtesans*, p. 77, for expression.

105. Julian Pitt-Rivers, *The Fate of Shechem or the Politics of Sex: Essays in the Anthropology of the Mediterranean* (Cambridge: Cambridge University Press, 1977); Bechtel, 'Shame as a Sanction'; and Gary Stansell, 'Honor and Shame in the David Narratives', *Semeia* 68 (1994), pp. 55-79.

106. Cf. Pierre Bourdieu, 'The Sentiment of Honor in Kabyle Society', in John G. Peristiany (ed.), *Honor and Shame: The Values of Mediterranean Society* (The Nature of Human Society; repr., Chicago: University of Chicago Press, 1974 [1966]), pp. 193-241.

the other not actually committed but representing all married women as potential adulteresses.

Such ambiguity is, perhaps, deliberate. Like other Commandments, the Seventh Word evokes a world that can be conjured at each individual's discretion. It also presupposes a community, or a neighborhood, in which social pressures play a major role of deterrence. In the Pentateuchal ordeal of the *soṭah* the husband's 'spirit of jealousy' seemingly materializes out of nowhere. But this also implies that it can come from anywhere: from neighbors, friends, and the woman's own behavior. In the biblical tales of adultery women are disappropriated and reappropriated. With every story, the narrative framework creates its specificity and constructs a discourse which has its internal logic. Thus, behind every case of adultery is an institutional discourse of marriage which postulates the identity of women in terms of tradability and loyalty.

The Hebrew Bible does not contain a ceremony of marriage. In words that amount to a solemn exchange Adam announces that:

> She is a bone of my bone and marrow of my marrow,
> She is woman, because from a man she has been formed. (Gen. 2.23)[107]

The traditional Roman formula of marriage ('Where you are Gaius, I am Gaia', *ubi tu Gaius, ibi ego Gaia*) presented the man as a giver of form and meaning to his wife, precisely as the Genesis verse posits, and as the rabbinic dictum quoted at the start of this chapter poignantly illustrates. In both, the generic name of 'wife' is a feminine facsimile of the husband.[108] The bond that ties a man to his wife, therefore, recalls a common beginning. It surpasses the temporality of the individual couple's life. In prophetic discourse this kind of marriage presupposes the relationship between Yahweh and Israel, a ubiquitous assumption that accounts, perhaps, for the temporary sexual renunciation that Moses imposes on the Israelites prior to the theophany at the Sinai (Exod. 19.15).[109]

From the very beginning of biblical 'history', female fertility is an object that must come under the control of man (Gen. 3.16). Because the body of woman bears the seeds of both legitimate and illegitimate paternity, its accessibility had to be severely limited. The arrival of the woman, as the arrival of marriage, symbolizes the mingling of the world of men with the sphere of women. The encroachment of one more man into the domestic scene of another heralds the breakdown of the basic structure of society, as based on the opposition between masculine and feminine and between the mutual appropriation of women through prescribed channels. Yet, laws cannot monitor the sentiments that ensure lasting and fruitful conjugality. Love and inborn loyalty cannot be legislated. To guarantee the arrangements of conjugality, law and lore explore the meaning of adultery within two iconic poles: the figure of the adulterer as a sinner, and the image of the adulteress as a traitor to her own body.

---

107. Cf. Hos. 2.21-2.
108. Loraux, *Born of the Earth*, p. 107.
109. E. Levine, 'On Exodus 21,10', pp. 163-65, on biblical marital ideology.

Chapter 8

STEALING HEARTS, THIEVING BODIES
(WORD EIGHT)

You shall not steal. (Exod. 20.15)

1. *What Does 'Stealing' Really Mean?*

Early 2002 catapulted a tiny town in Kansas to fame, or rather notoriety. Upon reading submissions from a group of sophomores, a biology teacher in a high school in the town of Piper turned to the know-all computer. Her search elicited the source of the precocious responses of her pupils. She rewarded their internet surfing with F(ail). After complaints by parents the school board, in a closed-door meeting, reversed her decision. She resigned in protest. Her resignation resounded through-out the media, from California to the Philippines and from New York to London (*New York Times*, 14 February 2002; *The Guardian*, 7 March 2002). At the time of writing, the matter has not been resolved. The town remains deeply divided. Nor are there teachers willing to step into so treacherous a ground.

In our terminology, the act of the sophomores is called 'plagiarism'. At a more basic level it is about theft of knowledge. What the enterprising pupils have done was to acquire the property of knowledge, legally, it would appear. They presented it, illegally, as their own property. Ironically, the case does not point out to either an identifiable victim or to a clear-cut diminution of tangible assets. Even more ironically, the thieves regarded themselves as the wounded party. Yet, their action constitutes if not a crime then certainly a concerted assault on the property of human knowledge. It also shows just how wide and fluid are the frontiers between the legal and illegal acquisition of material and mental goods. And it suggests that of the activities addressed in the Decalogue, stealing may be the most mundane of all, a transgression which transpires on a regular basis and is committed by a significant number of people.

In the present order of the Decalogue(s), theft follows murder and adultery, as though such transgressions are measured along a sliding scale of severity. Within this triad, stealing and adultery may not be entirely distinct, and both can lead to murder. Coveting, too, the subject of the Tenth Word, has the potential of incurring all three: adultery, murder and/or theft. What, then, is the point of including so many bans on ostensibly the same crime of stealing in the same code?[1] Confronting

---

1.   This question further assumes that חמד ('to covet'), which the Tenth Word prohibits, must refer to tangible objects rather than to a mental state, an assumption to which Stephen A. Kaufman,

such apparent duplicates in so short a document as the Decalogue, biblical scholars have concluded, as the rabbis had done centuries before, that the Eighth Word deals not with the basic act of stealing property but rather with the misappropriation of the human body.[2] In other words, the transgression envisaged in the Commandment relates to depriving an individual (specifically an adult Israelite male) of the free use of (his) own body through abduction and subjection to involuntary servitude.[3]

To account for this reading of the Eighth Word as a ban on abduction or man-stealing, scholars have relied on several arguments, including the Commandment's position in the text, namely its wedging between the prohibition on adultery, on one side, and on false witnessing, on the other side.[4] Since both adultery and perjury, it has been argued, are offences against individuals and not against inanimate objects, the Eighth Word commands perforce a similar scope, because all three precepts aspire to protect the basic rights of the male member of the covenant, namely his life, marriage and reputation. It has been further assumed that the curt Commandment 'originally' bore a specific object, a person rather than property. In this 'original' guise, the Commandment would have been something like: 'thou shalt not steal a man'. One problem with this interpretation is that the only biblical narratives which can be construed as abduction relate to the 'theft' not of adults but of babies.[5]

One can speculate further about missing objects of a transitive verb. It is possible, at least according to some, to contend that the Exodus Decalogue had been aimed at kidnapping while the Deuteronomy Decalogue shifted the object of stealing to property.[6] Through a process of inner-biblical interpretation, it would then

'The Structure of the Deuteronomic Law', *Maarav* 1 (1979), pp. 105-58 (145-55), strenuously objects. On the textual triad of murder–adultery–theft, see Richard Freund, 'Murder, Adultery and Theft', *SJOT* 2 (1989), pp. 72-80.

2. Albrecht Alt, 'Das Verbot des Diebstahls im Dekalog', in M. Noth (ed.), *Kleine Schriften zur Geschichte des Volkes Israel* (3 vols.; Munich: Beck, 1953–59), I, pp. 333-40, echoed in many of the standard commentaries and given the stamp of authority by von Rad, *Deuteronomy: A Commentary*, p. 59, and Martin Noth, *Exodus* (OTL; Philadelphia: Westminster Press, 1962), pp. 165-66. Alt's view is also supported by Phillips, *Ancient Israel's Criminal Law*, pp. 130-41, who assumes that the Decalogue's prohibition, or rather their violation, entailed a capital punishment. Cautious, if not dissenting voices, include H. Klein, 'Verbot des Menschendiebstahls im Dekalog: Prüfung einer These Albrecht Alt', *VT* 26 (1976), pp. 161-69; and Robert K. Gnuse, *You shall Not Steal: Community and Property in Biblical Traditions* (Maryknoll, NY: Orbis Books, 1985), who ultimately remains unconvinced, as do Stamm and Andrew, *The Ten Commandments*, p. 106. In general, Bernard S. Jackson, *Theft in Early Jewish Law* (Oxford: Clarendon Press, 1972). For the rabbinic interpretation see *b. Sanh.* 86a and the discussion of this text below.

3. Whether in this light the Commandment also contemplates the safeguarding of individual rights of ownership or the right to own one's own free body remains unclear; see Gerhard Wehmeier, 'The Prohibition of Theft in the Decalogue', *The Indian Journal of Theology* 26 (1977), pp. 181-91.

4. For Phillips, *Ancient Israel's Criminal Law*, pp. 131-35, the necessity to identify a capital crime rather than a tort further dictates a similar hypothesis.

5. Joseph and his brothers are hardly a case in point since the 'crime' is 'in-house', so to speak and, in fact, the criminals are not chastised. Ironically, their 'crime' achieves for the favored brother much more outside the home.

6. Wehmeier, 'Prohibition', p. 189.

appear that a prohibition which 'originally' had forbidden the deprivation of personal freedom changed to denote the unlawful removal of the possessions of an individual. This mutation, it is further argued, is reflected in the choice of a different verb in each of the Decalogues to describe coveting (but not stealing!), generating a further assumption to the effect that Deuteronomy's Eighth Word had taken the 'original' function of the Tenth.

Leaving aside, for the moment, modern scholarly ingenuity, it is worth noting that the rabbis in antiquity, puzzled by the same seeming insistence of the Decalogue on protecting basic rights at the cost of stylistic redundancy, debated the meaning of theft:

> Whence do we learn that there is a warning (or formal prohibition) to one who steals a person? R. Josia said: [we know it from the Eighth Commandment] You shall not steal. R. Johanan said: [rather we know this from the phrase: Because they are all my slaves whom I had brought out from the land of Egypt] you will not sell them as slaves (Lev. 25.42). Here there is no dispute. One master refers to the ban on stealing, the other on selling [a stolen person?].
>
> Our rabbis taught: You shall not steal (Exod. 20.15; Deut. 5.19). Scripture refers to a thief who steals humans. But you say that this may not necessarily be the case and that Scripture deals with the theft of money. Apply yourself to a study of the thirteen principles whereby the Torah is interpreted, including 'a matter is derived from its context'. And since Scripture speaks [in this context] of capital punishment this, too, is a matter relating to humans (and not to property).
>
> Another however taught: You shall not steal ([plural] Lev. 19.11). Scripture refers to one who steals property. You have reservations [about this interpretation] believing that Scripture deals with one who steals human beings as you rely on the thirteen principles?... [I maintain] that Scripture refers to money and hence that here, too, the matter relates to [theft of] property. (*b. Sanh.* 86a [Soncino])

Using Deut. 24.7 ('if one is found stealing a soul from among his own brothers, sons of Israel, treats him as a slave or sells him, let the thief die so that this evil be purged from among you') as a prooftext, a rabbinic majority advanced a theory of theft as abduction. Unlike modern biblical scholars, who regard the Eighth Word and its implied ban on abduction as an infringement of manhood and hence as a prohibition aimed primarily at curbing the 'stealing' of males, the rabbis ranged objects of kidnapping to include persons stolen in sleep, pregnant women, proselytes, manumitted slaves and even minors (*b. Sanh.* 85b). Rabbinic ruminations on theft went as far as contemplating an abduction of one woman by another! (*b. Sanh.* 85b). All these talmudic categories constitute, however, an expansion of rabbinic understanding of the act of stealing as, basically, the willful diminution of one's possessions by another.

At the heart of rabbinic perceptions of theft is a theology of restitution:

> A man who abducts another can return his theft and repent. A man who steals from another can return the loot and repent. But a man who comes on another man's wife causes her to become forbidden to her husband, banishes himself from the world. He has no remedy or repentance. (*b. Ḥag.* 9b [Soncino])

This comparative examination concludes that stealing a body or an object is a crime which carries the potential of definable and equitable compensation. By contrast, 'stealing' a man's wife (= adultery) is a wholly different proposition of theft. The invaded body of a married woman, once infringed upon, cannot be 'restored' to its pre-adultery state. Murder and adultery have no restitution. Plain theft does. This approach explains why biblical exegesis of the Eighth Word, when dealing with abduction, insists not so much on the act of stealing in itself as on the treatment of the stolen item.

Rabbinic speculations on the meaning of theft appear anchored in biblical episodes which lent themselves to an extraordinary range of thefts, from stealing the fruit of knowledge to hijacking primogeniture, and from kidnapping brothers to 'stealing' hearts and minds. A popularized rabbinic midrash on the Decalogue provides a narrative illustration of the broad meaning of stealing by linking the inhabitants of Paradise through theft, and by labeling the iconoclast Rachel a sinner for stealing idols from her own father:

> Come and see how much sin does a theft engender, how it turns beauty into ugliness, happiness into sadness, haughty into humble men, and the clothed into naked. In the garden of Eden no less than ten canopies, all made of precious stones, shielded Adam and Eve.[7] But because they stretched their hands in theft, stealing the fruit of the tree (אילן) of good and evil, the Lord was angry with them and ushered into the world forty curses, ten on Adam, ten on Eve, ten on the serpent, and ten on the earth.
>
> So, too, Rachel our mother, although stealing the idols in order to prevent her father from idolatry, nevertheless the sin barred her from burial in the cave of the righteous, as Jacob stated: *Whoever is found with your gods, he will not live.* (*Midrash Decalogue*; Gen. 31.32)[8]

With cautionary examples, the midrash transfers readers into metaphorical plains and domains of criminal activity. It implies that even in an idyllic existence the temptation to sin, specifically through stealing, is ever present, and that a daughter can transgress the boundaries of father–daughter relations by stealing from her own father. The rabbis knew, of course, that the verb גנב ('to steal'), as it appears in the Decalogue, is singularly absent from Genesis 3. They must have noted that its first usage is indeed in Gen. 31.19-20, which describes the departure of Jacob, Leah and Rachel from Laban's home, by stealth and at night. Neither tale (Gen. 3 nor 31) deals with either a theft of a mature Israelite male's body, or of a child, or with stealing ordinary material goods.

The social consequences of stealing in its broadest sense are clearly implied in the midrashic application of the term 'stealing' to the Genesis narrative of Adam and Eve. By juxtaposing the 'theft' of fruit from the tree of good and evil with Rachel's stealing of her father's idols, the midrash 'translates' the prohibition that

---

7.   Cf. the most elaborate description of the primordial wedding in *PRE* 11, quoted in Jeremy Cohen, *Be Fertile and Increse, Fill the Earth and Master It: The Ancient and Medieval Career of a Biblical Text* (Ithaca, NY: Cornell University Press, 1989), pp. 108-109.

8.   Jellinek, *s.v.*

Yahweh had issued in Paradise to the primordial couple into terms of stealing. Rabbinic exegesis suggests that a theft is not merely the appropriation of forbidden goods, but also an act that has far-reaching repercussions for social conventions: thefts subvert norms and transform the predictable into the unpredictable.

2. Between Man and Man: Exodus on Abduction

Whosoever steals a man, whether to sell or to keep him in bondage, is to be put to death. (Exod. 21.16)[9]

In the Covenant Code, abduction, like intentional and unintentional killing (Exod. 21.12-14) and battering of parents (21.15), entails capital punishment.[10] At stake in 21.16 seems to have been the right of free individuals to corporeal autonomy. In other words, the law aspires to regulate transfers from a state of physical freedom to that of bondage by outlawing whims of individuals, as already seen in the case of the Hebrew female slave (21.7-11).[11] Exodus 21.16 further complements the rules relating to the period of enslavement of 'Hebrew' male slaves.[12] Its formulation insists that any unauthorized change of status, particularly one which turns a free Israelite male into a slave against his will, is punishable by death.

This is a severe penalty which the Decalogue itself stops short of prescribing.[13] The severity of the punishment is especially striking in view of the general use of slave labor in ancient societies, an aspect which rendered trade in human beings a regular feature of the economy. For the narrators of the Exodus, however, the subject of slavery carried uncommon sensitivity. The God of the Decalogue was no mere deity but a liberator of slaves, as the First Word clearly announces. In this narrowly defined ecology the Pentateuch further stipulates, in theory at least, complete equality among (male) members of the covenant. In reality, Pentateuchal law recognizes absolute paternal authority over daughters, including their legal selling into concubinage (Exod. 21.6). Genesis also records the profitable sale of a young

---

9.   Cf. Sprinkle, *Covenant*, p. 73: 'he who kidnaps someone, whether he sells him or whether the person is found in his possession, may be put to death'; and Van Seters, *Law Book for the Diaspora*, p. 102: 'whoever kidnaps a person, whether he sells him or he (the victim) is found in his possession, he is to be put to death'.

10.   Sprinkle, *Covenant*, p. 76, further connects these by suggesting that stealing a person is typically an offense against parents. See also above Chapters 5 and 6.

11.   See above, Chapter 1. It is not clear, however, in spite of Phillips, *Ancient Israel's Criminal Law*, p. 131, whether the law further entails only sales outside the community although he is correct to suggest that such a transaction entails the permanent alienation of the abducted person. Nor do I find convincing Daube's notion of an expanded law which had originally been restricted to a sale but expanded to include wrongful possession (Daube, *Studies in Biblical Law*, p. 95). Morgenstern's suggestion of permanent possession seems more attractive; see Julian Morgenstern, 'The Book of the Covenant—Part II', *HUCA* 7 (1930), pp. 19-258 (189), 'The Book of the Covenant—Part III', *HUCA* 8-9 (1931–32), p. 1-150 (125).

12.   Exod. 21.2-6, and Chapter 1, above.

13.   In spite of scholarly assumptions which allocate capital punishment to all transgressions of the Words: e.g. Phillips, *Ancient Israel's Criminal Law*.

man by his own brothers (but without parental authorization) to slave traders (Gen. 37.25-28). Yet, according to Exod. 21.16, an unlawful seizure of one man by another with a view to profit through trading bodies and subjecting them to involuntary bondage merits death.

Stealing in the context of Exod. 21.16 implies not only a violation of the Eighth Word but also an undermining of acceptable social procedures which assign free or bonded status to individuals. There is no limit to buying Hebrew slaves, providing they are manumitted after six years. But there is no room for an arbitrary appropriation of this process through clandestine actions. The ban on stealing humans further develops the theme of freedom from servitude which the First Word incorporates, and which the regulations on slaves elaborate.[14]

That stealing extends from humans to animals and to inanimate objects is clearly evidenced in the regulations relating to theft of herd and of money. The difference resides in the recommended penalty. Exodus 21.37–22.16, a unit which deals with theft and damage to property, begins with theft of oxen and ends with the 'theft' of virginal hymen.[15] The laws show no mercy to a thief caught breaking in at night (22.1, death with no possibility of avenging) nor to one caught by daylight (22.2, death with the possibility of avenging or compensation or selling into slavery). Much attention is lavished on allocating appropriate compensation or punitive damages to the owner in case of a theft of animals, and on safeguarding a person suspected, unjustly, of betraying neighborly trust through stealing and lying.

Monetary compensation is also allocated by law in a case of a seduction of a virgin who had not been betrothed (Exod. 22.15-16). Here the law postulates the possible 'restoration' of a fractured hymen, either through marriage of the 'abductor' with the seduced woman, or through an adequate monetary compensation to her father, if he objects to the marriage. The inclusion of this type of a theft in the list of tangible objects of theft is revealing of the scope of stealing which the Eighth Word encompasses. 'Stealing' an intact hymen harms owners of property and families of marriageable daughters just as much as abduction undermines the ownership of an individual over her/his own body. Yet, whereas theft of property or of virginity can evidently be measured in monetary or marital terms and compensated accordingly, man-stealing requires that the very body of the thief provides the indemnification.[16]

When the law delves into the precise relations between thieves and victims, it depicts an all-male realm in which a temporary exchange of property is done on trust (Exod. 22.6-14). If this trust is betrayed, the theft itself becomes incidental in a complex web of communal relationship that binds members of the covenant to each other. This is why, when the accusing and the accused cannot settle the issue, a decision must be reached either through an ordeal of sorts (22.8) or through an oath (22.10)—both solutions apparently leaving the final arbitration beyond human

14. Sprinkle, *Covenant*, p. 81, and above, Chapter 1.

15. On the unity of these rules, Sprinkle, *Covenant*, pp. 129-59.

16. Deut. 22.28 unites the two clauses and imposes both monetary damages and marriage on a man who seduces an unbetrothed woman.

jurisdiction.[17] A lie, then, compounds the guilt of thieving. This intimate link between stealing and denying or theft and lying is precisely the theme of a ban which Lev. 19.11 enunciates and 5.21-26 elaborates. A theft, in this reading, is not merely a crime but also a sin which goes beyond material damage to either body or property. In the Levitical exposition of crimes, stealing undermines the very order of the society which the Pentateuch envisages by introducing a wedge into relations among covenant members and, through false swearing in God's name, also between God and Israel (Lev. 19.12, cf. 5.21-26).

Samples of stealing in Genesis–Numbers vary. The stories relating to Joseph provide an exegesis which obfuscates rather than illuminates the laws. Genesis 37 accounts for an abduction of one brother by his own siblings through jealousy, and Genesis 44 shows the ostensible victim of the theft planning a similar crime. Nor are the thieves punished, unless one considers a general famine (43.1) as a divinely induced penalty. By contrast, as the rabbis had indeed realized, the tale of Rachel supplies an important narrative commentary on the scope and nature of stealing.

3. *Rachel: Mediating Men by Theft*

Ancestral history in Genesis is marked by migrations, carefully calculated marital alliances and seemingly unpredictable appropriation of primogeniture. The case of Jacob is particularly interesting because the implementation of crucial transfers closely involves women. Jacob's usurpation of paternal blessing is carefully engineered by his mother, Rebecca, as is his escape route which leads to her paternal home in far-away Padan-Aram (Gen. 27–28). The favored son is packed off to prevent sibling murder as well as a misalliance.[18] But instead of one bride, Jacob secures two. And instead of the brides joining their husband in Abraham's promised land, the bridegroom initially stays with his in-laws.

From the start of the Jacob cycle rivalry, deception and apparent ignorance mark the progression of the protagonist from his parental home to his marital abode and back to Canaan.[19] At the center of this narrative are two thefts, one of property, the other of heart (Gen. 31.19-20). Because Laban appears reluctant to part with an industrious relative, at least according to 30.27-43, Yahweh must intervene to confirm the basic righteousness of Jacob's decision to sever ties with Laban and with his wives' home (31.3). The return to Canaan must be presented not as an arbitrary individual desire but as one which rehearses the action of Abraham himself (Gen. 12). In spite of divine approbation, parting with the host's property and relatives constitutes, as the narrator must have known, a violation of the rules of hospitality which protect the integrity of the host's household.

Jacob's adventures in Laban's land fit well into a pattern of ancient romances which feature a noble refugee in 'barbarous lands' presided over by a generous

---

17. There are no investigative procedures, nor reference to the testimony of at least two witnesses, as Deut. 19.15 demands in case of capital crimes.

18. See above, Chapter 6.

19. Jack M. Sasson, 'Love's Roots: On the Redaction of Genesis 30.14-24', in Marks and Good (eds.), *Love and Death in the Ancient Near East*, pp. 205-209.

local ruler who welcomes him warmly, going so far as to bestow on him the hand of his eldest daughter in marriage.[20] In such cases, it must be noted, the husband invariably joins the bride's family. If the foreigner eventually returns to his homeland he does not have the right to remove the wife, her children or her property from her paternal home.[21] This is the standard arrangement in a type of marriage called '*erebu*' in which a man lives with his wife in her father's household and must consequently leave as he had arrived, without family and property which had accrued since his arrival.[22] She remains 'the native lady' who cannot be transported against her will to her husband's land because there she may become an alien, laboring under the opprobrious disabilities of a 'foreign woman'.[23]

These are the rules that account for the otherwise inexplicable conference which Jacob holds with his wives, regarding his decision to leave their father's home (Gen. 31.4-16). In this meeting Jacob presents their father as a thief who had cheated him of rightful gain (31.7-8), himself as victim of paternal chicanery, and Yahweh as a judge who has sided with him (Jacob) (31.8-9). Notwithstanding this list of litanies, without the permission of Laban's daughters Jacob had no right to take them and their children with him. This is precisely why Leah and Rachel must 'renounce' their paternal home, as indeed they do by depicting themselves, and not Jacob, as Laban's victims (31.14-16).[24]

Genesis 30–31 hints at the dilemma of women who need to violate the rules of male hospitality in order to survive and to protect their interests. From Laban's daughters' point of view, their father had 'sold' them and had consumed the money paid to him instead of safeguarding it for their sake (3.15). In their eyes, such an attitude disqualifies him as a parent and consequently justifies their departure with Jacob.[25] Laban's daughters also insist that the property which Jacob had amassed in Laban's domain belongs to them and their sons, and that Laban had forfeited his parental right to decide their fate (31.16).

20.   Cf. the Egyptian romance of Sinuhe, in Miriam Lichtheim, *Ancient Egyptian Literature: A Book of Readings* (3 vols.; Berkeley: University of California Press, 1973–80), I, pp. 222-35. Joseph's tale is, of course, another variation on the same motives.

21.   Cyrus H. Gordon, 'The Marriage and Death of Sinuhe', in Marks and Good (eds.), *Love and Death in the Ancient Near East*, pp. 43-44 (44).

22.   Gordon, 'Marriage and Death'. Cf. the rules relating to a 'Hebrew' slave who marries a woman whom his master had bestowed on him (Exod. 21.4).

23.   Gordon, 'Marriage and Death', with Exod. 21.8-9 (discussed above, Chapter 1).

24.   I wonder if the 'renunciation' had to be effected by both or only by the eldest. If the latter is the case, the insertion of Rachel's name before Leah's in Gen. 31.14 suggests that Rachel acted out of place, as is also suggested by her theft of the תרפים. The text insists on verbs in the plural. Perhaps, then, the consent of both women had to be obtained, a case which still does not account for the appearance of Rachel's name before that of Leah.

25.   Exum, *Fragmented Women*, pp. 128-30, reads Rachel's theft as staking a claim to matrilineal descent (vs. Jacob's theft), with Esther Fuchs, '"For I Have the Way of Women": Deception, Gender and Ideology in Biblical Narrative', *Semeia* 42 (1988) (= J. Cheryl Exum and Johanna W.H. Bos [eds.], *Reasoning with the Foxes: Female Wit in a World of Male Power*), pp. 68-83, and Nancy Jay, *Throughout Your Generations Forever: Sacrifice, Religion and Paternity* (Chicago: Chicago University Press, 1992), pp. 106-107.

In spite of spousal consent, the departure is accompanied by stealth and darkness. Laban is absent (31.19). Jacob's actions are subsequently described as theft,
accompanied or heralded by another theft, Rachel's mystifying appropriation of
her father's תרפים:

> And Rachel stole the תרפים of her father. And Jacob outwitted (literally: stole the
> heart of) Laban the Aramean from whom he had concealed that he intended to flee.
> (Gen. 31.19-20)[26]

Symmetry of action and intention appears deliberate. By juxtaposing the two types
of theft the story equates Rachel's unlawful appropriation of paternal property with
Jacob's deceit of Laban, making both wife and husband ostensibly equally cul-
pable. Yet, if Jacob's 'theft' is accounted for, Rachel's remains inexplicable. If
Jacob's 'theft' is promptly discovered, that of Rachel remains concealed. Above all,
the two thefts differ in their mode of resolution. When Laban confronts Jacob over
his stealthy departure with wives, children and possessions he is irate but ultimately
accepts Jacob's excuse. No reconciliation or resolution accompanies Rachel's theft.

Why, then, does Rachel resort to theft? *Cui bono*? Who is to benefit from this
illegal transfer, especially when it is evidently never revealed? Moreover, the items
do not belong to a stranger, nor had they been entrusted by her to Laban's care or
by him to her care. From Laban's point of view, Jacob's departure, in his absence
and without his approval, with property to which he held, at best, a precarious
claim (including the תרפים) presents a triple theft (Gen. 31.26, 27, 30). The dialogue between the two men is instructive:

> (Laban:) What have you done, cheating me (literally, stealing my heart), and carry-
> ing away my daughters like captives of the sword? Why did you flee secretly and
> cheat me (literally, steal) and did not tell me so that I might have sent you away
> with mirth and songs, with tambourine and lyre?[27] Why did you not permit me to
> kiss my sons and my daughters farewell? You have acted foolishly indeed for it is
> in my power to do you harm. But the God of your father spoke to me last night
> saying, 'Take heed that you speak to Jacob neither good nor bad'. Now you have
> gone away because you longed greatly for your father's house. But why did you
> steal my gods?
>
> (Jacob:) Because I was afraid for I had thought that you would take your
> daughters from me by force (גזל). Anyone with whom you find your gods shall not
> live. In the presence of our kinsmen point out to what I have which is yours and
> take it. (Gen. 31.26-32 RSV [slightly modified])

26. תרפים have been variously identified as idols, divinatory items, ancestral figurines and, by
Laban, as his gods. See S. Smith, 'What were the Teraphim?', *JTS* 33 (1932), pp. 33-36; Joseph
Dan, 'Teraphim: From Popular Belief to a Folktale', *Scripta Hierosolymitana* 27 (1978), pp. 99-106;
Karel van der Toorn, 'The Nature of the Biblical Teraphim in the Light of the Cuneiform
Evidence', *CBQ* 52 (1990), pp. 203-22; Micahel Heltzer, 'New Light from Emar on Genesis 31:
The Theft of the Teraphim', in Manfried Dietrich and Ingo Kottspieper (eds.), *'Und Mose schrieb
dieses Lied auf': Studien zum Alten Testament und zum Alten Orient* (Festschrift Oswald Loretz;
Münster: Ugarit Verlag, 1998), pp. 357-62.

27. Cf. the merriment that accompanies the 'Song of the Sea' (Exod. 15) which commemorates
another hasty departure and a vain pursuit.

Amid these verbal skirmishes it may be asked: Why does Jacob not inform Laban that the return to his Canaanite home is a dictate of a deity? The answer seems to lie in the mode of marriage. Jacob could indeed have left (and Laban does not voice objection to Jacob's own departure) but not with Laban's daughters and grand-children. Even Yahweh's words do not empower the appropriation of wives and property which had accrued in Padan-Aram. Why, then, does Jacob not state openly that his wives had renounced their father's claim to themselves rather than con-fessing to fear of losing them? Perhaps because even the women's permission was insufficient to warrant departure without parental consent.

The scene, like that of Jacob's marriage(s), seems carefully crafted around two distinct and conflicting traditions, one providing for bridal severance from the parental home; the other espousing her retention. In spite of the support which both Leah and Rachel lend to Jacob, the text remains undecided. The decision is ulti-mately entrusted first to Yahweh, who urges Jacob to leave, and then to the תרפים, whose removal forfeits, it seems, Laban's claim to retain his daughters against their will.[28] The search for the תרפים, vain as it was bound to be, is merely a demonstra-tive gesture of paternal authority, as is Laban's response to Jacob's self-righteous rhetoric (Gen. 31.43).

The Genesis narrator casts Rachel as a wife who acts exactly like her husband, thus hinting that the items appropriated by Jacob were of equal value with the תרפים which Rachel stole. The two are linked not only through bonds of love but also through ties of transgression. Laban's accusation suggests that Jacob's mode of behavior had been as inappropriate as it was unpredictable, especially with regards to the theft of the תרפים. In Laban's paternal vision he (Laban) emerges as a de-voted father, imbued with laudable solicitude for the welfare of his daughters and their offspring.

When Laban enters Rachel's tent in his search for the תרפים, he gropes, like a blind man, throughout it (Gen. 31.34; cf. Deut. 28.29). Sitting on the loot, Rachel employs the same kind of self-righteous rhetoric that both her father and her hus-band had used throughout.[29] The text dryly asserts and reasserts that Laban 'did not find' the תרפים in Rachel's tent (Gen. 31.34, 35), highlighting the fragile nature of the familial bond that links all four participants in the 'divorce'. The confrontation between Rachel and Laban illuminates both the powerlessness, as well as the power, of women to navigate their path through the maze of rules which govern social

28. On the theft as a means to establish Jacob as family leader, see Cyrus H. Gordon, 'Biblical Customs and the Nuzu Tablets', *BA* 3 (1940), pp. 1-22; and Moshe Greenberg, 'Another Look at Rachel's Theft of the Teraphim', *JBL* 81 (1962), pp. 239-48. Cf. Ktziah Spanier, 'Rachel's Theft of the Teraphim, her Struggle for Family Primacy', *VT* 42 (1992), pp. 404-12, who sees it as means to establish Rachel's own position in Jacob's household. For Bal the possession of the תרפים repre-sents Rachel's transfer of paternal authority over child from grandfather to father, that is transi-tion from patrilocal to virilocal; see Mieke Bal, 'Tricky Thematics', *Semeia* 42 (1988) (= Exum and Bos [eds.], *Reasoning with the Foxes: Female Wit in a World of Male Power*), pp. 133-55 (151-52).

29. On the reference to menstruation as an editorial slander on Rachel, see Exum, *Fragmented Women*, p. 128, and Fuchs; '"For I Have the Way of Women"'.

norms between men. Her behavior suggests that the only constant in Rachel's life has been the love of her husband. Denied maternity, this love is, for years, a sole source of maintenance. Granted maternity, Rachel can act independently of both husband and father. For this, rather than for the theft itself, she is punished with both premature death and burial in isolation, as the midrash asserts.[30]

In the exchange between Jacob and Laban, after the vain search, the stolen 'gods' are no longer an object of discussion.[31] Reconciliation is achieved—between Jacob's rhetoric of injury and Laban's rhetoric of paternity—when the two men agree to erect a heap of stones to commemorate their newly struck covenant (Gen. 31.44). Jacob must pledge to treat Laban's daughters well. Barring love for Leah, this is exactly the way in which he had been treating them. Ultimately, then, the language of hospitality reasserts itself as Laban resumes the role of host and father that his own daughters have discarded.

At the heart of this biblical drama of theft is a woman who insists on the binding nature of the pact she had contracted, on her own, with a man, in spite of, and against, familial expectations and traditions. Rachel had been the first member of the family to meet Jacob, the first to be kissed by him, and the first to announce his arrival (Gen. 29.10-13). She was Jacob's desired bride. By stealing from her father, she reaffirms her decision to side with her husband contrary to local law. Her act also highlights the tragic nature of women's choice in an environment that fails to condone erotic spontaneity, male or female, unless it fits into a correct framework.

Rachel comes up against male ideology of kinship ties. Besides natural affection, these ties are based on mutual favors. Parents naturally love and care for their children but they also expect to benefit from them through reciprocal arrangements. This is one reason why childlessness is not only a source of personal sorrow and divine punishment but also a distinct disadvantage in a society that negotiates marital bodies as a vital form of exchange. Respect for parents, therefore, is one of the strongest obligations in biblical vision of covenant society. The greatest opprobrium is reserved for those who violate it.

Daughters and wives sustain the ties of friendship that connect men to each other either through kin or through bonds of hospitality. This is why Jacob can respond to Laban's chagrin by stating his fear lest Laban cheats him of his daughters (Gen. 31.31). And this is why a reconciliation between the two men is possible but not between father and daughter. Theft of an inalienable part of paternal property, then, introduces an irreparable breach of social rules and a permanent alienation from family and home. For Rachel there is no way back. Once she commits a crime against her father Rachel cannot retain her position as a daughter. Her situation is complicated by her need to conceal her theft not only from her father but also from her husband. Both are presented as wholly ignorant of the intention, action and

---

30. Cf. Daube, *Studies in Biblical Law*, pp. 216-17.

31. But the curse on the thief remains in effect. On Jacob's perception of the theft of the תרפים as a religious and criminal offense which carries capital punishment, see Heltzer, 'New Light'.

identity of the thief. Yet, the text inserts a comment about Jacob's apparent ignorance at a juncture (31.32) which suggests that the two men must have been aware
that either Leah or Rachel had committed the 'crime'.

Legally speaking, the 'crime' is insoluble. There were evidently no witnesses,
nor was the thief caught in action. Moreover, there is no restitution. Although the
הרפים are objects which, like other objects, should have carried a specific monetary value, biblical ideology cannot envisage a fourfold restitution, for example, of
idols or ancestral figurines. There is no adequate compensation, in this case, at least
none that a human judge can impose in accordance with existing regulations. Only
divine judgment can decide the magnitude and nature of the penalty. And while the
execution of the thief is clearly uncalled for, the consignment of Rachel to perpetual banishment from family burial provides a biblical forerunner of 'excommunication'. Buried on the road, Rachel is both forgotten and remembered. She is
excised from the familial cemetery and hence forgotten. But her lone monument on
the road reminds onlookers of the fate of a thief, motivated by love, whose fate
cannot be decided by human agents.

Although rabbinic readings construe Rachel's theft as an exemplary expression
of iconoclasm, the rabbis refused to ignore or condone the fact that her action
constituted a basic violation of the Eighth Word. As *Midrash Decalogue* suggests,
there is no redemption either for Rachel or for Eve. Because of her share in the
appropriation of forbidden fruit, Eve is penalized with perpetual pain of procreation
(Gen. 3.16). Because of her active participation in an affair that had to stay an all-
male matter, Rachel dies giving birth and remains barred from communal burial.[32]

Through stealing Laban's 'gods' Rachel carries an integral part of her home with
her to a new home in Canaan. Paradoxically, then, she carries with her the seeds of
idolatry to the promised land of her husband's ancestry, just as Eve had carried the
seeds of human knowledge from the Garden of Eden to human abodes.[33] Both
women are doomed to punitive separation, Eve from the paradisiacal scene of her
'crime', Rachel from the family she elected to join. Judged within a context of an
ideology which links man's value to his mode of burial, Rachel's interment in a
'diaspora' serves as a warning of the fate of women who tamper with the ideals of
manhood.[34]

32. 'The pathos of her death at so young an age is magnified by her lonely burial outside Beth-
lehem, apart from the other matriarchs and patriarchs' (Samuel H. Dresner, *Rachel* [Minneapolis:
Fortress Press, 1994], p. 101). On her subsequent prophetic 'redemption', see Susan Brown-Gutof,
'The Voice of Rachel in Jeremiah 31: A Calling to "Something New"', *Union Seminary Quarterly
Review* 45 (1991), pp. 177-90.

33. Gen. 35.4 refers to a burial ceremony in which Jacob inters foreign gods and their accou-
trements. These may have been none other than the הרפים. Perhaps, then, Rachel acknowledges
the theft.

34. Cf. the oracle of Huldah which assures Josiah a proper burial (2 Kgs 22); see also above,
Chapter 1. It is astonishing, and reflective of the redactor's biases, that Jacob gets away with 'stealing hearts' while Absalom, who does the same (2 Sam. 15.6), does not.

4. *Deuteronomy on Stealing Humans*

If a man is found stealing one (נפש) of his brethren, from among the people of
Israel, and if he ill treats him (and) or sells him, then the thief shall die. So you shall
purge the evil from the midst of you. (Deut. 24.7 RSV [slightly emended])

In the Deuteronomic reading of abduction, a thief is 'a stealer of life'.[35] By a
deliberate transfer of terminology, a kidnapper becomes a man who harms not only
the body of a 'brother' but also his soul, the very soul that must be focused on
loving God, as the *Shema* specifies (Deut. 6.5). The sale of such a person into
slavery is considered a violation of the very contract that binds Israel together. The
verb which describes the mistreatment of persons in kidnapped captivity, עמר, is
rare. It appears twice only, both in the context of Deuteronomic law: once in
conjunction with the so-called 'law of the beautiful captive' (21.14), and once in
this context of theft of humans. In both instances the verb signifies the arbitrary
handling of a helpless person in the power of another.[36]

Are 'stealers' of life and stealers of wives the same? Deuteronomy 21.11 casts
warriors who desire captive women for their beauty as men ruled by their passions.[37] The law provides for marriage between captor and captive after according a
period of mourning to the female captive. It also acknowledges the possibility of
the waning of the lust that had generated the union in the first place. This is why
regulations call on Israelite men who are married to these 'beautiful' captives not to
sell these women into slavery, lest they compound carnality with greed (21.14).
They are to set the women free, letting them go where they may will.

In this reading, the lot of a non-Israelite female, beautiful as she may have been,
hardly differs from that of a 'Hebrew' woman sold into slavery by her own father
(Exod. 21.11). But while Deuteronomy 21 calls on the captor-husband to release
his captive-wife, Exodus 21 encourages the buyer to keep his Hebrew maid-wife or
rather to preserve her marital rights.[38] In both cases the text tacitly acknowledges
the fact that humans are not born into slavery. Deuteronomy 21 further suggests
that the arbitrary disposal of female captives after marriage is as sinful as the
unlawful sale of abducted Israelites: both sets of rules (Deut. 21 and 24) deal with
property accrued either through war or as a result of an illegal action; and both
condemn the selling into slavery of human property acquired by aggression and
transgression. But Deuteronomy 21 does not specify a penalty for a man who does
sell a captive ex-wife; Deut. 24.7 consigns an abductor who had sold his male(?)
'loot' to death.

---

35.   Phillips, *Ancient Israel's Criminal Law*, p. 130.

36.   Phillips, *Ancient Israel's Criminal Law*, pp. 131-32, considers the meaning of the verb lost
and the context commercial, with Albrecht Alt, 'Zu Hit'ammer'', *VT* 2 (1952), pp. 153-59, where it
is defined as exercising power of disposal.

37.   According to Pressler, *View of Women*, p. 11, this law provides a means to marry where
normal procedures of marriage are unavailable or non-existing.

38.   See above, Chapter 2 §3.

Mitigating aggression, the laws relating to the mistreatment of beautiful captives and of Israelite 'brothers' negotiate a protocol of antagonism and dominance. As indications of male violence, these rules capture a crisis atmosphere of war and instability. They confront the dilemma of critical ethics in a culture in which slavery and war are endemic by making explicit the anxiety about cruelty to human beings. And they insist that inflicting violence on others by stealing their liberty signifies a general social and moral ill which, like contagious disease, must be cleansed.

Theft as tort is different.[39] Deuteronomy insists on honest dealings throughout, especially with the poor and fragile elements in society. It calls, however, for distinct, if not altogether contradictory, systems of retribution. Thus Deut. 24.16 allocates individual penalties for individuals crimes while 5.9 (and Exod. 20.6) calls on Yahweh to visit the sins of parents on their descendants. Motivated by the souvenirs of Egyptian slavery, Deuteronomic writer(s) rely on divine vindication to provide the dynamics that account for the social ordering of Israel as a just society (Deut. 24.18). This is one reason why stealing is a crime that cannot stand alone. Rather, it is a sin, a violation of the covenant, and an act that involves lying and unlawful arrogation (Josh. 7.11). תרפים, it would appear, symbolize a crisis of familial loyalty. By stealing paternal תרפים Rachel mediates a rift between males, and the transfer of authority from father to husband. The fate of the תרפים is never disclosed. But these objects of non-Yahwist veneration continue to haunt biblical narratives at the intersection of 'private' and 'national' interests. They surface, unaccountably, in the house of David himself (1 Sam. 19.11), where his wife uses them to fool her father and to save David's life. Nor is their source revealed.

5. *When Women Steal Hearts and Men Steal Women*

To complete the canvass of biblical notions of stealing, attention must focus on 1 Samuel 19, a text that has not been characterized in terms of theft although it bears a remarkable affinity with Genesis 31. Both narratives share the casting of תרפים as catalysts that lend drama to descriptions of male parting of ways, and both involve women as users or rather abusers of תרפים. In Genesis 31 the תרפים signify the final rift between Rachel and Laban; in 1 Samuel 19 they signal the estrangement of Michal from her father Saul.[40] 1 Samuel 19 follows the stormy relations between the two with David, Michal's beloved husband and Saul's enemy. On one occasion when Saul tries to catch David, Michal alerts David to the danger and facilitates his escape in the middle of the night. To fool the father's emissaries, she plants תרפים in the nuptial bed, further lying about her husband's

---

39. As Phillips, *Ancient Israel's Criminal Law*, would argue, one belongs to the realm of civil law the other of criminal.

40. The affinities between the tales of Michal and Rachel have been noticed. See, among many, Daniel Bodi, 'La tragédie de Mikal en tant que critique de la monarchie israélite et préfiguration de sa fin', *Foi et Vie* 95 (1996), pp. 65-105 (76-79). On aspects of Michal, see the articles in David J.A. Clines and Tamara C. Eskenazi (eds.), *Telling Queen Michal's Story: An Experiment in Comparative Interpretation* (JSOTSup, 119; Sheffield: JSOT Press, 1991).

whereabouts. When deception is revealed, father chides daughter. She justifies the
ruse by claiming that David had threatened to kill her (1 Sam. 19.17).[41]

According to the narrator, the 'crimes' were crimes committed out of passion; by
Michal's own account, they were sins of fear. Had Michal brought them with her,
the way Rachel had taken the תרפים from Laban's house? The issue bears no
relevance to the narrative. 1 Samuel 19 presents the clash between father and
daughter as a conflict over the (mis)appropriation of תרפים in terms which echo
the confrontation between Laban and Jacob over the theft of paternal trust (or
'heart'). Rachel's theft hastens a breach between males; Michal's deceit does the
same, and also prevents a murder.

The scene in Michal's bedroom is one folio in a triptych which follows the
growing rupture between the present and the future kings of Israel. First, the 'spirit
of Yahweh' (1 Sam. 19.9) cheats Saul of David's body; then Michal 'steals' his
body away from her father's guards; finally, Yahweh clouds Saul's wit, denuding
him of his proper attire (19.20-24). Only in the second part can the victim of the
'theft' confront the 'thief'. When this happens, Saul accuses Michal of cheating
him or, in his words, of 'stealing his heart' (19.17).

Multiple inversions are evident in the father–daughter scenery of 1 Samuel 19.
Saul expects his daughter, *qua* daughter and subject, to become an accomplice in
the killing of her own beloved husband. In his eyes daughters owe primary duty to
fathers rather than to husbands. Michal aids and abets her husband because she
'loves' him. She also uses the kind of objects (תרפים) which, in Genesis 31, hasten
rather than postpone confrontation between males. But Genesis 31 pits one man
(Laban) against another (Jacob) upon the discovery of a 'theft'. It also confronts
a father and a daughter over a theft that cannot be uncovered. 1 Samuel 19 pits
daughter and father because no reconciliation is possible between David and Saul.
The only 'reconciliation', implied but not stated, is between Saul and Michal, which
re-transfers the daughter once more into her father's sole authority and thence into
a second marriage.[42] David's stealthy departure, then, like Jacob's, suggests that
when relations between fathers-in-law and bridegrooms sour, the removal of hus-
band/son-in-law (with or without daughters/wife and their belongings) constitutes a
theft. It deprives a lawful male owner of power to arbitrate the fate of his daughters
and of the men incorporated in the paternal household by marriage.

Perhaps the most striking symmetry between the sagas of Rachel and Michal is
the narratological need to afflict the two women with sterility. In neither case does
marriage to a desirable and much-loved partner guarantee the 'happily ever after'.
Rachel blames Jacob for her unhappiness (Gen. 30.1). Michal is not given a chance
to indulge in marital intimacy with David after the scene in the bedroom in 1 Samuel 19. Because 'happiness' in biblical terms also depends on procreation, marriage
without children can result in spousal confrontation over reproduction or over
public exhibition.

---

41. Exum, *Fragmented Women*, pp. 21-27 and 42-50.
42. Cf. Samson's marriage and the subsequent giving of his wife to another, Judg. 14.

Nor is there an adequate compensation for the 'theft' of David's body. The legal aspects of the action are complicated by the fact that the 'abduction' was not perpetrated for a nefarious purpose, hence the 'abductor' is not punishable by law. Michal cannot be subjected to the law of restitution for in cases of kidnapping and enslavement the thief must die, although the law fails to provide for procedures of investigation. Because of the essential inapplicability of 'existing' regulations to Michal (and to Rachel), God must become the ultimate arbitrator. Since the 'criminals' in both instances are women, the 'natural' divine penalty is childlessness and early death, or death in childbirth, a penalty that exceeds the proportion of the 'crime'.

When familial relations are shaped around transgressions they proceed along various avenues: some predictable, others less so. David's very survival, hence the fulfillment of a divinely appointed scheme, depends on Michal's ingenuous use of the תרפים. Her device introduces a wedge into Saul's family and paves the way to the king's downfall. Saul's children defy paternal authority and acknowledge David's position as a viable substitute. Saul himself recognizes the shift when he throws his lance, yet again, not at David but at his own son (1 Sam. 20.33). Michal's initial act of paternal defiance leads, strangely enough, not to her separation from her father's home but to David's relegation to the status of a rejected spouse. His flight and marriage with Abigail are interpreted as a 'resignation' or unilateral divorce which allows Saul to select another husband for his daughter (25.44).

This would have been an odd, but perhaps not altogether an unpredictable ending of an affair which began with a woman's passionate love for her father's enemy, and continued with her 'theft' of her father's heart and husband's body. But since it seems easier to dispose of kings than of princesses, the tale of Michal continues beyond Saul's death into a reunion with David (2 Sam. 3.1-6) at the expense of her second husband, then a rupture (6.16-23) and finally death and the execution(?) of her children (21.8-9).[43] For David, Michal had become a trophy, like the foreskins of the Philistines whom he had killed to win her hand. In the only direct exchange between the spouses, David's words cast Michal as a transitory mediator between the disqualified dynasty and Yahweh's elect (6.21). After this, there can be only sterility and death for the woman.

Michal's brief saga begins with 'stealing' and ends with sterility. Its dramatic treatment unmasks the meaning of theft within a politico-familial context, in which what happens to individuals shapes the fate of the people. When do male thieves meet a fatal end? 'Never', is the short answer, particularly when they are favored by Yahweh and when the 'stolen' object is a desirable woman. The ramifications of the narrative that traces the incorporation of Bath Sheba into David's harem through adultery and murder (2 Sam. 11) have already been dealt with. But to convey the full range of narratological strategies, it is useful to refocus on Nathan's parable as it converges on hospitality, family, neighbors and on stealing.[44]

---

43. On the elimination of the last of the Saulides, including perhaps Michal's children, see Bodi, 'Mikal', pp. 93-96.

44. See above, Chapters 6 §6 and 7 §6.

To all intents and purposes, Nathan's exposition of the slaughter of a poor man's lamb to feast a rich man's guests appears barely relevant to either adultery or murder.[45] And both Nathan and David know that an ordinary case of theft of a single animal is hardly a matter worth either royal attention or prophetic time.[46] Yet, the appropriation of the lamb in Nathan's parable is not a mere theft—because it does not stop with an arbitrary transfer of an item of property from one household to another but proceeds to eliminate the loot.

In Nathan's parable, neighborly relations, if based on arbitrary thefts rather than on covenantal 'brotherhood', become a tragic parody. The rich man acts openly and out of manifest contempt for the poor man's property and sentiments, as did David when he 'summoned' Bath Sheba and later when he married her. If the proverbial image of a thief is of one who steals by night or sneaks by day, both the king and the nameless nabob of Nathan's parable exemplify the moral decadence which such behavior induces.[47] David need not conceal his desire for Bath Sheba; the rich man need not suppress his greed. Both 'females' were there for the taking.

Nathan's prophetic parable is tempered by an awareness of the transgressions inherent in political life. That adultery and theft are two sides of the same coin is evident. Theft generates unlawful access to forbidden items. It bridges distances by sinning, emphasizing the relations of possession to power. In a text like the Hebrew Bible, which continuously preaches benevolence, anxiety about the violence of criminal activities reflects concerns regarding repressive governments and suffering commoners. True mercy and moral fiber are superior to strength. But greed breeds theft, as lust breed adultery.

On balance, David's pragmatism, decisiveness and aggressiveness, perhaps commendable traits in a king, turn into abuse of power when the object of acquisitiveness is a woman. Michal's pragmatism turns against her, as does Rachel's. In dealings that hinge on male system of values, and especially on demonstrative authority over women (and by extension over their reproductive capacity), women who act like men are bound to meet a sore end. In Dtr exegesis of theft, the seriousness of the transgression gains momentum through gender affiliation. Thus, the stealing of the תרפים, a clandestine act which is only revealed to the reader, and the 'stealing' of paternal hearts through תרפים, when committed by women, become crimes requiring divine retribution. The presence of subversive women at moments that

---

45.   The asymmetry has been explained in various ways. For Gunkel, the parable was a late addition, Herman Gunkel, *Die Märchen im Alten Testament* (Tübingen: J.C.B. Mohr [Paul Siebeck], 1917 [repr. = Frankfurt: Athenäum, 1987]), pp. 46-47 (pp. 54-55 of the English edition, *The Folktale in the Old Testament* [trans. Michael D. Rutter, with an Introduction by John W. Rogerson; Historic Texts and Interpreters in Biblical Scholarship; Sheffield: Almond Press, 1987]). For Jones the same pericope reinforces the narratological message of an unacceptable abuse of power, see Gwilym H. Jones, *The Nathan Narratives* (JSOTSup, 80; Sheffield: JSOT Press, 1990), pp. 96-104. Adultery, of course, is a sort of a theft as well, as the rabbis correctly insisted.

46.   Uriel Simon, 'The Poor Man's Ewe Lamb: An Example of a Juridical Parable', *Bib* 48 (1967), pp. 207-42 (220-24).

47.   2 Sam. 12.12 compares David's secrecy with Yahweh's openness, but the adultery was hardly an unknown affair.

prove critical to both individual and 'national' interests serves as an index of the proper process of 'history', as decreed and designed by Yahweh.

6. *Stealing Babies*

In the debate over the precise scope of the Eighth Word, much ink has been spilt on showing the relevance of the Commandment to kidnapping. Yet, the only narrative samples that deal with 'abduction' focus not on the stealing of adults but of babies. One is the tale (or rather parable) of Solomon's judgment, pronounced in a case of a prostitute who 'abducts' or rather 'exchanges' a dead baby for a live one (1 Kgs 3.16-28). The other is the 'abduction' of a princely baby in order to save him from death (2 Kgs 11.2).[48] Neither case is, strictly speaking, a theft, nor does the 'abductor' or 'thief' meet the fate which the law assigns to kidnappers. But both texts question the legal ideology of theft by focusing on women as 'thieves' and on infants as 'stolen goods'.

1 Kings 3.16-28, a tale which focuses on two prostitutes and their babies, tests both the limits of motherhood and of royal wisdom.[49] Like the poor man of Nathan's parable, the two female plaintiffs have little to lose besides their babies. When one baby dies, the bereft mother 'steals' the baby of the other prostitute. Both approach the king. Adhering to the letter of the law, a royal verdict decreeing a fourfold restitution, for example, would have resulted in a paradoxical carving of the living baby into multiple fragments. Solomon's judgment, therefore, diverges significantly from the Deuteronomic ideology of a straightforward restitution for theft. His aim is to apply not legal rules but rather the 'predictable laws of maternal behavior'.[50] The king confronts both thief and victim. Because the case falls outside the legal parameters of theft, as defined in Exodus and Deuteronomy, Solomon must rely on his own intuition. Accordingly, there is neither investigation nor any other (recorded) court formality.

The confrontation between kings and maternity hints at the torments of a mother who might lose her baby twice, once through theft and once of her own accord in order to save him. It also highlights thieving greed. The abductor of 1 Kings 3 is ready to compound her theft with murder. More than any other tale of theft, that of the two prostitutes penetrates the trauma of theft. Yet, had a crime been committed? According to one woman, there had never been an abduction; according to the other woman, a crime had taken place. In her readings of the nightly events, her baby had been snatched and her motherhood subsequently denied. To crown her sufferings, she found herself consenting with the royal judgment, thus becoming twice victimized, by theft and by law. The abducting thief's acquiescence in the verdict, a paradoxical presentation of a criminal as a law-abiding 'citizen', is ultimately unpunished.

---

48. See also above, Chapters 2 §8 and 4 §6.

49. Stuart Lasine, 'The Riddle of Solomon's Judgement and the Riddle of Human Nature in the Hebrew Bible', *JSOT* 45 (1989), pp. 61-89 (70).

50. Lasine, 'The Riddle of Solomon's Judgment', p. 65.

Underlying the case is a crucial question: Does the law concede its limits when it touches on actions motivated by women's desire for motherhood? A comparison with Nathan's parable (2 Sam. 12), suggests two types of thieving greed: one 'positive', and hence condonable, the other negative, and hence unabsolvable. The rich man of Nathan's parable is motivated by pure greed of acquisition; the prostitute is moved by scarcity and by desire for maternity. Having lost her baby (through accidental mishandling, 1 Kgs 3.19), she becomes as impoverished as the parable's poor man who had lost his sole lamb through a deliberate action of his powerful neighbor. Solomon's experimental verdict tries out women's true commitment to motherhood. One fails the test; the other passes. The outcome, namely a reunion of 'true' mother with 'true' child, is especially striking because such a 'happy' end, although reinforcing biblical images of motherhood, also clashes with another biblical depiction of a woman who kills, seemingly unscrupulously and unhesitatingly, her own children and grandchildren in order to secure her own throne.

Queen Athalia has already been discussed.[51] In 2 Kings 11, Jehosheva, the enterprising 'abductor' of a royal baby, the last surviving scion of the family, disappears from the narrative as soon as her saving mission is accomplished. The rest of the tale is predictable—it required male mediation to bring the child out of hiding and to topple the 'wicked' queen. The high priest engineers the elevation of the child on his seventh birthday, on a Sabbath, as well as the execution of the queen. All of Israel subsequently celebrates the events with an idol-smashing feast. By one account, the woman who had stolen the baby from death, and the man who engineers the succession of this child to David's throne, were a wife–husband team (2 Chron. 22.11).

Gender perspectives render this episode particularly relevant to an examination of Dtr perceptions of 'theft'. From the start, the narrative contrasts 'bad' and 'good' women, primarily in terms of transgressions. Athalia becomes queen by virtue of royal blood and connections, but her reign is characterized as usurpation and she herself as a murderess. Jehosheva's abduction violates royal rules but its purpose justifies the 'crime'. The two royals, Athalia and Jehosheva, operate within a familial sphere in which the objects of death and theft are royal children and relatives. Here, the very identity of the participants, rather than the identity of the judge, determines both the ultimate judgment and the significance of the events. Athalia's execution of the princes of the land paves the way to the only period in biblical history in which the kingdom of David is ruled by a woman. Jehosheva's abduction of one royal baby ensures that this 'usurpation' is short lived, eternally stigmatized and unrepeatable.

Matters of maternity become an index of criminality in this deadly game over dynastic survival. At stake is a female's greed vs. a mother's inexplicable desire to kill her own family. Athalia's elimination of potential rivals becomes, in 2 Kings 11, a distortion of both the 'natural' political discourse which is invariably dominated by males, and of motherhood itself. Yet, such a measure is hardly an exception, as the bloody annals of the northern kingdom demonstrate (1 Kgs 15.29;

---

51.   See above, Chapters 2 §8 and 4 §6.

16.11; 2 Kgs 10.7). Because she is a woman, Athalia embodies unnatural mother-hood and unnatural rulership, even though her victims are not the children of her royal predecessor but her own kin. Jehosheva becomes an exemplary 'abductor', a woman whose maternal and national instincts combine to correct the course of wo/man-made history.

The story of stealing a legitimate candidate to the Davidic throne charts an un-explored venue of familial relations and law. The text ignores obvious questions: Why is Athalia ignorant of the escape of one child? How did Jehoiada the priest manage to conceal the child 'in the house of Yahweh' for no less than six years (2 Kgs 11.3)? Compared with the mere three months which Moses' mother had 'stolen away' from the pharaoh in Egypt, this is a remarkable feat indeed. In Exodus 2, as in 2 Kings 11, 'abductions' committed by mothers or female relatives, in defiance of rulers, highlight not only the contrasting scopes of 'criminality' but also the questionable character of the law itself.

Deuteronomy and Dtr narratives indicate that theft of goods and abduction of persons for no reason other than greed, undermine the development of a healthy society and economy.[52] When such thefts are practiced within a familial orbit, they have the potential of damaging the very foundations of the social order. Genesis 31 juxtaposes Jacob's theft of Laban's trust with Rachel's theft of תרפים, just as 1 Samuel 19 juxtaposes Michal's use of תרפים to 'steal' Saul's heart. Precisely because one 'crime' can be resolved by men while the other necessitates divine in-tervention, there is no clear-cut or 'legal' solution when women engage in theft. In Dtr dialogue of crime and femininity, women determine the social tone that modu-lates male ethics and authority.

---

52. Tate, 'Legal Traditions', p. 496.

Chapter 9

THE CONSTRAINTS OF DESIRE*
(WORD TEN)

You shall not covet your neighbor's house. You shall not covet your neighbor's wife, or his manservant, or his maidservant, or his ox, his ass, or anything that is your neighbor's. (Exod. 20.17)

You shall not covet your neighbor's wife. Neither shall you desire your neighbor's house, his field, or his manservant, his maidservant, his ass, or anything that belongs to your neighbor. (Deut. 5.21)

1. *Sins of the Soul*

By all accounts, the ending of the Decalogue appears odd. The presence of a ban on coveting in so curt a code implies an association between body and mind that fits an internal organ, the heart, into a series of 'external' sins. Such linkages breed endless ambiguities. Indeed, the very use of the term 'covet' (חמד) implies allusions to unbridled emotions which, if surfaced to the open, may lead to a transgression of any law. The root also denotes 'joy' or pleasure, and even beauty; in brief, precisely the attributes that occasion envy and kindle desire of ownership.

Demanding the exercise of self-control, the Tenth Commandment calls for hiding from the self as an entity that incorporates a potential to promote and to destroy life. In the developing ideology of ancient Israel, duties, obligations and affiliations between individuals, on the one hand, and between males and Yahweh, on the other, are basic tenets.[1] The Decalogue acknowledges the strength of household bonding through several Commandments. Its foundational vision is framed by two Commandments that reshape the meaning of a home/house (בית): the First which recasts Egypt as a 'house' of oppression; and the Tenth which casts the home as man's exclusive domain and as a metaphorical extension of the individual male member of the covenant.

---

*   The title of this chapter owes its inspiration to John J. Winkler, *The Constraints of Desire: The Anthropology of Sex and Gender in Ancient Greece* (New York: Routledge, 1990).

1.   Modern scholarly interpretations of the Tenth Commandments are, relatively, few and far between. Among the small number, see J.R. Coates, 'Thou Shalt Not Covet', *ZAW* 52 (1952), pp. 238-45; Alexander Rofé, 'The Tenth Commandment in the Light of Four Deuteronomic Laws', in Segal (ed.), *The Ten Commandments in History and Tradition*, pp. 45-65; Bernhard Lang, 'Du sollst nicht nach der Frau eines anderes verlangen: eine neue Deutung des 9ten und 10ten Gebots', *ZAW* 93 (1981), pp. 216-24.

Permanence of households depends on guaranteed economic stability, and on undisturbed generational continuity of children. To ensure both, the Decalogue attempts to eliminate tensions between the norms of public and private life which are felt in the competing claims of Yahweh and of the more traditional household. In the sphere of the family, which generally remains an area of tradition and conservatism, the Decalogue calls for respect of the younger towards the elder (Word Four), for a general day of rest (Word Five) and, above all, for the elimination of possible threats to the economic and reproductive viability of the household through 'desire' of others (Word Ten). More than any other Commandment, the Tenth indicates that a rejection of the laws is a rejection of an identity, the connotations of which extend to all parts of the Decalogue. In the Tenth Commandment, the emotionally and morally charged terminology of the family is appropriated to express the individual's relations to Yahweh and to Yahweh's laws.

An impressionistic view of the self makes both the 'house' and its dwellers inextricable components of male identity. The norms of Decalogue discourse converge on manhood as a manifestation of a state of mind. Compliance with the first nine Commandments parades manhood as well as ties and obligations to Yahweh, to own household and to other individuals. The Tenth Word reaffirms the responsibility to the self and, by extension, to the entire community. Its prohibition on desire promotes a specific form of socialization which entails not merely the preservation of familial integrity but also the development of a mentality of contentment. Since, ultimately, everything belongs to Yahweh, the banning of encroachment, even by thought, into another's realm becomes a claim for omnipotence and a plan for eternity. The negative formulation becomes a statement of repudiation of the greedy self. Because the Tenth Commandment appears to reduplicate practically all the other nine, it reinforces the negative and disowns the emotions that may lead to excess.

Renunciation of the innermost self is accomplished with the help of all the other Commandments which deny negativities. The prohibitions which the Decalogue articulates make hearing and thinking succumb into an irresistible association. The sequence of avoiding or preventing theft, adultery, murder and formal injustice imposes itself, through the Tenth Commandment, with greater force, because the Commandment designates the objects of desire that may result in subsequent offences.

The role model of manhood as repository of mental wholesomeness evokes a context of understanding in which there is a complex interplay between 'law' and ideology. The question of the integration of the individual (male) into the community becomes essential because temptation, in this reading, alienates man from his environment. To belong to an essentially male group, attitudes, as well as behavior, are being tested. To think and act rightly is respectful, constituting a basic recognition of values that ought not to be compromised. The Tenth Commandment ponders on what is right and what is expedient, or on pragmatic values and duties. And it is precisely the obligation to Yahweh and to the self that the Tenth Commandment extols in favor of a set of values that sets apart the covenant community from its non-Israelite environment.

A man's house (including land), wife, slaves and animals, name the elements that constitute rank, class and social status. The Commandment provides a concise abstract of the obligations of owners of households to both the hierarchical orders of community and of family. It delineates the family as a locus of tension and of conflict rather than of harmony by questioning even the secure meaning of key words, such as 'house', 'wife', 'slaves', in the discourse of social order, and the meaning of ownership.

In institutionalizing a sin that eludes visual manifestation, the Tenth Commandment delineates humans as surfaces sheltering that which must be repressed. The aim of preventing coveting is, paradoxically, to ensure self-amnesia which will overlook what one sees with one's own eyes. Aspiring to extract the heart in order to reconstruct a new type of Israelite, the Commandment suggests that greed breeds greed, and that a greedy man will succumb to the same lot that he would inflict on others. This is why the desire to posses is more threatening than the prospect of other transgressions.

A sense of honor is touted as the means to resolve tension between standard human emotions and Yahweh's ideology. Hence, this ending must be read in the light of the beginning, because both outline how human values relate to the Decalogue's perception of liberation and to Israel as a 'holy nation'. The Tenth Commandment enjoins the sacrifice of humanity's true nature and feelings in order to live out a myth of a society that is clean of sin. As Yahweh reorders history, divine Commandments reshape the passage of events and human relations. In espousing collective civic values, as well as specific household decisions, the Decalogue provides a range of iniquities and of values. But only the Tenth Commandment resolves the tension between the community and the individual by banning sinful thoughts.

The visualization of a society without sin promotes values that are not merely those of the family but also of a collective ethos. In order to maintain what is right and to avoid conflict in the system, the Tenth Commandment insists on a commitment to the self and to the collective. But it also plants seeds of doubt about the very possibility of compliance. Such skepticism stands in contrast with the assuredness of the opening statement of the Decalogue. Having instated the divinity as God of liberation (with the First Commandment), the Tenth Commandment shows that what might evolve is not always clear, and that neither positive 'laws' nor negative invariably reconcile ideology with reality.

Conceptualizing coveting encodes a system of differences in which each household is positively constituted in opposition to other households. The picture projected is of a homogenous collective identity that responds to a call to subscribe to a 'constitution' that outlaws even stray thoughts. Actions, words and even contemplation become objects of self-control and of self-criticism. An image of uniform manhood, deeply committed to Yahweh's domestic ideology, emerges. Although banal, it is nevertheless crucial. An evaluation of the Tenth Commandment depends, therefore, on patent or potential transgressions. Underlying the inquiry are questions such as: What does it mean to fit into society? And: What is the meaning of reversing its norms?

In spite of its idealization of a fictitious parity, the Tenth Commandment draws the sharpest dichotomy between legal theories and practical realities, recognizing, perhaps, that the ultimate seat of transgression, as of compliance, cannot solely be fear of the letter of the law but a deeper commitment to the morality that Yahwism attempts to instill in its followers. To achieve male identity, the Hebrew Bible carefully considers actions and attitudes that inform manhood. The Tenth Commandment's ban on covert desire reduces the scope of hazardous emotions to one: greed. It depicts a Yahwist orbit that is, ideally, free from desire, other than the one to serve Yahweh. In this trajectory, socialized urges, such as sex, become projections of negativities, and paradigms of preventive actions.

2. *Coveting Foreign Women: The Seeds of Idolatry*

> Beware lest you cut a covenant with the inhabitants of the land to which you arrive lest it becomes a lure among you. Rather, their altars you shall smash, their shrines (pillars) you shall destroy, and their *asherot* you shall cut down. You shall not bow to another god because Yahweh whose name is jealous is a jealous God. [Beware] lest you cut a covenant with the peoples of the land because when they prostitute themselves in worshipping their gods and sacrifice to their gods, they will invite you and you will eat of their sacrifice, take wives from among their daughters for your sons and [when] these daughters prostitute after their gods they will make your sons likewise prostitute before their gods… (Exod. 34.12-16)

> I will cast out nations before you and enlarge your borders. Neither shall any man desire (יַחְמֹד) your land when you go up to appear before Yahweh your God three times a year. (Exod. 34.24)

Exodus 34 examines the implications of the thematic preoccupation of the Decalogue with other gods and with other people's possessions by exploring the results of association with non-Israelites.[2] In this exploration, foreign women are invested with power which Israelite women rarely enjoy. They are desirable as sexual partners, and they can dissociate their lovers from their learned behavior. Precisely because the text does not indulge readers in visions of children of such alliances, the potency of foreign women, not as potential mothers but as influential spouses, is especially striking.

Beyond the mechanics of scenes involving idolatry and iconoclasm, the context of Exodus 34 suggests a wider and more emblematic set of significations which refer both to the conditions of the ritual itself and to the conditions of sexual association. Participation in local rituals means a mimetic action that engages Israelite males not only in sex but also in rites which are a deadly version of initiation, indeed a parody of the covenant itself. Through images of illicit sex and banned idolatry, the text projects the peculiar dynamism of a drama of coveting which unfolds through undesirable friendships and intercourse. Allusions to conflicts generated by the particularities of sexual association help to draw a portraiture of

---

2. The chapter has traditionally been analyzed as a one component of the unity that Exod. 32–34 ostensibly project; see Edward G. Newing, 'Up and Down—In and Out: Moses on Mount Sinai—The Literary Unity of Exodus 32–4', *AusBR* 41 (1993), pp. 18-34.

law-breaking that amplifies the enormity of transgressing the prescribed orbit of the
Tenth Commandment.

Covenants with locals (Exod. 34.12 uses the term ברית, which also applies to
the relationship between Yahweh and Israel) breed the coveting of local women.
These, in turn, insist on sharing in their sacred rites, henceforth introducing confusion, conflicts, tensions and ambiguities that challenge the masculine patterns that
articulate the world of men. As Exodus 34 extends the meaning of self-control to
relations with non-Israelites, its regulations equate gender behavior of foreigners as
though this, in itself, was another deplorable aspect of the forbidden. This notion of
the interchangeability of men and women in the 'pagan' world is especially striking
in the context of a Commandment that, like the Tenth, carefully juxtaposes categories of the controlled (wives, female servants, male servants, animals) with the man
in charge, the dominant male of the household.

Foreigners, then, even more than covetous Israelites, stand for physical and cultural instability that renders men weaker than women. 'Foreign' cults are a source
of disturbing power over their followers, and potentially over Yahweh's own
people. Both cults and peoples, and especially women who embody an alternate
mode of existence, must be therefore dissociated from covenant male members.
The boundaries of unwarranted desire are set, however, beyond the perimeters
ostensibly envisioned in the Decalogue. Exodus 34 delineates the outlining zones of
Israelite religion in terms that are as fluid as women's bodies, and as equally open
to entry/exit from/into the outside. Consequently, they require fixity and control.

The text (Exod. 34) traces the disastrous consequences of an ill-advised transformation of Israelite males under the spell of women who, paradoxically, display
remarkable if erroneous commitment to their own gods. The fact that Exodus 34
envisions men desiring women, but not women desiring men, exposes one of the
most marked features of the biblical anti-pagan rhetoric, namely the assimilation of
idolatry with foreign women. By an ironic twist, the legal landscape of Exodus 34
conjures non-Israelite households as harmonious loci of dutiful daughters who aid
and abet their fathers in luring Israelite males away from the path of righteousness.

To manipulate the rash effects of idolatry, Exodus 34 makes 'prostitution' an
inherited and inherent trait of foreigners, transmitted, like a disease, from fathers to
daughters. In suggesting a certain kind of sickness or 'madness', the text highlights
the irrational and the emotional aspects of 'paganism' which, in pernicious opposition to Yahwism, is cast as a meaningless assortment of inane objects worshipped
by mindless men and women.[3] As Exodus 34 codifies the 'other' in terms of undesirable sexual partners, it vests sex with foreign women with a legal terminology
that effectively outlaws the women, their fathers and this type of association.[4]

At a theoretical level, the proposition of casting locals, women and men alike, as
single-dimensional creatures bent on idolatry and sex, aims at fueling an antagonism between Israel and the non-Israelite environment. But this is as misleading as

---

3.   Harrelson, *The Ten Commandments*, p. 126, sees in the ban an attempt to curb the hanker-
ing after the ways of others which he defines as 'sick and dangerous desire'.

4.   G.N. Knoppers, 'Sex, Religion, and Politics', pp. 121-41, explores sexual associations and
marriage with foreign women as a Deuteronomic theme, based on both Exod. 34 and Deut. 7.

the symmetry that the Tenth Commandment applies to all households, regardless of size and contents. On the level of practice, the asymmetry between Israel and the 'other' is often more apparent than real.

From the outset of the biblical narrative, the self that is really at stake is to be identified with the male. Both Exodus 34 and the Tenth Commandment explore the male project of selfhood. They promote self-sufficiency by allocating to women the roles of catalysts, agents, instruments, spoilers and destroyers. Paradoxically, women are presented as anti-models, as well as hidden models for the masculine self. The demand for male identity and self-esteem suggests that mental content-ment, expressed in singular absence of crimes generated by greed, is to be obtained by ignoring the outside.

In what appears, at first, as a drastic over-simplification of the lessons of devia-tion, Numbers 25 delineates the repercussions of breaking the constraints that the Tenth Commandment imposes.[5] The text, deliberately, fails to differentiate between Moabite and Midianite women, because foreign females, in general, equate to disaster. Moreover, in Numbers 25 these women are not accompanied by males of their own ethnicity. Acting on their own, they become referents of the traits that biblical society routinely associates with the feminine domain.

Viewed from afar, and through a late redactional lens, these women are repre-sented as bodies with solely a sense of physical reality. Their spatial distribution, first in the margins of the camp and then in its midst, projects a relational tension between the inside and outside. The distinct stories, deliberately juxtaposed in Numbers 25, of a well-known single mixed couple, on the one hand, with the sex-ual adventures of numerous unnamed Israelite males, on the other hand, contrive to elevate the ordinary to a level of an unforgettable and unforgivable example of the violation of not one but of several Commandments.

Because the Tenth Commandment, like Numbers 25, emphasizes the outer dimensions of an inner weakness, both narrative and law suggest an unnatural state, the opposite of their ideal of strength and integrity. Exodus 34 and Numbers 25 conjure Israelites who are reduced to helpless and passive condition, constrained by their desire for the 'other'. At the end of one tale in Numbers 25 the camp is strewn with corpses of numerous Israelite males, victims of divine wrath, of divinely in-duced plague, and of their own desire. The deadly sight affords a spectacle of the punishment that Exodus 34 and the Tenth Commandment only imply. It also suppresses the way of women which Exodus 34 and Numbers 25 define as nothing beyond sex and idolatry.

3. *Coveting Knowledge and Sowing the Seeds of Human Morality*

The 'history' of the first human couple begins with an erotic pursuit of knowledge. In the vocabulary of Genesis, knowledge is desire (חמדה or תאוה), specifically aimed (in Gen. 3) at consuming a desirable item of food which generates discern-

---

5. See above, Chapter 6 §4, and my 'The Rape of Cozbi'.

ment. The trees that God plants to keep *adam* company in Paradise, including the
forbidden one (2.9, 17), are 'delight to the sight and delicious to the palate' (2.9).
The root of 'delight' (נחמד) in this phrase is the same as that which denotes illicit
desire in the Tenth Commandment.

The Genesis codification of the unknown in terms of delight/desire delineates a
dream of a world with *adam* alone at its center, a place where he might even achieve
everything other than morality and immortality. With the coming of woman in Gen.
2.21-23, human susceptibility to deceit illustrates how desire leads to disaster. On
the advice of a snake, woman 'comes to a realization' that the forbidden fruit is
indeed delightful to the eye (תאוה לעינים) but not, as yet, tested by the palate.

Curiously, Gen. 3.6 employs the terminology of Deuteronomy (5.17), rather than
that of the Exodus Decalogue, to describe the object of covetousness. The narrative
thus cajoles both texts as it confirms the intrinsic weakness of human nature when
confronted with the desirable. The trees are symbols of a process that potentially
corrupts and erases trust. Yet, they are no illusion. In a realm where serpents talk
like humans, and woman is both thoughtful and articulate, the silence of trees
appears a mischievous illusion of a creation.

Although Genesis 3 confirms the conventional dictum that woman's natural
potential for virtue is inferior to man's, she is nevertheless an active force in the
world of man. By a series of juxtapositions and innuendoes, the serpent is enrolled
as a trickster and the woman becomes his unwitting apprentice. As the serpent
deceptively passes for the appearance of truth, appealing to the inferior parts of the
self, she, and consequently man, yield to emotions and pleasures of make-believe.
The text stresses a certain sensual pleasure attendant on the experience that specifically associates it with the feminine.

Once assimilated, the fruit shares the same field of reference that likens the
woman's gesture to a false imitation of domestic justice. She knows what foods are
best for the body, because the apple, besides contentment, also engenders knowledge. The result is an awareness of deceptive appearances, which emerges with the
emotional power of nudity. When man excuses himself, he is shown to be weak and
incapable of remaining steadfast to himself. Nor is he able to exercise self-control
by pondering rationally the events that had happened and the consequences of
'greed'. Man gives way to a host of conflicting emotions that ill suit the model of
manliness that the Decalogue and covenant require. Worst of all, he is enticed by
woman to share in the pleasure of identifying and sympathizing with her state after
she had introduced a cognitive complexity which undermined the principles that
had regulated human's first realm.

Genesis 3 shows the 'other' as a composite of woman and reptile in order to
idealize man who is, in fact, weaker and inferior to the self. His lack of strength is
codified according to the conventional terms of society under the name of 'law'.
Recalling Genesis, the Tenth Commandment includes the cognate negative traits of
cowardice, fearfulness and emotional liability that coveting incorporates. Implicitly,
it also embeds a ban on imitating woman. As the Genesis narrative strives to remove
confusion sown by serpent and by woman, it strips gender categories to bare bones.
God's verdict stabilizes the mobility of the scene of desire. At the most inclusive

level, the divine dictum ordains that no woman can play more than one part (wife/ mother), leaving man to shape his destiny between birth 'from the earth', human conception, and death.

Adam, who is allowed to discover his weakness, or rather lack of internal strength in Paradise, is also given an opportunity to transcend it by reasserting the male through the pastoral and through overcoming the feminine. In the end, Genesis 3, like the Decalogue, reasserts paternal structures of authority. In coveting elements of God's realm, 'woman' and *adam* act as transgressors of the Tenth Commandment which focuses on other men's houses as entities that mobilize a shift from the passive to the active, and from mastery over the self and others to surrender to desire. Understood as a component of covenant theology, covetousness expands a sinful awareness of the world and the self. It tests masculine values to find out how adequate are all the other forms of self-control, and to show that manliness need not compete with others.

4. *Deuteronomy's Ideology of Coveting: Why is Woman First?*

An examination of the two sets of the Tenth Commandment, in Exodus 20 and Deuteronomy 5, suggests that the order of the forbidden indicates scales of desire. Deuteronomy 5.21 ranks wives of other men as primary objects of covetousness. Only then it lists the house, field, male slave, female slave, ox, ass, and 'all that the neighbor owns' as other forbidden items. Motivated by horror of appropriation, the Deuteronomy Commandment elevates women as the most desirable objects of coveting. It also implies that covert coveting of other men's wives is more pervasive and more complex than the rest of the listed inventory.

Hinting at the conflict which violation engenders, Deuteronomy's Tenth Commandment constructs crisis with women as its symptom and major cause. Through this permutation, Deuteronomy returns to the problem of the self. As it searches for the make-up of Israelite manhood, Deuteronomy imagines the 'other' not merely as another man in possession of coveted wife, but also as the woman herself. She becomes a fugitive phantom of the self, an image that plays an essential role in formulating self-definition.

Literally read, the Deuteronomic opposition of wife vs. the rest (i.e. house, slaves, animals) proves a signpost and a riddle. The wife of another man turns out to be both one and many, doubled in the role of wife and mother. She is also a symbol of broken brotherhood and of problematic progeny. Her position in the Tenth Commandment is ambiguous: she is one among many, since the Commandment envisions wives as integral components of Israelite households; yet her identity is not her own but determined by affiliation with a man. In the end, the fusion of subject and object of the Commandment, of the Israelite men who covet and of men whose possessions are coveted, is reduced to an artificial polarization.

Deuteronomy 5 employs two verbs to describe coveting: one (חמד) specifically applied to women, the other (תאוה) embraces the sentiments that kindle greed for other men's houses, fields, slaves and animals. Coveting, then, appears to take two faces, the one that leads to the estrangement of a wife from her husband, and another that entails the unlawful appropriation of property. In a world that ideally obeys the law, the rule regarding coveting provides a new and final variation on the theme of desire. Failure to obey disqualifies men from membership. It also undermines the integrity of other men's claim to membership. Violation brings out the effacement of identity, as well as the shaking of the foundation of the family which had been problematic from its very inception.

Impulse generates trespassing, in itself a repeated and repeatable pattern, especially with regards to forbidden female space. To reconfirm the essential identity of the covenant member, the law maintains an obdurate constancy of a willful self whose power can bring gain to the self but loss to the community. Enacted on a 'neighbor's' territory, desire indicates transformation of both. By specifically changing avenues of coveting, the Deuteronomic version of the Tenth Commandment provides a paradigm of transgressive behavior that complements and contradicts the Decalogue's vision of manhood. It shows that the establishment of relations between males entails fundamental problems that require the inculcation of the morality of ownership at its deepest level.

With the establishment of critical distinctions, not only between male individuals but also between objects of illicit desire, the Tenth Commandment evolves a set of juridical principles that distinguish between legal and religious responsibilities, and between act and intention. It arranges a triangular relationship of man, another man and another man's wife, to furnish the most instructive example of how conventions assign a specific identity to a specific violation. Echoing the Seventh Commandment, the Tenth, in its frank ideological way, sets the sanction in a framework that looks at the intention that precedes the action.[6] Together, the Tenth and the Seventh Commandments disallow conflict among covenant members by encumbering with theological meaning the plain fact that there is no justification for an adulterous enterprise.

In agreeing to honor the Commandments, the Israelites leave themselves open to admonition on both juridical and theological grounds. If they can see the error of their ways by monitoring desire, they can be linked to one another in a unique way. The contrast between those who adhere and those who violate is at its most extreme through coveting other males' wives. Venting religious indignation at misguided thoughts, the Tenth Commandment responds to fears of a higher justice by placing women in the most prominent position in the text. Despite the irregular nature of the forbidden transaction, the Commandment is primarily concerned with the welfare of men. It accords women a status based on their affiliation with a specific male and on their marital status, assuming a most negative color by launching a double attack on covetousness and on adultery.

The Tenth Commandment characterizes Israel as a place of negation where even the inner-self is subject to criticism. On the most literal level, the Deuteronomic Tenth Commandment demonstrates the closest stage to a deconstruction of the self through the mental examination that each man must undergo. To be deserving of

---

6.   In general, see Bernard S. Jackson, 'Liability for Mere Intention in Early Jewish Law', *HUCA* 42 (1971), pp. 197-225 (reprinted in *idem, Essays in Jewish and Comparative Legal History* [Leiden: E.J. Brill, 1975], pp. 202-34).

Yahweh's patronage means the conscious choice of Yahwist precepts at their most demanding. In this version the problem of adultery is posed as a choice between belonging and alienation. Upon conclusion, the enemy is still a woman. If there are terms on which Israelite manhood continues to be rescued by Yahweh, it is through the banishment of both the image and the body of women, a complete excision.

If the Commandment is transgressed, Israel becomes a locus corrupt beyond redemption, as the prophets so often assert.[7] To remain intact as a Yahwist enclosure, Israelite males must stay within closely confined perimeters because only within these limits can inextricable and ever-present conflicts be resolved. For the Deuteronomic redactor, the paradigm of a closed system that vigorously protects its psychological and social boundaries is one that also protects its physical space, domicile inclusive. The importance of fencing off the home cannot be underestimated, because coveting is an underlying pattern of social and moral disease that has, in this reading, far-reaching implications for the general good. The Tenth Commandment locks Israelite males into a priority which vacillates between the extremes of rigid exclusion, and the radicalization of differences between individuals, between men and women and, by implication, between Israel and the gentile other.

Marriage, the institution that normally regulates relations between non-kin and circulates women, emerges in Deuteronomy 5 as the most conspicuous symptom of this maladaptive system. It may bring danger both in the form of excessive endogamy (= 'incest') or in the shape of an excessive exogamy, namely the search and introduction of outside or 'foreign' brides. In spite, then, of a myth of collective male solidarity, a fundamental cleavage between covenant and family remains. This is what the Tenth Commandment suggests, in one sense. The Commandment also presents a hidden analogy between covenant and family, based on common origins and on the common ideal of self-referential autonomy. To violate the Tenth Commandment entails a confusion of the relations between families. An individual who cannot rule himself is incapable of maintaining an unequivocal identity. In surrendering to hidden constraints the covetous Israelite must surrender the kinship that identifies him as a member of Yahweh's group.

5. *Covet a Woman; Covet a Kingdom*

Then Adoniah, son of Hagith, came to Bath Sheba, the mother of Solomon. She asked him: 'Do you come peacefully?' He said: 'In peace'. Then he added: 'I have something to say to you'. 'Say on'. 'You know that the kingdom was mine and that all Israel had fully expected me to reign. However, the kingdom has turned about and become my brother's, for it was his from the Lord. And now I have one request to make of you; do not refuse me.' 'Say on', she urged. And he said: 'Pray ask King Solomon, since you he will not refuse, to give me Abishag the Shunammite as my wife'. And Bath Sheba said: 'Very well. I will speak on your behalf to the king.'

---

7.   Gunther Wittenberg, 'The Tenth Commandment in the Old Testament', *Journal of Theology for Southern Africa* 22 (1978), pp. 3-17 (12-15).

So she went to King Solomon to speak to him on behalf of Adoniah. And the king rose to meet her, and bowed down to her. Then he sat on his throne and had her seated on his right, as the king's mother. Then she said: 'I have one small request to make of you; do not refuse me'. And the king said to her: 'Make your request, my mother, for I will not refuse you'. 'Let Abishag the Shunammite be given to Adoniah, your brother, as his wife.' King Solomon answered his mother: 'Why do you ask Abishag the Shunammite for Adoniah? Ask for him the kingdom also. For he is my elder brother and on his side are Abiathar the priest and Joab the son of Zeruiah.' Then King Solomon swore by the Lord, saying: 'Let God do this to me and more also, if this word does not cost Adoniah his life!' (1 Kgs 2.13-23)

The scenario, a contrived intimacy of mother and son within the public setting of a palace, is suggestive of two Decalogue Commandments. It shows a king resorting to the power of the Third Commandment in order to maintain the security of a throne threatened by a violation of the Tenth Commandment. The pressure of events reveals Bath Sheba as a person who confuses the relationship between a coveted concubine of a deceased king, and her own position in the king's household. She seems naïve to the point of incredulity. Confronted with a meek Adonijah, who in fact shares with her and with her own son the desire to rule, Bath Sheba agrees to act as his messenger.[8]

Metaphors of marital mediation by women are rare. Marriage brokers are invariably male. Bath Sheba has to invent a language that brings the Tenth Commandment to its fullest resonance. Her presentation recasts Adoniah's 'confession' of Solomon's superiority. She acknowledges her son's power of dispensing favors. Adonijah surrenders, in theory, the political kingship that he had craved by virtue of primogeniture. His request, however, demonstrates that he had not relinquished his craving for sibling equality, if not for the throne itself. As they play for the highest stake, the two brothers clash over the invisible Abishag in a deadly confrontation initiated by a woman who herself had once been an object of illicit desire.[9]

Irony is palpable. Having secured the succession for her son, Bath Sheba is apparently lured into divesting him of his kingdom. But Solomon is not like his half-sister Tamar. He sees through pretenses. The fate of Abishag does not concern him, as long as she remains attached to the memory of the dead David but unattached to any one of his living sons. Between the actual throne of Solomon and the potential scepter of Adonijah, the religious, political and familial issues con-

8.   In general, see Burke O. Long, 'A Darkness between Brothers: Solomon and Adonijah', *JSOT* 19 (1981), pp. 79-94; and Tomoo Ishida, 'Adonijah, the Son of Haggith, and his Supporters: An Inquiry into Problems about History and Historiography', in Richard E. Friedman and Hugh G.M. Williamson (eds.), *The Future of Biblical Studies: The Hebrew Scriptures* (Atlanta: Scholars Press, 1987), pp. 165-87. On the Adonijah affair as part of the vexed 'history' of David's succession, see, among many, Douglas A. Knight, 'Moral Values and Literary Traditions: The Case of the Succession Narrative (2 Samuel 9–20; 1 Kings 1–2)', *Semeia* 34 (1985), pp. 7-23; and Jeffrey S. Rogers, 'Narrative Stock and Deuteronomistic Elaborations in 1 Kings 2', *CBQ* 50 (1988), pp. 398-413.

9.   On Abishag, a woman without words, see Adele Berlin, 'Characterization in Biblical Narratives: David's Wives', *JSOT* 23 (1982), pp. 69-85. See also, Kenneth A. Stone, 'Sexual Power and Political Prestige: The Case of the Disputed Concubines', *BR* 10 (1994), pp. 28-31, 52-53.

verge on the same point—the transfer of a coveted woman from one household to another.

There are no differences between the two brothers. Both are results of the muddled history of David's amorous and marital pursuits, and both share its marked features. Adonijah refuses to accept the differentiation between himself and Solomon which, for him, is based solely on divine favor. His appeal to Bath Sheba also conveys his acknowledgment of her role as a kingmaker. He is about to play out yet another version of the self-destructive impulses that had characterized David the monarch. Not being in a position to covet and to kill, Adonijah uses the strategies that Amnon had employed. To further his aims, he resorts to the feminine and to the employment of the female.

When Adonijah and Bath Sheba invoke his brotherhood with Solomon they are referring to a common paternal stock. His projected alliance with Abishag is cast as a pious act of a dutiful son towards a deceased father, and the request itself as an admission of inferiority. The lessons that Solomon had learnt from the past decode Adonijah's message as a threat and as an act of enmity. Abishag embodies not love but potential disinheritance. In Solomon's interpretation of his mother's request, Adonijah crosses the boundaries of the Tenth Commandment by coveting a woman under the authority another man. In entering the realm of the forbidden, Adonijah decrees death for himself, and a metaphorical one for the king's mother. At the very same time both verify the inherent power of Abishag to transfer the throne.

By his existence Adonijah is not a threat. But if allied with Abishag he becomes an intruder who can undermine Solomon's royal status. Both Abishag and Bath Sheba are pawns in a game played by two men who understand each other not through words but through intentions. According to Adonijah, he had the popular vote, but Solomon had Yahweh's ear. According to Solomon, Adoniah had powerful allies, the advantage of age and, if he obtained Abishag, also the kingdom. Closely associated with the issue of legitimacy, the question of Abishag's virginity becomes a final catalyst in a fraternal rivalry. This is why 1 Kings 1, the prelude to the tale of David's succession and death, juxtaposes two seemingly unrelated factors: David's impotence and Adonijah's assumption of kingly apparel. In the knotted plot that follows, the interplay of crossed interference by Bath Sheba (twice), by a prophet and by Adonijah, is dominated by the shadow of Abishag, a coveted woman who is never heard. Her dilemma cannot be resolved through Adonijah. He is the one man for whom she represents a forbidden desire, an object to be coveted not for its own sake but for what she stands for.

Within the compass of the dramatic time of the scene, events seem to echo the moments in the history of the Davidic dynasty in which desirable and desired women punctuate the interaction of men. Adonijah's birth makes him eligible. Bath Sheba's intervention insures that David designates her son as his heir. Forbidden female spaces confirm the ambiguity of Adonijah's status in the community. Desiring intimacy with his father's last 'wife', he hopes to reorder his relations with his kin. He approaches Bath Sheba with conciliatory gesture and words, stopping short of approaching Solomon himself. The fratricidal destiny that characterizes the family is to be reasserted. Participants believe that they possess the vantage point of knowledge and experience. Adonijah is confident of reinterpreting the past as he evaluates the present and future through a constructive interplay with the women of the house. Solomon unmasks this anomaly.

In a male discourse of legitimacy, Abishag is a value that cannot be summarized in terms of beauty alone. Although a definite outsider, a factor which her absence enhances, she assumes the role of a mediator between the past and the present, a potential arbiter of monarchical claims. Even after Solomon's elevation, the hope for posterity which Abishag's intact hymen carries plunges the drama into its deadly end. In attempting to create his destiny in his own terms Adonijah craves the forbidden. To be specific, the permissible in one man's eye is tantamount to a deadly craving in another's. Repudiating his brother and consigning Abishag to oblivion, Solomon also rejects the mother who had assumed the role of familial mediator. The structure of the episode confirms the new orientation of the kingdom. The interchange has been revealing. With Adonijah and his supporters out of the way, Solomon's throne is secure and the shift of allegiance is complete.

Deuteronomy's Tenth Commandment sets aside women from the rest of man's immediate environment to emphasize both the interchangeability of woman with other items of property, and to highlight the close connection between them. Few tales convey the full spectrum of the message of the Tenth Commandment as effectively as this last chapter in the bloody saga of David's succession. Along these narrative lines, women provide a moral dimension to political actions which, in themselves, are a repetition of ancient patterns that embody transgressions.

The Tenth Commandment espouses a law of marriage that distributes women, one by one, into masculine households. In its dream of a just community, women must stay in a fixed domain where they can bear sons who resemble their fathers. Such an ecology suppresses sexuality, conceiving one specific combination as essential for a sexual union. There is no reproduction outside a home where an ideal man is one who is a Yahwist, a truthful friend, a respected father and a complete master over his entire household. This is why the Hebrew Bible insists on an asymmetry of sexes, rather than on separation, and this is why this asymmetry is etched into the Tenth Commandment. The Decalogue adapts itself to this disequilibrium to enable males to monopolize the status of 'men'.

Chapter 10

ARE WE, WOMEN, THE ADDRESSEES?
COLLECTED AND CLOSING REFLECTIONS

I remembered what Ramos once said, over a cognac, about women challenging men. All women come from one of two different lines, the Judaeo-Christian and the Greek. Those from the Judeo-Christian line are descended from Eve, whom God had made from Adam's rib in order to serve man, tempt him and accompany him in his fall and ruin. Those from the Greek line are descended from Athena, whom Zeus had plucked from his own brain, and those women never miss a chance to remind men that they were sprung from the head of a god and had nothing to do with men's insides or with their damnation.

—Luis Fernando Verissimo, *The Club of Angels*[1]

At the core of the Ten Commandments stand Yahweh and the individual Israelite. Males only? From the very start of the recorded 'history' of hu/mankind conflicting reflections on creation generate conflicting messages about basic issues, such as the place of women, the division of the sexes, and the forms of kinship. From the Garden of Eden to the futile attempt of Josiah to recreate the Judean kingdom in purely Yahwist terms, the Hebrew Bible uses womanly presence to amplify the tension between a man's private interest and his public loyalty to other men. Where women appear as a *leitmotif*, narratives and laws project a powerful moral language which deters men from the temptation to betray the common good while serving as a weapon against men who had done so. Acting in the best interests of the self, of others and of Yahweh means resisting the temptation of avarice, of murder, of adultery and of apostasy.

Genesis 1 casts both female and male as an artifice, crafted simultaneously by a divine hand. Genesis 2 reassembles males even before the idea of woman occurs. In the redactional order of Genesis 2 a differential chronology appears to determine the place of women in a created cosmos. With Adam, a mere 'clay cunningly compounded',[2] and Eve, a bone clad in flesh, a problematic symbiosis ensued. As a result, throughout the Bible the text maintains two competing and complementary representations of the sexes. To understand how these connect, how they fashion Israelite identity and how they construct their own safeguards, the Decalogue, framed as the timeless word of God, provides a pivotal point of departure.

---

1. Luis Fernando Verissimo, *The Club of Angels* (trans. Margaret Costa; New York: New Directions, 2002), p. 96.

2. For the expression see Epictetus, *Discourses* 1.1.11.

Aspiring to instruct Israelites how to live in harmony with God and with each other, the Hebrew Bible develops its own language to match its legal system and to record its aberrations. As soon as the text outlines its laws with succinctness inspiring compliance, perspectives shift to indicate the opposite. In Exodus 20, the Israelites voice obedience; in Exodus 32 they hasten to violate the First Commandment. A tissue of tales of conflict and discord emerges, each projecting a composite landscape of legal positivities and narratological negativities. All are strewn with sets of dualities: Yahweh vs. other gods; Yahweh vs. Israel; Israelites vs. the 'other'; men vs. men; and women vs. men.

Charting a map of permissible and of unlawful behaviors, the Decalogue delineates the horizons of the body and of the mind and how to administer both. Its overall message suggests a perpetual dualism between body and soul, each subject to human urges but also to human control. The Commandments dictate how the body is to be kept well tuned by avoiding a series of basic crimes, and how the mind must refine itself to avoid participation in the liability of the flesh. But between laws that shape behavior and behaviors shaped by law, between the dos and the don'ts, confusion ensues. Emblematic of this constant textual *agon* is the biblical concept of gender.

By appealing to the past and to posterity, the Ten Commandments determine themes and structures of narratives designed to illuminate their scope and the repercussions of transgression. Both laws and narratives share the same point of view—they assert Yahweh's pre-eminence over all other divinities and Israel's moral superiority over its gentile environment. They further seek to provide a basis for Yahweh's universal power and to bear witness to its grandeur. Because the Hebrew Bible displays divine exploits as mirroring human morals, the function of the Decalogue, a catalogue of moral paradigms, is to obviate the need for a constant demonstration of God's strength.

Like speech without a reply, the Decalogue intends to arouse in its listeners both submission and respect. It justifies and it threatens, and the threat comes close to being a contradiction. This contradiction is inherent in the very biblical notion of superiority exerted by Israelite males over equals, and especially over women. Such assumptions create an inevitable gap between the aims of the law and its actual effect, or between legal theories and narrative 'realities'.

Validating an obsessive virile morality, the Hebrew Bible never completely excludes women from its circle of glorification of God and of man. Reminding Israelite males of Israel's moral superiority, the Decalogue revives and sustains male need to lay claim to this rank by self-control and by control of their surrounding, womenfolk above all. Allied narratives, especially tales featuring women as models of either submission or defiance, presuppose the existence of an audience who needs to be convinced. They convey confidence in the persuasive power of the text itself.

The Decalogue posits a stable environment where social order is adjusted to the needs of society whose individuals possess a discipline that directs body and soul to focus on a specific divinity. A restrictive code, it applies primarily to men but its import extends to women and its lessons are driven most forcibly through narratives that extend to women. Here, the richness of conceptions of manhood is enriched by a concomitant poverty of the conceptions of womanhood.

Revolving around themes of the Decalogue, narratological situations delineate the frontiers of behavior and of manliness. The choice of narratives to be part of the grand scheme of Israelite annals, as that of precepts to be included in the Decalogue and other legal collections, stresses the paradox of a text that claims hegemony over others while being addressed solely to Israelite males. The very resemblance of many laws to general, non-Israelite, moral precepts reinforces the ambiguity of this fundamental charter of Israelite identity. The Yahweh of the Decalogue is a god who, like an ancient Near Eastern monarch, issues laws to control morality, to crush vice, to protect marriage and to secure property. By the tightening of discipline, the Decalogue opens a chasm between Israel and its gentile environment, as it does between men and women.

Both women and men are socialized through the inexorable cycle of birth and death, a temporal framework of repeated social practices that include, for men, marriage, sacrifice and property. A completion of manhood means full membership in the covenant. A complete man is one integrated through a series of rituals and confirmed by a covenant oath. The Hebrew Bible provides a few but vivid glimpses of what it was like to be a woman in the communities for whom the Decalogue became a central text. These insights suggest that women were disturbingly amphibious creatures who were neither fully at home amid covenant men nor quite disqualified from full membership in covenant congregations. They were persons, the quintessential 'other', who had accumulated the attributes that the Decalogue both endorses and denounces.

As they take cognizance of Israel's uniqueness, the Commandments also imply recognition of the 'other', wives, daughters, neighbors, female and male slave, and polytheists, each posing a threat to covenant completeness, external and/or internal. Whatever transpires when a male Israelite encounters this 'other', the laws lend a *de facto* canonization to conflicts which perpetuate the distinctions that narratives explore, and vice versa. Linking law with 'actualities', stories expound the implied or explicit presence of the 'other' as a shaping factor of each Commandment. They show how the 'other' in every guise, as a spectator, listener, interlocutor, foreigner or female, sheds light on the aims of the laws.

The juxtaposition of laws and narratives, a hallmark of Pentateuchal and Dtr redactional hands, bears witness to the uneasy relations within one's own household and with the outside world. Even the spell of the moment of the theophany itself is soon dissipated by the gathering of female ornaments to fashion a calf of gold. Whereas the Decalogue tends to suppress the living multiplicity of the Israelite landscape in the name of covenant unity, the narratives, and especially those featuring a female protagonist, highlight the diversity and variety that brim under the smooth surface of the law. The strategy, adopted in this study, of contrasting legal perspectives with their literary variations reflects the constant advocating of male hegemony, even as a rhetorical model.

Reconstructing the history of Israel from mythical creation beginnings, the story of Israel draws on traditions that attest the vitality of the law as a paradigm of a hegemonic discourse. Contrasting images of idealized males with descriptions of law-breaking and of betrayal suggest that the Decalogue's declaration of manhood constitutes wishful thinking, a sort of a timeless ornamental flourish which precariously balances masculinity with a denial of its effectiveness. A systematic examination of the Decalogue in light of the biblical corpus of female personifications, from wily wives to the murderous queens, from obedient daughters to recalcitrant spouses, from 'witches' to prophetess, from mothers to daughters and from Israelite to foreign, places at our disposal a valuable index for comparing Israelite entities, women and men.

The Decalogue sets out to equalize all male Israelites; redacted narratives set out to neutralize all women, both by omission and by circumscribed depictions. In the redacted Hebrew Bible the covenant assumes a male role as a contract between Yahweh, a male divinity, and male Israelites. Ostensibly, at least, there is no room in this construct for the female element to assume a decisive function. Removed from representation, the law becomes genderless. But narratives which involve women, although serving a myth which justifies the exclusion of women, generate a landscape that remains flagrantly imbalanced. Since covenant affiliation coexists with a collective and undifferentiated male identity, it makes all Israelites interchangeable husbands of Israelite or foreign women, fathers of obedient or disobedient daughters, and sons of devoted mothers. And although the Decalogue employs a specific male form of address, narratives hover precariously on a transcendence of the distinction between male and female.

In the Bible, male morality is often presented by its defenders as a reaction to the supposed immorality of the idolatrous world, especially of Egypt, the womb from which Israel had been expelled to be adopted by Yahweh's merciful precepts. Biblical narratives project women, the idolatrous other, sinners and transgressors of laws, as potent stereotypes who induce social disorder while codes of legal morality endeavor to maintain the identity of the Israelite group. Both laws and narratives separate believing families from the imagined dissoluteness of idolatrous neighbors and of their own subversive women. Neither, however, could renounce women altogether.

There is, after all, a harmony in the dissonance between laws and narratives. Justice, divine and human, implies not so much confounding the tension as maintaining it. Inherent discord becomes a unifying commonality, even a victory of human-made language over the visible and invisible threats that women represent. To give the upper hand to the negative reasserts, temporarily, the positive, as well as desired peace and concord. As a model of civic and religious joining, the Decalogue expounds and confronts covenant agreement and disagreement. Narratives highlight how the dissimilar coexists with an effort to cover over clashing elements by a legal discourse of the same.

What, then, is a 'perfect fit' or a Decalogue's ideal Israelite? In the book of Genesis, ancestors resolve discord by harnessing an ancestress to plans of survival. In the wilderness, harmony is achieved only through opposition. Miriam's defiance of Moses' divinely conferred authority (Num. 12), while mirroring the Israelites' own sentiments (Exod. 32), highlights the ambivalence of the post-Egypt social order. David's marriages with Michal and with Bath Sheba, rather than providing a model of integrating women into the community of men, are accompanied by misfortune and disorder. They hardly encourage a model of inextricably marital mixture as a symbol of covenant conjugality.

Within the covenant society relations between men and women are shaped by laws which articulate conscription and rigid structures. Narratological notions of the human person, on the other hand, generate unconventional attitudes that allow women to act as men, positioning women as catalysts of male minds and bodies. Seen from a woman's point of view, the Decalogue describes a landscape that abides by a correctness that engulfs precise social structures and a precise counter-world. In this counter-world women challenge the authority of men who had been selected by Yahweh to lead Israel—they carry out plans that their powerful husbands shy from executing, and they make dints in a male-made chain of regulations. These challenges delineate an alternate landscape in which adultery leads from an ordinary home to a royal palace (Gen. 12; 20; 26; 2 Sam. 11) and respect for parental vows brings the extinction of a household (Judg. 11).

Female tragedy in the Bible is organized around a litany of anguish and iniquities, beginning with the untimely death of Rachel at birth and Jacob's discarding of the name she had given the newly born, continuing through the unlawful appropriation of women through rape and forced mating (Judg. 19 and 21), and ending with a woman's usurpation of David's own throne (2 Kgs 11). Willingly or forcibly, women are invited to participate in the production of male conceived and enacted dramas which revolve on rapes, murders, wars and abductions. By their very sexual identity women are taught to recognize their role as catalyst of crimes. Paradoxical as this may appear, in these self-referential presentations women dramatize concrete events, manifesting the parameters of transgression.

Narratives consistently 'elevate' women in order to promote male unity by expounding on female spheres of interaction. The striking female imagery in all these stories is that of a personified female 'other', a promoter and sharer of idolatry, adultery and of loyalty/disloyalty (Num. 25; Gen. 12; 20; 26; 1 Sam. 19; 2 Sam. 12), a swearer of false oaths (Josh. 2; Judg. 4), a planner of or participant in murders (Judg. 4; 1 Kgs 19; 2 Kgs 11), an object of male violence (Judg. 19; 1 Kgs 14), but also a singer of divine triumphs (Exod. 15), a leader of Israelite armies (Judg. 4) and an authorized seer of royal doom (1 Sam. 28; 2 Kgs 22). Active participation of women in acts which reflect obedience (Judg. 11) and defiance provides 'actuality' to the Decalogue's legal orbits.

Female fleeting images, with their repetitiveness and uniqueness, are calculated to both bridge and project a yawning gap between legal abstractions and narrative representations. Although the feminine 'other' takes many different forms, she always plays the same role in relations to the ideal Israelite manhood. She is a foil and necessary correlative to both positive and negative masculinity. Excessively condemned (Cozbi, Jezebel, Athalia) or extravagantly praised (Rahab, Jael, Ruth), the women cast as actors and activators in episodes that endorse the participatory range of the Commandments share the same underlying principles which group all possible forms of 'foreignness' in womanhood.

Where women are directly engaged, concern for deportment and for the integrity of their bodies converges to ban the coveting of, and sex with other men's wives. The state of motherhood, as that of fatherhood, becomes the standard of correct familial relations. To bring the family and the self under control, the Decalogue attempts to counteract the dangers that might accompany daily life by means of judiciously chosen regimen of rules. The positive effect of abiding by the law ensures the kind of horizontal and vertical connections that link males across society to each other, to the younger generation, and to women. The Commandments are framed in the second person masculine not merely because they reflect a male-oriented society but also because they entrust males with the guardianship of the female body.

Within the carefully wrought microcosm of Israelite covenant, the physical integrity of the female body becomes a charged symbol. Loss of virginity is a bad omen. Extra-marital affairs are ominous. Violated female bodies stand for male infamy. Taking human frailty for granted, the Decalogue makes adultery, forbidden desires, theft, murder and false testimony objects of reprobation and mnemonics of self-definition. It aspires to ensure that no free man becomes so weakened by desire as to step out of the ferociously maintained hierarchy which places all free Israelite males above women, slaves, foreigners and resident aliens. It is a code that bonds men by the exercise of power over others and over the self.

Family, habitation and habit determine the degree of connectedness and hence the shape of society. The Fourth Word condemns irrational cruelty; others (the Sixth, Seventh and Tenth) condemn menacing greed, while the Fourth Word implicitly castigates erratic savagery which disallows rest on the Sabbath. To curb these human passions, the First reminds Israel of its submissive past, the Second of the dangers of idolatry, and the Third and the Ninth of the unlawful use of the divine name. In the resulting social order, the environment is adjusted to the needs of society and of a discipline that directs body and soul to focus on Yahweh. Yet, as the Fifth Word recognizes, the mere fact of physical birth does not guarantee either 'family' or covenant. Both constructs demand that adolescence be steadily directed towards preservation of kinship and Yahwist ideology.

Sexuality becomes a problem of parents who are held responsible for their daughter's lapse into fornication (Deut. 22). And although marriage could be dissolved upon a husbands' whim and will, conjugality reflects covenant ideology. Hence, as long as marriage lasts it has to be exclusive, and a married man has to content his desires at home, with his own wives, concubines and maidservants. Marriage and childbirth provide the fulfillment and completion of a woman's life when she is clearly and completely separated from the male sphere and as she adopts the role by which she is essentially defined. The word 'woman' (אִשָּׁה) applies to both 'woman' and 'wife'. Placed inside humanity, woman can weaken manhood, yet is indispensable. This is why both the Decalogue and its allied narratives draw a map of moral fertility and sterility, casting the Ten Words as a text which governs and frames other laws, as well as substantiating their stories.

To 'normalize' society, refraining from inappropriate acts becomes a Decalogue model of behavior. The important thing is to avoid apostasy, idolatry, false oath, disrespect for parents, desecration of the Sabbath, theft, murder, adultery and inversion of court proceedings. This can be done by vigilantly refraining from transgressions by monitoring the self. The Decalogue's register of crimes and sins acquires radicalism through narrative expressions. A forbidden territory, often manned by women, charts negative spheres of pollution. In the course of constant covenant renewals, women are cut out so that the collective male can be wholly subject to God. And the reiteration of this gesture of suppression emphasizes the gap between legal theories and the random recollection of women that strives to erase them without thinking.

The community of property and wives that characterizes the Genesis patriarchal pattern aims at survival. The community that Yahweh liberates from Egypt, destined to die in the desert, requires the image of a settled society which is directed by law. The Decalogue provides negative justice by banning basic crimes, as well as positive justice by insisting on the practice of 'citizenship'. Such a juxtaposition highlights human existence as a continuous struggle. It postulates an agonistic culture, open struggles between equal male adversaries and unequal, male and female, opposing viewpoints. In all these encounters Yahweh is constituted as the supreme arbiter because, in spite of the plethora of rules, the process of arbitration monitors and organizes society.

A decade ago Athalya Brenner asked whether women were/are the addressees of the Ten Commandments, and in *Standing Again at Sinai*, Judith Plaskow explored how women shaped successive presentations of the Sinaitic theophany. My study stems from the concerns raised by these two scholars. It also addresses the uneasy coexistence of feminist and 'mainstream' biblical scholarship by exploring the Ten Commandments as a mainstay of both law and lore. Taking women as subjects and objects of legal and narratological texts, I have intentionally placed the feminine at the heart of a biblical vision of a thoroughly masculine version of humanity. It seems to me that only in this 'unnatural' setting it is possible to explore in full how notions of sexual difference, rather than of sexual equality, framed concepts of patriarchal oppression of women.

Endeavoring to employ the Ten Commandments as a key to the formation of a moral language of concord and of discord, this study tried to shed light on moral consensus and representative conventions, as well as on subversions. Whether these conventions shaped social reality, or reality shaped ideology is interesting but impenetrable. What remains vital is the biblical rhetoric which positions Yahweh as the ultimate arbiter of morality in order to promote ideals of harmony, domestic and public. With this rhetoric the Hebrew Bible further advances a new group of men to a new kind of power—based not on might but on what is morally right.

In the ceaseless struggle among males over standing in the community, the public reputation of one's womenfolk (or lack of it) emerges as a critical component of manhood. The Decalogue implies that all men were subject to a divine and public scrutiny, and that a façade of exemplary behavior was, in itself, insufficient. Public as well as private gestures furnished a font of resources of manly conduct. Both males and females would have been seen, by themselves and by others, as two representative dimensions of the household, two sides of the same coin. To sustain his authority, a man's ability to dissociate himself from the weaknesses enumerated in the Decalogue was critical. To maintain social stability, the covenant required a continuous demonstration of the individual's trustworthiness. An undisciplined man, and by extension woman, meant lack of control over the self and, by extension, over the household. By exposing the faults of the female members of his family a male broadcast his support for the common values of a community which severely chastised adulterous wives, wayward daughters, and defiant sisters.

The role of women as constitutive of our understanding of biblical ethics indicates that the experience or self-understanding of the female part of the human race, as articulated in the Hebrew Bible, is both vital and faulty. Acknowledging this inherent limitation of our source, I have nevertheless ventured to explore the conventions by which gender-specific characteristics were assigned to women and to men. I believed it possible, through the Ten Commandments, to pave one avenue of integrating attention to gender in 'mainstream' scholarship because both laws and narratives tell us something about relations between men and women, as well as between men and other men.

Reading the Decalogue in light of gender visibility and invisibility, of domestic ideology, of covenant concord and discord, this study suggests that women bore a prominent symbolic function within the rhetoric of manhood as arbitrators of masculine virtue. If what is argued is true, the implications for our understanding of the history of women in biblical antiquity are far reaching. They indicate that accounts of female behavior were shaped to suit a judgment of male character and that consequently their reflections of reality are distorted. On the other hand, these distortions would have elicited a more accurate picture of how these women understood themselves.

The present investigation into the dynamics of the Decalogue and its projections of Israelite identity has accompanied the emergence of the individual Israelite through processes of social interaction as one who is constituted and reconstituted through various practices in which s/he participates. This means that as narrators and redactors positioned their protagonists, they also positioned themselves and provided an interpretative scheme which allows for alternative discourses. Challenging individuals to comply and to defy the Commandments, redactional recasting of male figures and their female counterparts aspires to maintain the common good which the Decalogue sublimates.

In this new topography of the Decalogues the household is positioned as a locus of legitimate and illegitimate modes of interaction. I examined in tandem legal language and concomitant tales, within the respective context of Genesis–Numbers and the Dtr History, in order to scale down the ideals of human identity to the level of the individual. Because of the monumental place of the Bible in Western tradition, the biblical notion of the individual obscures for us the centrality of the group which shaped this identity. In the Exodus narrative of the epiphany, the emphasis is on the collective; the Dtr History refocuses on the individual.

Women are never seen as autonomous social agents in such constellations. They are, however, arbiters of morality for individual males as they are for the kin group.

The continuing allure of female stereotypes, from obedient daughters to chaste wives, and from whores to 'witches', provides an underlying unity of the Astonishing variety of views which the Bible expresses. The arrival of woman (Gen. 2) enabled biblical authors and redactors to abet a claim to modes of identity which are gender-based. As rhetorical figures, women are pliant and volatile. Their ambiguity indicates that we cannot afford the luxury of inattention to the complexities that gender engages and to the centrality of women in a shifting landscape of moralities and modalities.

BIBLIOGRAPHY

Abma, R., *Bonds of Love: Methodic Studies of Prophetic Texts with Marriage Imagery: Isaiah 50.1-3 and 54.1-10, Hosea 1–3, Jeremiah 2–3* (Assen: Van Gorcum, 1999).

Abu Lughod, Lila, *Veiled Sentiments: Honor and Poetry in a Bedouin Society* (Berkeley: University of California Press, 1987).

—*Writing Women's World: Bedouin Stories* (Berkeley: University of California Press, 1993).

Ackerman, Susan, *Warrior, Dancer, Seductress, Queen: Women in Judges and in Biblical Israel* (New York: Doubleday, 1998).

—'What if Judges had been Written by a Philistine?', *BibInt* 8 (2000), pp. 33-41.

Aitken, Kenneth T., 'The Wooing of Rebekah: A Study in the Development of the Tradition', *JSOT* 30 (1984), pp. 3-23.

Albright, William F., *Archaeology and the Religion of Israel* (Baltimore: Johns Hopkins University Press, 5th edn, 1968).

Alexander, Desmond T., 'Are the Wife/Sister Incidents of Genesis Literary Compositional Variants?', *VT* 42 (1992), pp. 145-53.

Allard, Michel, 'Note sur la formule Ehyeh aser Ehyeh', *Recherches de science religieuse* 44 (1957), pp. 79-86.

Alt, Albrecht, 'Das Verbot des Diebstahls im Dekalog', in Martin Noth (ed.), *Kleine Schriften zur Geschichte des Volkes Israel* (3 vols.; Munich: Beck, 1953–59), I, pp. 333-40.

—'Zu Hit'ammer'', *VT* 2 (1952), pp. 153-59.

Alter, Robert, *The Art of Biblical Narrative* (New York: Basic Books, 1981).

—'How Convention Helps Us Read: The Case of the Bible's Annunciation Type-Scene', *Prooftexts* 3 (1983), pp. 115-30.

—'Sacred History and Prose Fiction', in Friedman (ed.), *The Creation of Sacred Literature*, pp. 7-24.

Amit, Yairah, 'Judges 4: Its Contents and Form', *JSOT* 39 (1987), pp. 89-111.

—'The Shunammite, the Shulamite, and the Professor between Midrash and Midrash', *JSOT* 93 (2001), pp. 77-91.

Andersen, Francis I., 'Socio-Juridical Background of the Naboth Incident', *JBL* 85 (1966), pp. 46-57.

Ariès, Philip, *Centuries of Childhood: A Social History of Family Life* (trans. Robert Baldick; New York: Knopf, 1962).

Arnaoutoglou, Ilias, *Ancient Greek Laws: A Sourcebook* (London: Routledge, 1998).

Aschkenasy, Nehama, *Woman at the Window: Biblical Tales of Oppression and Escape* (Detroit: Wayne State University Press, 1998).

Assmann, Jan, *Moses the Egyptian: The Memory of Egypt in Western Monotheism* (Cambridge, MA: Harvard University Press, 1997).

Auld, Graeme A., 'Sabbath, Work and Creation: מלאכה Reconsidered', *Henoch* 8 (1986), pp. 273-80.

Ausloos, Hans, 'Exod 23.20-33 and the "War of YHWH"', *Bib* 80 (1999), pp. 555-63.

Bach, Alice, 'Breaking Free of the Biblical Frame-Up: Uncovering the Woman in Genesis 39', in Brenner (ed.), *A Feminist Companion to Genesis*, pp. 318-42.

—'Reading Allowed: Feminist Biblical Criticism Approaching the Millennium', *CRBS* 1 (1993), pp. 191-215.

Bahrani, Zainab, *Women of Babylon: Gender and Representation in Mesopotamia* (London: Routledge, 2001).

Bailey, Randall C., *David in Love and in War: The Pursuit of Power in 2 Samuel 10–12* (JSOTSup, 75; Sheffield: JSOT Press, 1990).

Bal, Mieke, 'A Body of Writing: Judges 19', in Brenner (ed.), *A Feminist Companion to Judges*, pp. 208-30.

—*Death and Dissymmetry: The Politics of Coherence in the Book of Judges* (Chicago: Chicago University Press, 1988).

—*Lethal Love: Feminist Literary Readings of Biblical Love Stories* (Bloomington: Indiana University Press, 1987).

—'Lots of Writing', in Brenner (ed.), *A Feminist Companion to Ruth and Esther*, pp. 212-38.

—*Murder and Difference: Gender, Genre and Scholarship on Sisera's Death* (trans. Matthew Gumpert; Bloomington: Indiana University Press, 1988).

—'Reading as Empowerment: The Bible from a Feminist Perspective', in Barry N. Olshen and Yael S. Feldman (eds.), *Approaches to Teaching the Hebrew Bible as Literature in Translation* (New York: Modern Language Association of America, 1989), pp. 87-92.

—'Scared to Death: Metaphor, Theory and the Adventure of Scholarship', in David Jasper and Mark Ledbetter (eds.), *In Good Company: Essay in Honor of Robert Detweiler* (Atlanta: Scholars Press, 1994), pp. 11-31.

—'Tricky Thematics', in Exum and Bos (eds.), *Reasoning with the Foxes*, pp. 133-55.

Bal, Mieke (ed.), *Anti-Covenant: Counter-Reading Women's Lives in the Hebrew Bible* (Bible and Literature, 22; Sheffield: Almond Press, 1989).

Barrick, William D., 'The Mosaic Covenant', *The Master's Seminary Journal* 10 (1999), pp. 213-32.

Barstad, Hans M., 'Is the Hebrew Bible a Hellenistic Book? Or: Niels Peter Lemche, Herodotus, and the Persians', *Transeuphratène* 23 (2002), pp. 129-51.

Barthes, Roland, *The Pleasure of the Text* (trans. Richard Miller; New York: Hill & Wang, 1975).

Barton, John (ed.), *Cambridge Companion to Biblical Interpretation* (Cambridge: Cambridge University Press, 1998).

Batto, Bernard F., 'The Institution of Marriage in Genesis 2 and in Atrahasis', *CBQ* 62 (2000), pp. 621-31.

Baumann, Gerlinde, 'Connected by Marriage, Adultery and Violence: The Prophetic Marriage Metaphor in the Book of Twelve and in the Major Prophets', *SBLSP* 38 (1999), pp. 552-69.

—*Liebe und Gewalt: die Ehe als Metaphor für das Verhältnis JHWH und Israel in den Prophetenbüchern* (Stuttgart: Katholisches Bibelwerk, 2000).

Bechtel, Lyn M., 'Shame as a Sanction of Social Control in Biblical Israel: Judicial, Political and Social Shaming', *JSOT* 49 (1991), pp. 47-76.

Beck, Martin, *Elia und die Monolatrie: Ein Beitrag zur religionsgeschichte Rückfrage nach dem Vorprophetischen Jahwe-Glauben* (Berlin: W. de Gruyter, 1999).

Bellefontaine, Elizabeth, 'Deuteronomy 21:18-21: Reviewing the Case of the Rebellious Son', *JSOT* 13 (1979), pp. 13-31.

Benjamin, Don C., 'Israel's God: Mother and Midwife', *BTB* 19 (1989), pp. 115-20.

Benjamin, Don C., and Victor H. Matthews, *Social World of Ancient Israel 1250–587 BCE* (Peabody, MA: Hendrickson, 1993).

Benjamin, Walter, 'On the Concept of History', in *Selected Writings*. IV. *1938–1940* (trans. Edmund Jephcott *et al.*; eds. Howard Eiland and Michael W. Jennings; Cambridge, MA: Belknap, 2003), pp. 389-97

Benveniste, Emile, *Problèmes de linguistique générale* (2 vols.; Paris: Gallimard, 1974).

—*Vocabulaire des institutions indo-européenes* (2 vols.; Paris: Minuit, 1969).

Berlin, Adele, 'Characterization in Biblical Narratives: David's Wives', *JSOT* 23 (1982), pp. 69-85.

—*Poetics and Interpretation of Biblical Narratives* (Bible and Literature, 9; Sheffield: Almond Press, 1983 [repr. Winona Lake, IN: Eisenbrauns, 1994]).

Berlinerblau, J., 'The "Popular Religion" Paradigm in Old Testament Research', *JSOT* 60 (1993), pp. 3-26.

Beyerlin, Walter, *Near Eastern Religious Texts Relating to the Old Testament* (trans. John Bowden; Philadelphia: Westminster Press, 1978).

Biddle, Mark E., 'The "Endangered Ancestress" and the Blessing for the Nations', *JBL* 109 (1990), pp. 599-611.

Bird, Phyllis A., 'The Harlot as Heroine: Narrative Art and Social Presupposition in Three Old Testament Texts', in Anne M. Solomon *et al.* (eds.), *Narrative Research on the Hebrew Bible* [= *Semeia* 46 (1989)], pp. 119-39.

—'Images of Women in the Old Testament', in Rosemary R. Ruether (ed.), *Religion and Sexism: Images of Women in the Jewish and Christian Traditions* (New York: Simon & Schuster, 1974), pp. 41-88.

—'The Place of Women in the Israelite Cultus', in Miller, Hanson and McBride (eds.), *Ancient Israelite Religion*, pp. 397-419.

—'Translating Sexist Language as a Theological and Cultural Problem', *Union Seminary Quarterly Review* 42 (1988), pp. 89-95.

Blayney, Jan, 'Theories of Conception in the Ancient Roman World', in Beryl Rawson (ed.), *The Family in Ancient Rome: New Perspectives* (London: Routledge, 1992), pp. 230-36.

Blenkinsopp, Joseph, 'Deuteronomy and the Politics of Post-Mortem Existence', *VT* 45 (1995), pp. 1-16.

Boda, Mark J., *Praying the Tradition: The Origin, and Use of Tradition in Nehemiah 9* (Berlin: W. de Gruyter, 1999).

Bodi, Daniel, 'La tragédie de Mikal en tant que critique de la monarchie israélite et préfiguration de sa fin', *Foi et Vie* 95 (1996), pp. 65-105.

Boer, Ronald, 'Culture, Ethics and Identity in Reading Ruth: A Response to Donaldson, Dube, McKinlay and Brenner', in Brenner (ed.), *A Feminist Companion to Ruth and Esther*, pp. 163-70.

Bohmbach, Karla G., 'Conventions/Contraventions: The Meanings of Public and Private for the Judges 19 Concubine', *JSOT* 83 (1999), pp. 83-98.

Boorer, Suzanne, *The Promise of the Land as Oath: A Key to the Formation of the Pentateuch* (Berlin: W. de Gruyter, 1992).

Bourdieu, Pierre, *The Logic of Practice* (trans. Richard Nice; Stanford: Stanford University Press, 1990).

—'The Sentiment of Honor in Kabyle Society', in John G. Peristiany (ed.), *Honor and Shame: The Values of Mediterranean Society* (The Nature of Human Society; repr., Chicago: University of Chicago Press, 1974 [1966]), pp. 193-241.

Boyarin, Daniel, *Unheroic Conduct: The Rise of Heterosexuality and the Invention of the Jewish Man* (Berkeley: University of California Press, 1997).

Braulik, Georg, 'Die Abfolge der Gesetze in Deuteronomium 12–26 und der Dekalog', in Norbert Lohfink (ed.), *Das Deuteronomium: Enstehung, Gestalt und Botschaft* (Leuven: Peeters, 1985), pp. 61-138.

—'Das Deuteronomium', in Erich Zenger (ed.), *Die Tora als Kanon fur Juden und Christen* (Freiburg: Herder, 1996), pp. 61-138.

—'Haben in Israel auch Frauen geopfert? Beobachtungen am Deuteronomium', in Siegfried Kreuzer and Kurt Lüthi (eds.), *Zur Aktualität des Alten Testaments: Festschrift für Georg Sauer* (Frankfurt: Peter Lang, 1992), pp. 19-28.

Brenner, Athalya, 'The Decalogue—Am I an Addressee?', in *idem* (ed.), *A Feminist Companion to Exodus–Deuteronomy*, pp. 255-58.

—'On Incest', in *idem* (ed.), *A Feminist Companion to Exodus–Deuteronomy*, pp. 113-38.

—'On Reading the Hebrew Bible as a Feminist Woman: Introduction to the Song of Songs', in *idem* (ed.), *A Feminist Companion to the Song of Songs* (The Feminist Companion to the Bible, 1; Sheffield: JSOT Press, 1993), pp. 11-27.

Brenner, Athalya (ed.), *A Feminist Companion to Exodus–Deuteronomy* (The Feminist Companion to the Bible, 6; Sheffield: Sheffield Academic Press, 1994).

—*A Feminist Companion to Genesis* (The Feminist Companion to the Bible, 2; Sheffield: Sheffield Academic Press, 1993).

—*A Feminist Companion to Judges* (The Feminist Companion to the Bible, 5, 2nd Series; Sheffield: Sheffield Academic Press, 1993).

—*A Feminist Companion to Ruth and Esther* (The Feminist Companion to the Bible, 2nd Series, 3; Sheffield: Sheffield Academic Press, 1999).

—*The Israelite Woman: Social Role and Literary Type in Biblical Narrative* (The Biblical Seminar, 2; Sheffield: JSOT Press, 1985).

Brenner, Athalya, and Fokkelien van Dijk-Hemmes, *On Gendering Texts: Female and Male Voices in the Hebrew Bible* (Leiden: E.J. Brill, 1993).

Brenner, Athalya, and Carole Fontaine (eds.), *A Feminist Companion to Reading the Bible: Approaches, Methods and Strategies* (The Feminist Companion to the Bible, 11; Sheffield: Sheffield Academic Press, 1997).

Brettler, Mark, Zvi, 'Women and Psalms: Toward an Understanding of the Role of Women's Prayer in the Israelite Cult', in Matthews, Levinson and Frymer-Kensky (eds.), *Gender and Law*, pp. 25-56.

Brichto, Herbert C., 'The Case of the *Sota* and a Reconsideration of Biblical "Law"', *HUCA* 46 (1975), pp. 55-70.

—'The Worship of the Golden Calf: A Literary Analysis of a Fable on Idolatry', *HUCA* 54 (1983), pp. 1-44.

Briend, Jacque, 'Honoré ton père et ta mère', *Christus* 122 (1984), n.p.

Brody, Saul N., *The Disease of the Soul: Leprosy in Medieval Literature* (Ithaca, NY: Cornell University Press, 1974).

Brooks, Simcha S., 'Was there a Concubine at Gibeah?', *Bulletin of the Anglo-Israel Archaeological Society* 15 (1996–97), pp. 31-40.

Brown, John P., 'The Role of Women and the Treaty in the Ancient World', *BZ* 25 (1981), pp. 1-28.

Brown-Gutoff, Susan E., 'The Voice of Rachel in Jeremiah 31: A Calling to "Something New"', *USQR* 45 (1991), pp. 177-90.

Brueggemann, Walter, *Deuteronomy* (Abingdon Old Testament Commentaries; Nashville: Abingdon Press, 2001).

—*Genesis* (Interpretation; Atlanta: John Knox Press, 1982).

—'The Shrill Voice of the Wounded Party', *HBT* 21 (1999), pp. 1-25.

Buber, Martin, *Moses* (Tel Aviv: Schocken Books, 1963 [Hebrew]) (published in English as *Moses: The Revelation and the Covenant* [New York: Harper Row, 1958]).

Burns, Rita J., *Has the Lord Indeed Spoken Only Through Moses? A Study of the Biblical Portrait of Miriam* (Atlanta: Scholars Press, 1987).

Butler, Judith P., *Gender Trouble: Feminism and the Subversion of Identity* (New York: Routledge, 1990).

Bynum, Caroline Walker, *Fragmentation and Redemption: Essays on Gender and the Human Body in Medieval Religion* (New York: Zone Books, 1991).

Calderon, Ruth, *The Market, the Home, the Heart* (Jerusalem: Keter, 2001 [Hebrew]).

Camp, Claudia V., 'The Female Sage in Ancient Israel and in the Biblical Wisdom Literature', in John G. Gammie and Leo G. Perdue (eds.), *The Sage in Israel and in the Ancient Near East* (Winona Lake, IN: Eisenbrauns, 1990), pp. 185-203.

—'Understanding a Patriarchy: Women in Second Century Jerusalem through the Eyes of Ben Sira', in Amy Jill Levine (ed.), *'Women like This': New Perspectives on Jewish Women in the Greco-Roman World* (Atlanta: Scholars Press, 1991), pp. 1-39.

—*Wise, Strange and Holy: The Strange Woman and the Making of the Bible* (JSOTSup, 320; Sheffield: Sheffield Academic Press, 2000).

—'The Wise Women of 2 Samuel: A Role Model for Early Israel', *CBQ* 43 (1981), pp. 14-29.

Campbell, Anthony F. and Mark A. O'Brien, *Unfolding the Deuteronomistic History: Origins, Upgrades, Present Text* (Minneapolis: Fortress Press, 2000).

Carmichael, Calum M., 'Biblical Laws of Talion', *HAR* 9 (1985), pp. 107-26.

—*The Laws of Deuteronomy* (Ithaca, NY: Cornell University Press, 1974).

—*The Origins of Biblical Law: The Decalogues and the Book of the Covenant* (Ithaca, NY: Cornell University Press, 1992).

—*Women, Law and the Genesis Traditions* (Edinburgh: Edinburgh University Press, 1979).

Carr, David M., 'Controversy and Convergence in Recent studies of the Formation of the Pentateuch', *RelSRev* 23 (1997), pp. 22-31.

Carrón, Julián, 'Honor your Father and your Mother', *Communio* 22 (1995), pp. 28-43.

Cazelles, Henri, *Etudes sur le code de l'alliance* (Paris: Letouzey et Ané, 1946).

Certeau, Michel de, *The Writing of History* (trans. Tom Conley; New York: Columbia University Press, 1988).

Charpin, Dominique *et al.*, *Archives épistolaires de Mari* I/2 (Archives royales de Mari, 26; Paris: Editions Recherches sur les Civilisations, 1988).

Childs, Brevard S., *The Book of Exodus: A Critical, Theological Commentary* (OTL; Philadelphia: Westminster Press, 1974).

—*Memory and Tradition in Israel* (London: SCM Press, 1962).

Chinitz, Jacob, 'The Ten and the Torah', *JBQ* 27 (1999), pp. 186-91.

Chirichigno, Gregory C., *Debt-Slavery in Israel and the Ancient Near East* (JSOTSup, 141; Sheffield: JSOT Press, 1993).

Clines, David J.A., 'The Ancestor in Danger: But not the Same Danger', in *idem*, *What Does Eve Do to Help? And Other Readerly Questions to the Old Testament* (JSOTSup, 94; Sheffield: JSOT Press, 1990), pp. 67-84.

—'The Ten Commandments: Reading from Left to Right', in Jon Davies, Graham Harvey and Wilfred G.E. Watson (eds.), *Words Remembered, Texts Renewed: Essays in Honor of John F.A. Sawyer* (JSOTSup, 195; Sheffield, Sheffield Academic Press, 1995), pp. 97-112.

Clines, David J.A., and Tamara C. Eskenazi (eds.), *Telling Queen Michal's Story: An Experiment in Comparative Interpretation* (JSOTSup, 119; Sheffield: JSOT Press, 1991).

Coats, George W., *From Canaan to Egypt: Structural and Theological Context for the Joseph Story* (Catholic Biblical Quarterly Monograph Series, 4; Washington: Catholic Biblical Association of America, 1976).

—*Rebellion in the Wilderness* (Nashville: Abingdon Press, 1968).

Coates, J.R., 'Thou Shalt Not Covet', *ZAW* 52 (1934), pp. 238-39.

Coggins, Richard J., *Introducing the Old Testament* (Oxford: Oxford University Press, 2nd edn, 2001).

Cohen, Jeremy, *'Be Fertile and Increase, Fill the Earth and Master It': The Ancient and Medieval Career of a Biblical Text* (Ithaca, NY: Cornell University Press, 1989).

Cohen, Shaye J.D., 'Solomon and the Daughter of Pharaoh: Intermarriage, Conversion, and the Impurity of Women', *JANES* 16-17 (1984–85), pp. 23-37.

Cohn, Robert L., *2 Kings* (Berit Olam; Collegeville, MN: Liturgical Press, 2000).

Conrad, Diethelm, *Studien zum Altargesetz: Ex. 20.24-26* (Marburg: H. Kombächer, 1968).

Coogan, Michael D., 'Canaanite Origins and Lineage: Reflections on the Religion of Ancient Israel', in Miller, Paul and McBride (eds.), *Ancient Israelite Religion*, pp. 115-24.

Cook, Stanley A., 'A Pre-Masoretic Biblical Papyrus', *Proceedings of the Society of Biblical Archaeology* 5 (1903), pp. 34-56.

Croatto, Severino J., '¿Como releer la Biblia desde su contexto socio-politico?', *Revista Biblica* 53 (1991), pp. 193-212.

Cross, Frank M., *Canaanite Myth and Hebrew Epic: Essays on the History of the Religion of Israel* (Cambridge, MA: Harvard University Press, 1973).

—'A Response to Zakovitch's 'Successful Failure of Israelite Intelligence', in Niditch (ed.), *Text and Tradition*, pp. 99-106.

Crüsemann, Frank, *Bewahrung der Freiheit: Das Thema des Dekalogs in socialgeschichlicher Perspektive* (Munich: Chr. Kaiser Verlag, 1983).

—*The Torah: Theology and Social History of Old Testament Law* (trans. Allan W. Mahnke; Minneapolis: Fortress Press, 1996).

Dan, Joseph, 'Teraphim: From Popular Belief to a Folktale', *Scripta Hierosolymitana* 27 (1978), pp. 99-106.

Darr, Katheryn P., *Isaiah's Vision and the Family of God* (Louisville, KY: Westminster/John Knox Press, 1994).

Daube, David, 'Biblical Landmarks in the Struggle for Women's Rights', *Juridical Review* 23 (1978), pp. 177-97.

—'The Culture of Deuteronomy', *Orita* 3 (1969), pp. 43-50.

—*Studies in Biblical Law* (Cambridge: Cambridge University Press, 1947 [repr. New York: Ktav, 1969]).

Davidson, James, *Courtesans and Fishcakes: The Consuming Passions of Classical Athens* (New York: HarperCollins, 1999).

Davies, Eryl W., *Numbers* (NCBC; Grand Rapids: Eerdmans, 1995).

Dawn, Moira J., *Keeping the Sabbath Wholly: Ceasing, Resting, Embracing, Feasting* (Grand Rapids: Eerdmans, 1989).

Day, Peggy L., 'Adulterous Jerusalem's Imagined Demise: Death of a Metaphor in Ezekiel XVI', *VT* 50 (2000), pp. 285-309.

—'From the Child is Born the Woman: The Story of Jephthah's Daughter', in *idem* (ed.), *Gender and Difference in Ancient Israel*, pp. 58-74.

Day, Peggy L. (ed.), *Gender and Difference in Ancient Israel* (Minneapolis: Fortress Press, 1989).

Deem, Ariella, 'The Goddess Anath and Some Biblical Hebrew Cruces', *JSS* 23 (1978), pp. 25-30.

Dempster, Stephen, 'The Deuteronomic Formula *kî yimmatse* in the Light of Biblical and Ancient Near Eastern Law: An Evaluation of David Daube's Theory', *RB* 91 (1984), pp. 188-211.

Derby, Josiah, 'The Third Commandment', *JBQ* 21 (1993), pp. 24-27.

Dever, William G., 'Revisionist Israel Revisited: A Rejoinder to Niels Peter Lemche', *CRBS* 4 (1996), pp. 35-50.

Dijk-Hemmes, Fokkelien van, 'The Great Woman of Shunem and the Man of God: A Dual Interpretation of 2 Kings 4.8-37', in Athalya Brenner (ed.), *A Feminist Companion to Samuel and Kings* (The Feminist Companion to the Bible, 5; Sheffield: Sheffield Academic Press, 1994), pp. 218-30.

—'Sarai's Exile: A Gender-Motivated Reading of Genesis 12.10–13.2', in Brenner (ed.), *A Feminist Companion to Genesis*, pp. 222-34.

—'Tamar and the Limits of Patriarchy: Between Rape and Seduction (2 Samuel 13 and Genesis 38)', in Bal (ed.), *Anti-Covenant*, pp. 135-56.

Dohmen, Christoph, *Das Bilderverbot: Seine Entstehung und seine Entwicklung im Alten Testament* (Bonner biblische Beiträge, 62; Bonn: Hanstein, 2nd edn, 1987 [1985]).

—'כבד, כבודת', in *ThWAT*, IV, pp. 13-40 (English translation = *TDOT*, VII, pp. 13-38).

Douglas, Mary, *In the Wilderness: The Doctrine of Defilement in the Book of Numbers* (JSOTSup, 158; Sheffield: JSOT Press, 1993).

—*Leviticus as Literature* (Oxford: Oxford University Press, 1999).

Dozeman, Thomas B., *God on the Mountain: A Study of the Redaction, Theology and Canon in Exodus 19–24* (Atlanta: Scholars Press, 1989).

Dresner, Samuel H., *Rachel* (Minneapolis: Fortress Press, 1994).

Durham, J., *Exodus* (WBC, 2; Waco, TX: Word Books, 1987).

Edelmann, Ronald, 'Exodus 32:18', *JTS* 1 (1950), p. 56

—'To ענות: Exodus xxxii.18', *VT* 16 (1966), p. 355.

Eilberg-Schwartz, Howard, *God's Phallus: and Other Problems for Men and Monotheism* (Boston: Beacon Press, 1994).

—*The Savage in Judaism: An Anthropology of Israelite Religion and Ancient Judaism* (Bloomington: Indiana University Press, 1990).

Elssner, Thomas R., *Das Namensmissbrauch-Verbot: Bedeutung, Enstehung, und frühe Wirkungsgeschichte* (Leipzig: Benno, 1999)

Eskenazi, Tamara C., 'Nehemiah 9–10: Structure and Significance', *Journal of Hebrew Scriptures* 3 (2000–2001), available online at <http://www.arts.ualberta.ca/JHS/Articles/article_21.htm>.

Eskenazi, Tamara C., Daniel J. Herrington and William H. Shea (eds.), *The Sabbath in Jewish and Christian Traditions* (New York: Crossroad, 1991).

Evans, Craig A., and James A. Sanders (eds.), *The Function of Scripture in Early Jewish and Christian Tradition* (JSNTSup, 154; Sheffield: Sheffield Academic Press, 1998).

Exum, J. Cheryl, 'Feminist Study of the Old Testament', in Andrew D.H. Mayes (ed.), *Text in Context* (Oxford: Oxford University Press, 2000), pp. 86-115.

—*Fragmented Women: Feminist (Sub)versions of Biblical Narratives* (Valley Forge: Trinity International, 1993).

—'Samson's Women', in *idem*, *Fragmented Women*, pp. 61-93.

—'The Tragic Vision and Biblical Narratives: The Case of Jephthah', in *idem* (ed.), *Signs and Wonders*, pp. 59-83.

—'Who's Afraid of "the Endangered Ancestress"?', in *idem*, *Fragmented Women*, pp. 148-69.

Exum, J. Cheryl (ed.), *Signs and Wonders: Biblical Texts in Literary Focus* (Atlanta: Scholars Press, 1989).

Exum, J. Cheryl, and Johanna W.H. Bos (eds.), *Reasoning with the Foxes: Female Wit in a World of Male Power* (= *Semeia* 42 [1988]).

Fensham, Charles F., 'The Son of a Handmaid in Northwest Semitic', *VT* 19 (1969), pp. 312-21.

Féral, Josette, 'The Powers of Difference', in Hester Eisenstein and Alice Jardine (eds.), *The Future of Difference* (New Brunswick: Rutgers University Press, 1985), pp. 88-94.

Fewell, Danna N., 'The Gift: World Alteration and Obligation in 2 Kings 4:8-37', in Saul M. Olyan and Robert C. Culley (eds.), *Wise and Discerning Mind: Essays in Honor of Burke Long* (Providence: Brown Judaic Studies, 2000), pp. 109-23.

Fewell, Danna N. (ed.), *Reading between Texts: Intertextuality and the Hebrew Bible* (Louisville, KY: Westminster/John Knox Press, 1992).

Fewell, Danna N., and David M. Gunn, *Gender, Power and Promise: The Subject of the Bible's First Story* (Nashville: Abingdon Press, 1993).

Finkelstein, Israel, 'The Archaeology of the United Monarchy: An Alternative View', *Levant* 28 (1996), pp. 177-87.

Finkelstein, Jacob J., 'Sex Offenses in Sumerian Laws', *Journal of the American Oriental Society* 86 (1966), pp. 355-72.

Fischer, Irmtraud, 'The Book of Ruth: A "Feminist" Commentary to the Torah?', in Brenner (ed.), *A Feminist Companion to Ruth and Esther*, pp. 24-49.

—*Die Erzeltern Israels: Feministisch-thelogische Studien zu Genesis 12–36* (Berlin: W. de Gruyter, 1994).

Fishbane, Michael, 'Accusations of Adultery: A Study of Law and Scribal Practice in Numbers 11–31', *HUCA* 45 (1974), pp. 25-45.

—*Biblical Interpretation in Ancient Israel* (Oxford: Clarendon Press, 1985).

—*Text and Texture: Close Reading of Selected Biblical Texts* (New York: Schocken Books, 1979).

Fleishman, Joseph, *Parent and Child in the Ancient Near East and the Bible* (Jerusalem: Magnes Press, 1999 [Hebrew]).

Fokkelman, J.P., *Narrative Art and Poetry in the Books of Samuel: A Full Interpretation Based on Stylistic and Structural Analysis* (Studia Semitica Neerlandica, 20, 23, 27, 31; 4 vols.; Assen: Van Gorcum, 1981–93).

—*Narrative Art in Genesis: Specimens of Stylistic and Structural Analyses* (The Biblical Seminar, 12; Sheffield: JSOT Press, 2nd edn, 1991 [1st edn = Assen: Van Gorcum, 1975]).

Forrest, W.G., *A History of Sparta* (New York: Norton, 1968).

Frankel, David, 'The Destruction of the Golden Calf: A New Solution', *VT* 44 (1994), pp. 330-39.

Freedman, David N., *The Nine Commandments: Uncovering a Hidden Pattern of Crime and Punishment in the Hebrew Bible* (New York: Doubleday, 2000).

Fretheim Terence E., *First and Second Kings* (Westminster Bible Companion; Louisville, KY: Westminster/John Knox Press, 1st edn, 1999).

Freund, Richard A., 'The Decalogue in Early Judaism and Christianity', in Evans and Sanders (eds.), *The Function of Scripture*, pp. 124-41.

—'Murder, Adultery and Theft', *SJOT* 2 (1989), pp. 72-80.

—'Naming Names: Some Observations on "Nameless Women" Traditions in the MT, LXX and Hellenistic Literature', *SJOT* 6 (1992), pp. 213-32.

Friedman, Richard E., 'Sacred History and Theology: The Redaction of the Torah', in *idem* (ed.), *The Creation of Sacred Literature*, pp. 25-34.

Friedman, Richard E. (ed.), *The Creation of Sacred Literature: Composition and Redaction of the Biblical Text* (Berkeley: University of California Press, 1981).

Frymer-Kensky, Tikva, 'The Bible and Women's Studies', in Lynn Davidman and Shelly Tenenbaum (eds.), *Feminist Perspectives on Jewish Studies* (New Haven: Yale University Press, 1994), pp. 16-39.

—*In the Wake of the Goddesses: Women, Culture and the Biblical Transformation of Pagan Myth* (New York: Schocken Books, 1992).

—'Law and Philosophy: The Case of Sex in the Bible', *Semeia* 45 (1989), pp. 89-102.

—'Pollution, Purification, and Purgation in Biblical Israel', in Carol L. Meyers and M. O'Connor (eds.), *The Word of the Lord Shall Go Forth: Essays in Honor of David Noel Freedman* (Winona Lake, IN: Eisenbrauns, 1983), pp. 399-414.

—'Rahab', in Meyers *et al.* (eds.), *Women in Scripture*, p. 141.

—'Reading Rahab', in Mordechai Cogan, Barry L. Eichler and Jeffrey H. Tigay (eds.), *Tehilla LeMoshe: Biblical and Judaic Studies in Honor of Moshe Greenberg* (Winona Lake, IN: Eisenbrauns, 1997), pp. 57-72.

—*Victors, Victims, Virgins and Voice: Reading the Women of the Bible* (New York: Schocken Books, 2002).

—'Virginity in the Bible', in Matthews, Levinson and Frymer-Kensky (eds.), *Gender and Law*, pp. 79-96.

Fuchs, Esther, ' "For I Have the Way of Women": Deception, Gender and Ideology in Biblical Narrative', *Semeia* 42 (1988) (= Exum and Bos [eds.], *Reasoning with the Foxes*), pp. 68-83.

—'The Literary Characterization of Mothers and Sexual Politics in the Hebrew Bible', in Adela Yarbro Collins (ed.), *Feminist Perspectives on Biblical Scholarship* (Chico, CA: Scholars Press, 1985), pp. 117-36.

Gafni, Reuven, 'Leprosy as Penalty in the Bible and in Rabbinic Writings', *Megadim* 30 (1999), pp. 23-33 (Hebrew).

Gallop, Jane, *Thinking Through the Body* (New York: Columbia University Press, 1988).

García López, Fèlix, 'Analyze littéraire de Deutéronomie V–XI', *RB* 85 (1978), pp. 37-39.

—'Del "Yavista" al "Deuteronomista": Estudio critico de Genesis 24', *RB* 87 (1980), pp. 242-73.

—'Narración y ley en los escritos sacerdotales del Penateuco', *Estudios Bíblicos* 57 (1999), pp. 271-87.

Gardner, Jane F., and Thomas Wiedeman (eds.), *The Roman Household: A Sourcebook* (London: Routledge, 1991).

Garsiel, Moshe, 'The Story of David and Bath Sheba: A Different Approach', *CBQ* 55 (1993), pp. 244-62.

Geller, S.A., 'The God of the Covenant', in Barbara N. Porter (ed.), *One God or Many? Concepts of Divinity in the Ancient World* (Chebeague, ME: Casco Bay Assyriological Institute, 2000), pp. 273-319.

—*Sacred Enigmas: Literary Religion in the Hebrew Bible* (London: Routledge, 1996).

Gernet, Louis, *Recherches sur le développement juridique et moral de la pensée grecque* (Paris: Ernest Leroux, 1917).

Gevirtz, Stanley, 'Lamech's Song to his Wives (Genesis 4:23-4)', in Richard S. Hess and David T. Tsumura (eds.), *I Studied Inscriptions before the Flood: Ancient Near Eastern, Literary and Linguistic Approaches to Genesis 1–11* (Winona Lake, IN: Eisenbrauns, 1994), pp. 405-15.

Gillmayr-Bucher, Susanne, 'The Woman of their Dreams: The Image of Rebekah in Genesis 24', in Philips R. Davies and David J.A. Clines (eds.), *World of Genesis* (JSOTSup, 257; Sheffield: Sheffield Academic Press, 1998), pp. 90-101.

Gilmore, David, *Aggression and Community: Paradoxes of Andalusian Culture* (New Haven: Yale University Press, 1987).

—*Manhood in the Making: Cultural Concepts of Masculinity* (New Haven: Yale University Press, 1990).

Glatt-Gilad, David A., 'The Role of Huldah's Prophecy in the Chronicler's Portrayal of Josiah's Reform', *Bib* 77 (1996), pp. 16-31.

Gleason, Maud W., *Making Men: Sophists and Self-Representation in Ancient Rome* (Princeton, NJ: Princeton University Press, 1995).

Glotz, Gustave, 'Le serment', in *idem, Etudes sociales et juridique* (Paris: Hachette, 1906).

Gnuse, Robert, *You shall Not Steal: Community and Property in Biblical Tradition* (Maryknoll, NY: Orbis Books, 1985).

Good, Robert M., 'Exodus 32:18', in Marks and Good (eds.), *Love and Death in the Ancient Near East*, pp. 137-42.

Gordon, Cyrus H., 'Biblical Customs and the Nuzu Tablets', *BA* 3 (1940), pp. 1-22.

—'The Marriage and Death of Sinuhe', in Marks and Good (eds.), *Love and Death in the Ancient Near East*, pp. 43-44.

Goshen-Gottstein, Moshe, 'Abraham-Lover or Beloved of God', in Marks and Good (eds.), *Love and Death in the Ancient Near East*, pp. 101-104.

Gottwald, Norman K., 'Triumphalist versus Anti-Triumphalist Versions of Early Israel: A Response to Articles by Lemche and Dever in Volume 4 (1996)', *CRBS* 5 (1997), pp. 15-42.

Goulder, Michael D., 'Ruth: A Homily on Deuteronomy 22–25?', in Heather H. McKay and David J.A. Clines (eds.), *Of Prophets' Visions and the Wisdom of the Sages: Essays in Honour of R.N. Whybray* (JSOTSup, 162; Sheffield: JSOT Press, 1993), pp. 307-19.

Gowan, Donald E., *Theology in Exodus: Biblical Theology in the Form of a Commentary* (Louisville, KY: Westminster/John Knox Press, 1994).

Grabbe, Lester L. (ed.), *Can a 'History of Israel' be Written?* (JSOTSup, 245; Sheffield: Sheffield Academic Press, 1997).

Gradwohl, Roland, 'Nissal und hissil als Rechtsbegriffe im Sklavenrecht', *ZAW* 111 (1999), pp. 187-95.

Graupner, Axel, 'Zum Verhältnis der beiden Dekalogfassungen Exod. 20 und Dtn 5', *ZAW* 99 (1987), pp. 311-15.

Gray, George B., *A Critical and Exegetical Commentary on Numbers* (ICC; Edinburgh: T. & T. Clark, 1903).

Gray, John, *I and II Kings* (London: SCM Press, 3rd edn, 1977).

Gray, Mark, 'Amnon: A Chip Off the Old Block? Rhetorical Strategy in 2 Samuel 13.7-15. The Rape of Tamar and the Humiliation of the Poor', *JSOT* 77 (1998), pp. 39-54.

Greenberg, Moshe, 'Another Look at Rachel's Theft of the Teraphim', *JBL* 81 (1962), pp. 239-48.

—'Some Postulates of Biblical Criminal Law', in Menahem Haran (ed.), *Yehezkel Kaufmann Jubilee Volume* (Jerusalem: Magnes Press, 1960), pp. 5-28.

Greene, Mark, 'Enigma Variations: Aspects of the Samson Story, Judges 13–16', *Vox Evangelica* 21 (1991), pp. 53-79.

Greengus, Samuel, 'Old Babylonian Marriage Ceremonies and Rites', *Journal of Cuneiform Studies* 20 (1966), pp. 55-72.

—'A Textbook Case of Adultery in Ancient Mesopotamia', *HUCA* 40-41 (1969–70), pp. 33-44.

Grenfell, Bernard *et al.* (eds.), *The Tebtunis Papyri* (4 vols.; London: Oxford University Press, 1902–).

Gressman, Hugo, *Mose und seine Zeit: ein Kommentar zu den Mose-Sagen* (Göttingen: Vandenhoeck & Ruprecht, 1913).

Grottanelli, Cristiano, 'Making Room for the Written Law', *History of Religions* 34 (1994), pp. 246-64 (repr. in *idem*, *Kings and Prophets* [New York: Oxford University Press, 1999], pp. 185-201).

Gruber, Mayer I., 'Hebrew Qedesah and her Canaanite and Akkadian Cognates', *UF* 18 (1986), pp. 133-48.

—*The Motherhood of God and Other Studies* (Atlanta: Scholars Press, 1992).

Gunkel, Herman, *Die Märchen im Alten Testament* (Tübingen: J.C.B. Mohr [Paul Siebeck], 1917 [repr. = Frankfurt: Athenäum, 1987]) (published in English as *The Folktale in the Old Testament* [trans. Michael D. Rutter, with an Introduction by John W. Rogerson; Historic Texts and Interpreters in Biblical Scholarship; Sheffield: Almond Press, 1987]).

—*Genesis* (trans. Mark E. Biddle; Macon: Mercer University Press, 1997).

Gunn, David M., 'Bathsheba Goes Bathing in Hollywood: Words, Images and Social Locations', *Semeia* 74 (1996), pp. 75-101.

Gunn, David M., and Danna N. Fewell, *Narrative in the Hebrew Bible* (Oxford: Clarendon Press, 1993).

—*The Story of King David: Genre and Interpretation* (JSOTSup, 6; Sheffield: JSOT, 1978).

Haas, Peter J., '"Die, She Shall Surely Die": The Structure of Homicide in Biblical Law', *Semeia* 45 (1989), pp. 67-87.

Haberman, Bonna Devora, 'The Suspected Adulteress: A Study of Textual Embodiment', *Prooftexts*, 20 (2000), pp. 12-42.

Hadley, Judith M., *The Cult of Ashera in Ancient Israel and Judah: Evidence for a Hebrew Goddess* (Cambridge: Cambridge University Press, 2000).

Hahn, Joachim, *Das 'Goldene Kalb': Die Jahwe-Verehrung bei Stierbildern in der Geschichte Israels* (Frankfurt: Peter Lang, 1981 [2nd edn = 1987]).

Halbertal, Moshe, and Avishai Margalit, *Idolatry* (trans. Naomi Goldblum; Cambridge, MA: Harvard University Press, 1992).

Hallo, William H., 'The Birth of Kings', in Marks and Good (eds.), *Love and Death in the Ancient Near East*, pp. 45-52.

—'New Moons and Sabbaths: A Case Study in the Contrastive Approach', *HUCA* 48 (1977), pp. 1-18.

Harman, Allan M., 'The Interpretation of the Third Commandment', *The Reformed Theological Review* 47 (1988), pp. 1-7.

Harrelson, Walter, *The Ten Commandments and Human Rights* (Philadelphia: Fortress Press, 1980).

Harries, Jill, *Law and Empire in Late Antiquity* (Cambridge, MA: Cambridge University Press, 1999).

Hart, Ian, 'Genesis 1:1–2:2 as a Prologue to the Book of Genesis', *TynBul* 46 (1995), pp. 315-36.

Hasel, Gerhard F., 'Sabbath', in *ABD*, V, pp. 849-56.

—'The Sabbath in the Pentateuch', in Kenneth A. Strand (ed.), *The Sabbath in Scripture and History* (Washington, DC: Review and Herald Publishing Association, 1982), pp. 21-43.

Hauptman, Judith, *Rereading the Rabbis. A Woman's Voice* (Boulder, CO: Westview Press, 1998).

—'Women Reading Talmud', in Rina Levine-Melammed (ed.), *Lift Up Your Voice: Women's Voices and Feminist Interpretation in Jewish Studies* (Tel Aviv: Yedioth, 2001), pp. 28-40 (Hebrew).

Hawk, Daniel L., *Every Promise Fulfilled: Contesting Plots in Joshua* (Louisville, KY: Westminster Press, 1991).

Heger, Paul, *The Three Biblical Altar Laws: Developments in the Sacrificial Cult in Practice and Theology; Political and Economic Background* (Berlin: W. de Gruyter, 1999).

Heltzer, Michael, 'New Light from Emar on Genesis 31: The Theft of the Teraphim', in Manfried Dietrich and Ingo Kottsieper (eds.), *'Und Mose schrieb dieses Lied auf': Studien zum Alten Testament und zum Alten Orient* (Festschrift Oswald Loretz; Münster: Ugarit Verlag, 1998), pp. 357-62.

Hendel, Ronald S., *The Text of Genesis I–II: Textual Studies and Critical Edition* (New York: Oxford University Press, 1998).

—'Worldmaking in Ancient Israel', *JSOT* 56 (1992), pp. 3-18.

Herzfeld, Michael, *The Poetics of Manhood: Contest and Identity in a Cretan Mountain Village* (Princeton, NJ: Princeton University Press, 1985).

Hess, Richard S., Gordon J. Wenham and Philip E. Satterthwaite (eds.), *He Swore an Oath: Biblical Themes from Genesis 12–50* (Carlisle: Paternoster Press, 1994).

Hezser, Catherine, 'The Codification of Legal Knowledge in Late Antiquity: The Talmud Yerushalmi and Roman Law Codes', in Peter Schäfer (ed.), *The Talmud Yerushalmi and Graeco-Roman Culture* (Tübingen: J.C.B. Mohr [Paul Siebeck], 1998), pp. 581-641.

Hoffman, Lawrence A., *Covenant of Blood: Circumcision and Gender in Rabbinic Judaism* (Chicago: Chicago University Press, 1996).

Hoffman, Yair, *The Doctrine of the Exodus in the Bible* (Tel Aviv: Tel Aviv University Press, 1983 [Hebrew]).

Hoffner, Harry A., 'Symbols for Masculinity and Femininity: Their Use in Ancient Near Eastern Sympathetic Magic', *JBL* 85 (1966), pp. 326-34.

Holt, Else K., '"Urged On by his Wife Jezebel": A Literary Reading of 1 Kgs 18 in Context', *SJOT* 9 (1995), pp. 83-96.

Horbury, William, 'Women in the Synagogue', in *idem et al.* (eds.), *The Cambridge Ancient History of Judaism* (3 vols.; Cambridge: Cambridge University Press, 1999), III, pp. 376-401.

Horst, Pieter W. van der, 'Tamar in Pseudo-Philo's Biblical History', in Brenner (ed.), *A Feminist Companion to Genesis*, pp. 300-304.

Hossfeld, Frank-Lothar, *Der Dekalog: seine späten Fassung, die originale Komposition und seine Vorstufen* (Freiburg: Universitätverlag, 1982).

Houtman, Cornelis, *Exodus* (trans. Sierf Wuudsra; Historical Commentary on the Old Testament; 3 vols.; Leuven: Peeters, 1993-2000).

Hudson, Don M., 'Living in a Land of Epithets: Anonymity in Judges 19–21', *JSOT* 62 (1994), pp. 49-66.

Humphreys, W.L., 'The Story of Jephthah and the Tragic Vision: A Reply to J. Cheryl Exum', in Exum (ed.), *Signs and Wonders*, pp. 85-96.

Hurowitz, Victor A., 'His Master Shall Pierce his Ear with an Awl (Exodus 21:6): Marking Slaves in the Bible in Light of Akkadian Sources', *Proceedings of the American Academy of Jewish Research* 58 (1992), pp. 47-77.

Hyatt, Philip J., *Exodus* (NCBC; Grand Rapids: Eerdmans, rev. edn, 1980 [1971]).

Ishida, Tomoo, 'Adonijah, the Son of Haggith, and his Supporters: An Inquiry into Problems about History and Historiography', in Richard E. Friedman and Hugh G.M. Williamson (eds.), *The Future of Biblical Studies: The Hebrew Scriptures* (Atlanta: Scholars Press, 1987), pp. 165-87.

Jackson, Bernard S., 'The Ceremonial and the Judicial: Biblical Law as Sign and Symbol', *JSOT* 30 (1984), pp. 25-50.

—*Essays in Jewish and Comparative Legal History* (Leiden: E.J. Brill, 1975).

—'Justice or Righteousness in the Bible: Rule of Law or Royal Paternalism', *ZABR* 4 (1998), pp. 218-62.

—'Liability for Mere Intention in Early Jewish Law', *HUCA* 42 (1971), pp. 197-225 (reprinted in *idem, Essays in Jewish and Comparative Legal History* [Leiden: E.J. Brill, 1975], pp. 202-34).

—'Reflections on Biblical Criminal Law', *JJS* 24 (1973), pp. 8-38.

—*Theft in Early Jewish Law* (Oxford: Clarendon Press, 1972).

Janzen, Gerald J., 'The Character of the Calf and its Cult in Exodus 32', *CBQ* 52 (1990), pp. 597-607.

—*Exodus* (WBC, 2; Louisville, KY: Westminster Press, 1997).

—'Song of Moses, Song of Miriam: Who is Seconding Whom?', in Brenner (ed.), *A Feminist Companion to Exodus–Deuteronomy*, pp. 187-99.

Jay, Nancy B., *Throughout Your Generations Forever: Sacrifice, Religion and Paternity* (Chicago: Chicago University Press, 1992).

Jellinek, Adolph, *Bet ha-Midrasch* (Jerusalem: Wahrmann Books, 1967 [Hebrew]).

Jenson, Philip P., *Graded Holiness: A Key to the Priestly Conception of the World* (JSOTSup, 106; Sheffield: JSOT Press, 1992).

Jepsen, Alfred., 'Amah und schiphchah', *VT* 8 (1958), pp. 293-97.

Jobbling, David, 'A Bettered Woman: Elisha and the Shunammite in the Deuteronomic Work', in Fiona C. Black, Roland Boer and Erin Runions (eds.), *The Labour of Reading: Desire, Alienation and Biblical Interpretation* (Atlanta: SBL, 1999), pp. 177-92.

Johnstone, William, 'The Decalogue and the Redaction of the Sinai Pericope in Exodus', *ZAW* 100 (1988), pp. 361-85.

—'The "Ten Commandments": Some Recent Interpretations', *Expository Times* 100 (1988–89), pp. 453-61.

Jones, Gwilym H., *The Nathan Narratives* (JSOTSup, 80; Sheffield: JSOT Press, 1990).

Jones-Warsaw, Kaola, 'Toward a Womanist Hermeneutic: A Reading of Judges 19–21', in Brenner (ed.), *A Feminist Companion to Judges*, pp. 172-86.

Jüngling, H.W., *Richter 1: ein Plädoyer für das Königtum* (Rome: Biblical Institute Press, 1981).

Kadishson Schieber, Ava, *Soundless Roar* (Evanston: Northwestern University Press, 2002).

Kaiser, Otto, *Der Gott des Alten Testament; Theologie des Alten Testament. II. Jahwe, de Gott Israels, Schöpfer der Welt und des Menschen* (Göttingen: Vandenhoeck & Ruprecht, 1998).

Kamuf, Peggy, 'Author of a Crime', in Brenner (ed.), *A Feminist Companion to Judges*, pp. 187-207.

Kapelrud, Arvid S., 'Some Recent Points of View on the Time and Origin of the Decalogue', *Studia Theologica* 18 (1964), pp. 81-90.

Kaufman, Stephen A., 'The Structure of the Deuteronomic Law', *Maarav* 1 (1979), pp. 105-58.

Kaufmann, Yehezkel, *The Religion of Israel: From its Beginnings to the Babylonian Exile* (trans. Moshe Greenberg; Chicago: Chicago University Press, 1960).

Keller, Carl A., *Das Wort OTH als offenbarungszeichen Gottes* (Basel: Buchdrukerei Hoenen, 1946).

Keller, Martin, *Untersuchungen zur deuteronomisch-deuteronomistischen Namenstheologie* (Weinheim: Beltz, 1996).

Kessler, John, 'Sexuality and Politics: The Motif of the Displaced Husband in the Books of Samuel', *CBQ* 62 (2000), pp. 409-23.

Kilian, Rudolf, *Die vorpriesterlichen Abrahams-Überlieferungen: literarkritisch und traditionsgeschichtlich untersucht* (Bonn: Hanstein, 1966).

Kirkpatrick, Shane, 'Questions of Honor in the Book of Judges', *Koinonia* 10 (1998), pp. 19-40.

Klein, H., 'Verbot des Menschendiebstahls im Dekalog: Prüfung einer These Albrecht Alt', *VT* 26 (1976), pp. 161-69.

Klein, Ralph W., 'Back to the Future: The Tabernacle in the Book of Exodus' (unpublished paper available from <www.ot-studies.com>).

Knight, Douglas A., 'Moral Values and Literary Traditions: The Case of the Succession Narrative (2 Samuel 9–20; 1 Kings 1–2)', *Semeia* 34 (1985), pp. 7-23.

Knohl, Israel, *The Sanctuary of Silence: The Priestly Torah and the Holiness School* (Minneapolis: Fortress Press, 1995).

Knoppers, Annelies, 'Using the Body to Endorse Meanings about Gender', in Mary Stewart Van Leeuwen *et al.* (eds.), *After Eden: Facing the Challenge of Gender Reconciliation* (Grand Rapids: Eerdmans, 1993), pp. 268-98.

Knoppers, Gary N., 'Aaron's Calf and Jeroboam's Calves', in Astrid B. Beck *et al.* (eds.), *Fortunate the Eyes that See: Essays in Honor of David Noel Freedman* (Grand Rapids: Eerdmans, 1995), pp. 92-104.

—'Intermarriage, Social Complexity, and Ethnic Diversity in the Genealogy of Judah', *JBL* 120 (2001), pp. 15-30.

—'Rethinking the Relationships between Deuteronomy and the Deuteronomistic History: The Case of Kings', *CBQ* 63 (2001), pp. 393-415.

—'Sex, Religion, and Politics: The Deuteronomist on Intermarriage', *HAR* 14 (1994), pp. 121-41.

Koch, Klaus, *The Growth of Biblical Tradition: The Form-Critical Method* (trans. S.M. Cupitt; New York: Charles Scribner's Sons, 1969).

Koehler, Ludwig and Walter Baumgartner, *A Bilingual Dictionary of the Hebrew and Aramaic Old Testament* (Leiden: E.J. Brill, 1998).

Kraemer, Ross S., *When Joseph Met Aseneth: A Late Antique Tale of the Biblical Partiarach and his Egyptian Wife Reconsidered* (New York: Oxford University Press, 1998).

Kraus, Hans-Joachim, *Worship in Israel: A Cultic History of the Old Testament* (trans. Geoffrey Buswell; Oxford: Basil Blackwell, 1966).

Kristeva, Julia, *Polylogues* (Collection Tel quel; Paris: Seuil, 1977).

Kugel, James L., *In Potiphar's House: The Interpretative Life of Biblical Texts* (San Francisco: Harper & Row, 1990; Cambridge, MA: Harvard University Press, 2nd edn, 1994).

Kuhrt, Amelie, 'Israel: The Formation of a Small Levantine State c.1200–900', in *idem*, *The Ancient Near East* (2 vols.; London: Routledge, 1995), II, pp. 417-72.

Kunin, Seth D., *The Logic of Incest: A Structuralist Analysis of Hebrew Mythology* (JSOTSup, 185; Sheffield: Sheffield Academic Press, 1995).

Laberge, Léo, 'Sabbat: étymologie et origines', *Science et ésprit* 44 (1992), pp. 185-204.

Lang, Bernhard, 'The Decalogue in the Light of a Newly Published Palaeo-Hebrew Inscription (Hebrew Ostracon Moussaieff no. 1)', *JSOT* 77 (1998), pp. 21-25.

—'Du sollst nicht nach der Frau eines anderes verlangen: eine neue Deutung des 9ten und 10ten Gebots', *ZAW* 93 (1981), pp. 216-24.

—'Das Verbot des Meineids im Dekalog', *Theologische Quartalschrift* 161 (1981), pp. 97-105.

Lanner, Laurel, 'Cannibal Mothers and Me: A Mother's Reading of 2 Kings 6.24–7.20', *JSOT* 85 (1999), pp. 107-16.

Lasine, Stuart, 'Guest and Host in Judges 19: Lot's Hospitality in an Inverted World', *JSOT* 29 (1984), pp. 37-59.

—'Jehoram and the Cannibal Mothers (2 Kings 6.24-33): Solomon's Judgment in an Inverted World', *JSOT* 50 (1991), pp. 27-53.

—'Melodrama as Parable: The Story of the Poor Man's Ewe-Lamb and the Unmasking of David's Topsy-Turvy Emotions', *HAR* 8 (1984), pp. 101-24.

—'The Riddle of Solomon's Judgment and the Riddle of Human Nature in the Hebrew Bible', *JSOT* 45 (1989), pp. 61-86.

Lasserre, Guy, 'Quelques études recentes sur le code de l'alliance', *Revue de theologie et de philosophie* 125 (1993), pp. 267-76.

Lefkowitz, Mary L., and Maureen B. Fant, *Women's Life in Greece and Rome* (Baltimore: The Johns Hopkins University Press, 1982).

Lemaire, Andre, 'Le décalogue. Essai d'histoire de la rédaction', in Andre Caquot and Mathias Delcor (eds.), *Mélanges bibliques et orientaux en l'honneur de M.H. Cazelles* (Kevelaer: Butzon & Bercker, 1981), pp. 259-95.

Lemche, Niels P., 'Early Israel Revisited', *CRBS* 4 (1996), pp. 9-34.

—'Manumission of Slaves—the Fallow Year—the Sabbatical Year—the Jubilee Year', *VT* 26 (1976), pp. 38-59.

Lerner, Gerda, *The Creation of Patriarchy* (New York: Oxford University Press, 1986).

Lerner, Miron B., 'On the Midrashim on the Decalogue', in Yaakov Sussman and David Rosenthal (eds.), *Mehqerei Talmud. I. Talmudic Studies* (Jerusalem: Magnes Press, 1990–93), pp. 217-36 (Hebrew).

Levenson, Jon D., 'The Theologies of Commandment in Biblical Israel', *HTR* 73 (1980), pp. 17-33.

Levin, Cristoph., 'Der Dekalog am Sinai', *VT* 35 (1985), pp. 165-91.

Levine, Baruch A., *In the Presence of the Lord: A Study of Cult and Some Cultic Terms in Ancient Israel* (Leiden: E.J. Brill, 1974).

—*Leviticus* (JPS Torah Commentary; Philadelphia: Jewish Publication Society of America, 1989).

Levine, Etan, 'On Exodus 21,10: "Onah and Biblical Marriage"', *ZABR* 5 (1999), pp. 133-64.

—'On Intra-Familial Institutions of the Bible', *Bib* 57 (1976), pp. 54-59.

Levinson, Bernard M., 'The Right Chorale: From the Poetics to the Hermeneutics of the Hebrew Bible', in Jason P. Rosenblatt and Joseph C. Sitterson (eds.), *Not in Heaven: Coherence and Complexity in Biblical Narrative* (Bloomington: Indiana University Press, 1991), pp. 129-53.

Levison, Jack, 'An-Other Woman: Joseph and Potiphar's Wife—Staging the Body Politic', *JQR* 87 (1997), pp. 269-301.

Lichtheim, Miriam, *Ancient Egyptian Literature: A Book of Readings* (3 vols.; Berkeley: University of California Press, 1973–80).

Lipiński, Edward, 'The Syro-Palestinian Iconography of Woman and Goddess (review article)', *Zhumal prikladnoaai khimi* 36 (1986), pp. 87-96.

Loades, Ann, 'Feminist Interpretation', in John Barton (ed.), *Cambridge Companion to Biblical Interpretation* (Cambridge: Cambridge University Press, 1998), pp. 81-94.

Loewenstamm, Samuel E., 'The Making and Destruction of the Golden Calf', *Bib* 48 (1967), pp. 481-90.

—'The Making and Destruction of the Golden Calf. A Rejoinder', *Bib* 56 (1975), pp. 330-43.

Lohfink, Norbert, '*d*(*w*)*t* im Deuteronomium und in den Königsbüchern', *BZ* 35 (1991), pp. 86-93.

Long, Burke O., 'A Darkness between Brothers: Solomon and Adonijah', *JSOT* 19 (1981), pp. 79-94.

—'Sacred Geography as Narrative Structure in 2 Kings 11', in Wright, Freedman and Hurvitz (eds.), *Pomegranates and Golden Bells*, pp. 231-38.

—'The Shunammite Woman: In the Shadow of the Prophet?', *BR* 7 (1991), pp. 12-25.

Loraux, Nicole, *Born of the Earth: Myth and Politics in Athens* (trans. S. Stewart; Ithaca, NY: Cornell University Press, 2000).

—*The Children of Athena: Athenian Ideas about Citizenship and the Division between the Sexes* (trans. Caroline Levine; Princeton, NJ: Princeton University Press, 1993).

—*The Divided City: On Memory and Forgetting in Ancient Athens* (trans. Corinne Pache and Jeff Fort; New York: Zone Books, 2002).

—*The Experiences of Teresias: The Feminine and the Greek Man* (trans. Paula Wissing; Princeton, NJ: Princeton University Press, 1995).

Loza, José, *Las palabras de Yahvé. Estudio del Decálogo* (México: Universidad Pontificia, 1989).

Lyke, Larry L., *King David with the Wise Woman of Tekoa: The Resonance of Tradition in Parabolic Narrative* (JSOTSup, 255; Sheffield: Sheffield Academic Press, 1997).

Magen, Yitzhak., 'Mount Gerizim during the Roman and Byzantine Period', *Qadmoniot* 120 (2000), pp. 133-43 (Hebrew).

Mandel, P., 'The Servant, the Man, and the Master: An Inquiry into the Rhetoric of Genesis 24', *Jerusalem Studies in Hebrew Literature (= Mehkarei Yerushalayim beSifrut Ivrit)* 10-11 (1988), pp. 613-27 (Hebrew).

Mann, Thomas W., *Deuteronomy* (WBC, 5; Louisville, KY: Westminster/John Knox Press, 1995).

Manor, Dale W., 'A Brief History of Levirate Marriage as it Relates to the Bible', *Restoration Quarterly* 27 (1984), pp. 129-42.

Márai, Sándor, *Embers* (trans. Caroline Brown Janeway [from the German translation, *Die Glut as Embers*, of the Hungarian original, *A gyertyák csonkig égnek*] New York: Viking, 2001).

Margalit, Baruch, 'The Meaning and Significance of Asherah', *VT* 40 (1990), pp. 264-97.

Marks, John H., and Robert M. Good (eds.), *Love and Death in the Ancient Near East: Essays in Honor of Marvin H. Pope* (Guilford, CT: Four Quarters Publishing, 1987).

Matthews, Victor H., 'Honor and Shame in Gender-Related Legal Situations in the Hebrew Bible', in Matthews, Levinson and Frymer-Kensky (eds.), *Gender and Law*, pp. 97-112.

Matthews, Victor H., and Don C. Benjamin, *Honor and Shame in the World of the Bible* (Semeia, 68; Atlanta, GA: Scholars Press, 1994).

Matthews, Victor H., Bernard M. Levinson and Tikva Frymer-Kensky, *Gender and Law in the Hebrew Bible and the Ancient Near East* (JSOTSup, 262; Sheffield: Sheffield Academic Press, 1998).

Matties, Gordon H., 'Reading Rahab's Story beyond the Moral of the Story', *Direction* 24 (1995), pp. 57-70.

Mayer, Werner R., *Untersuchungen zur Formensprache der babylonischen 'Gebetsbeschwörungen'* (Rome: Biblical Institute Press, 1976).

Mayes, Andrew D.H., *Deuteronomy* (NCBC; London: Oliphants; Grand Rapids: Eerdmans, 1979).

—'Deuteronomy 5 and the Decalogue', *Proceedings of the Irish Biblical Association* 4 (1980), pp. 68-83.

Mazar, Amihai, 'Iron Age Chronology: A Reply to I. Finkelstein', *Levant* 29 (1997), pp. 157-67.

McBride, Dean S., 'Perspective and Context in the Study of Pentateuchal Legislation', in James L. Mays *et al.* (eds.), *Old Testament Interpretation: Past, Present and Future: Essays in Honor of Gene M. Tucker* (Nashville: Abingdon Press, 1995), pp. 47-59.

McCarter, Kyle P., 'Aspects of the Religion of the Israelite Monarchy: Biblical and Epigraphic Data', in Miller, Hanson and McBride (eds.), *Ancient Israelite Religion*, pp. 137-55.

—*II Samuel* (AB, 9; New York: Doubleday, 1984).

McClenney-Sadler, M.G., 'Women in Incest Regulations', in Meyers *et al.* (eds.), *Women in Scripture*, pp. 206-208.

McKane, William, 'Poison, Trial by Ordeal and the Cup of Wrath', *VT* 30 (1980), pp. 474-92.

McKay, Heather A., 'New Moon or Sabbath?', in Eskenazi, Herrington and Shea (eds.), *The Sabbath in Jewish and Christian Traditions*, pp. 12-27.

McKeating, Henry, 'The Development of the Law on Homicide in Ancient Israel', *VT* 25 (1975), pp. 46-68.

—'Sanctions Against Adultery in Ancient Israelite Society, with Some Reflections on Methodology in the Study of Old Testament Ethics', *JSOT* 11 (1979), pp. 57-72.

McKenzie, John L., *The World of the Judges* (Englewood Cliffs: Prentice Hall, 1966).

McKenzie, Steven L., *The Trouble with Kings: The Composition of the Books of Kings in the Deuteronomistic History* (Leiden: E.J. Brill, 1991).

McKinlay, Judith E., 'Rahab: A Hero/ine', *BibInt* 7 (1999), pp. 44-57.

Meier, Samuel A., 'The Sabbath and Purification Cycles', in Eskenazi, Herrington and Shea (eds.), *The Sabbath in Jewish and Christian Traditions*, pp. 3-11.

Mendenhall, George E., *Law and Covenant in Israel and the Ancient Near East* (Pittsburgh: Biblical Colloquium, 1955).

Mettinger, Tryggve N.D., *The Dethronement of Sabaoth: Studies in the Shem and Kabod Theologies* (Coniectanea Biblica Old Testament, 18; trans. Frederick H. Cryer; Lund: C.W.K. Gleerup, 1982).

—'Israelite Aniconism: Developments and Origins', in van der Toorn (ed.), *The Image and the Book*, pp. 173-204.

Meyers, Carol L., *Discovering Eve: Ancient Israelite Women in Context* (New York: Oxford University Press, 1988).

—'The Family in Early Israel', in Perdue *et al.* (eds.), *Families in Ancient Israel*, pp. 1-47.

—'"Women of the Neighborhood (Ruth 4.17)": Informal Female Networks in Ancient Israel', in Brenner (ed.), *A Feminist Companion to Ruth and Esther*, pp. 110-27.

Meyers, Carol *et al.* (eds.), *Women in Scripture: A Dictionary of Named and Unnamed Women in the Hebrew Bible, the Apocryphal/Deuterocanonical Books, and the New Testament* (Boston: Houghton Mifflin, 2000).

Milgrom, Jacob, 'A Husband's Pride, A Mob's Prejudice: The Public Ordeal Undergone by a Suspected Adulteress in Numbers 5', *BR* 12 (1996), p. 21.

—*Numbers* (JPS Torah Commentary; Philadelphia: Jewish Publication Society of America, 1990).

Miller, Patrick D., 'The Place of the Decalogue in the Old Testament and its Law', *Int* 43 (1989), pp. 229-42.

Miller, Patrick D., Paul D. Hanson and S. Dean McBride (eds.), *Ancient Israelite Religion: Essays in Honor of Frank Moore Cross* (Philadelphia: Fortress Press, 1987).

Mink, Louis O., 'Modes of Comprehension and the Unity of Knowledge', in Brian Fay *et al.* (eds.), *Historical Understanding* (Ithaca, NY: Cornell University Press, 1987), pp. 35-41.

Moberly, R.W.L., *At the Mountain of God: Story and Theology in Exodus 32–34* (JSOTSup, 22; Sheffield: JSOT Press, 1983).

Moor, Johannes C. de, *The Rise of Yahwism* (Leuven: Peeters, 1990).

Moor, Johannes C. de (ed.), *Synchronic or Diachronic? A Debate on Method in Old Testament Exegesis* (Oudtestamentische studiën, 34; Leiden: E.J. Brill, 1995).

Moran, William. L., 'The Ancient Near Eastern Background of the Love of God in Deuteronomy', *CBQ* 25 (1963), pp. 77-87.

—'The Conclusion of the Decalogue (Exod. 20.17 = Deut. 5.21)', *CBQ* 29 (1967), pp. 543-54.

Morgenstern, Julian, 'The "Bloody Husband"(?) (Exod. 4:24-26) Once Again', *HUCA* 34 (1963), pp. 35-70.

—'The Book of the Covenant—Part II', *HUCA* 7 (1930), pp. 19-258.

—'The Book of the Covenant—Part III', *HUCA* 8–9 (1931–32), pp. 1-150.

Muffs, Yochanan, *Love and Joy: Law, Language and Religion in Ancient Israel* (New York: Jewish Theological Seminary, 1992).

Nakanose, Shigeyuki, *Josiah's Passover: Sociology and the Liberating Bible* (Maryknoll, NY: Orbis Books, 1993).

Naumann, Thomas, 'David als exemplarischer Konig: Der Fall Urijas (2 Sam. 11) vor dem Hintergrund altorientalischer Erzahltradition', in Albert de Pury and Thomas Römer (eds.), *Die Sogenannte Thronfolgegeschichte Davids* (Freiburg: Universitätsverlag, 2000), pp. 136-67.

Neef, Heinz-Dieter, 'Deboraerzahlung und Deboralied: Beobachtungen zum Verhaltnis von Jdc. IV und V', *VT* 44 (1994), pp. 47-59.

—'Jephta und seine Tochter (Jbc XI 29-40), *VT* 49 (1999), pp. 206-17.

Newing, Edward G., 'Up and Down—In and Out: Moses on Mount Sinai—The Literary Unity of Exodus 32-4', *AusBR* 41 (1993), pp. 18-34.

Newman, Judith H., 'Nehemiah 9 and the Scripturalization of Prayer in the Second Temple Period', in Evans and Sanders (eds.), *The Function of Scripture*, pp. 112-23.

Nicholson, George W., 'The Decalogue as the Direct Address of God', *VT* 27 (1977), pp. 422-33.

Nicol, George G., 'The Alleged Rape of Bath Sheba: Some Observations on Ambiguity in Biblical Narratives', *JSOT* 73 (1997), pp. 43-54.

—'David, Abigail and Bathsheba, Nabal and Uriah: Transformations within a Triangle', *SJOT* 12 (1998), pp. 130-45.

Niditch, S., 'Eroticism and Death in the Tale of Jael', in Day (ed.), *Gender and Difference in Ancient Israel*, pp. 43-57.

—'The "Sodomite" Theme in Judges 19–20: Family, Community and Disintegration', *CBQ* 44 (1982), pp. 365-76.

—'The Three Wife–Sister Tales of Genesis', in *idem*, *Underdogs and Tricksters: A Prelude to Biblical Folklore* (San Francisco: Harper & Row, 1987), pp. 23-69.

—'War, Women and Defilement in Numbers 31', *Semeia* 61 (1993), pp. 39-57.

—'The Wronged Woman Righted: An Analysis of Genesis 38', *HTR* 72 (1979), pp. 143-49.

Niditch, Susan (ed.), *Text and Tradition: The Hebrew Bible and Folklore* (Atlanta: Scholars Press, 1990).

Niehr, Herbert 'Grundzüge der Forschung zur Gerichtsorganisation Israels', *BZ* 31 (1987), pp. 206-27.

Nielsen, Eduard, *The Ten Commandments in New Perspective* (London: SCM Press, 1968).

Noordtzij, A., *Numbers* (trans. Ed van der Maas; Bible Student's Commentary; Grand Rapids: Zondervan, 1983).

Noth, Martin, *The Deuteronomistic History* (JSOTSup, 15; Sheffield: JSOT Press, 2nd edn, 1991).

—*Exodus: A Commentary* (OTL; Philadelphia: Westminster Press, 1962).

—*A History of Pentateuchal Traditions* (trans. Bernhard W. Anderson; Englewood Cliffs: Prentice Hall, 1972).

—*Leviticus* (trans. J.E. Anderson; London: SCM Press, 1965).

—*Numbers: A Commentary* (trans. J. D. Martin; OTL; Philadelphia, Westminster Press, 1968).

Nussbaum, Martha C., *The Therapy of Desire: Theory and Practice in Hellenistic Ethics* (Princeton, NJ: Princeton University Press, 1994).

O'Connell, Robert H., 'Deut. IX 7–X 7-11: Paneled Structure, Double Rehearsal and the Rhetoric of Covenant Rebuke', *VT* 42 (1992), pp. 492-509.

Olmo Lete, Gregorio del, *Canaanite Religion according to Liturgical Texts of Ugarit* (trans. Wilfred G.E. Watson; Bethesda: CDL Press, 1999).

Olson, Dennis T., *Numbers* (Interpretation; Louisville, KY: John Knox Press, 1996).

Olyan, Saul M., *Asherah and the Cult of Yahweh in Israel* (Atlanta: Scholars Press, 1988).

—*Rites and Rank: Hierarchy in Biblical Representations of Cult* (Princeton, NJ: Princeton University Press, 2000).

Organ, Barbara E., 'Pursuing Phineas: A Synchronic Reading', *CBQ* 63 (2001), pp. 203-18.

Osborne, Robin., *Greece in the Making, 1200–479* (London: Routledge, 1996).

Otto, Eckhard, *Das Deuteronomium: Politische Theologie und Rechsreform in Juda and Assyrien* (Berlin: W. de Gruyter, 1999).

—'False Weights in the Scales of Biblical Justice? Different Views of Women from Patriarchal Hierarchy to Religious Equality in the Book of Deuteronomy', in Matthews, Levinson and Frymer-Kensky (eds.), *Gender and Law*, pp. 128-46.

—'Forschungen zur Priesterschrift', *Theologische Rundshau* 62 (1997), pp. 1-50.

—'Review of Pressler, *View of Women*', *Theologische Literaturzeitung* 119 (1994), pp. 983-86.

—'Town and Rural Countryside in Ancient Israelite Law: Reception and Redaction in Cuneiform and Israelite Law', *JSOT* 57 (1993), pp. 3-22.

Otwell, John H., *And Sarah Laughed: The Status of Women in the Old Testament* (Philadelphia: Westminster Press, 1977).

Partner, Nancy, 'No Sex, No Gender', *Speculum* 68 (1993), pp. 419-43.

Patrick, Dale, *Old Testament Law* (Atlanta: John Knox Press, 1985).

—'The Rhetorical Collective Responsibility in Deuteronomic Law', in Wright, Freedman and Hurvitz (eds.), *Pomegranates and Golden Bells*, pp. 421-36.

Paul, Shalom, 'Euphemistically "Speaking" and a Covetous Eye', *HUCA* 14 (1994), pp. 193-204.

—'Exod. 21.10: A Threefold Maintenance Clause', *JNES* 28 (1969), pp. 48-53.

—*Studies in the Book of Covenant in the Light of Cuneiform and Biblical Laws* (Leiden: E.J. Brill, 1970).

Perdue, Leo G. *et al.* (eds.), *Families in Ancient Israel* (Louisville, KY: Westminster/John Knox Press, 1997).

Peter-Contesse, Rene, 'Was Potiphar a Eunuch?', *The Bible Translator* 47 (1996), pp. 142-46.

Petersen, David L., 'A Thrice-Told Tale: Genre, Theme, and Motif in Genesis 12, 20, 26', *BibRes* 18 (1973), pp. 30-43.

Pettey, Richard J., *Asherah, Goddess of Israel* (New York: Peter Lang, 1990).

Phillips, Anthony, *Ancient Israel's Criminal Law: A New Approach to the Decalogue* (Oxford: Basil Blackwell, 1970).

—'Another Look at Murder', *JJS* 28 (1977), pp. 105-26.

Pitt-Rivers, Julian, *The Fate of Shechem or the Politics of Sex: Essay in the Anthropology of the Mediterranean* (Cambridge: Cambridge University Press, 1977).

Plaskow, Judith, *Standing Again at Sinai: Judaism from a Feminist Perspective* (San Francisco: Harper & Row, 1990).

Plate, Brent S., Edna M. and Rodríguez Mangual, 'The Gift that Stops Giving: Hélène Cixous's "Gift" and the Shunammite Woman', *BibInt* 7 (1999), pp. 113-32.

Polzin, Robert, 'The Ancestress of Israel in Danger', *Semeia* 3 (1975), pp. 81-98.

Posner, Gabriel, 'Anonymity in Genesis: The Pattern of a Literary Technique', *Nahalah* 2 (2000), pp. 103-29.

Pressler, Carolyn, *The View of Women found in the Deuteronomic Family Laws* (Berlin: W. de Gruyter, 1993).

—'Wives and Daughters, Bond and Free: Views of Women in the Slave Laws of Exod 21.2-11', in Matthews, Levinson and Frymer-Kensky (eds.), *Gender and Law*, pp. 147-72.

Rad, Gerhard von, *Deuteronomy: A Commentary* (trans. Dorothea Barton; OTL; Philadelphia: Westminster Press, 1966).

—*Genesis* (trans. John H. Marks; Philadelphia: Fortress Press, 1961).

—*Old Testament Theology* (trans. D.M.G. Stalker; 2 vols.; Edinburgh: Oliver & Boyd, 1962).

—*Studies in Deuteronomy* (trans. David Stalker; London: SCM Press, 1963).

Radding, Charles M., *A World Made by Men: Cognition and Society 400–1200* (Chapel Hill: University of North Carolina Press, 1985).

Rashkow, Ilona N., 'Intertextuality, Transference and the Reader in/of Genesis 12 and 20', in Fewell (ed.), *Reading between Texts*, pp. 57-73.

Redford, Donald B., *A Study of the Biblical Story of Joseph (Genesis 37–50)* (VTSup, 20; Leiden: E.J. Brill, 1970).

Reinhartz, Adele, *Why Ask my Name? Anonymity and Identity in Biblical Narratives* (New York: Oxford University Press, 1998).

Rendtorff, Rolf, 'Directions in Pentateuchal Studies', *CRBS* 5 (1997), pp. 43-65.

Robertson, Edward, 'The Altar of Earth', *JJS* 1 (1948), pp. 12-21.

Robinson, Gnana, *The Origin and Development of the Old Testament Sabbath: A Comparative Exegetical Approach* (Bern: Peter Lang, 1988).

Rodd, Cyril S., *Glimpses of a Strange Land: Studies in Old Testament Ethics* (Edinburgh: T. & T. Clark, 2001).

Rofé, Alexander, 'Family and Sex Laws in Deuteronomy and the Book of the Covenant', *Henoch* 9 (1987), pp. 131-59.

—'The Tenth Commandment in the Light of Four Deuteronomic Laws', in Segal and Levi (eds.), *The Ten Commandments in History and Tradition*, pp. 45-65.

—'The Vineyard of Naboth: The Origin and Message of the Story', *VT* 38 (1988), pp. 89-104.

Rogers, Jeffrey S., 'Narrative Stock and Deuteronomistic Elaborations in 1 Kings 2', *CBQ* 50 (1988), pp. 398-413.

Römer, Thomas, 'La formation du Penateuque selon l'exégèse historico-critique', in Christian-B. Amphoux and Jean Margain (eds.), *Les premières traditions de la Bible* (Lausanne: du Zebre, 1996), pp. 17-55.

—'Why Would the Deuteronomists Tell about the Sacrifice of Jephthah's Daughter?', *JSOT* 77 (1998), pp. 27-38.

Roncace, Mark, 'Elisha and the Woman of Shunem: 2 Kings 4.8-37 and 8.1-6 Read in Conjunction', *JSOT* 91 (2000), pp. 109-27.

Rosaldo, Michelle Z., 'Women, Culture and Society: A Theoretical Overview', in Rosaldo and Lamphere (eds.), *Woman, Culture and Society*, pp. 17-42.

Rosaldo, Michelle Z., and Louise Lamphere (eds.), *Woman, Culture and Society* (Standford: Stanford University Press, 1974).

Rosenblit, Barbara E., 'David, Bat Sheva, and the Fifty First Psalm', *Cross Current* 45 (1995), pp. 326-40.

Rotenstreich, N., 'The Decalogue and Man as *Homo Vocatus*', in Segal and Levi (eds.), *The Ten Commandments in History and Tradition*, pp. 247-59.

Roth, Martha T., 'Gender and Law: A Case Study from Ancient Mesopotamia', in Matthews, Levinson and Frymer-Kensky (eds.), *Gender and Law*, pp. 173-84.

—' "She Will Die by the Iron Dagger": Adultery and Neo-Babylonian Marriage', *Journal of the Economic and Social History of the Orient* 31 (1988), pp. 186-206.

Roth, Wolfgang M.W., 'The Wooing of Rebekah: A Tradition-Critical Study of Genesis 24', *CBQ* 34 (1972), pp. 177-87.

Sakenfeld, Katherine D., 'Feminist Perspectives on Bible and Theology: An Introduction to Selected Issues and Literature', *Int* 42 (1988), pp. 5-18.

—'Feminist Uses of Biblical Materials', in Letty M. Russel (ed.), *Feminist Interpretation of the Bible* (Philadelphia: Fortress Press, 1985), pp. 55-64.

—'Love (OT)', in *ABD*, VI, pp. 375-81.

Sanday, Peggy R., 'Female Status in the Public Domain', in Rosaldo and Lamphere (eds.), *Woman, Culture and Society*, pp. 189-206.

Saporetti, Claudio, *The Middle Assyrian Laws* (Malibu: Undena Publications, 1984).

Sarna, Nahum M., *Exploring Exodus: The Heritage of Biblical Israel* (New York: Schocken Books, 1986).

Sasson, Jack M., 'Bovine Symbolism in the Exodus Narrative', *VT* 18 (1968), pp. 380-87.

—'Love's Roots: On the Redaction of Genesis 30:14-24', in Marks and Good (eds.), *Love and Death in the Ancient Near East*, pp. 205-209.

—*Ruth: A New Translation with a Philological Commentary and a Formalist-Folklorist Interpretation* (Baltimore: Johns Hopkins University Press, 1979 [2nd edn = Sheffield: JSOT Press, 1989]).

Sawyer, Deborah F., *God, Gender and the Bible* (London: Routledge, 2002).

Schenker, Adrian, 'La profanation d'images cultuelles dans la guerre. Raisons explicites et raison implicites de l'aniconisme israélite dans les textes de la Bible', *RB* 108 (2001), pp. 321-30.

Schmitt, Hans-Christoph, 'Die Erzählung vom Goldenen Kalb. Ex.32 und das Deuteronomistische Geschichtswerk', in Steven L. McKenzie and Thomas Römer (eds.), *Rethinking the Foundations: Historiography in the Ancient World and the Bible—Essays in Honor of John Van Seters* (Berlin: W. de Gruyter, 2000), pp. 235-50.

Schneidau, Herbert N., *Sacred Discontent: The Bible and Western Tradition* (Baton Rouge: Louisiana State University Press, 1976).

Schniedewind, William M., *Society and the Promise of David: The Reception History of 2 Samuel 7:1-17* (New York: Oxford University Press, 1999).

Schottroff, Louise, Silvia Schroer and Marie-Therese Wacker, *Feminist Interpretation: The Bible in Women's Perspective* (trans. Martin and Barbara Rumscheidt; Minneapolis: Fortress Press, 1998).

Schottroff, Willy, *Gedenken im alten Orient und im Alten Testament: die Wurzel Zakar im semitischen Sprachkreis* (Neukirchen–Vluyn: Neukirchen Verlag, 1964).

Schüssler Fiorenza, Elizabeth, *Wisdom Ways: Introducing Feminist Biblical Interpretation* (Maryknoll, NY: Orbis Books, 2001).

Schwartz, Baruch J., 'The Prohibition Concerning the "Eating" of Blood in Leviticus', in Gary A. Anderson and Saul M. Olyan (eds.), *Priesthood and Cult in Ancient Israel* (JSOTSup, 125; Sheffield: JSOT Press, 1991), pp. 34-66.

Schwartz, Regina M., 'Adultery in the House of David: The Metanarrative of Biblical Scholarship and the Narratives of the Bible', *Semeia* 54 (1991), pp. 35-55.

Segal, Ben-Zion, and Gerson Levi (eds.), *The Ten Commandments in History and Tradition* (Jerusalem: Magnes Press, 1990).

Setel, Drorah O'Donnell, 'Exodus', in Carol A. Newsom and Sharon H. Ringe (eds.), *Women's Bible Commentary* (Louisville, KY: Westminster/John Knox Press, 1992), pp. 26-35.

Sheres, Ita, *Dinah's Rebellion: A Biblical Parable for Our Time* (New York: Crossroad, 1990).

Shields, Mary E., 'Subverting a Man of God, Elevating a Woman: Role and Power Reversals in 2 Kings 4', *JSOT* 58 (1993), pp. 59-69.

Shrager, Miriam Y., 'A Unique Biblical Law', *Dor le Dor* 15 (1987), pp. 190-94.

Siebert-Hommes, Joppie, *Let the Daughters Live: The Literary Architecture of Exodus 1–2 as a Key for Interpretation* (Leiden: E.J. Brill, 1998).

—'The Widow of Zarephath and the Great Woman of Shunem: A Comparative Analysis of Two Stories', in Bob Becking and Meindert Dijkstra (eds.), *On Reading Prophetic Texts: Gender-Specific and Related Studies in Memory of Fokkelien van Dijk-Hemmes* (Leiden: E.J. Brill, 1996), pp. 231-50.

Simon, U., 'The Poor Man's Ewe Lamb: An Example of a Juridical Parable', *Bib* 48 (1967), pp. 207-42.

Sivan, Hagith, 'Dating the Decalogue' (forthcoming).

—*Dinah's Daughters: Gender and Judaism from the Hebrew Bible to Late Antiquity* (Philadelphia: University of Pennsylvania Press, 2002).

—'From Jezebel to Esther: Fashioning Images of Queenship in the Hebrew Bible', *Bib* 82 (2001), pp. 477-95.

—'Moses the Persian? Exodus 2, the "Other" and Biblical "Mnemohistory"', *ZAW* 116 (forthcoming).

—'The Rape of Cozbi', *VT* 51 (2001), pp. 69-80.

—'The Silent Women of Yehud', *JJS* 51 (2000), pp. 3-18.

Ska, Jean L., 'Biblical Law and the Origins of Democracy', (unpublished paper delivered at AAR 2001, text accessible from <www.biblicallaw.org>).

—*Introduction à la lecture du Pentateuque. Clés pour l'interprétation des cinq premiers livres de la Bible* (Paris: Cerf, 2000), pp. 28-30.

Slager, Donald L., 'The Figurative Use of Terms for "Adultery" and "Prostitution" in the Old Testament', *Bible Translator* 51 (2000), pp. 431-38.

Smith, Carol, 'Samson and Delilah: A Parable of Power?', *JSOT* 76 (1997), pp. 45-57.

Smith, Jenny, 'The Discourse Structure of the Rape of Tamar (2 Samuel 12:1-22)', *Vox Evangelica* 20 (1990), pp. 21-42.

Smith, Jonathan Z., 'The Garments of Shame', in *idem, Map is Not Territory: Studies in the History of Religion* (Studies in Judaism in Late Antiquity, 23; Leiden: E.J. Brill, 1978), pp. 1-23.

Smith, Ralph L., 'Covenant and Law in Exodus', *Southwestern Journal of Theology* 20 (1977), pp. 33-41.

Smith, S., 'What were the Teraphim?', *JTS* 33 (1932), pp. 33-36.

Snaith, Norman H., *Leviticus and Numbers* (The Century Bible; London: Thomas Nelson, 1967), pp. 234-35.

Soroudi, Sorour S., 'Judeo-Persian Religious Oath Formulas as Compared with Non-Jewish Iranian Traditions', *Irano-Judaica* 2 (1990), pp. 166-83.

Spanier, Kitziah, 'Rachel's Theft of the Teraphim, her Struggle for Family Primacy', *VT* 42 (1992), pp. 404-12.

Speiser, E.A., *Genesis* (AB, 1; Garden City, NY: Doubleday, 1964).

—'The Wife–Sister Motif in the Patriarchal Narratives', in Alexander Altmann (ed.), *Studies and Texts*. I. *Biblical and Other Studies* (Cambridge, MA: Harvard University Press, 1963), pp. 15-28 (repr. in J.J. Finkelstein and Moshe Greenberg [eds.], *Oriental and Biblical Studies: Collected Writings of Ephraim A. Speiser* [Philadelphia: University of Pennsylvania Press, 1969], pp. 62-82).

Sprinkle, Joe M., *'The Book of the Covenant': A Literary Approach* (JSOTSup, 174; Sheffield: JSOT Press, 1994).

Stade, B., 'Beiträge zur Pentateuchkritik (3: "Die Eiferopferthora")', *ZAW* 15 (1895), pp. 166-78.

Stahl, Nanette, *Law and Liminality in the Bible* (JSOTSup, 202; Sheffield: Sheffield Academic Press, 1995).

Stamm, Jakob and Maurice E. Andrew, *The Ten Commandments in Recent Research* (London: SCM Press, 1967).

Stansell, Gary, 'Honor and Shame in the David Narratives', *Semeia* 68 (1994), pp. 55-79.

Stanton, Elizabeth Cady, *The Woman's Bible* (New York: European Publishing Company, 1895 [latest repr. 1993]).

Steiner, E. (ed.), *Forms of Desire: Sexual Orientation and the Social Constructionist Controversy* (New York: Routledge, 1990).

Steinberg, Naomi, *Kinship and Marriage in Genesis: A Household Economics Perspective* (Minneapolis: Fortress Press, 1993).

Sternberg, Meir, *The Poetics of Biblical Narrative: Ideological Literature and the Drama of Reading* (Bloomington: Indiana University Press, 1985).

Stone, Kenneth A., *Sex, Honor and Power in the Deuteronomistic History: A Narratological and Anthropological Analysis* (JSOTSup, 234; Sheffield: Sheffield Academic Press, 1996).

—'Sexual Power and Political Prestige: The Case of the Disputed Concubines', *BR* 10 (1994), pp. 28-31, 52-53.

Streete, Gail P., *The Strange Woman: Power and Sex in the Bible* (Louisville, KY: Westminster/John Knox Press, 1997).

Stulman, Louis, 'Encroachment in Deuteronomy: An Analysis of the Social World of the D Code', *JBL* 109 (1990), pp. 613-32.

—'Sex and Familial Crimes in the D Code: A Witness to Mores in Transition', *JSOT* 53 (1992), pp. 47-63.

Talstra, Eep, 'Deuteronomy 9 and 10: Synchronic and Diachronic Observations', in de Moor (ed.), *Synchronic or Diachronic*, pp. 187-210.

Tate, Marvin E., 'The Legal Traditions of the Book of Exodus', *Review and Expositor* 74 (1977), pp. 483-509.

Teubal, Savina J., *Hagar the Egyptian: The Lost Traditions of the Matriarchs* (San Francisco: Harper & Row, 1990).

—'Sarah and Hagar: Matriarchs and Visionaries', in Brenner (ed.), *A Feminist Companion to Genesis*, pp. 235-50.

Teugels, Lieve, 'The Anonymous Matchmaker: An Inquiry into the Characterization of the Servant in Genesis 24', *JSOT* 65 (1995), pp. 12-23.

—'"A Strong Woman, Who Can Find?": A Study of the Characterization in Genesis 24, with Some Perspectives on the General Presentation of Isaac and Rebekah in the Genesis Narratives', *JSOT* 63 (1994), pp. 89-104.

Thürmer-Rohr, Cristina, *Vagabonding: Feminist Thinking Cut Loose* (trans. Lise Weil; Boston: Beacon Press, 1991).

Tigay, Jeffrey H., *Deuteronomy* (JPS Torah Commentary; Philadelphia: John Knox Press, 1996).

—'Israelite Religion: The Onomastic and Epigraphic Evidence', in Miller, Hanson and McBride (eds.), *Ancient Israelite Religion*, pp. 157-94.

Toews, Wesley I., *Monarchy and Religious Institution Under Jeroboam I* (Atlanta: Scholars Press, 1993).

Toorn, Karel van der, *From her Cradle to her Grave: The Role of Religion in the Life of the Israelite and the Babylonian Woman* (trans. Sara J. Denning-Bolle; The Biblical Seminar, 23; Sheffield: JSOT Press, 1994).

—'The Iconic Book: Analogies between the Babylonian Cult of Images and the Veneration of the Torah', *idem* (ed.), *The Image and the Book*, pp. 229-48.

—'The Nature of the Biblical Teraphim in the Light of the Cuneiform Evidence', *CBQ* 52 (1990), pp. 203-22.

Toorn, Karel van der (ed.), *The Image and the Book: Iconic Cults, Aniconism, and the Rise of Book Religion in Israel and the Ancient Near East* (Leuven: Peeters, 1997).

Trenchard, Warren C., *Ben Sira's View of Women: A Literary Analysis* (Chico, CA: Scholars Press, 1982).

Trible, Phyllis, 'Bringing Miriam out of the Shadows', in Brenner (ed.), *A Feminist Companion to Exodus–Deuteronomy*, pp. 166-99 (first published in *BR* 5 [1989], pp. 14-25).

—'The Daughter of Jephthah: An Inhuman Sacrifice', in *idem*, *Texts of Terror*, pp. 92-116.

—'Exegesis for Storytellers and Other Strangers', *JBL* 114 (1995), pp. 3-19.

—'Feminist Hermeneutics and Bible Studies', in Ann Loades (ed.), *Feminist Theology: A Reader* (Louisville, KY: Westminster/John Knox Press, 1990), n.p.

—*God and the Rhetoric of Sexuality* (Philadelphia: Fortress Press, 1978).

—'The Odd Couple: Elijah and Jezebel', in Christina Büchmann and Celina Spiegel (eds.), *Out of the Garden: Women Writes on the Bible* (New York: Fawcett Columbine, 1994), pp. 166-79.

—*Texts of Terror: Literary-Feminist Readings of Biblical Narratives* (Philadelphia: Fortress Press, 1984).

Tsevat, Matitiahu, 'The Basic Meaning of the Biblical Sabbath', *ZAW* 84 (1972), pp. 447-59.

Tucker, Gene M., 'The Rahab Saga', in James M. Efird (ed.), *The Use of the Old Testament in the New and Other Essays: Studies in Honor of William G. Stinespring* (Durham: Duke University Press, 1972), pp. 66-86.

Turner, Mary D., 'Rebekah: Ancestor of Faith', *Lexington Theological Quarterly* 20 (1985), pp. 42-50.

Uehlinger, C., 'Anthropomorphic Cult statuary in Iron Age Palestine and the Search for Yahweh's Cult Image', in van der Toorn (ed.), *The Image and the Book*, pp. 97-155.

Van Seters, John, *Abraham in History and Tradition* (New Haven: Yale University Press, 1975).

—'Comparison of Babylonian Codes with the Covenant Code and its Implications for the Study of Hebrew Law' (unpublished paper delivered at SBL 2001, electronic version available from <www.biblicallaw.org>).

—*A Law Book for the Diaspora: Revision in the Study of the Covenant Code* (Oxford: Oxford University Press, 2002).

—'The Law of the Hebrew Slave', *ZAW* 108 (1996), pp. 534-46.

Van Wolde, Ellen J., 'Telling and Retelling: The Words of the Servant in Genesis 24', in Johannes C. de Moor (ed.), *Synchronic or Diachronic?*, pp. 227-44.

—'Texts in Dialogue with Texts: Intertextuality in the Ruth and Tamar Narratives', *BibInt* 5 (1997), pp. 1-28.

—'Ya'el in Judges 4', *ZAW* 107 (1995), pp. 240-46.

Vaux, Roland de, *Ancient Israel: Its life and Institutions* (trans. John McHugh; London: Longman, 1961).

Vegetti, Silvia Finzi, *Mothering: Toward a New Psychoanalytic Construction* (trans. Kathrine Jason; New York, Guilford Press, 1996).

Veijola, Timo, 'Bundestheologische Redaktion im Deuteronomium', in *idem* (ed.), *Das Deuteronomium und seine Querbeziehungen* (Helsinki: Finnische Exegetische Gesellschaft, 1996), pp. 242-276

Verissimo, Luis Fernando, *The Club of Angels* (trans. Margaret Costa; New York; New Directions, 2002).

Vervenne, Marc, 'Current Tendencies and Developments in the Study of the Book of Exodus', in *idem* (ed.), *Studies in the Book of Exodus: Redaction–Reception–Interpretation* (Leuven: Peeters, 1996), pp. 47-54.

—'The Question of "Deuteronomic" Elements in Genesis to Numbers', in Florentino García Martínez *et al.* (eds.), *Studies in Deuteronomy in Honour of C.J. Labuschagne on the Occasion of his 65th Birthday* (VTSup, 53; Leiden: E.J. Brill, 1994), pp. 243-68.

Viberg, Åke, *Symbols of Law: A Contextual Analysis of Legal Symbolic Acts in the Old Testament* (Stockholm: Almquist & Wiksell, 1992).

Wacker, Marie-Therese, 'Historical, Hermeneutical, and Methodological Foundations', in Schottroff, Schroer and Wacker (eds.), *Feminist Interpretation*, pp. 1-82.

Wagenaar, Jan A., 'The Cessation of Manna: Editorial Frames for the Wilderness Wandering in Exodus 16,35 and Joshua 5,10-12', *ZAW* 112 (2000), pp. 192-209.

—'"Give in the Hand of your Maidservant the Property": Some Remarks on the Second Ostracon from the Collection of Moussaieff', *ZABR* 5 (1999), pp. 15-27.

Walsh, Jerome T., 'Methods and Meanings: Multiple Studies of I Kings 21', *JBL* 111 (1992), pp. 199-201.

Watts, James H., *Reading Law: The Rhetorical Shaping of the Pentateuch* (The Biblical Seminar, 59; Sheffield: Sheffield Academic Press, 1999)

Weems, Renita J., *Battered Love: Marriage, Sex and Violence in the Hebrew Prophets* (Minneapolis: Fortress Press, 1995).

—*Just a Sister Away: A Womanist Vision of Women's Relationship in the Bible* (San Diego: LuraMedia, 1988).

Wegner, Judith Romney, *Chattel or Person? The Status of Women in the Mishnah* (New York: Oxford University Press, 1988).

Wehmeier, Gerhard, 'The Prohibition of Theft in the Decalogue', *Indian Journal of Theology* 26 (1977), pp. 181-91.

Weinfeld, Moshe, 'The Decalogue: Its Significance, Uniqueness, and Place in Israel's Tradition', in Edwin Firmage, Bernard G. Weiss and John W. Welch (eds.), *Religion and Law: Biblical-Judaic and Islamic Perspectives* (Winona Lake, IN: Eisenbrauns, 1990), pp. 3-47.

—*Deuteronomy and the Deuteronomistic School* (Oxford: Clarendon Press, 1972).

—*From Joshua to Josiah: Turning Points in the History of Israel from the Conquest of the Land until the Fall of Judah* (Jerusalem: Magnes Press, 1992 [Hebrew]).

—'The Loyalty Oath in the Ancient Near East', *UF* 8 (1977), pp. 379-414.

—'Sabbatical Year and Jubilee in the Pentateuchal Laws and their Ancient Near Eastern Background', in Timo Veijola (ed.), *The Law in the Bible and in its Environment* (Helsinki: Finish Exegetical Society, 1990), pp. 39-62.

—'Sarah in the House of Abimelech (Gen. 20) in the Light of Assyrian Law and the Genesis Apocryphon', *Tarbiz* 52 (1982), pp. 639-42 (Hebrew) (repr. as 'Sarah and Abimelech (Gen. 20) Against the Background of an Assyrian Law and the Genesis Apocryphon', in A. Delcor [ed.], *Melanges Bibliques et Orientaux en l'Honneur de Mathias Delcor* [Kevelaer: Butzon & Bercker, 1985], pp. 431-36).

—'The Uniqueness of the Decalogue and its Place in Jewish Tradition', in Segal and Levi (eds.), *The Ten Commandments in History and Tradition*, pp. 1-44.

Wellhausen, Julius, *Prolegomena to the History of Israel* (Atlanta: Scholars Press, 1994 [repr. of English trans.]).

Wenham, Gordon J., 'Betulah: A Girl of Marriageable Age', *VT* 22 (1972), pp. 326-48.

—'The Gap Between Law and Ethics in the Bible', *JJS* 48 (1997), pp. 17-29.

Wesselius, Jan-Wim, 'Towards a New History of Israel', *Journal of Hebrew Scripture* 3 (2000–2001), pp. 2-21.

Westbrook, Raymond, 'Adultery in Ancient Near Eastern Laws', *RB* 97 (1990), pp. 542-80.

—'The Female Slave', in Matthews, Levinson and Frymer-Kensky (eds.), *Gender and Law*, pp. 214-38.

Westermann, Claus, *Genesis* (3 vols.; Neukirchen–Vluyn: Neukirchener Verlag, 1974).

—'כבד', in *THAT*, I, pp. 794-812 (English translation = *TLOT*, II, pp. 590-602).

White, Marsha, 'Naboth's Vineyard and Jehu's Coup: The Legitimation of a Dynastic Extermination', *VT* 44 (1994), pp. 66-76.

Wiggins, Steve A., *A Reassessment of Ashera: A Study according to the Textual Sources of the First Two Millennia BCE* (Kevelaer: Butzon & Bercker, 1993).

Willey, Patricia K., 'The Importunate Woman of Tekoa and How She Got her Way', in Fewell (ed.), *Reading between Texts*, pp. 115-31.

Williams, James G., 'The Beautiful and the Barren: Conventions in Biblical Type-Scenes', *JSOT* 17 (1980), pp. 107-19.

Wilson, Robert R., 'Enforcing the Covenant: The Mechanisms of Judicial Authority in Early Israel', in Herbert B. Huffmon, F.A. Spina and A.R.W. Green (eds.), *The Quest for the Kingdom of God: Studies in Honor of George E. Mendenhall* (Winona Lake, IN: Eisenbrauns, 1983), pp. 58-75.

—*Genealogy and History in the Biblical World* (New Haven: Yale University Press, 1977).

—'Israel's Judicial System in the Pre-Exilic Period', *JQR* 74 (1983), pp. 229-48.

—*Prophecy and Society in Ancient Israel* (Philadelphia: Fortress Press, 1980).

Winkler, John J., *The Constraints of Desire: The Anthropology of Sex and Gender in Ancient Greece* (New York: Routledge, 1990).

Winter, Urs, *Frau und Göttin: Exegetische und Ikonographische Studien zum weiblischen Gottesbild im Alten Israel und in desssen Umwelt* (Freiburg: Universitätsverlag, 1983).

Wittenberg, Gunther, 'The Tenth Commandment in the Old Testament', *Journal of Theology for Southern Africa* 22 (1978), pp. 3-17.

Wray, David, *Catullus and the Poetics of Roman Manhood* (Cambridge: Cambridge University Press, 2001).

Wright, Christopher J.H., 'The Israelite Household and the Decalogue: The Social Background and Significance of Some Commandments', *TynBul* 30 (1979), pp. 101-24.

Wright, David P., David Noel Freedman and Avi Hurvitz (eds.), *Pomegranates and Golden Bells: Studies in Honor of Jacob Milgrom* (Winona Lake, IN: Eisenbrauns, 1995).

Yaron, Reuven, 'On Divorce in Old Testament Times', *Revue internationale des droits de l'antiquite* 3 (1957), pp. 117-28.

Yee, Gale A., 'By the Hand of a Woman: The Metaphor of the Woman Warrior in Judges 4', *Semeia* 61 (1993), pp. 99-132.

Zakovitch, Yair, 'Humor and Theology or the Successful Failure of Israelite Intelligence', in Niditch (ed.), *Text and Tradition*, pp. 75-98.

—*The Life of Samson (Judges 13–16): A Critical Literary Analysis* (Jerusalem: Magnes Press, 1982 [Hebrew]).

—'Through the Looking Glass: Reflections/Inversions of Genesis Stories in the Bible', *BibInt* 1 (1993), pp. 139-52.

Zenger, Erich, 'Die Bücher der Tora/des Pentateuch', in *idem et al.* (eds.), *Einleitung in das Alte Testament* (Stuttgart: W. Kohlhammer, 3rd edn, 1998), pp. 66-124, 142-76.

Zimmerli, Walther, 'Das Zweites Gebot', in *idem* (ed.), *Göttes Offenbarung: gesammelte Aufsätze zum Alten Testament* (Munich: Chr. Kaiser Verlag, 1963), pp. 234-48.

—*Old Testament Theology in Outline* (Edinburgh: T. & T. Clark, 1978).

Zipor, Moshe A., 'The Deuteronomic Account of the Golden Calf and its Reverberation in Other Parts of the Book of Deuteronomy', *ZAW* 108 (1996), pp. 20-33.

Žižek, Slavoj, *The Metastases of Enjoyment: Six Essays on Women and Causality* (New York: Verso, 1994).

—*The Sublime Object of Ideology* (London: Verso, 1989).

Zlotnick, Helena, see under Sivan.

INDEXES

INDEX OF REFERENCES

OLD TESTAMENT

OTHER ANCIENT REFERENCES

INDEX OF AUTHORS